KU-735-376

"When children are traumatised within their families, they learn to fear relationships. They learn to control rather than engage with others. The therapist wants to help children to feel safe enough to trust in healthy relationships. The therapist needs to discover the child's story – the inside and the outside and to help the child to communicate this to safe parents. The child discovers that it is safe to feel vulnerable and that expressing this vulnerability can lead to comfort and nurture. How do we help children to feel safe with us and use this to discover the child's story? Often we talk with them, and in talking with them we can move too fast. 'Slow down to get there quicker' is a mantra I am fond of telling my trainees. Children are doers more than they are talkers, and when we join them in doing we find we are able to discover the story at the child's pace. Karen Treisman has given us a wonderful book to help us to do this.

Full of ideas, exercises, and compassionate ways of joining with children to fully discover who they are, and to help them to manage difficulties that they are experiencing. This is grounded in the best of what we know about relational trauma.

This book and accompanying resources will enhance the most creative of us, and be a rich resource for those of us who doubt our own creativity. It will give all of us ways to go slower, to help children to feel safe enough to reveal their own story, and to find the confidence to allow us to share this story with their safe parents. Now healing can begin. My treasure box is certainly richer for having this book on my shelf."

– Dr. Kim S. Golding, clinical psychologist and author

"As a Treasure Box, Treisman has created exactly what it says on the tin. Embedded in the relational world of development, this book takes us on a journey of thoughtful, sensitive, creative, and deeply moving interventions. The lives and minds of children and young people can only be enriched if we embed this magic in our work."

– John Simmonds, OBE, Director of Policy, Research,
and Development at CoramBAAF, London

"'Relational trauma requires relational repair' says Dr. Treisman throughout her book and it's a mantra worth repeating. Her book explains what relational repair really involves, from creating safety and regulation, to exploring complex and layered emotions to tackling rage and sleep disturbances. It is packed with ideas and materials to guide and support therapeutic conversations, much of which could be used by therapeutic parents. What I especially love is the combination of compassion both for child and parent and its insistence on a sound, scientific approach. The pictures, the pebbles, the glue and the glitter are all set within a robust trauma-informed framework that reflect the emotional complexity of building a meaningful relationship with a traumatised child.

For those who labour at the coalface of relational repair, it is a nourishing read that will top up your therapeutic tank and make you feel just that little bit more encouraged and cherished and perhaps even vindicated. It deserves to be widely read by all those involved in supporting the healing of relationally traumatised children from commissioners, policy makers and academics right up to foster carers and adoptive parents."

– Sally Donovan, author and editor of Adoption Today

"When we lift the lid on a child's trauma it can feel overwhelming and impossible to address. Dr. Karen Treisman's accessible, insightful, and resource laden book will change this for ever for every practitioner, therapist, parent, and carer, and the precious children they support."

– Jane Evans, Childhood Trauma and Parenting Expert, author of Cyril Squirrel Finds Out About Love *and* How Are You Feeling Today Baby Bear?

"This book is an extraordinary achievement. It is packed with myriad tools, methods, and suggestions that will be indispensable to therapists, parents, and anyone working with traumatised kids. Most importantly, the book's simplicity is deceptive as every page is built on the firm foundations of the latest science and a deep understanding of the effects of developmental trauma. I predict this will be a book that trauma therapists will be scared to leave home without."

– Dr. Graham Music, consultant psychotherapist, Tavistock Clinic and author of Nurturing Natures

A Therapeutic Treasure Box for Working with Children and Adolescents with Developmental Trauma

The accompanying PDF can be accessed from www.jkp.com/voucher
using the code TREISMANTREASURE

by the same author

A Therapeutic Treasure Deck of Sentence Completion and Feelings Cards
Karen Treisman
ISBN 978 1 78592 398 2

of related interest

The Big Book of Therapeutic Activity Ideas for Children and Teens
Inspiring Arts-Based Activities and Character Education Curricula
Lindsey Joiner
ISBN 978 1 84905 865 0
eISBN 978 0 85700 447 5

The Big Book of EVEN MORE Therapeutic Activity Ideas for Children and Teens
Inspiring Arts-Based Activities and Character Education Curricula
Lindsey Joiner
ISBN 978 1 84905 749 3
eISBN 978 1 78450 196 9

The Art Activity Book for Psychotherapeutic Work
100 Illustrated CBT and Psychodynamic Handouts for Creative Therapeutic Work
Jennifer Guest
ISBN 978 1 78592 301 2
eISBN 978 1 78450 607 0

The CBT Art Activity Book
100 Illustrated Handouts for Creative Therapeutic Work
Jennifer Guest
ISBN 978 1 84905 665 6

Using Stories to Build Bridges with Traumatized Children
Creative Ideas for Therapy, Life Story Work, Direct Work and Parenting
Kim S. Golding
ISBN 978 1 84905 540 6
eISBN 978 0 85700 961 6

Clinical Exercises for Treating Traumatic Stress in Children and Adolescents
Practical Guidance and Ready-To-Use Resources
Damion J. Grasso
ISBN 978 1 84905 949 7
eISBN 978 0 85700 768 1

A THERAPEUTIC TREASURE BOX FOR WORKING WITH CHILDREN AND ADOLESCENTS WITH DEVELOPMENTAL TRAUMA

Creative Techniques and Activities

DR. KAREN TREISMAN

Jessica Kingsley *Publishers*
London and Philadelphia

First published in 2017
by Jessica Kingsley Publishers
73 Collier Street
London N1 9BE, UK
and
400 Market Street, Suite 400
Philadelphia, PA 19106, USA

www.jkp.com

Copyright © Karen Treisman 2018

All rights reserved. No part of this publication may be reproduced in any material form (including photocopying, storing in any medium by electronic means or transmitting) without the written permission of the copyright owner except in accordance with the provisions of the law or under terms of a licence issued in the UK by the Copyright Licensing Agency Ltd. www.cla.co.uk or in overseas territories by the relevant reproduction rights organisation, for details see www.ifrro. org. Applications for the copyright owner's written permission to reproduce any part of this publication should be addressed to the publisher.

Warning: The doing of an unauthorised act in relation to a copyright work may result in both a civil claim for damages and criminal prosecution.

All pages marked + may be photocopied and downloaded from www.jkp.com/voucher for personal use with this programme, but may not be reproduced for any other purposes without the permission of the publisher.

Library of Congress Cataloging in Publication Data
A CIP catalog record for this book is available from the Library of Congress

British Library Cataloguing in Publication Data
A CIP catalogue record for this book is available from the British Library

ISBN 978 1 78592 263 3
eISBN 978 1 78450 553 0

Printed and bound in Great Britain

To my family and friends – my treasure box of relational riches –
and to the amazing, inspiring families, children,
and colleagues I have been honoured to work with and learn from.

Acknowledgements

Thank you to my amazing family, my mum, dad, Nicky, Loren, and Dan, for their constant love, support, faith, and encouragement. You continuously filled and continue to fill my treasure box up with positive memories, experiences, and special moments.

I also want to thank my granny Ellen, who played a hugely influential part in me seeing the world through an artist's lens and in bringing out my creative and imaginative side. This then continued to be embedded by my one-in-a-million mum.

I want to thank my incredible friends and supporters, who I am beyond fortunate to be surrounded by. I wish I could mention so many more of them, but a special thanks to Ayo Sodeke, Oliver Suendermann, Elizabeth Stevens, Cyra Neave, Lili Ly, Amy Woolf, Katie Poll, Michelle Avraham, and Katherine Levinger.

I also want to say a special thank you to Rachel Falk, who has been a shining light and a beacon of support and energy throughout the journey of writing this book. I want to give a shout out to my other amazing girls from Islington: Katie, Chantal, Laura O, and Laura T.

A big thank you to Stephen Jones, Simeon Hance, and the whole Jessica Kingsley Publishers team, who have been beyond a pleasure to work with, and I'm so pleased to be part of your collection of authors.

A special thank you to Emma Metcalfe for her beautiful, thoughtful, and powerful illustrations, and for bringing my concepts alive.

And lastly, but most importantly, to the amazing children and families who I have been honoured and blessed to work with and to learn from.

Contents

Worksheets

Photos

Table

Figures

Illustrations

Boxes

CHAPTER 1

Introduction to Using the Book, Guiding Principles, and Underpinning Rationale

This chapter will offer a range of factors and principles to hold in mind when implementing the strategies described in this book. These should be referred to and considered when reading the following chapters and when applying the included tools and techniques. After some of these factors and principles have been presented, a range of reasons and a rationale for why using creative and expressive tools in the context of relational and developmental trauma may be useful will be discussed.

It should be noted that a wealth of photos and pictures have been included in this book. All of these images are recreations and examples of children's art and are not original pieces. Therefore, no actual therapy work was used in this book in order to preserve children's privacy, confidentiality, and anonymity and respect their therapy journey.

The accompanying online materials (such as the worksheets) can be accessed at www.jkp.com/voucher using the code TREISMANTREASURE.

Pitfalls, planning, preparation, principles, and overall factors to be mindful of when implementing the strategies in this book

(Please note that these should be referred to and interwoven with all of the chapters that follow.)

The target audience and the terms used

The mentioned strategies in this book are primarily intended for use by relational and trauma-informed practitioners and clinicians. However, many of the ideas will also apply and be extremely useful (directly or indirectly) to a whole range of people within the Team Around the Child, including teachers, youth workers, parents, foster carers, kinship carers, adoptive parents, special guardians, independent reviewing officers, virtual school workers, residential workers, and so forth. However, when used in this way, this should be done with care and caution, as this book is not a replacement for therapy, or for clinical supervision/support.

Moreover, it is acknowledged that at different times the terms "parent", "carer" or "caregiver" are used interchangeably throughout this book. This is to reflect the diversity of "parenting" constellations that are likely to be found within this context; therefore, it is important that the most fitting term (suggested and selected by the client) is used for each unique, individual case.

Unique individuals within unique contexts

The activities, exercises, and tools described in this book are by no means prescriptive or exhaustive. There is no magic bullet or cookie-cutter approach for supporting such complexity and diversity. They are offered as guides and suggestions, and with the intention of encouraging further expression and exploration. Each strategy detailed can be adjusted, changed, and adapted according to the unique individual, therapist, and context. The included tools are intended to offer some possibilities, but it is hoped that the reader will also draw on their own knowledge, language, creativity, and playfulness to bring the strategies to life, to adapt them, and to make them more meaningful and tailored for the individual/s.

Moreover, I am also mindful that I have a personal leaning towards the arts and crafts. This can colour my therapeutic lens and therapeutic style and has inevitably influenced and shaped the included and selected tools within this book. However, it is acknowledged that this type of working does not suit everyone, so it is important to find a style that clicks and resonates for that particular client, at that particular time, and feels comfortable and appealing to them and to you. Within this, although many arts-based activities are included in the book, the concepts themselves, and the aims of the activities, can be creatively transferred and applied using different mediums to a range of other methods or styles.

Informed by assessment, formulation, and code of conduct

Each described idea needs to be thought about carefully, sensitively, and reflectively before implementing it; the magic and the effectiveness of the ideas relies on the relationship, the clinical skills, and the process that facilitate them. This process will be expanded on in the following sections. This includes taking into consideration the experience, knowledge, skills, and uniqueness of the individual practitioner, child, family, relationships, and wider context. Therefore, these need to be informed by a thorough trauma/relational/child development/neurobiology-informed assessment, a working formulation, clinical judgement, clinical skill, one's professional code of conduct, safeguarding procedures, and high-quality supervision. Moreover, they need to consider what has already been tried, tested, successful, trickier, etc., and what is within the skill and knowledge of the person implementing the strategy.

In addition, these tools and ideas are intended as complementary activities to other existing therapies, models, and therapeutic approaches; therefore, it is important to think about how they can be naturally interwoven with the other approaches and skills that you ordinarily employ.

Being mindful of the potential impact of the exercises, and the importance of familiarising and practising the tools before implementing them

It is also worth holding in mind that each activity, as with all therapeutic techniques, can be triggering or evoke a range of responses/emotions in the child, carer, and therapist. Therefore, the tools should be implemented with intentionality, care, thought, reflection, and caution. Practitioners also need to consider the rationale for employing the tool before doing so, anticipate to the best of their ability what different responses they may meet, and plan and prepare for how they will respond to these.

Within this, it is recommended that the tools are practised beforehand and that practitioners familiarise themselves with them first and try them on themselves and colleagues before applying them within a clinical context.

Believing and investing in the tools

Therapists need to believe and buy in, to some degree, to the strategies, or the underlying rationale behind them, in order to feel confident and efficacious in consistently implementing them and to convey this belief, genuineness, hope, and confidence to the child/family. This is important in supporting children and their caregivers to feel held in safe hands and in hopeful minds. Therefore, before implementing the tools, it is important to reflect on one's confidence, beliefs around the tools, and understanding of them and, where appropriate, to reflect on the potential barriers or unaligned values. This also relates to caregivers when therapists are suggesting strategies for them to carry out; thought needs to be put into how much the caregivers believe in it, what barriers there might be, what fears they might have, what they have already tried, etc. These beliefs, blocks, values, and attributions are likely to significantly impact the way strategies are implemented and how successful and effective they will be.

Part of a bigger process: exhale, expand, and embed

The ideas offered are not intended to be standalone tools. They are part of a bigger process and are proposed to be a springboard for future thickening of the tools and of more detailed, rich expression, exploration, expansion, and explanation. It is often the process, the sense-making, the meaning-making, and the embedding of a concept that are more important than the content itself. I find the saying "Exhale, Expand, and Embed" useful. Examples are peppered throughout the book of how to expand, exhale, and embed; however, an example follows of some of the clinical skills that are useful and important in optimising, thickening, and embedding the tools.

Even the simplest task can be expanded on and cemented further by drawing on one's clinical knowledge, relational style, and counselling skills. For instance, asking a child to draw/write their thoughts and feelings on a polystyrene head, a hat, or speech bubbles (see Photo 4.15) is a fairly straightforward and accessible task; however, the therapeutic bit comes in the way in which the practitioner brings in some of the following therapeutic skills.

- Responding to and making sense of the child's verbal and non-verbal communication.

- Slowing down, pausing, and respecting the gradual process of the therapeutic process.

- Reflecting on the process (where necessary by adjusting the pace, tone, and levels of arousal and intensity including setting the scene and warming the context).

- Making links, patterns, and connections.

- Identifying and, where appropriate, labelling tentatively and sensitively the child's feelings/needs, the feelings in the room, and the feelings/patterns within the relationship (including the unspoken and unexpressed needs and feelings).

- Actively listening and engaging using the whole-brain and whole-body.

- Asking open-ended exploratory and Socratic questions.

- Not making assumptions or judgements.

- Taking a position of curiosity and of "not knowing", and respecting and appreciating the child/parent as an "expert of their own experiences".

- Picking up on pertinent themes and cues (including those subtler, more-difficult-to-decipher ones).

- Showing and embodying empathy, sensitivity, compassion, and understanding.

- Framing, punctuating, magnifying, and expanding on certain relevant areas.

- Bringing in some psychoeducation or new information where appropriate.

- Subsequently, finding ways to embed and enrich the concepts in the point above through creative and expressive means and through thickening discussions (examples of ways to expand and embed creatively are given throughout the book).

The magic is in the process, not just the product

Building on the above, it is often easy when creating something to get caught up in having a clear idea of where you want to get to with it, what the finished product should look like, or that there is a right or wrong or good or bad way of doing things (this is also often wrapped up in our own experiences of completing tasks, learning, creating, etc.). In the case of the strategies presented in this book, it is helpful to keep an open mind and to focus and reflect on the process, the relational dynamic, and the journey, rather than on the end product. As said previously, each child/parent/family/therapist will interpret the activity differently and will take it to different places. It is amazing that when I implement a strategy, sometimes even the same strategy several times with the same child at different stages of the therapy, I am often pleasantly surprised by the diversity, differences in the doing of it, and end result.

Relational trauma requires relational repair – keeping the relationship at the centre

Crucially, each idea is written with the intention that the therapeutic relationship is, or the key relationship/s are, at the centre of all of them. The relationships are the glue and the magic that make the strategies meaningful, purposeful, and therapeutic. This is in line with the sayings "Relational trauma requires relational repair" (Treisman, 2016, p.17) and "Relational repair requires safe hands, thinking minds, and regulated bodies" (Treisman, 2016, p.17). Without the relationship to anchor to, the strategies are empty and tokenistic, and they lose their essence and intention. Therefore, it is important to have (or be working towards and conveying) a safe, responsive, sensitive, compassionate, mindful, containing, empathetic, reflective, trusting, and consistent underpinning relationship first in order to guide, enrich, and ground the work.

The therapist needs to be genuinely interested and invested in the child and to work towards developing a positive relationship with them; co-creating a feeling of safety and of permissiveness within the relationship so that the child feels free to express themselves completely. This relationship ideally will offer the child/carer a different experience of doing and being in a relationship and of being mentalised within the context of an attachment relationship. Within this, depending on the context, it is essential that the relationships around the child, and those that are most important to the child, are prioritised and supported (Chapter 6).

Relational and developmental trauma framework and child development base

These tools will be most effective and meaningful when implemented by or supported by people who have an increased awareness, sensitivity, and knowledge around the multi-layered impact that developmental and relational trauma, loss, and toxic stress can have on the child, caregivers, therapists, and the surrounding systems (e.g. schools and organisations), and vice versa. Some of these concepts and theoretical underpinnings are written about in more detail in *Working with Relational and Developmental Trauma in Children and Adolescents* (Treisman, 2016).

Prioritising and establishing multi-levelled safety first

In the same vein, for children to be able to think, learn, and explore, they need to feel and start to believe that they are safe and that they can trust. They need to begin to be supported to not be in a continual and dominant state of dysregulation and high arousal and in fear/survival mode. Therefore, their multi-levelled whole-brain-body safety needs to be prioritised and centralised (see Chapter 3 on multi-levelled safety). Establishing, maintaining, and expanding on their multi-levelled safety is, in many ways, the foundation and roots on which all other interventions should build and anchor, especially as physical, emotional, and relational safety, trust, and security are the cornerstones of any positive therapeutic relationship and of any therapeutic re-parenting experience. The child needs to feel that they are in a place and relationship that can offer them a physical, emotional, and symbolic second-chance secure base and second-chance safe haven (e.g. safe hands, thinking minds, and regulating bodies). (See Chapter 3 for various strategies and explanations around multi-levelled safety.)

In addition, it should be held in mind that this multi-levelled safety feeds into all aspects of therapy, from the setting up of the sessions and discussing confidentiality and boundaries, to ensuring that the child is not leaving the session dysregulated and in a heightened state of arousal. Within this, the child should never feel coerced or forced to engage in the sessions or tasks. They should know their exit strategy – for example, if they want to have a brain break or to finish the session early. For some, it can be helpful to have a cue word, a hand signal, or a communication card that they can use if things are feeling too much (see Chapter 3 for a range of tools to support the development of multi-levelled safety).

Viewing behaviour within a context and as a form of communication

There are specific chapters on certain behaviours or on presenting difficulties, such as Chapter 8 on outbursts and dysregulation and Chapter 9 on nightmares and worries. It is also important to keep in mind that this book takes the position that behaviours are on a continuum, are not in a vacuum, and, therefore, need to be considered within their context and within a wider frame and lens. Thus, this posits that rather than taking behaviours at face value, it is helpful to view behaviours as forms of multi-layered communication that tells a story and often provides us with a map of and clues about the child's inner worlds and unexpressed needs. Different ways of bringing this concept to life will be expanded on and discussed throughout the book. Within this, this book also takes the position that the impact of the behaviour, how stressful the behaviour is perceived to be, and what attributions and sense-making are made around the behaviour are also crucial to consider (see Box 6.4, as well as "Assessment of behaviour" in Chapter 8 of *working with Relational and Developmental Trauma in Children and Adolescents* (Treisman, 2016), for an expansion on thinking about behaviours).

> For example, a three-year-old taking sweets from a supermarket would be viewed differently to the same behaviour being displayed by a 15-year-old. A child who has a couple of nightmares per month would be viewed differently to a child who is having nightmares every night that result in them being scared to go to bed.

Holding in mind what ghosts, angels, and other relational dynamic children/families are bringing into the room

Within the context of relational and developmental trauma, children have often been soaked in secrecy and mistrust and most likely have felt that things were done to and about them. Thus, they have often learned that adults are unreliable, abusive, unpredictable, absent, the source of fear, and so on (see Chapters 3, 4, and 6 for further explanation and discussion). Therefore, it is likely that these experiences, learned beliefs, scripts, relationships to adults, and "help" would have contributed to and coloured children's perception of therapy, "support", and themselves. Holding, being aware, validating, and responding to the complexity of what influences one's relationship to people, to "support/therapy", and to what they may be bringing into the room with them feels integral. Within a relational approach, it is important to hold in mind that we all bring lots of "people" into the "room" with us (e.g. previous relationships, values, belief systems, and ghosts and angels of the past) (Fraiberg, Adelson, and Shapiro, 1975; Lieberman *et al.*, 2005). Therapists can also bring these relationships in with them. Some case examples of the way relationships, ghosts of the past, values, and dynamics can colour the therapeutic process, and children's relationship to support, will follow.

It took Phillip close to three years to disclose that he had been repeatedly raped by his older cousin. This was so wrapped up in cultural and gender-based fears around rape being a sin, strongly embedded beliefs about family loyalty, and self-stigma that as a result of the rape he was "dirty, spoiled, weak, and gay".

After years of relational starvation, verbal humiliation, and shame, Nathan's self-esteem and self-worth were so low that he felt he was "unlovable and disposable". Therefore, he bravely shared early on that he did not feel that he deserved to be in therapy and that there were others who deserved it a lot more. Nathan then shared that he felt that regardless of what was done, he knew that he was a "lost cause", "broken", and a "waste of space".

In the context of relational and developmental trauma, and having been soaked in toxic stress, Glenda had learned that the only way she could survive and preserve herself was by disconnecting, zoning out, and dissociating. She had adapted by functioning predominantly in a protective mist and by keeping others at bay and at a distance. Therefore, she entered the therapy room in that foggy bubble, encircled by a blocking mist.

Being raised in a house dominated by alcohol and extreme domestic violence and subsequently being placed in six foster care placements that had all broken down, Bessie had learned through repeated experiences that adults, particularly those in positions of power, were dangerous, not to be trusted, and were abusive. These core beliefs and interpretative lenses travelled with her into the therapy room and were expected of, transferred, and projected onto the therapist.

Facing the buried anger, resentment, complicated grief (Abraham's father was executed in Iran), and disappointment that Abraham felt towards his father for choosing politics over his family was too painful, threatening, and terrifying for him. Instead, in a form of protective dissociation and splitting, he hung on to his father as perfect and, subsequently, idealised him.

Nina had been told time and time again to never speak of the abuse that she had faced and threatened that, if she did, she and her family would be harmed. These words haunted her like black ghosts as she entered the therapy room.

In Jamie's family, there was a strong family script around secrets staying within the family, blood being thicker than water, and not speaking about difficult aspects (i.e. pushing things under the carpet). Therefore, he went into the therapy room with these messages symbolically wrapped around him.

Working with hesitance and cautiousness

Due to the experience of relational trauma and ruptured trust and safety, it is expected that many children/parents will be hesitant or cautious about the process and the described activities. This is completely understandable and just offers a clue into their previous experiences, belief systems, fears, expectations, and templates. Therefore, it is about validating, acknowledging, and empathising with this experience, and finding a way to explore this, meet them where they are at, establish some sense of trust and safety, and go at their own pace, rather than insisting or forcing them to do any of the creative activities. The activities are intended to be organic, helpful, and collaborative, to increase a sense of mastery and agency, and not to feed into a sense of powerlessness or helplessness or to insist on a rigid way of doing things. The activities or questions should not feel intrusive or like an interrogation; they should be delivered with sensitivity, fun, space, compassion, and matched rhythm. As previously stated, the context needs to be warmed first, and a foundation of physical, emotional, and relational trust and safety prioritised and established.

The activities, tone of the session, relationship, and overall therapy experience need to be part of a continual feedback loop (the good, the bad, and the ugly), where the young person has endless opportunities to collaborate, shape, and drive their own therapy journey. This can include asking questions about questions. Some example questions will follow. This also acknowledges, once again, that each child/situation/therapist is unique and that what might be useful for one person, at a particular time and in a particular context, may not resonate or be useful for another person, at that time and in that context.

I have a question in mind, but I am not sure what you will think of it… How was that question/topic/activity for you? Were there any questions you would have liked me to ask that I didn't ask? What do you think about…? If you were going to ask a friend about that, what or how would you ask them? Were there questions I asked/things I did that weren't helpful? How would we know if I was working in a way with you that was not helpful/that did not fit for you/that felt…?

Non-verbal communication and whole-body listening

Throughout the sessions, and when implementing the tasks, it is also important to think carefully about body language, body positioning, tone of voice, facial expressions, and how one is conveying verbally and non-verbally the qualities of containment, responsiveness, sensitivity, warmth, being genuine, being present, and being caring. This is crucial, as children who have experienced relational and developmental trauma have finely attuned antennae for picking up and sometimes misinterpreting signals of threat (see Chapters 3, 4, and 8). There should also be clear messages conveyed to them that you are there to listen to them, to hear them, and to learn from them and with them, and that what they say is really important.

Explaining the rationale, linking to other concepts, and gaining consent

It is also important, as with all therapeutic interventions, that we carefully set up the idea, give some rationale and context to it, and have meaningfully received the young person's informed consent before going ahead with the specific strategy. This might include gaining the child's understanding, sense-making about why they are there for therapy, and being transparent about the assessment purpose, practicalities, process, and your and their role. Some questions to consider are listed below.

How do you (practise out loud with colleagues) explain your role, expectations, and the purpose of therapy to a three-year-old child, seven-year-old child, 12-year old adolescent, 17-year-old adolescent, parent, teacher, or colleague from another discipline? How might this be different, or similar, when explaining the concepts to a child/family where English is their second language or to a child who has a learning disability? How might this be different, or similar, when explaining the concepts to a child/family who has had several years of therapy previously or is surrounded by other professionals?

So, for example, other ways of gaining consent, explaining rationales, and increasing children's understanding and comfort may include discussing the "elephant in the room", giving some psychoeducation ideas, having myth-busting conversations (e.g. "All therapists want you to do is cry", "You want to take me away from my parents", "Therapists can read your mind", "Coming to therapy means I am weak"), and encouraging curious questioning (e.g. "If I was in your shoes I might…" or "Some children tell me they worry about…"). This includes an acknowledgement of what was described in the previous sections about what fears, hopes, expectations, and worries children/caregivers might be coming into the room with, alongside their ghosts/angels of the past, values, attributions, beliefs, etc.

Timing and location

It is important to consider the timing, both in terms of whether the current time is the right time and stage within the child's/family's life to be embarking on therapy and whether the actual practical timing is suitable. For example: Does the child have exams coming up? Is the child about to have a big change in their life, such as moving placements, change of contact arrangements, or changing schools? Have they just finished another course of therapy or are they about to start another type of therapy? Is there other work that needs to be done before therapy, with the child directly or with the family/system? Is the case involved in, or about to be involved in, court? Is the child about to move out of the local area?

Once that decision has been made, it is important to reflect more practically on the best time and best location to see the child. For example: Are they at their best in the mornings? Is there a favourite lesson that they don't want to miss? Has the child had the opportunity to eat, so that they are not feeling hungry or uncomfortable during the session (this can be retriggering of past experiences of being hungry or deprived, or of not being looked after)? Where will they be going after the session, and how will this work if difficult topics have been discussed?

This also extends to the location and environmental surroundings of the sessions. Where will the sessions be held? Is this an appropriate place where the child feels safe? Is this place quiet and not overly stimulating? Is this a place where the session won't be disrupted and where the child has a sense of privacy? Is this a place that can be used regularly and consistently? If the child becomes dysregulated and distressed, will they have to be in this place at other times (e.g. their bedroom)? If there is little choice available due to service provisions, how can this place be made as appropriate as possible, and the less-than-ideal nature be named and acknowledged to the child?

Greetings and hellos

The way we first introduce and welcome a child can make a big difference and can set the scene and warm the context for the introduction and the implementation of the described tools. First impressions count. So, it is important to be genuine, attuned, warm, and friendly and to be mindful of what the child might be feeling when coming to see a stranger/authority figure/therapist. This can come with all sorts of fears, worries, expectations, discourses, stigmas, and assumptions, which inevitably can influence engagement and progress.

It is also worth checking out what they like to be called and how they like to be referred to (i.e. pronunciation of their name, nicknames, middle names, abbreviations, etc.) and how they would like their caregivers to be referred to (e.g. mum, mother, foster carer, aunty, by their name, etc.).

Being prepared and handling items with care

Although many of us are working in busy contexts, and in under-resourced services, it is advisable to be prepared for the session: physically, cognitively, emotionally, and practically. Being prepared sends a strong message to the client that you have kept them in mind and that you value your time with them. This is also more likely to support them in feeling more contained and regulated.

For example: Have you brought the right equipment, measures, tools, and resources that you need with you? Have you set up the room ready for the session in a way that feels comfortable to them? Have you reviewed the previous session summary and notes? Have you remembered to bring anything that you told the child you would bring? Have you de-rolled from the previous session with another client, a bad journey, or a difficult staff meeting before entering the new session? Have you considered what themes or topics might be discussed? Have you had time to anticipate the child's response, triggers, or potential barriers? If administering measures, have you tried them out on yourself and familiarised yourself with them?

Moreover, it is also important to remember that creative and expressive sessions tend to take more time and preparation. Therefore, it is helpful to make sure that you leave yourself enough time to source the items, set them up, and pack them away after the session.

It is also important that the child sees that you take care of the items, value them, and look after them; this sends important messages to them about being in safe hands, being nurtured, and being valued. This can be partially shown through the caring and thoughtful way in which the items are packed up and handled. This can also be enhanced by having conversations about where the items will be kept, why they are kept there, and how they will be looked after in between sessions. Some children may benefit from actually being taken to the place where their items are kept or being shown a photo of the place where they are kept.

Areas of difference and selection of materials

The concepts discussed and the activities presented throughout the book should be tailored to the individual child's likes, ability, cultural background, and learning style (e.g. visual, kinaesthetic, auditory, etc.). Within this, it is useful to bear in mind that some children will require more scaffolding, time, and mediated learning than others. For example, some children may need more props, examples, multiple choice options, and/or ready-made worksheets, etc. It is also vital to consider and adapt the activities to the child's social, emotional, and developmental age and stage, rather than to their chronological age.

Moreover, the materials selected should be child-friendly and culturally sensitive and should consider areas of diversity (e.g. race, gender, religion, sexuality, class, culture, education, age, disability, ability, spirituality, and so forth). For example: having dolls or papers in a range of different colours, using non-people props such as animals, having miniatures that represent different cultural ways of grieving and processing death, or having options for different constellations of families to represent same-sex couples or single-parent households. It is also important to have items in a range of different shapes, sizes, and colours, to allow for children to have a choice, and to be able to have a variety of ways to express levels of difference.

Additionally, when selecting or introducing materials, practitioners should be sensitive to the child's lived experience and triggers, and adapt accordingly. For example, some exercises that require touch, such as drawing around the child's body for the body-mapping exercise, may feel like too much or be too invasive for some children. So another activity should be selected, and exploratory and acknowledging discussions should be had around this; and/or alternatives should be used, such as a teddy, a body cut-out, or them drawing around the adult instead.

Starting small and in a manageable way

A lot of ideas and strategies are offered in the chapters that follow. These can seem overwhelming and can convey the message that "the difficulty" is unmanageable and big. Therefore, it is important to start by selecting a small, manageable amount (think SMART goals; see Chapter 5), and then to implement them as a trial to ascertain whether or not they are helpful. It is useful to offer a couple of options to a young person/parent and to support them in having ownership and mastery over which ones they would like to try and to be led by their ideas, suggestions, and choices. This narrowing-down process should also be informed by a thorough assessment, clinical judgement, and the individual client, and through supervision. It is also helpful to read and re-read the sections again to familiarise yourself with the strategies and to start to narrow down which ones might be most appropriate at a particular given time.

Routine and structure

Within the context of relational and developmental trauma, children have often experienced inconsistent, chaotic, and unpredictable environments; therefore, it is important to have some routine, consistency, and structure within the session (not in a rigid, inflexible way). This might include having a welcome and review of the week, some warm-up and easing-into-the-activity time, and having sufficient time to reflect on the process, pack away, and ensure that the child is not leaving the session dysregulated and in a heightened state of arousal (additional ideas are offered in Chapters 3, 6, and 8).

Children often have not fully grasped the concept of time and orientation, particularly those who have experienced trauma, which often impacts one's time stamper, memory recall, and orientation. Therefore, they should know that there is a clear beginning, middle, and end to the sessions. This can be aided by having a child-friendly clock, countdown conversations, and therapy anchors and rituals (see Chapter 3).

Balanced with strengths and lightness

Generally, therapy should allow for children to dip in and out of the intensity and for there also to be moments of lightness, playfulness, fun, and humour. In addition, as with all of the mentioned strategies, it is important to ensure that there is a range of positive, mixed, and negative expressions/questions/phrasings to demonstrate the whole spectrum and to open the space for rich and diverse feeling discussions. For example: when asking about times when the child has felt scared and angry, it is also important to ask about times when they have felt happy, proud, and excited; and similarly, when exploring difficult moments, it is also important to reflect on fulfilling positive moments (see Chapter 5).

Monitoring and evaluating tools

It is important as a reflective-scientist practitioner to monitor and evaluate the effectiveness, helpfulness, and appropriateness of the tools and their delivery from the perspective of the child, their surrounding adults, and the practitioner. This ideally will be through the use of both qualitative and quantitative means of measurement and through multiple sources of information and output.

Recording their journey through making a personal folder or box

Different clinicians work differently; however, I find it helpful to have/make a box or a personal folder for each child where they can keep their work together and have a record of their journey. This can be named, labelled, and decorated by them. I find taking photos of their work (with their permission) helpful for having pictures that can be used in other strategies, such as on their sensory box or safe place poster, as a visual record of their therapy journey and in case the original gets lost/damaged.

Why creative and expressive tools and techniques might be helpful in the context of relational and developmental trauma and when working with young people

- When working with children and adolescents, it feels crucial to make therapy more playful, interesting, enjoyable, interactive, and fun in order to increase engagement and accessibility and to lessen the likelihood of the child feeling on the spot and/or threatened. Creative techniques and play are more universal and therefore tend to be more familiar and less intimidating to children. Expressive means also allow the child and therapist to have a project/task to focus on, which naturally creates some distance, space, and externalisation, which can make the feelings or memories feel less overwhelming and support the child to feel less exposed.

- Creative and expressive techniques can work helpfully across language, learning, and cultural borders, which can increase their accessibility and reach.

- Creative and expressive techniques can take into account all different types of learning and engaging styles. Therefore, embedding concepts in multiple ways increases the likelihood of the concepts making sense, being absorbed, being remembered, and being internalised. It also gives more opportunities for the concepts and metaphors to be tailored, individualised, and played with in a way that fits. Examples of expanding, exhaling, and embedding concepts using the arts will be presented throughout this book. However, one follows:

    Externalising and talking about butterflies in one's tummy using words may be helpful. However drawing butterflies in one's tummy, labelling them with the different worry names, making a body-map of what it feels like with and without the butterflies in one's tummy, watching videos of butterflies, sticking labels of the different worries in the shapes of butterflies in one's tummy, playing and acting out butterflies in one's tummy, and using a butterfly puppet are likely to embed this concept further and enrich the discussions around it.

    The premise also is that if these creative and expressive strategies are done within the context of a safe, regulating relationship, they not only provide the child with rich relational memories that it is hoped can then be internalised, but they also offer the child a reparative relational experience and opportunities to feel differently when in a relationship – where the child's needs and wants are listened to and responded to by a thinking, attuned, and sensitive adult. The creative tool may be the tangible outcome, but it is the relational quality and interaction that surrounds the process that is the true magic. It is also hoped that through the co-regulation and co-construction processes (all core parts of the creative tools) being internalised and anchored to, the child can gradually move on to self-regulation and, subsequently, transfer these relational templates to other future relationships and interactions.

- Trauma occurs in a wider context, and is often encoded in sensory and embodied modes, such as through pictures, sounds, smells, sensations, and images. So, it makes sense when addressing trauma and difficult memories to work at a creative contextual, embodied, sementic, narrative and sensory level (e.g. visual, kinaesthetic, tactile, olfactory, affective, and auditory), where children can engage all of their senses in a relational, safe, contained, and connected way and through somatic attunement and whole-brain-body connection.

- Building on the above, studies have shown that trauma and toxic stress can impact the communication between the left and right brain. Positively, creative techniques address this notion by utilising both sides of the brain and by supporting the core aim of most trauma therapies, which is to connect, link, increase the flow and integrate. This includes supporting and promoting the connection, communication, and integration between the left and the right brain, the mind and the body, thoughts and feelings, and the bottom of the brain and the top of the brain. Creative means also support the engagement of the child's sensory, motor, limbic/emotional, and arousal systems, as well as soothing their lower parts of the brain, releasing tension, grounding and regulating them, and activating their relaxation responses.

- In addition to the above, trauma can impact the Broca's region of the brain, which is where language is predominantly held. This is one of the reasons why trauma is often referred to as being a silent terror and why people often say that no words were able to come out of their mouth during a traumatic event. This relationship with language is also relevant for children who experienced trauma when they were pre-verbal, and, therefore, instead of the trauma being encoded in words, it tends to be encoded into images and senses and within their bodies. This fits with the quotes "The body keeps the score" (Van der Kolk, 2014) and "The body remembers" (Rothschild, 2000). Therefore, children often do not have the language to describe, name, or make sense of their experiences, so creative means can also be helpful in accessing far more than just words and can promote a whole-brain-body approach. This echoes the saying: a picture tells a thousand words. Often a picture can give a window into a child's emotional landscape and into their inner world.

- Trauma has also often contributed to the child being and/or feeling powerless, helpless, trapped, and out of control. This sense of powerlessness can be responded to through creative means. Creative means and tools can support the child to have some mastery and control over both the process and the finished product. They can support the child to be their own author of their story and to be the painter of their own canvas.

- Creative expressions can also provide the child with something concrete that they can take home, destroy, use to feel bigger than "the piece of paper", and have control over.

- Creative expressions can create both a physical and metaphorical container for the child but also act as a transitional object that they can take and adapt into their everyday life and use after the sessions/therapy comes to an end.

- Creative means are also a concrete and visual representation of the work done and the journey travelled within the sessions. They can be a powerful visual journey and tracking system of the changes and discoveries that have been made (see Chapter 10).

- Last but by no means least, having concrete creations can also support and be added to other therapy strategies, such as positive affirmation cards, prompt cards, a sensory box, and relaxation strategies (examples are provided throughout this book).

CHAPTER 2

Tools for Supporting the Assessment and Engagement of and Building Rapport with Young People

Introduction

The assessment type, style, and length will depend on and vary according to numerous factors, including the therapist's modality and training, length of time available, goals and focus of the work, and service context. This chapter will offer therapists some practical and creative tools that can be interwoven and incorporated into the assessment and into the engagement/getting-to-know-the-child tasks. These should be employed alongside, and in conjunction with, some of the strategies described in Chapters 3, 4, and 5, which are complementary and interlinked.

It may be helpful to revisit this chapter after reading Chapters 3, 4, and 5, and to be informed and guided by Chapter 1, which discusses underpinning principles, factors to be mindful of, and common pitfalls to consider when implementing the strategies and tools discussed throughout the book.

For interested readers, Table 2.1 at the end of this chapter offers a summary of some of the key assessment areas to consider in the context of relational and developmental trauma, with some sample questions included. A more detailed discussion of planning and undertaking attachment and trauma-informed assessments, and a summary of common attachment and trauma measures, is given in Chapter 5 of *Working with Relational and Developmental Trauma in Children and Adolescents* (Treisman, 2016).

Some practical, creative, and expressive assessment tools and techniques will now be presented. These are intended to be interwoven with other existing assessment tools and methods.

Practical, expressive, and creative assessment tools and techniques

Free playing and drawing

Free playing and drawing can be helpful from an observational and building-rapport perspective, and it can also contribute to valuable information-gathering. Example observations and questions that might be reflected on are listed below.

What is the nature and quality of the child's play – for example, is it hyper-vigilant/ controlling/intrusive/compulsive/chaotic/repetitive/rigid/restrictive/of an adult nature? Are there particular themes that emerge in the child's play or in the way/style in which they play? How and where does the child position themselves in relation to other items/ people/the room? How does the child respond to, look after, and/or interact with the toys and equipment? Which mediums and materials is the child drawn to or vice versa? How does the child respond to instructions, directions, and boundaries? How does the child interact with you as the therapist? How does the child respond to questions about their play or about their art? What are the feelings/sensations/tone in the room? How does the child respond to having their play tracked or to having their feelings named? How does the child talk about the finished product (e.g. proud, and wants to take it home or give it to the therapist; or rip it up, devalue it, etc.)?

This free-playing time might also give a window into certain aspects, such as: the child's emotional, social, and developmental age; how a child manages transitions, starts and ends tasks, regulates their emotions, manages anxieties, keeps to boundaries, engages in imaginative play, and so forth.

Free playing can also create opportunities for children to gain some mastery and to become familiar with the therapy space, the boundaries, and the materials. Optimally, children should have a range of resources available (these will vary depending on their "age/stage", preferences, learning style, and cultural background, and the theoretical approach employed), which they can use to express an array of feelings and themes (see Chapter 1). For example, having angel wings, a skeleton, a coffin, and so forth to represent death; having a wishing well, dream catcher, genie, fishbone, horse shoe, or dandelion to represent wishes, hopes, and dreams. It is also important, as stated in Chapter 1, to have a range of shapes and sizes to allow for children to express different levels of intensity, etc.

Common therapy items (there are likely to be fewer if you are working portably) might include puppets, masks, Play-Doh, a dressing-up kit, drawing/painting equipment, board games, a medical kit, a dolls' house, puzzles, clay, a sand tray, LEGO®, and miniatures.

Free playing and free drawing can also be useful, as just following the child, tracking and commenting on what they are doing in a connected and attuned way and reflecting and naming the associated feelings in a tentative, curious way, can be very powerful in itself. However, throughout the session, or in a different session, it can also be helpful to use follow-up questions (open-ended and from a position of curiosity) that can map onto the child's play. For example, a child who is playing with animals might be asked questions such as: If you could be an animal, which one would you most/least want to be, and why? If… (pointing to a specific animal) could talk, what do you think it would say? A child drawn to the Spider-Man figure might be asked: What is Spider-Man doing/thinking/feeling? If you could be a superhero, which would you be? What powers would you want to have? What powers do you have already? A child who has drawn a picture of a scary scene might be asked: If you were to give your drawing a title, what would it be? Can you tell me about your drawing? If your drawing could talk, what would it say?

Shared and co-constructing activities

Shared activities can be useful and informative, as well as enhancing the concepts of co-creating, taking turns (follow and leader), reciprocal roles, and the serve-and-return process. This might include exercises such as: co-creating a picture/story/song (see Photo 2.1), or building something together, like a LEGO® building, a tower, or a den.

Another fun way of engaging with a child through a shared activity is using the squiggle exercise (Winnicott, 1968). This is where the therapist draws a squiggle and the child adds to it, and so on. This can be enhanced by using Play-Doh or pipe cleaners, which can be added to the lines, as illustrated in Photo 2.2. This exercise can also provide interesting information on the way in which the child follows instructions and on their relationship to being a follower, or a leader, when in the presence of another adult.

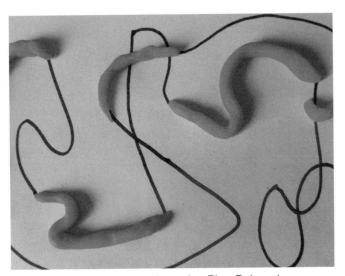

Photo 2.2 A squiggle exercise using Play-Doh and pens

Photo 2.1 Co-constructed drawing

Getting to know the child and all-about-me tasks

Although getting to know the child is a process that will grow and develop throughout the therapeutic journey, it feels important to try to spend some time, and take an enhanced interest early on, in getting to know the specific child as a valued and unique individual. This feels important in conveying the message to the child that they are a whole person with lots of different parts and layers to them and that they are much more than the "trauma", being a "child in foster care", having "witnessed domestic violence", or the "tricky behaviours".

This engagement and getting-to-know-you process is worked towards through the feelings in the room, the body language, the questions asked, and setting the scene of the therapy and of the relationship. However, in addition this can also be worked towards through specific getting-to-know-you exercises. These exercises are also helpful in supporting the therapist to show the child that they are both being kept in mind and held within the therapist's memory bank. For example,

"I remember we changed our first appointment, because you were watching the football. Which team do you support? How long have you supported them for? Who is your favourite player?"

There are lots of "All About Me" computer programs, colouring books, and interactive books widely available, which can be great and effective. Personally, I like to make my own; although this is time consuming, it allows for more flexibility when tailoring it for the particular child. The questions will vary depending on the child, but may include things like: What is your favourite food? Who is your favourite singer? What is your favourite season in the year? What is your favourite colour? What makes you feel excited? Describe yourself in three words. (See Worksheet 2.7/*A Therapeutic Treasure Deck of Sentence Completion and Feelings Cards* (Treisman, 2017) for some other sentence-completion questions.) These questions ideally should be tailored to a child's identified interest/passion/hobby. For example, if the child likes Dora the Explorer, you may ask why and what they like about Dora, and then go on to ask questions such as: What is in (child's name) the Explorer's world? If Dora met you, what would you tell her about yourself?

Some individualised "All About Me" exercises include: 1) making or using "All About Me" quizzes/crosswords/games; 2) making an "All About Me" treasure hunt; 3) designing an "All About Me" book/comic/PowerPoint presentation; 4) making an "All About Me" collage Photo 2.8); 5) telling or making an "All About Me" story/movie/song; or 6) supporting children to make an "All About Me" book using the letters of the alphabet (e.g. "A is for America, as it is top of my wish list, B is for bowling, as it is one of my favourite things to do, C is for cat, as I love my cat who is called Silky", and so forth).

Several other "All About Me" ideas and examples are listed below (additional ideas are also described in Chapter 4).

- Supporting the child to write about or draw all of the different parts of their identity/personality on pieces of a puzzle (see Worksheet 2.3), on Russian dolls (see Photo 2.3), on a LEGO® block sculpture, on a puzzle person/doll/body cut-out (see Worksheet 2.2, Photo 2.4, and Photo 2.9) or on a patchwork pattern (see Worksheet 2.4).

- Supporting the child to draw around their hands and then write on each finger different parts of their identity and the range of things that they like and are interested in (see "Self-esteem and sensory hand" in Chapter 5).

- Selecting something a child likes and using this as a template for writing more about themselves and their likes, dislikes, interests, etc. Examples include writing these things on: different stripes of a rainbow (see Photo 2.7 and Worksheet 2.5), different parts of a globe of the world (see Photo 2.5), components of a racing track, fairground rides, planets in a galaxy, toppings on a pizza, and/or bricks in a graffiti wall (see Photo 2.6).

- Making an "All About Me" game using different coloured sweets, such as jelly beans or Smarties, or different coloured pipe cleaners, pebbles, or buttons, where each colour represents a question (e.g. red represents your favourite colour or blue represents your favourite song (see Photo 2.10)).

- Writing "All About Me" questions on a ball and throwing it to the child; each time they catch it they answer the question nearest where their hands have landed.

- Making "All About Me" cards (Worksheet 2.6 can be used here), placing them in a pattern on the floor, and then throwing sticky fingers at them. The child answers the question nearest to where the sticky finger lands (see Photo 4.22 for an example of using this type of format with a feeling focus).

- Asking the child to bring in an item that they think is special or represents them in some way and then supporting them to tell a story about it.

- Giving the child a disposable camera and asking them to take photos that give you a sense of a "Day in the Life of…", "… World", "Walking the World from My Shoes", or "My Life from My Eyes".

- Playing games such as Connect Four, pick-up sticks, or Jenga, and then asking an "All About Me" question after each turn.

The child's response can later be used to inform other tools, for example putting inside or decorating their sensory or treasure box (see Chapter 3). Some examples are given below.

A young person who loves snow, and finds it regulating, is supported to make a personalised snow globe to put in their sensory box. A child who expresses that religion is important to them has prayers and other religious rituals incorporated into their session, their coping card, and the overall tasks. A child who likes graffiti is supported to express some of their interests/feelings through canvas, spray paints, and comic strips.

Photo 2.3 Each Russian doll representing a different part of the child's personality and identity

Photo 2.4 "All About Me" doll using fabric pens

Photo 2.5 A child displaying lots of the things they like, which make them happy and are part of what makes them who they are, using the world globe: Charlotte's World

Photo 2.6 A young person displaying his likes and interests on a graffiti-style identity wall

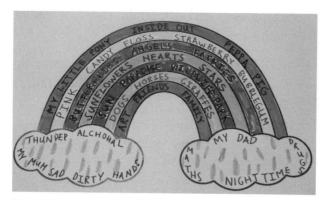

Photo 2.7 A young person displaying her likes and interests on the stripes of a rainbow and capturing some of the things that are difficult on the clouds

Photo 2.8 An "All About Me" collage

Photo 2.9 "All About Me" person puzzle (see Worksheet 2.3 for template) and "All About Me" collage combined

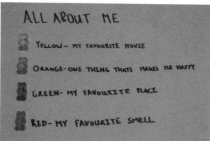

Photo 2.10 An "All About Me" game using sweets

Photo 2.11 "All About Me" through different pieces of a puzzle

Story of my name

Another exercise that can be a useful way of engaging children/carers and getting to know them a bit better is to ask them to introduce themselves by drawing the stories, meanings, associations, connections, and feelings about their name. This often opens up a lot of rich discussions and provides the child with a vehicle to begin to talk about themselves, their identity, and their story (an example of this follows, using my own name). This also can be a less threatening way of talking about themselves than if they are asked directly. As with all of these tools, this exercise can also bring about lots of questions and emotions, especially for those children in foster care or who were named after someone who has died or who they have/had a difficult relationship with. Therefore, it should be used sensitively and reflectively.

The photo below (Photo 2.12) is of my own quick drawing of my full name. When describing the picture to others, I might describe how Karen, which comes from the name Katherine, means pure maiden, hence the angel drawing. I also explain that, in South Africa, Karen is pronounced Kar, instead of Ka as it is in the UK, and that I actually prefer the sound of the Kar pronunciation. I discuss how although I like it as a name, I don't feel it fully suits me or captures who I am as a person and that I wish that I had a more unusual dynamic name. I also speak of how I like the letter "K" and how the "K" was selected by my parents, as it represents two of my family members who were in the Holocaust. I then discuss the name Treisman, how it represents both parts of my Jewish and South African identity, how it is my dad's name, and how, as one of three girls, it holds even more significance for passing on and preserving the family name. I then might discuss how I chose the green, blue, and orange colours to symbolise nature and the world, which links to my love of travelling and of being at one with nature.

Take a moment to think how much more you now feel you know about me having read the above than had I just introduced myself as "Karen" and left it at that. If you feel comfortable, try and do this with your own name and introduce your picture of your name to others. What did you notice? What did you learn? How easy or difficult was this exercise to do? As with all the tools, it is important to remember that there are no right and wrong ways of doing them, as everyone's pictures and interpretations will be unique to them.

Photo 2.12 The story of my name

A different version of this exercise, or an extension, is to support the child to draw their initials of their full name and then to turn the initials into a picture (see Photo 2.13).

Photo 2.13 Initials of my name turned into a picture

Family sculpts, genograms, and eco-maps

Creating a family sculpt, genogram, or eco-map can be a fantastic way of identifying, exploring, and reflecting on family patterns, scripts, themes, dynamics, and relationships. Ideally, genograms should include three generations (this can be more difficult for children who have been in care, bereaved, and/or adopted, etc.). It also can be helpful to incorporate people who have died, imaginary friends, other important people, pets, etc. It can be useful to get the child to place their "worst enemy" or the "person they don't like" on to the map, as this can support them in putting distance between them and also in making space for expressing negative feelings.

To increase the engagement and child-friendliness of these tools, it can be great to use a range of materials to represent the different people and relationships, such as miniatures (see Photo 2.14), Play-Doh, stickers (Photo 2.15), and/or buttons. Using a variety of materials positively can elicit a wealth of richer information (Why did they choose a particular figurine to represent a family member/their role/their characteristics? What might the positioning and distance of the placement of the figurines represent? What are the similarities and differences between the choice of figurines?), which can be expanded on through various questions. See Worksheet 2.6 for a selection of sample questions that can be used when creating a genogram or a cultural genogram.

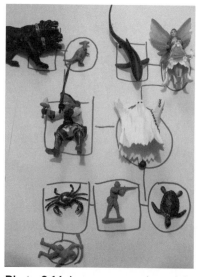

Photo 2.14 A genogram using miniatures

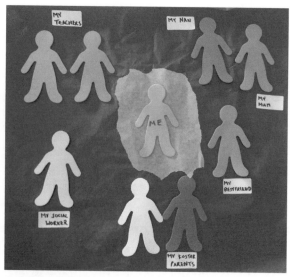

Photo 2.15 An eco-map using people stickers

Directive exercises using the arts

In addition to the free drawing/free playing described, it can be useful during the assessment and engaging stage, and throughout therapy, to use and incorporate a range of art-based directive exercises. Materials and mediums might include using pens, paint, clay, sculpts, collages, sand trays, puppets, music, toys, masks, photography, puppets, miniatures, stickers, and so forth.

An array of different tools based on using these mediums and providing children with different ways of expressing themselves are discussed throughout this book; however, the following points offer some suggestions of directive arts-based activities that may be helpful during the assessment and engagement process. It is important to hold in mind that the selection and appropriateness of these will be dependent on the assessment, relationship, individual child, and initial formulation. Some of the presented ideas may be quick exercises and others may span over several weeks and it could be beneficial to repeat them several times.

The art-based directive tasks are intended as starting points and scaffolding anchors; however, it is the process, thickening, and making-sense discussions and questions that make the task meaningful and relational rather than purely the end product or content (see Chapter 1 for further explanation around the therapeutic process). It is hoped that some of the tasks will offer a window into the child's inner world and therefore will subsequently inform future exercises.

An example of how one might expand on one of the following tasks is presented. This uses the example of a sand tray; however, these types of questions could be adapted for any type of medium/task.

Can you please tell me the name and the story of your sand tray world? What is happening in your sand tray world (chosen name would be used instead here)? Tell me about your sand tray world. If you could change one part of… (name of sand tray world), which part would you change, if any? If I stepped in to… (name of sand tray world), what do you think I might feel/see/hear/notice? What is it like looking at your world/what do you feel/ notice? Can you tell me about this part (pointing to a specific part)? What would … say to… (facilitate a conversation between two different figurines)?

Some examples of art-based directive tasks follow. Children can be asked to draw, sculpt, mould, collage, make, use sand, etc.

A self-portrait

Self-portrait (see Photo 2.16) drawing can be very informative and useful; including in areas around self-concept, self-esteem, identity, etc.

Self-portrait exercises can also be expanded by supporting children to make dual portraits (see Photo 2.18), where half of their face represents how they see themselves and the other half represents how they think others see them. (This type of dual concept can also be implemented by using inside/outside masks or boxes; see Photo 2.17 for an illustration of this, and Chapter 4 for more details and other photographed examples.)

This exercise can also be extended by asking children to draw a "then, now, and future" self-portrait image (see Photo 2.22 and Chapter 5).

Other additions to self-portrait expressive exercises include supporting children to express their identity and their portrait on to: a blank clock, a paper plate, or an actual mirror (where they can either draw on two sides of the mirror or on half of it).

Their family (in general) or their family portrait (see Photos 2.19 and 2.20)

Family portraits/sculpts can also provide a wealth of information and insight (although it is important, as with all the tasks, to interpret and reflect on them tentatively, cautiously, and with a multi-perspective critical lens).

Family portraits can be extended in a variety of ways including: asking the child to *depict the family doing something or an activity together* (e.g. doing the washing, playing together, eating together, going out, etc.); supporting the child to *think about their family at their best and their family at their worst*; asking children to *represent their family using a wide range of miniatures and figurines.*

Their house or a house in general

This can also be expanded by using Worksheet 4.16 in Chapter 4, where each room represents a different feeling, or Worksheet 4.17, where each TV and channel represent a different feeling.

Discussions around houses can also be supported by using a dolls' house (this can be optimised even further by making a dolls' house together out of household items). To enrich discussions and expand the understanding, questions that may be asked (dependent on the assessment, the goals/aims of the session, on the individual, and on the relationship) include: Who lives in the house? If your house had a name, what would it be? Can you tell me about... (pointing to a room or figurine)? What would I see if I looked into your house at...? What is your favourite place in the house? Who looks after the house? Can you please show me dinnertime/bedtime/playtime?

Feelings

Children can be supported to make/draw/sculpt a representation in sand, through collage, in a sculpt, or through drawing of, for example, how you feel now or what does... (a particular emotion) look like/feel like? See below for examples, as well as Chapter 4 for a range of feeling-focused exercises.

- Their world (see Photo 2.21).

- "My perfect day", "my typical day", or "my worst day".

- A tree or a garden.

- A superhero or a magical being/creature.

- Their externalised representation of the "difficulty", e.g. "headache" (see Photo 2.23), "worries", and/or "the anger".

- An "inside my head" or "my head of thoughts and emotions" collage/hat/head sculpture (see Chapter 4 for a description of this exercise).

- An "I am, I have, and I need" three-column collage or drawing.

- A or their safe place (see Chapter 3).

Photo 2.16 A replica self-portrait by a child who described himself as "spotty, ugly, big nosed, and with fangs"

Photo 2.17 Inside/outside feelings masks

Photo 2.18 A dual portrait drawing

Photo 2.19 Family sculpt using miniatures

In Photo 2.19 the child represented her father as a clock and described this as being due to his "prison sentence looming". She also represented her mother as being "very busy like an octopus". Interestingly, she also chose the same figurine (without detail or facial expressions) yet different colours for herself and for her sister.

Photo 2.20 A replica of a child's drawing of her family

In Photo 2.20 notice the distance and togetherness of the different family members in this drawing. This child shared that the left figure was her step-dad, the middle figure was her mother, and the three figures on the right were her siblings. She also placed her dog in the drawing next to her siblings. She did not place herself in the drawing. It is interesting to reflect on (in a cautious, reflective, and multi-perspective lens way) what not placing herself in the picture might mean about her sense of self, sense of belonging, wishes, and identity.

Photo 2.21 A recreation of a child's world in sand

Photo 2.22 A then, now, and future image

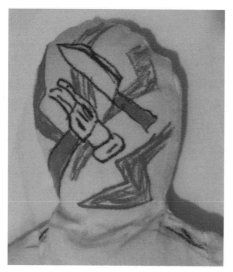

Photo 2.23 Externalised headache represented on a doll

Expressing, identifying, and expanding on a range of feelings

Chapter 4 offers specific ideas around supporting the identification and expression of feelings, and therefore, to avoid repetition, these should be referred to in conjunction with this chapter and will not be discussed here. However, it is important to mention that many of the tools mentioned in Chapter 4 can be used effectively during the assessment and engaging stage, such as the body-mapping exercises, a patchwork of feelings, the head of thoughts and emotions, a jar/box of feelings, a feelings puzzle, sentence-completion cards (see Worksheet 2.7), and feelings games. For many children, creating a feelings foundation and feelings language is the most important aspect, and this needs to be supported and prioritised before anything else can be moved on to.

Children's goals, wishes, hopes, and dreams for therapy, themselves, their relationships, and their lives

It is important to explore with the child their overall wishes, hopes, and goals and to zoom in on what they would like to change or to be different during or at the end of therapy. Questions that can support these discussions are listed below.

When we leave this room, what, if anything, would you have liked to have thought about/ achieved? When we come to the end of therapy, what, if anything, would you like to be different? If you could fast forward time, or travel into the future, what would you like to see/notice/to have happened? What news from the future would you like a fortune teller to tell you? What do you feel is the main reason we are here today? What are you hoping will have changed? What would you like to be doing/to see that you are not doing/seeing at the moment? How will you know when that has happened/been achieved? What are your wishes for yourself, for your relationships, for the world around you? If you could ask your wishing wizard/genie/dreaming dragon for some wishes, or some dreams to come true, what would they be?

The solution-focused miracle question (De Shazer, 2012) can also be a great way to expand on the above questions. There are lots of different variations of the miracle question; however, an example of one version follows here.

If you woke up tomorrow and a miracle happened and your main difficulties had disappeared, what would be different about the way you act, feel, and think? Walk me through what your day would look like after the difficulties had vanished?

The miracle question and wider discussions about children's wishes, hopes, dreams, and aspirations can be complemented by using actual props (puppets, masks, and miniatures), and making or drawing things like: magic wands, genies, fortune-teller balls, wishing dust, wishing fairies, dream catchers, a wishing well, or wishing dandelions (see Chapter 5). Sometimes I introduce a character, such as a "wishing wizard", "dreaming dragon", or "dreaming dandelion", to support these discussions. You may like to use the templates provided in Worksheets 2.8 or 2.9, or you may prefer to make your own.

It is recommended that you thicken the discussions of each wish or goal so that they become and feel richer and more energised. See Chapter 5 for examples of enriching conversations around wishes and dreams. This eliciting of wishes also gives an opportunity to try to support the child/family to set and fine tune their goals and expectations by thinking SMART (Specific, Measurable, Achievable, Realistic, and Time-limited). See Worksheet 5.6 for more information on creating SMART goals.

Similarly, it is also important to ask the young person/parent about their fears, worries, and apprehensions and to foster an atmosphere of ongoing open feedback and curiosity. For example: How would we know if I was working in a way with you that was not helpful/that did not fit for you/that felt…? See Chapter 1 for additional questions about eliciting feedback.

Scaling and measuring

In order to get more of a sense of the nature of the difficulty or of its baseline, to know where interventions should begin to target, and to have a guide of measuring change, it can be helpful to use measuring or scaling questions.

For example: On a scale from 0–10, where 0 is really, really sad and 10 is super happy, where would you place yourself? Then let's say the child says "five", you might say: Five, what does five look like/mean to you/what makes you say five? What is keeping you from being zero, one, or two (identifying protective factors)? What do you think might help you to move up a bit to a six or a seven? Can you think of a time when you were a... (number)?

For some children, the concept of scaling and measuring can be tricky, so it is worth thinking about how you can make this more accessible and more child-friendly. For example, you might use post-it notes or tape and place them at different points across the room, or you might use different size LEGO® towers (see Photo 2.24), varying sizes of Play-Doh balls (see Photo 2.25), different levels of colour intensity in containers of liquid (see Photo 2.26), different size pieces in a pie, or different symbols, such as a small dot moving through to a big circle.

It can also be useful and enriching to support the child to draw/sculpt/collage their responses. An example is given below.

Using tape to make different levels of intensity and to assist the scaling questions: Annemarie described how she felt she was currently at a two. She was supported to draw and represent what being at number two looked and felt like. She was then supported to draw and represent what she thought was keeping her at two, instead of being at zero or at one, so, in essence, identifying some of her protective factors. She was then asked to draw and represent herself at a six or seven, to discuss what components and steps it would take to support her to move there, and what being at six or seven might look like/feel like/mean. These changing numbers and images were discussed regularly and used as a check-in measure. At the end of therapy, Annemarie was supported to make a gallery of her scaling images, which visually captured her journey and growth.

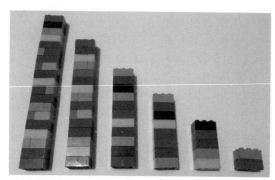

Photo 2.24 Measuring feelings using LEGO® and Play-Doh

Photo 2.25 Measuring feelings using Play-Doh circles

Photo 2.26 Measuring feelings using different colour intensity of liquid

Visual timeline, path, paper chain, or comic strip

Creating a visual timeline (see Photo 2.27), such as on a road, a movement map, or a path, can be beneficial during the assessment period. This might be of the child's overall life (birth till the current time), or around a more specific section, such as their "journey with the nightmares", "time since starting school", "foster placement journey", etc.

Within the creating-their-journey process, it can also be helpful for children to label and give a title to each stage on their map. Children may also want to assign different symbols (chosen by the child; however, options can be offered) to represent different times and different feelings, such as using the sun and rain, snakes and ladders, flowers and weeds, diamonds and coal, sharks and dolphins, spikes and curves, etc. In addition, a great way to bring a timeline and journey to life can be through using sensory materials, such as velvet, glitter, or silk for a happy time, and sandpaper or rocks for more difficult times.

When making their timeline, older children might prefer to collage or to use creative journaling to chart their different life stages. It feels important when creating timelines and journeys to make sure that there is space left at the end of any picture. This symbolises and sends the message to the young person that there is still the future – more journey to come and more opportunities for change and development.

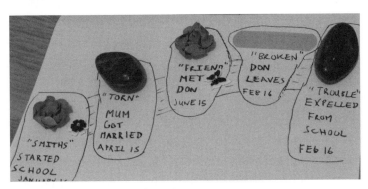

Photo 2.27 Material timeline of recent events

Along the same lines, it can be valuable to use interactive ways of discussing a chain of events, or a series of situations, such as making a paper chain (see Photo 2.28), a domino representation (see Photo 2.29), or a comic strip. This can be particularly helpful if there has been a specific incident that you want to understand in more detail, such as the child getting excluded from school or a presenting difficulty recently escalating. This can also be enhanced by using the "thoughts, feelings, physical sensations, and behaviours" concept described in Worksheet 4.20, or the "head, heart, and hands" concept described in Worksheet 4.21.

Photo 2.28 Chain of events

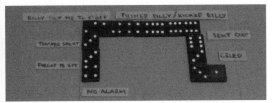

Photo 2.29 Chain of events using dominoes

Worksheet 2.1
Assessment areas and questions to consider when undertaking an attachment and trauma-informed assessment

Table 2.1 (adapted from Chapter 5 in *Working with Relational and Developmental Trauma in Children and Adolescents* – Treisman, 2016) discusses a variety of areas that can be considered when assessing a child/family who has experienced relational and developmental trauma. These questions and areas will vary depending on the child's "age", the unique child and situation, and the assessment/therapy goals. The appropriateness and usefulness of the questions, including how best to frame, deliver, and measure them, should be carefully considered. The included questions are by no means an exhaustive or prescriptive list, and the majority of areas overlap and are interwoven. Some of the questions are phrased with the term "mother"; however, it is acknowledged that families come in all different constellations, and therefore it is as important to ask these questions about any key attachment figure/caregiver.

Some areas might need to be expanded and magnified, whereas others might not be relevant for the specific child/family in question (imagine a camera capturing as much of the backdrop as possible with a wide-angle lens compared with taking a zoomed-in shot). Additionally, some questions might be kept in mind as part of a working hypothesis, but not asked, or answers to others may be sought through previous information-gathering. Ideally, an assessor will work systematically to build a wider picture, connect the dots, and interweave the patchwork pieces in order to form some sort of coherent narrative, working hypotheses, and initial formulation. This can also be usefully captured in a conceptual map that visually represents the integrated framework.

A thorough assessment acknowledges that parenting and behaviour does not occur within a vacuum and is contextually embedded and, therefore, will develop a formulation based on the interplay and relationship between multiple factors. When assessing, it is important to hold the dual lens of attachment and trauma within a wider frame of mental health and child development.

Copyright © Karen Treisman – *A Therapeutic Treasure Box for Working with Children and Adolescents with Developmental Trauma* – 2018

Table 2.1 Assessment questions and areas of consideration

Assessing area	Example questions	Additional considerations
In-utero and post-natal	Did the mother have antenatal care and what support systems and services were available/used during her pregnancy? How was the pregnancy? How was the pregnancy described? Were there any stressors, traumas, losses, accidents, injuries, and/or violent situations reported during the pregnancy? Did the mother smoke, drink alcohol, take medications, and/or use substances during the pregnancy? Was the pregnancy planned? What were the parents' feelings, thoughts, reactions, and responses about the pregnancy/baby/gender? What was the "mother's" prenatal attachment and reflective function about the baby like to the baby? For example, cognitive attachment (e.g. the ability to conceptualise the foetus as a person or be able to differentiate them from themselves), emotional attachment (e.g. an empathic affectionate bond), attachment behaviours (e.g. responding and interacting with the foetus), and self-care practices (e.g. maintaining good health). How was the labour and delivery? Were there any complications or concerns (e.g. baby's growth, weight, or oxygen supply)? What was the "parent's" reaction and responses to the baby? How was the baby's name selected? What was the nature and quality of the "mother–baby" relationship following arrival?	If not a first-time mother, there may be important questions about past pregnancies, motherhood, termination, and/or miscarriage experiences. The following may be helpful supporting measures: • The Pregnancy Interview (Slade *et al.* 2007) • Parent Development Interview (Slade *et al.* 2003) • Parental Reflective Functioning Questionnaire (Luyten *et al.*, 2017) • This is My Baby Interview (Bates *et al.*, 1998) • Maternal Attachment Inventory (Muller, 1994) • Maternal Foetal Attachment Scale (Cranley, 1981) • Maternal Antenatal Attachment Scale (Condon, 1993) • Postpartum Bonding Questionnaire (Brocklington *et al.* 2001) • Mother–Infant Bonding Scale. (Kumar *et al.* 1997)

Copyright © Karen Treisman – *A Therapeutic Treasure Box for Working with Children and Adolescents with Developmental Trauma – 2018*

Assessing area	Example questions	Additional considerations
Developmental trajectory	Did the child experience trauma, loss, and/or toxic stress during their development (including the in-utero period)? Was the child exposed to toxins during their development (e.g. drugs, nicotine, medication, alcohol, or household products)? Did the child meet their developmental milestones? Were/are there any developmental delays/learning disabilities/difficulties or pre-existing medical conditions? What core experiences and skills did they miss out on during their development? What are their emotional, social, and developmental needs? How will these change as they develop?	This should be supported by observations and multiple reports from professionals (e.g. the health visitor, nursery worker, GP, etc.). This should also ideally be complemented by Sensory and Developmental Profile questionnaires and measures. Some examples are listed below. • Infant–Toddler Social and Emotional Assessment (ITSEA and BITSEA) (Carter and Briggs-Gowan, 2005), ages 1–3 years. • The Bayley Scales of Infant Development (Bayley, 2006), 1–42 months. • Ages and Stages Questionnaires (Squires, Bricker, and Twombly, 2002) – different versions available ranging from 6 to 60 months old. • The Communication and Symbolic Behaviour Scales Developmental Profile (Wetherby and Prizant, 2001), ages 6–24 months.
Family factors	Who is in the child's family/ies? What do we know about the family experiences of trauma, genetic factors, life stressors, conflictual relationships, attachment relationships, mental and physical health diagnoses, learning disability diagnoses, criminal activity, and use of substances? What impact might these have had on the child? What is the quality and nature of the family's support system? What is the family's structure and organisation (i.e. subsystems, cohesion, hierarchies, boundaries, and roles)? What are the family patterns of communication, conflict-resolution, decision-making, help-seeking, and problem-solving? What are the shared family models, beliefs, values, stories, and inter-/multi-generational legacies? What are the families' strengths, skills, protective factors, and resiliencies?	Genograms or eco-maps can be beneficial tools to aid these questions. The term "family" should be thought of in a broad sense; this may include cousins, foster carers, nanny, etc. Sibling and extended family relationships should also be considered.

Copyright © Karen Treisman – *A Therapeutic Treasure Box for Working with Children and Adolescents with Developmental Trauma* – 2018

| Parenting and attachment experience | Who were the child's primary carers? Is this similar or different now?

What does the parent/parenting experience mean to the child?

What was the home atmosphere like?

What parenting styles/models/quality/relational templates/behavioural management did they receive?

Have these been shaped or changed over time? If so, how?

How did the parenting meet the different developmental stages of the changing child? | These questions should be informed by parenting measures, rich descriptions, specific examples, and observations of parent–child interactions.

Observations should include a variety of tasks and settings that allow for children's attachment systems to be activated and for there to be live examples of managing high-intensity arousal and separation and for co-construction to be seen.

Observations may include:

• stressful times of the day such as mealtimes or the morning routine

• watching the family build a LEGO® structure or play a game together

• naming the family rules or each member's likes and dislikes

• seeing the child's responses when separated from and reunited with their primary caregiver or when approached by a stranger.

Children's representations may be sought in numerous ways, such as drawing a picture of their family, making a family sculpt, sentence-completion tasks, or telling a story.

Some useful measures might include the following.

• Strange Situation (Ainsworth *et al.*, 1978), 11–24 months, adapted versions available.

• Separation anxiety tests (various versions available).

• CARE-Index Infancy and CARE-Index Toddler (Crittenden, 2004).

• Assessment-Q Set (Waters, 1995), 11 months to five years.

• Narrative story stems (various formats available).

• The Attachment Doll Play Interview for Pre-schoolers (Oppenheim, 1997).

• School-aged assessment of attachment (Crittenden, Kozlowska, and Landini 2010), 6–13 years.

• Attachment Interview for Childhood and Adolescence (Ammaniti *et al.*, 2000), 10–16 years.

• The Child Attachment Interview (Target, Fonagy, and Shmueli-Goetz, 2003), approximately 8–13 years. |

Copyright © Karen Treisman – *A Therapeutic Treasure Box for Working with Children and Adolescents with Developmental Trauma* – 2018

Assessing area	Example questions	Additional considerations
Relationships	Who are/were the key relationships in the child's life? What are the different types of relationships the child has? What relational losses and relational riches have they experienced? What are their patterns of relating to others? What have they learned about "doing and being in" relationships? How are their interpersonal and social skills?	Consider "family", professional, and peer relationships. Some measures that can complement this component, along with the parenting experience, are listed here. • Adult Attachment Interview (George, Kaplan, and Main 1985). Adapted and modified versions available. • Working Model of the Child Interview (Zeanah and Benoit, 1995). • Parent Development Interview (Slade *et al.*, 2004). • Caregiving Interview (George and Solomon, 2008). • The Adult–Adolescent Parenting Inventory (Bavolek and Keene, 2001). • The Parenting Role Interview (Bifulco *et al.*, 2008). • The Insightfulness Assessment (Koren-Karie and Oppenheim, 2004). • This is My Baby (Bates and Dozier, 1998). • Parental Reflective Functioning Questionnaire (Luyten *et al.*, 2009). • Mayer–Salovey–Caruso Emotional Intelligence Test (Mayer *et al.*, 2003). • Emotional Availability Scales (Biringen, 2008). • The Difficulties in Emotional Regulation Scale (Gratz and Roemer, 2004). • Parent–Child Relationship Inventory (Gerard, 1994). • Parent–Infant Relationship Global Assessment (ZERO TO THREE, 2005), ages 0–3. • Parent–Infant Relational Assessment Tool (PIRAT) (Broughton, 2010). • NCAST Parent–Child Interaction and Teaching Scales (Mischenko, Cheater, and Street, 2004). • Marschak Interaction Method (Marschak, 1960). • Parenting Stress Index (Abidin, 1995). • The Parenting Daily Hassles Scale (Crinic and Greenberg, 1990). • Parenting Sense of Competence (Johnston and Mash, 1989).

Copyright © Karen Treisman – *A Therapeutic Treasure Box for Working with Children and Adolescents with Developmental Trauma* – 2018

			• Maternal Self-Efficacy Scale (Teti and Gelfand, 1991).
			• Family Environment Scale (Moos and Moos, 1983).
			• Family Relationship Index (Holahan and Moos, 1983).
			• Family Adaptability and Cohesion Scale (Olsen, Gorall, and Tiesel, 2006).
			• Home Observation for Measurement of the Environment (Caldwell and Bradley, 1984).
Service history and relationship to professional support		What is the child/family's relationship to services/professionals? What services have been involved? What other interventions/assessments have taken place, and how were these experienced and responded to?	This might be supported by drawing their service journey, map, or chronology. It can be useful to explore their conceptualisations/beliefs/hopes/worries/expectations about, for example, "therapy". Where appropriate, this might include questions around capacity, motivation, and readiness to change.
Placement history		If the child was or is placed in care: What was the reason they were removed? What has/was their placement history been? What separations, losses, and transitions have they experienced? How have they managed and responded to these? What have their relationships with their caregivers been? What was the quality of the placement/s? What was their understanding of the placement/s and of being in care? Have they experienced multiple placements? If so, why and how were these managed? What are their contact arrangements?	Chronologies and life-story books can be helpful here.

Copyright © Karen Treisman – *A Therapeutic Treasure Box for Working with Children and Adolescents with Developmental Trauma – 2018*

Assessing area	Example questions	Additional considerations
Traumas and losses	What age was the child when the traumas occurred? What was the nature/frequency/severity/duration of the traumas? How did the traumas come to light? What were the child's and others' responses to the traumas? What was the child's relationship to the person/people who carried out the traumas? What are their feelings (positive and negative) towards them? What consequences were there of the traumas and losses? What were the child's/family's understanding, sense-making, attributions, and meaning-making about the traumas? What might the child's core beliefs, internal working models, and sense of self be? What was the child's experience of shame and blame? What have they learned about emotional and behavioural arousal-regulation? How have they learned to manage stress, frustration, impulses, feeling out of control, and transitions? What is their ability to trust or to feel safe? What is the child's relationship like with their body and sensory world?	These questions take into account some of the eight domains proposed to be affected by complex trauma. These include attachment, biology, affect regulation, dissociation, behavioural control, cognition, and self-concept (Cook *et al.*, 2005). Some trauma and dissociation measures are listed here. • Clinician-administered PTSD Scale (Nader *et al.*, 1996), ages 8–18. • Children's PTSD Inventory (Saigh *et al.*, 2000), ages 6–18. • UCLA Trauma Reminders Inventory (Steinberg *et al.*, 2013), ages 7–12, and an adolescent version available. • Child PTSD Symptom Scale (Foa *et al.*, 2001), ages 8–18. • Trauma Symptom Checklist for Children (Briere, 2005), different age versions available. • PTSD Semi-Structured Interview and Observation Record for Infants and Young Children (Sheeringa and Zeanah, 1994), ages 0–7. • Children's Impact of Traumatic Events Scale (Wolfe *et al.*, 1991), ages 8–16. • Child's Reactions to Traumatic Event Scale (Jones, Fletcher, and Ribbe, 2002), ages 6–18. • Structured Interview for Disorders of Extreme Stress (SIDES), adolescent version (Pelcovitz *et al.*, 1997), ages 12–18. • The Angie/Andy Cartoon Trauma Scale (Praver *et al.*, 2000), ages 6–12. • Child Dissociative Checklist (Putnam, Helmers, and Trickett, 1993), ages 5–12. • The Child Dissociative Experience Scale (Stolbach, 1997). • Children's Perceptual Alterations Scale (Evers-Szostak and Sanders, 1992), ages 8–12. • Adolescent Dissociative Experiences Scale (Armstrong *et al.*, 1997), ages 11–18.

Copyright © Karen Treisman – *A Therapeutic Treasure Box for Working with Children and Adolescents with Developmental Trauma* – 2018

Presenting difficulties and subsequent impact	Define the presenting difficulty. What is it and what does it look like? Can you give an example of when it happened? When did the presenting difficulty start and how long has it been occurring for? How frequently does it occur? When does it occur and not occur? What patterns, triggers, hotspots, and variables (environmental, sensory, autobiographical, physical, cognitive, relational, emotional, situational) make the presenting difficulty bigger, smaller, absent, present, etc.? What is the impact of the difficulty on the child and those around them (e.g. self-care, self-presentation, sleep, eating, mood, school life, relationships, learning, hobbies, daily-living skills, self-esteem, etc.)? How stressful is the difficulty to the child and to their Team Around the Child? What is the difficulty making trickier or stopping the child/caregivers from doing? What are the child's sense-making, meaning-making, attributions, and explanations about the difficulty? How do these fit with their Team Around the Child's views? What might the difficulty be communicating and what story is it telling? What function might it be serving? (See Box 6.4 and "Behaviour as communication" in Chapter 8.) What responses has the difficulty received? What interventions/messages/strategies have been put in place to address the difficulty?	It can be helpful to visually map, chart, diarise, and/or track the behaviour. Scaling questions can also be useful here. Some behaviour-based measures are listed here. • Children's Global Assessment Scale (Shaffer, Gould, and Brasic, 1983), ages 4–16. • DAWBA (Goodman, Ford, and Richards, 2000), ages 5–17. • The Behaviour Assessment System for Children (Reynolds and Kamphaus, 2004). • The Achenbach System of Empirically Based Assessment includes an integrated set of rating forms for children age 1.5 through to adulthood (Achenbach, 2009). • Vineland Adaptive Behaviour Scales (Sparrow, Cicchetti, and Balla, 2005), different age range versions available.
Education and recreation	How is the child doing in school (socially, academically, behaviourally, emotionally)? How are their cognitive and executive function skills? How are their play, peer, and social skills (including relationships with teachers)? Have they had any additional input, such as one-to-one support, neuropsychological assessment, speech and language support, and/or behavioural support? What extracurricular activities/interests do they have?	Some useful cognitive and executive function measures include the following. • Wechsler Preschool and Primary Scale of Intelligence (WPSSI) (Wechsler, 1967). • Wechsler Intelligence Scale for Children (WISC) (Wechsler, 1991). • The Developmental NEuroPSYchological Assessment (NEPSY) (Korkman, Kirk, and Kemp, 1998). • The Kaufman Assessment Battery for Children (Kaufman and Kaufman, 2004). Particular domains of cognitive functioning, for example executive functioning, may need to be investigated further by specific measures.

Copyright © Karen Treisman – *A Therapeutic Treasure Box for Working with Children and Adolescents with Developmental Trauma* – 2018

Assessing area	Example questions	Additional considerations
Strengths, positive qualities, and protective factors	What are/were the protective factors? What has and is going well? What positive steps forward have they already made? What adversities have they survived? What are their strengths, skills, resiliencies, protective factors, positive qualities, coping strategies, and interests? What motivates them? What makes them light up and feel good? What are their hopes, dreams, and ambitions?	See Chapter 5.
Risk and safety	What areas of risk, child protection, and safety need to be taken into account and assessed (e.g. suicidal ideation/self-harm/self-neglect/social withdrawal/non-compliance with medication/going missing/criminal activity/antisocial behaviour/violence/sexual exploitation/substance abuse/behaviour of a sexual nature)? What safety plans and risk assessments are in place? How are these working and being monitored?	These areas may differ if categorised into sections of parental, child, and social risk factors and separated as historical or current risk factors (static vs. dynamic).
Contextual factors	What are the important systemic, contextual, and organisational dynamics (e.g. cultural, financial, social, political, familial, gender, religious, and organisational factors)?	An example: Jala reported to her teacher that she was having nightmares. Her teacher interpreted these as distressing and referred Jala to a therapist. Jala made sense of these nightmares differently; she saw them as reflecting her spiritual status whereby her ancestors were conveying powerful messages to her. Jala also shared that she had experienced female genital mutilation (FGM). This coincided with a new governmental focus on FGM, coupled with the therapist having a specialist interest in FGM. Jala required an interpreter. She also practised Islam, a key part of her identity. Jala's immigration status was being reviewed, and she was living in temporary housing. How would these wider factors impact and colour the assessment and responses?

Copyright © Karen Treisman – *A Therapeutic Treasure Box for Working with Children and Adolescents with Developmental Trauma* – 2018

Copyright © Karen Treisman – *A Therapeutic Treasure Box for Working with Children and Adolescents with Developmental Trauma* – 2018

Worksheet 2.3
"All About Me" puzzle

Copyright © Karen Treisman – *A Therapeutic Treasure Box for Working with Children and Adolescents with Developmental Trauma* – 2018

My patchwork of ...

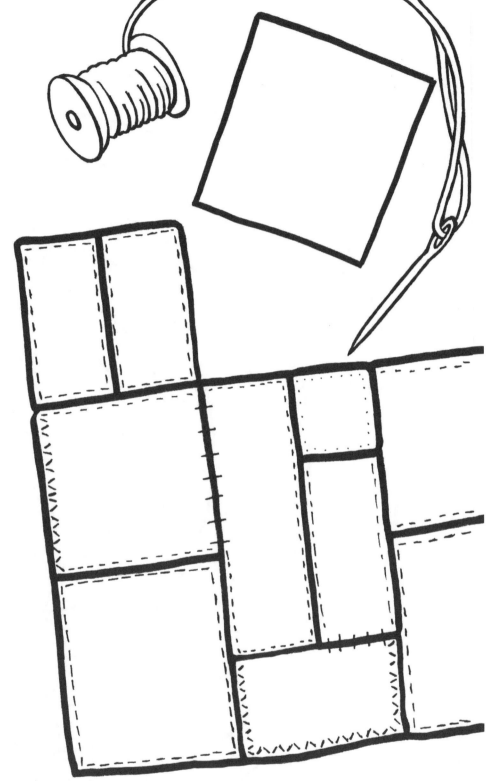

Copyright © Karen Treisman – *A Therapeutic Treasure Box for Working with Children and Adolescents with Developmental Trauma – 2018*

Worksheet 2.5
"All About Me" rainbow

Copyright © Karen Treisman – *A Therapeutic Treasure Box for Working with Children and Adolescents with Developmental Trauma* – 2018

Worksheet 2.6
Genograms and cultural genograms

This worksheet includes some sample questions that can be asked when co-creating genograms and cultural genograms. (Note: It is not an exhaustive or prescriptive list and needs to be tailored to the individual.) Example words and phrasings are included; however, these need to be adjusted and individualised for the unique person/family. As stated in previous sections, it is optimal to use interactive and child-friendly materials to bring the genograms alive and to gather additional information, such as using figurines, puppets, stickers, and/or pebbles.

> » Who is in your family?

> » What are their connections and relationships to each other?

> » Can you tell me a bit about… (name)?

> » If you were to describe… (name) in three words, how would you describe them?

> » What kind of relationship does… (name) have with… (name)? (The child may want to choose a symbol or type of pattern to capture this – they then can make a key for the different symbols.)

> » Who on here are you "closest to" and why?

> » Who are you "least close to" and why?

> » Who do you have the "most fun" with?

> » How do you do being a "boy"?

> » How does your family do "praise"?

> » Who shows "the anger" the most?

> » Who else feels the same about… (name)? Who else agrees with… (name)?

> » Who do you think you are most like/different to?

> » Is anyone else interested in "football" (replace the word football)?

> » How is the way your "mum" responds to you when you are "sad" different from how your "grandma" responds?

> » Who do you know the least about? If they were here, what questions would you ask?

> » Are there any patterns or themes you notice?

> » Is there anything that surprised you or interested you when creating your genogram?

> » How are/were "emotions" dealt with, expressed, and managed in your family? What stories and messages are/were there about "emotions"? (Replace the word "emotions" with the intended focus, for example death, loss, secrets, mental health, police, learning disability, stigma, etc.)

Copyright © Karen Treisman – *A Therapeutic Treasure Box for Working with Children and Adolescents with Developmental Trauma – 2018*

» How was/is "affection" shown in your family? (Replace the word "affection" with the intended focus, for example anger, love, pride, shame, disappointment, etc.)

» How were/are "differences/conflicts" managed and responded to in your family? (Replace the words "differences/conflicts" with the intended focus, for example disobedience, expressions of sexuality, successes, achievements, mistakes, etc.)

» How do/did you celebrate achievements/birthdays/successes in your family?

» What was... (a family member's) experiences of "school"? (Replace the word "school" with the intended focus, for example mental health, racism, loss, trauma, making friends, rejection, bullying, etc.)

» What do you think... (a family member's) experience of being "parented" was? How is this similar or different to... (name)?

» How, if at all, do you think... (a family member's) experiences impacted... (name)? For example: How, if at all, do you think your grandmother's experiences of deprivation and war impacted and influenced your father's relationship to money? How, if at all, do you think your mother's experiences of physical chastisement influenced her relationship to discipline and behavioural management?

» What stories of strength and resilience are there in your family?

» Can you tell me a story of one of your family members showing a strength or something you are proud to share?

Cultural genograms

Cultural genograms expand on the above. They further facilitate an exploration of life themes whilst attending to, and mapping out, areas of historical, geographical, and cultural processes and identity that have occurred in the family life-cycle. They can be a sensitive way to explore areas of difference and similarities, such as (this list is not exhaustive) religion, spirituality, culture, ability, education, class, age, sexuality, gender, and race, as well as creating an opportunity to explore children's representations, multigenerational legacies, and cultural conceptualisations. Cultural genograms can also be helpful in identifying patterns, including those around shame, pride, acceptance, rejection, historical hostility, and transmission of trauma, and they can be key in gathering a deeper understanding of how the child/family positions themselves within their wider socio-political context and community.

The following questions should be interwoven with the questions above (they need to be tailored to the individual child, goals, presenting difficulty, relationship, etc.).

» What "hardships" did your "grandmother" experience and what was her sense-making around these? (Replace the word "hardships" with the intended focus, for example losses, traumas, obstacles, etc.)

» How was "mental health" viewed by... (name)? (Replace the words "mental health" with the intended focus, for example HIV/AIDS, marriage, death, divorce, abuse, discipline, etc.)

Copyright © Karen Treisman – *A Therapeutic Treasure Box for Working with Children and Adolescents with Developmental Trauma* – 2018

» What role did and does "gender" play within the family? (Replace the word "gender" with the intended focus, for example sexuality, culture, birth order, etc.)

» How do you do being a "girl"?

» How does your family do "praise"?

» How is...understood in your culture? (Fill in the blank with the intended focus, for example HIV/AIDS, marriage, death, divorce, abuse, discipline, crying, sex, etc.)

» What "emotions" are valued or avoided in... (name)? (Replace the word "emotions" with the intended focus.)

» What "religious rituals, values, or beliefs" did you grow up with? (Replace the words "religious rituals, values, or beliefs" with the intended focus, for example beliefs around death, beliefs around divorce, beliefs around sex, beliefs around being a woman, etc.)

» What or who influenced the development of these beliefs and values?

» What would happen if these beliefs or values were challenged or disagreed with?

» What "collective traumas and losses" has... (name) experienced? (Replace the words "collective traumas and losses" with the intended focus.)

» How have family values changed over time?

» What stories within your family/community/identified cultural group are there of "strength and resilience"? (Replace the words "strength and resilience" with the intended focus, for example bravery, overcoming adversity, hardship, discrimination, persecution, etc.)

Copyright © Karen Treisman – *A Therapeutic Treasure Box for Working with Children and Adolescents with Developmental Trauma* – 2018

Worksheet 2.7
Sentence-completion ideas

These will vary depending on the individual and on the focus of the work. Only a few should be selected at a time. These can be used as suggestions or can be cut up and made into sentence-completion cards (see *A Therapeutic Treasure Deck of Sentence Completion and Feelings Cards*, Treisman 2017).

"I feel happy when…"
"I miss…"
"I love…"
"I cry when…"
"My favourite place is…"
"My favourite colour is…"
"My favourite time of year/season is…"
"My favourite animal is…"
"My favourite sport/team is…"
"My favourite item is…"
"My favourite TV shows/movies are…"
"If I could close my eyes and be transported to any place, I would go to…"
"If I ruled the world, I would…"
"I wish my family would…"
"I think my 'parents' should…" (Replace the word "parents" with another focus, for example father, mother, sister, teacher, etc.).
"My 'family' make me feel…" (Replace the word "family" with another focus, for example friends, teachers, foster carers, etc.)
"I wish I had…"
"I wish I could…"
"It's a great day when…"
"I'm happiest when…"
"I feel good when…"
"I am most proud of…"
"Someone I look up to is…"
"If I could go back in time to a moment, I would go back to…"
"If I could play one moment over and over again, I would play…"

Copyright © Karen Treisman – *A Therapeutic Treasure Box for Working with Children and Adolescents with Developmental Trauma* – 2018

"If I could be someone else for the day, I would be…"
"…puts a smile on my face."
"The things that make the 'anger' visit are…" (Replace the word "anger" with other emotions.)
"The things that make the 'sadness' visit are…" (Replace the word "sadness" with other emotions.)
"The things that make the 'worry/fear' visit are…" (Replace the words "worry/fear" with other emotions.)
"The things that make the 'excitement/joy' visit are…" (Replace the words "excitement/joy" with other emotions.)
"I feel 'scared' when…" (Replace the word "scared" with other emotions such as sadness/angry/happy/embarrassed/excited.)
"I feel 'angry' when…" (Replace the word "angry" with other emotions.)
"I feel 'sad' when…" (Replace the word "sad" with other emotions.)
"I feel 'excited/joyful' when…" (Replace the words "excited/joyful" with other emotions.)
"I feel 'frustrated' when…" (Replace the word "frustrated" with other emotions.)
"When I feel 'scared' I…" (Replace the word "scared" with other emotions such as sadness/angry/happy/embarrassed/excited.)
"When I feel 'angry' I…" (Replace the word "angry" with other emotions – think about what you do, say, feel, and show.)
"When I feel 'sad' I…" (Replace the word "sad" with other emotions – think about what you do, say, feel, and show.)
"When I feel 'frustrated' I…" (Replace the word "frustrated" with other emotions – think about what you do, say, feel, and show.)
"When I feel 'excited/happy' I…" (Replace the words "excited/happy" with other emotions – think about what you do, say, feel, and show.)
"I think a lot about…"
"I try not to think about…"
"The things that get under my skin are…"
"The things that I am fighting for are…"
"The things that are most important to me are…"
"Before I go to sleep, I think about…"
"When I am home…"
"The thing I need is…"
"If people could truly see inside me, they would see…"
"I wish people knew about me that…"
"The thing I would change is…"
"I keep myself safe by…"

Copyright © Karen Treisman – A Therapeutic Treasure Box for Working with Children and Adolescents with Developmental Trauma – 2018

My wishes for...
are...

Copyright © Karen Treisman – *A Therapeutic Treasure Box for Working with Children and Adolescents with Developmental Trauma – 2018*

Worksheet 2.9
Wishing wizard or dreaming dragon

? What does my Wishing Wizard or Dreaming Dragon look like?

Draw, sculpt, write, and collage to show your responses.

? What does my Wishing Wizard or Dreaming Dragon sound like/smell like?

? What does my Wishing Wizard or Dreaming Dragon do and help me with?

Draw, sculpt, write, and collage to show your responses.

? What messages do I have to give to my Wishing Wizard or Dreaming Dragon?

Copyright © Karen Treisman – *A Therapeutic Treasure Box for Working with Children and Adolescents with Developmental Trauma – 2018*

CHAPTER 3

Working Towards Establishing Multi-Levelled Safety (Inner Safety, Emotional Safety, Physical Safety, Felt Safety)

Introduction and why establishing safety is fundamental to interventions within the context of relational and developmental trauma

Experience-dependent brain and trauma as multi-sensory experience

During the critical sensitive periods of childhood, including the pregnancy stage, the brain develops at an incredible growth rate. Like a sponge or a muscle, the experience-dependent brain constantly absorbs new experiences and is positively and/or negatively shaped by interactions, relationships, and its surrounding environment (e.g. the neurobiology of attachment). This is noteworthy, as many children who have experienced relational and developmental trauma have been soaked, trapped, and left in a state of fear and toxic stress (surviving shark-infested waters – see Box 3.1) over a long period of time, often without the presence of a safe, regulating, responsive, and containing adult. For some, this fear or sense of being unsafe, or of not being safe enough, started during their in-utero experience (pregnancy). Their in-utero experience might have been characterised by hostility, fear, toxic stress, unresponsiveness, ambivalence, and threat (e.g. domestic violence, exposure to substances, homelessness, sexual abuse, verbal aggression, etc.). This is vital, as the womb is a child's first classroom, teaching experience, introduction to the world, and lesson of what it is like to be in a relationship and to be connected to another person.

Illustration 3.1 The womb as a warzone

Within a relational and developmental trauma context, children have often been left in overwhelming seas of emotional, sensorial (Figure 3.1), and physiological waves, including changes in chemicals such as adrenaline, cortisol, and serotonin. The case examples and Figure 3.1 below illustrate some of these emotional, sensorial and physiological waves.

Case examples are given below and additional examples can be found in Chapter 8. Try, in as safe a way as possible, to put yourself in the child's shoes or to see the world through the child's eyes and lived experiences as you read.

Eye contact (intrusive, intense, and threatening versus limited and avoidant)

Mouth (shouting/verbal abuse, open wide versus silence)

Hearing/ears (shouting/screaming verbal abuse, aggression, crying, loud noises, banging, items breaking, blaring music, police sirens, etc. versus silence)

Nose/smelling (urine, cigarettes, dirt, blood, alcohol, faeces, distinct smells associated with the trauma, e.g. perfume, etc.)

Feeling (too much touching, too little touching, pain, cold/hot, wet, pressure, etc.)

Body sensations (sweating, heart pounding, tense muscles, hungry, cold, wet, feeling trapped, stiff, dizzy, in pain, nauseous, frozen, out of control, etc.)

Brain/cognitive (fearful, threatened, angry, scared, sad, confused, dreading, helpless, powerless, frozen, trapped, blame, shame, etc.)

Figure 3.1 Some examples of the multi-sensory elements of trauma (not exhaustive)

Four-year-old Sebastian leapt down the stairs unsupported and unsupervised. He lost his grip and fell down the stairs, ending up in a ball-like shape wedged against the wall. Sebastian cried and held on to his leg in pain. His father initially ignored his cries and then eventually, as this escalated, began to laugh at and humiliate him: "It doesn't take a rocket scientist to walk down the stairs, you're so clumsy, stop being a baby, and get up."

Baby Rosa was held in the arms of her mother (Carol), who was at the same time experiencing extreme verbal hostility and physical aggression from her partner. Carol's fear levels continued to rise, and she became lost in her own survival mode and dysregulation. Therefore, at that time, despite Rosa crying for a prolonged period, Carol was unable to provide Rosa with the sense of containment, safety, sensitivity, regulation, and security that she needed.

Three-year-old Charlie sat helplessly in his playpen, whilst his mother was repeatedly kicked and thrown around the room by his uncle. He was experiencing a sensory overload of trauma (see Figure 3.1). He could hear the sounds of the household items banging and falling, his uncle shouting in an aggressive manner, and his mother screaming. He also could smell the strong scents of cigarette smoke and the unwashed surroundings, which included his own urine-drenched clothes. At the same time, he was contending with the sensations of his beating heart, his body being frozen and literally trapped within the playpen, the hunger pains in his stomach, and the images and facial expressions of fear and pain on his mother's face.

Nine-year-old Maisy was experiencing bullying in school. Each day she feared going into class, and the daily comments and personal attacks felt more piercing and intense. When she returned home from school, she retreated into her bedroom. When asked how she was, or how her day had been, she used to respond "Good", with a smile on her face. Maisy's father was struggling with chronic depression following the sudden death of her mother. Maisy had learned to keep her feelings to herself and to portray a happy persona, in order to protect her father from any further pain and to not send him into a deeper depression.

Four-year-old Kenya would try everything in her power to get some sort of response from her mother. However, despite endless efforts, Mary rarely responded or engaged with Kenya. She would provide her with basic care, but struggled to provide her with stimulation or relational interaction. Kenya was faced with being looked through and often being on the receiving end of a still face. (The "Still Face Experiment" video clip on YouTube by Dr Edward Tronick is a powerful example of this.)

As illustrated by the case examples, relational and developmental trauma is a multi-layered and multi-sensory experience that permeates all different levels of functioning and processing. Children like Charlie and Rosa did not consistently and reliably have the experience of feeling physically or emotionally safe, secure, and protected (including from a sensory level). They often did not have the same opportunities to internalise a sense of safety, security, relational trust, a grounding anchor, or an internal regulator.

Reflecting on the experiences of children like Charlie and Rosa gives a small window into their lived experiences; a snapshot rather than the film. However, it begins to give one a sense of how children's sense of safety and felt safety can be impacted within the context of relational and developmental trauma.

What do you do when you feel unsafe/distressed/upset/threatened/in danger? How does it feel in your mind and body? Do you have someone/something to turn to? What would it feel like if that person wasn't there, if you didn't have someone to turn to, or if that person was sometimes the source of the distress? Do you have an internalised sense/image/memory of being safe and what safety feels like? Do you have built-in coping strategies to support you when feeling unsafe/distressed/upset/threatened? How did you learn these coping skills and how did they develop and get reinforced?

For many of these children, the very person/people who were supposed to be their source of comfort, safety, and trust (e.g. their secure base and their safe haven) instead were at times their source of fear, abuse, rejection, pain, and danger. These fear- and trauma-based experiences and negative relational interactions have often been reinforced and embedded time and time again over long periods. Thus, children like Charlie and Rosa have often had to find survival and coping strategies to keep themselves, and at times others such as siblings, alive, safe, and protected.

For many children, these survival and coping strategies included having to learn how to keep others at a distance, shut people out, avoid relationships, and/or control relationships to avoid further pain (e.g. "If I let myself enjoy something or let it in, it will be taken away, used against me, or destroyed", "It is better to attack than to be attacked", "The closer someone gets to me, the more chance there is of getting hurt or of being in danger"). See Worksheet 3.1 for a visual representation of some of the common ways in which children/adults may have learned to keep themselves safe.

Instead of having a phobia of spiders, injections, or small spaces, some of these children have phobias that have been formed around a fear of relationships, closeness, and intimacy. To some children, people, relationships, intimacy, and closeness pose the biggest threat (relational trauma – see *Working with Relational and Developmental Trauma in Children and Adolescents* (Treisman, 2016)), as this is what they have learned through repeated experiences and missed connections.

What is your phobia? How often do you come face-to-face with your phobia? What happens in your body and mind when confronted with your phobia? How easy or difficult is it to avoid or get away from your phobia? Imagine how similar or different this would be, if your phobia was relationships, closeness, and intimacy?

Building on this concept, children are often repeatedly told by surrounding adults that they are safe, but they may struggle to understand what feeling safe is, to be able to feel safe, to trust this message, or to truly believe that they are, and will continue to be, safe. This can be likened to someone who is scared of sharks being told that it is OK because a particular shark is friendly or is not hungry, or a child who has been surrounded and trapped in shark-infested waters being put in a swimming pool or an area with dolphins and expecting them to naturally and instinctively feel safe (see Box 3.1). Generally, children's trauma jackets and trauma lenses travel with them across situations and environments.

Box 3.1 **Reflective exercises metaphors of relational and developmental trauma**

(Adapted from *Working with Relational and Developmental Trauma in Children and Adolescents* – Treisman, 2016.)

Two metaphors that resonate for me when thinking about relational and developmental trauma and loss are *shark-infested waters* (e.g. abuse/frightening parenting) and *desolate islands* (e.g. neglect/relational poverty). The following text builds on these concepts; however, it is acknowledged that metaphors fit differently with different people. If these don't work for you, can you think of others that do resonate?

Shark-infested waters

Imagine swimming, or being on the edge of, *shark-infested waters*. Put yourself in the shoes of a child who is surrounded by, trapped, and powerless around these big, fast, and unpredictable sharks: waiting, anticipating, expecting, and/or fearing being attacked; feeling frightened, under threat, outnumbered, and on edge. Visualise each brush of seaweed, lurking shadow, or ripple in the water sending your body, and mind, into overdrive.

How might you try to navigate and survive these shark-infested waters? When in shark-infested waters, what do you/can you do? Do you a) swim away, b) punch the shark or wrestle it, c) stay incredibly still, d) try and make friends with the sharks, e) succumb to the sharks, f) scream for help, and/or g) pretend to be a feared shark yourself? What if you don't have the physical strength or the knowledge to fight or swim away from the sharks?

Illustration 3.2 Shark-infested waters

How would it change your responses and meaning-making if the sharks were sometimes friendly or even turned out to be dolphins? What might it be like to be taken out of the shark-infested waters and to subsequently be put in a swimming pool (e.g. foster care)? What if you were then returned to the shark-infested waters? If someone told you that the next shark you met was friendly, would you believe or trust them? What if someone asked you to do synchronised swimming or aqua aerobics whilst in these shark-infested waters? What or who would be your source of comfort, anchor, or lifeboat?

Desolate islands

Some children who experience neglect and relational poverty might feel like they are stuck or stranded on a lonely, dry, empty, and *desolate island*: a place where one feels disconnected, disengaged, and invisible. The lack of water and nourishment can be likened to being starved and deprived of relational riches and interpersonal treasures. Neglect, although often side-lined, compared with physical or sexual abuse, should be fore-fronted due to its powerful, far-reaching impact on developing children.

Illustration 3.3 A desolate island

What would you do to survive on a desolate island? How long would you look for hidden treasures or buried food? How would you learn new skills without people teaching or encouraging you on your journey? What might it be like to go from a desolate island into shark-infested waters and back again? In the context of relational and developmental trauma, children have often had to function in hyper or hypo-aroused states, or more often have had to oscillate between the two. What might it feel like if your island was suddenly re-inhabited with new people or through an arduous journey you were taken to a more populated island?

Survival mode and safety

Children who feel unsafe and fearful (in shark-infested waters and/or on desolate islands) have often had to spend more time in the lower building blocks of their brain (fight, flight, or freeze survival/reptilian part). This can mean that the survival part of their brain has been regularly activated and strengthened, like a well-exercised muscle. However, because they have had to invest so much energy on this and spend so much time in their survival brain, they are likely to have had restricted opportunities for exploring, playing, being curious, engaging, and learning. Those parts of their brains (e.g. thinking, learning, and exploring parts) have not been taken to the gym, strengthened, and exercised in the same way. Thus, those parts of their brains, such as their "thinking brain" and other higher-order skills such as consequential thinking or perspective-taking, are likely to have been underutilised, underdeveloped, and, at times, offline.

As illustrated in Figure 3.2, this can be likened to being on a seesaw: when the feelings of fear, danger, insecurity, and threat go up, learning, thinking, and curiosity tend to go down. Similarly, when the arousal and dysregulation levels go up, cognitive ability, reflective function, and thinking tend to go down. This reminds me of an old quote by Sir James Dewar: "Minds are like parachutes. They only function when they are open." *Think about what happens to your thinking, regulation abilities, and decision-making abilities when you are in a position of danger/ threat/extreme fear/toxic stress?*

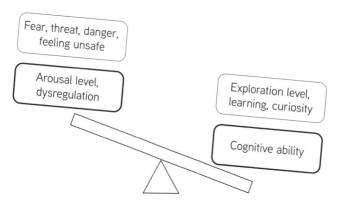

Figure 3.2 Seesaw: when fear and arousal levels go up, exploration, learning, and cognitive ability tend to go down

The above offers some explanation as to why these children can have sensitive defence systems (overly sensitised), can be hyper-vigilant, be preoccupied with detecting and surviving threats, and have a poorer ability to self-regulate, process, and modulate affect and sensory stimuli (Koomar, 2009). This also sheds some light on why children exposed to repeated toxic stress are often more easily triggered, have a lower window of tolerance for high-intensity emotions (Siegel, 2012), can take longer to return to their baseline, and can present at times with an out-of-sync emotional equilibrium. These children can experience regular hijacking of their limbic systems (e.g. emotions and drives) like a constantly beeping burglar alarm or threat radar.

For many of these children (taking into account the multi-sensory experience of trauma and the lessened opportunities during their critical sensitive periods for developing regulating, sensory, and transition skills), their world can often feel too loud, too big, or too bright, like a fairground or a disco. Therefore, one drop of an emotion can feel to them like a vast, all-consuming ocean that can override their inhibitory systems. They are often more vigilant for threats and signs of danger, like a constantly scanning threat/danger-detecting magnet.

This is heightened in children who are pre-verbal at the time of the trauma and who naturally function more in the right-brain hemisphere (the feeling and sensing hemisphere). Consequently, trauma is more likely to be embedded and encoded within the body and the arousal regulation systems and to be re-experienced or relived through bodily sensations and movements. In essence, the body may remember what the mind wants to forget. This may also result in increased sensitisation to subtle affective and sensory reminders of the traumatic event, which may easily set off false alarms (Fisher, 2006).

In addition to the above, many of these children have often been in situations of extreme unpredictability, uncertainty, and inconsistency and left with an overwhelming sense of feeling powerless and out of control (see Box 3.1). This sense of fear and feeling unsafe, and having to be at a higher arousal/alert level, can become their norm, their baseline, and/or their internalised sense of being. Therefore, this fear and sense of unsafety, like a trauma jacket or trauma lens, can follow them into different environments, for example into a new foster placement, on the football pitch, in the therapy room, or at school. Through repeated and reinforced experiences, their trauma jacket often had to have more layers added to it and be more tightly sewn on and firmly zipped up to ensure that they were kept safe and protected. Therefore, children who have experienced relational and developmental trauma are often frozen by fear and can feel unsafe physically, socially, psychologically, spiritually, and cognitively (for a more detailed explanation see Chapters 1–3 in *Working with Relational and Developmental Trauma in Children and Adolescents* – Treisman, 2016).

Having provided some basis for why multi-levelled safety is crucial in the context of relational and developmental trauma, some of the implications for practice and ways to enhance safety within the therapeutic process will now be offered and a variety of creative, expressive, and practical ways for supporting the development of multi-levelled safety will be presented. Please see Chapter 1 for a discussion and tips on some of the guiding principles, considerations, and factors to be mindful of when implementing the described strategies.

Implications for practice

With the above in mind, for children to be able to think, learn, and explore, they need to *feel and believe that they are safe and can trust* and not be in a continual and dominant state of physiological and emotional dysregulation, and high arousal and in fear mode. Their nervous system and arousal states need to be acknowledged, calmed, supported, and regulated first. As well as the child needing to have an embodied and somatic experience of safety so that they can internalize what this feeling of safety means and is like. Therefore, their *multi-levelled, whole-brain-body safety* needs to be prioritised and centralised. Establishing, maintaining, and expanding on their multi-levelled safety in many ways is the foundation and roots from which all other interventions should build on and anchor to; physical, emotional, and relational safety are the cornerstones of any positive therapeutic relationship and any therapeutic re-parenting experience. Without safety, everything else fades into the background and exists on fragile ground. The more regulated, organised, and grounded children are; the more able they will be to be able to learn, develop, engage, and flourish.

Therefore, the child needs to feel that they are in a place and relationship that can offer them a physical, emotional, and symbolic second-chance secure base and second-chance safe haven (e.g. safe hands, thinking minds, and regulating bodies). This relational safety and relational sociostatus needs to provide the child with a sense of containment, patience, curiousness, openness, nurturance, empathy, acceptance, responsiveness, sensitivity, consistency, predictability and more.

These places/relationships ideally will support the child to be able to move out of their survival brain and fear system and to move towards being able to be in their thinking brain, where they can explore, think, reflect, and breathe. These places/relationships need to offer the child the experience of being valued, mentalised, understood, and held in a thinking mind and a space where they feel able to share all parts of themselves.

Actively working towards establishing safety within the therapeutic process

A sense of safety can begin to be established by having *therapeutic anchors*, such as seeing the child at the same time and in the same room each week. This is also enhanced by having *some structure in the session*, such as consistent welcoming and ending rituals, clear limitations, boundaries, and unambiguous expectations for the space/room, relationship, and materials. This may include incorporating props, such as child-friendly timers or clocks, so that the child knows how much time they have remaining in the session.

It also feels important that *the concept of safety/a safe place/safe person is explicitly and implicitly communicated* to the young person, with permissive messages so that the child can feel free to express or show all sides of themselves.

A specific example of this, within a therapy context, is when seven-year-old Evie flinched when I leant over to get the crayons. I was able to say to her, "I noticed that when I leant over you flinched, and I wonder if you thought I was going to hurt you. I want you to know that you are safe in this room and that I will not hurt you, but I can imagine that it might be hard to believe or to trust what I am saying, so from now on, each time I lean over, I will let you know before I do it and…" This then led us to further discussions around her past experiences, relationships to adults, memories of being hurt, and her fight, flight, or freeze responses.

This explicit sense of safety can also be worked towards by using multiple ways of *explaining safety-related concepts* and the rationale of the session tasks to the young person (e.g. through psychoeducation). Examples of this will be peppered throughout the chapter. In addition to these explorations, where appropriate, having *a reciprocal* (shared and two-sided) *verbal and/or written agreement* can also facilitate embedding the notion of expectations and of safety. For example, "I will ensure that I...", "I promise you that...", "Each session I will...", "Together we can...", etc. This should include concepts around confidentiality and information-sharing. Some children might like to turn this agreement into a rules or ways-of-being poster, book, or door sign that they design and decorate. They also might like to sign this document with something like a special-seal stamp, their favourites stickers, or their handprint. It can be helpful to state that this document is a work in progress and that new thoughts, rules, and agreements can be added throughout your time together.

It is also important to have a focus on exploring and identifying the child's/ parent's *multi-layered and multi-sensory triggers* and in turn finding ways to both reduce the child's feelings of danger/threat and increase their feelings of safety (Worksheets 3.2, 3.7, 3.8, and 3.9 support this process). Additionally, and often in line with a child's triggers and hotspots, it can be useful to identify a *hand signal or another mode of communication* for the child to use if the sessions are feeling too much, if they want to leave, if they would like to have a break, etc. Some children may not be in a place where they feel able to identify their triggers and/or to use a cue word, so it is important that the surrounding adults remain attuned, responsive, and sensitive to the child's cues and different ways of communicating their distress so that they can support them in this regulating process (these are often non-verbal through their body and facial expressions).

It is also vital that *sessions are ended* in a careful way and that the child is not left to leave the room in a dysregulated, heightened, or distressed place. For some children, a detailed, collaborative, step-by-step *safety and coping plan* can be very useful, particularly in the context of specific risks, such as self-harming, low mood, substance abuse, or being involved in a domestic violence relationship.

The rest of this chapter will offer additional ideas and strategies to further explore and embed this concept of multi-levelled safety and to support the co-creation of a safe space. These should be integrated and complementary to the other therapy models and skills that you ordinarily practise and implement. Please be guided by the principles, pitfalls, and factors to be mindful of (described in Chapter 1) so that these are implemented with care and under supervision.

Practical and creative strategies for contributing to the feeling of multi-levelled safety

Conversations about safety and safety collages, images, poems, and sculpts

Before considering some practical strategies for contributing to the feeling of safety, it feels integral to have discussions with the young person about what safety means to them, to gain an understanding of their sense and definition of safety, and to subsequently expand on this concept. The concept of safety may be alien to them and may hold different meanings and associations. Worksheets 3.3 and 3.4 offer some ways to guide these conversations around safety.

These discussions can be further embedded by creating safety collages and/or posters (using magazines, newspapers, photos, materials, and images from the internet). These can be child-directed, or the young person can be supported to create a collage/poster around a guided topic, such as: "I feel safe when...", "The things that make me feel safe are...", "I would feel safe if...", "Safety is...", and "Times that I felt safe were...".

Alternatively, these titles and themes can be expressed through drawings, poems, raps, stories, songs, sculpts, etc. Each young person will be drawn to different mediums, and it is recommended that you are guided by their preferences.

Creating a place of safety (physical)

"Therapists" need actively to *talk to children about safety* and to *have a place of safety* for the child to go to. Ideally, this should be twofold: an *actual physical place of safety* and an *imaginary place of safety*.

Places of safety should be easily accessible and provide children with a sense of calm and containment. Some homes/schools/centres will have an allocated place, such as a *sensory room*, whilst others will have something like a *special space, thinking tent, calm cave, cosy corner*, or *zen zone*. Of course, this may need to be on a smaller scale according to budget and space, but there are lots of creative ways in which one can have the intended effect without having a designated room.

It can be engaging to support the child to have more ownership by them *naming or decorating* their own safe space. One child aptly named his safe space "Cloud Corner", whilst another who used hers to re-ground chose "Tree Time".

Equipment varies and ideally should be tailored to the individual child's regulation, trauma and sensory needs, preferences, and triggers; however they may include: weighted blankets, cushions, water items, bubble machines, lava lamps, rocking chairs/rocking horse, spinning chair, a tunnel/tube, a den/mini house, a swing, massaging items, sensory boxes (see further below for a step-by-step guide on making sensory and regulating boxes), beanbags, calming lighting, aromatherapy scent kit, and soothing music (e.g. white noise, wind chimes, and/or the ocean).

Some children will naturally gravitate towards or take themselves unaided to their safe place, whereas others may need a *way of communicating* when they need their safe place. This might include a hand signal, a cue word, a traffic-light system, and a movement/exit card. Others may not yet have the ability to recognise when they are dysregulated, so the surrounding adults will need to actively support them with this.

As with all new strategies, the safe space should be introduced to the child when they are in a thinking, regulated place. Following this, and whilst in a thinking space, children should have a few turns at *practising and role-playing* how and when to use their safe space. Some children might prefer to practise and/or role-play putting their favourite toy into the safe space before they have a go themselves. The safe space should be emphasised as a safe, positive space and not used as a place of punishment.

During the introduction or preparation of the safe space, this can be a perfect time to interweave some psychoeducation around safety, the impact of trauma, dysregulation, anxiety, etc. This can also be a positive opportunity to think alongside the child about some specific past times when a safe space might have been helpful and why (be their memory bank, e.g. "Remember last week when you said you felt... and you did..."). This can include reflecting on some of their and your own multi-sensory triggers (see Worksheet 3.2). These times and ideas can then be strengthened by writing them down, drawing them, sculpting them, representing them in sand, creating a social story, or making a reminder poster (e.g. "Times when I can use my safe place" or "My safe place makes me feel..."). Other creative and expressive extensions of bringing a safe place alive and embedding it further will be detailed in the following sections.

Creating a safe place (cognitive/imaginary) and using creative methods to embed the concept

Safe place imagery and factors to be mindful of

Support the young person in thinking of a cognitive/imaginary safe place. To do this, the child needs to understand the concept of safety. If this is not the case, steps to support them around their understanding of safety may need to take place before proceeding.

This safe place should be a place where they have felt happy, safe, and calm, which gives them positive and warming associations and feelings. Everyone needs a place where they can feel safe and gain an inner sense of safety, like an emotional haven.

If the child notices any negative links or images entering when selecting a safe, calming, and positive place, try to support them in thinking of a different place. This is why it is generally optimal to select a place where the child was alone and outside of their house. Often, somewhere like a bedroom, or a person such as a parent, can hold mixed and complex feelings and associations that can intrude on the intended positive safe space. Along this line, adolescents often select a place with a girlfriend/boyfriend, which ideally should be avoided, because if these relationships end the young person is left without a safe space or with a contaminated safe space.

If the young person cannot think of a place where they felt/feel safe, which is fairly common within a relational and developmental trauma context, then if appropriate (this depends on the assessment and relationship) you can try to support them in thinking about and creating an imaginary, magical, and fantasy safe place (see Photo 3.5). This might be inspired by TV programmes, magazines, stories they have heard, books, dreams, etc.

Once a safe place has been identified, it is helpful to talk with the child about the multi-sensory details and description of their safe place (the smells, sounds, tastes, feelings, thoughts, and body sensations) and then to support them to return to that safe place (see below for step-by-step guidance followed by different ways of creatively extending the concept of a safe place).

Please note that, as a self-care (see Chapter 7) and regulation exercise, it can be beneficial to create your own safe place as a practitioner or to support others in the Team Around the Child to do so.

The safe place exercise: a step-by-step guide

Once the child has identified their safe place, the following steps can be carried out. Start by getting the child to sit or lie down in a comfortable position in a quiet place. Encourage them to take some intentional deep, slow breaths (this process can be complemented by other breathing and relaxation techniques). If they feel comfortable to do so, they can choose to close their eyes and with each breath notice the tension drifting away. Some children find having an item such as a weighted blanket, cuddly toy, or transitional object can support them to feel more comfortable during this exercise.

Support the child in imagining that they are in their safe place that they have described. They may need you to support them in retelling the details or connecting with the feelings that they previously identified. They may find it helpful to have their cue word said to them.

Some children can go straight to their safe place, by simply closing their eyes or saying their cue words whereas others may like to imagine that they are a) flying there on a magic carpet/aeroplane/helicopter/hot air balloon b) using a bridge/secret passage/magic key, and/or c) using a hidden door to get there (see Photo 3.6).

Get the child to look around them whilst they are in their safe place and to experience their safe place from a multi-sensory perspective. What colours, shapes, smells, sounds, temperature, movement, and sights do they notice?

Support them to notice the physical sensations within their body. Where in their body do they feel the physical sensations of being relaxed/calm/happy? What do those sensations feel like? If these sensations were a shape/colour/item/object, what would they be?

Support the child in thinking about all the different emotions that they experience and feel when they have connected with their safe place. Support them in breathing in those warm, relaxing, calming, happy feelings and in breathing out the more difficult and distressing feelings.

Whilst they are in their peaceful and safe place, they might choose to give their safe place a name, a title, or a word/phrase that they can use to bring that image back whenever they feel the need or desire to be back there (like a cue/trigger word).

They can choose to stay and soak in their safe place, and equally they can leave whenever they want to. They just need to open their eyes and be supported to slowly become aware of where they are in the present moment.

Afterwards, it can be helpful to think about, reflect on, and evaluate the experience of the exercise. This exercise should be practised on a regular basis.

The safe place exercise: creative and expressive extensions

As with all techniques, in order to keep the safe place "alive" and to embed the learning, it can be helpful to represent and expand on the safe place by using creative and expressive means. This also has the dual aim of being done in a relationship-based context, which it is hoped can be attuned, containing, responsive, playful, and subsequently internalised.

- Make a visual poster/canvas/collage of the safe place using magazines, photos, drawings, etc. (see Photo 3.3).

- Draw/paint/mosaic the safe place.

- Sculpt the safe place. This could be using clay/Play-Doh/everyday items/pipe cleaners, etc.

- Make or design the key, bridge, tunnel, hidden door, magic carpet, and/or fairy gates that can be used to enter into the safe place (see Photo 3.6).

- Make or design a safe place inspired pillow case or blanket. This could be by using fabric pens or iron-ons to decorate it or transferring actual photos or images on to a pillow case/blanket/doodle teddy bear, etc. (see Photos 3.1 and 3.2).

- Have a reminder script/story of the safe place. This could be extended by the therapist/caregiver putting a voice recording on their smartphone, a DVD, or a USB that assists the child to be able to journey into their safe place.

- Make a mini representative of the safe place so that it can travel with the child. For example, it can be placed in a photo key ring/on a postcard/in a jar/in a snow globe.

- Choose a piece of music that is related to the safe place. Some children may want to write or choreograph their own associated safe place song/music/dance.

- Make a body-map that explores the child's feelings when they feel unsafe/distressed and then make a comparison body-map of how they feel when they are in their safe place (see Photo 3.4). You can have discussions such as: If your body could talk, what would it say? Where in your body do you feel a sense of safety? What does that feeling feel like? If that feeling was a colour/item/shape, what would it be?

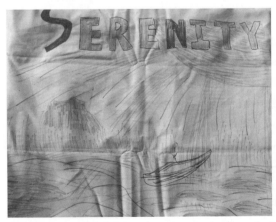 

Photos 3.1 and 3.2 Safe place inspired pillow designs

Photo 3.3 A safe place poster/photo montage

Photo 3.4 Body-mapping differences in the safe place and when the anger visits: "How I felt last night when…" and "How I feel when I am in my safe place"

Photo 3.5 Imaginary and fantasy safe place of a magical mermaid

Photo 3.6 A decorated fairy gate and magic key to enter the safe place

A safe place for an item/object

Some children might find it useful to make/design/ decorate a safe place for an animal/item/object (see Photo 3.7). They can also be supported to choose a name for this place and item. This exercise can facilitate a lot of conversations around what safety is, what safety looks like, what safety feels like emotionally and physically, and how safety can be achieved (Worksheets 3.3 and 3.4 can aid this process too). This also gives the child an opportunity to have some mastery over keeping something/someone else safe and possibly acting out and expressing some of the ways in which they would have liked/like to be kept safe themselves. Some children might like to tell a story, make a comic strip, or use puppets to show their "creature" being in trouble or being scared and then coming out of the other end and feeling safe.

Photo 3.7 A safe place for Lila

When carrying out this exercise, it is important that the child has a selection of various colours, shapes, and materials to select both the item/object that will be kept safe and the environment that the item/object will be placed in.

It is also crucial to have conversations with the child about what or who will look after the item during and in between the sessions and how they will do that. (This agreement will vary depending on the child and context.)

Safety tour

Children's sense of safety and their ability to feel and believe that they are safe should not be assumed or underestimated. Therefore, it can also be helpful to provide children and adolescents with a *safety tour*. This might be at one or multiple places, such as at school, in the playground, at home, at a new placement, or in the therapy room/building.

This might include lots of different outings, conversations, and activities. For example, depending on the environment, the child can be shown how the alarm system works, the CCTV cameras, the security person, the double-glazed windows, the locks on the door, the sign-in book, neighbourhood watch, limited number of keys, and so on.

The child may need to walk through this tour several times and be supported in asking safety-related questions. Some children may enjoy having a disposable or digital camera to take photos of the different elements of safety and then putting them together in a book/worksheet/story format.

Photos 3.8–3.10 Different elements of safety that could be incorporated into a safety-themed story

Creating a calming, soothing, and self-regulating box

Photos 3.11 and 3.12 The outside and the inside of my own calming sensory box

A "safe box", "happy box", "calming box", "sensory box", or "soothing box" can support a young person in learning different self-soothing, self-nurturing, and self-regulating coping strategies. This technique of designing a "calming sensory box" is intended to be used within the context of other evidence-based approaches and is one of numerous sensory approaches available. It has different aims that target multiple areas, including to:

- allow children to develop some concrete, playful, creative, and proactive strategies to manage their bodies and emotions effectively

- engage and build rapport with the young person whilst showing them that their needs and wants are important and being listened to by a thinking adult

- promote a sense of external and internal safety, which is fundamental for enabling exploration, curiosity, and attachment

- support young people to gradually and in a safe, containing way widen their window of tolerance and to support them in finding a more manageable arousal zone

- support the child in focusing on, tolerating, grounding, modulating, and sustaining a connection to their internal states

- engage the child's subcortical systems (sensory, motor, limbic/emotional, and autonomic arousal), soothe their lower parts of the brain, and activate their body's relaxation and stress reduction response; this multi-sensory approach (visual, kinaesthetic, tactile, olfactory, affective, and auditory) is particularly important given the multi-sensory nature of trauma and disrupted attachments

- encourage their nervous system to process and integrate sensory input in organised and meaningful ways

- create a physical container and a transitional object that has been made with the therapist or within the caregiver relationship and therefore has relational elements including co-regulation and co-construction, which it is hoped can be internalised and anchored to

- give children a space and task in which they can gain some mastery and control and be active agents within their coping process

- have a concrete means that enables other therapy strategies such as positive affirmation cards, prompt cards, and relaxation strategies to be incorporated into the contents of the box.

A step-by-step guide to creating a "regulating box"

1. Discuss the rationale of the box in a child-friendly, normalising, and accessible way. This can be usefully linked to psychoeducation around the brain, fight, flight, or freeze responses, and dysregulation. Ask whether this is something that the child thinks may be helpful and is willing to engage with. The more they are involved and invested in the process, the better.

2. Support the child to choose or bring in a shoebox, plastic container, or trinket box, which will form the basis of the exercise. Please note some children might prefer to use/make a different form of container; this is encouraged, as it offers them mastery and choice over all the elements. This might be a jar, a star-shaped box, or a bag (try and ensure that the selected container is big enough to fit the intended contents and durable enough to last a substantial time).

3. Have discussions about what things make the child feel calm, relaxed, nurtured, safe, happy, and warm. Use prompt cards, sentence-completion tasks (see *A Therapeutic Treasure Deck of Sentence Completion and Feelings Cards*, Treisman 2017), "All About Me" type questions, and other creative techniques to support the child in answering these questions (see Chapter 2). Questions can range from their favourite season during the year to their best meal, their biggest role model, their favourite hobby, their favourite song, etc. Try to incorporate a range of questions that include enquiring about all of their senses, such as what things they might like to smell, touch, hear, do, taste, and see (see Worksheet 3.5 on identifying sensory likes and Worksheet 3.6 on creating a "sensory hand"). Children may like to draw, make a collage, or write on these worksheets or they may like to cut out the headings and place objects/items that are associated with each sense next to them. The images should be calming, positive, and strength-focused. If the child brings up negative images, acknowledge, validate, discuss, and memory bank them for other future tasks.

    Be mindful that some young people will need scaffolding, prompting, and reassurance to facilitate this process, so it is handy to have a few suggestions up your sleeve and to have memory banked some things that they/surrounding adults have said that they like or have helped them to integrate and incorporate.

4. Depending on the child's wishes, and on the assessment of their needs, the therapist/caregiver/supporting adult or child (or this might be a mutual task) should collect a range of images/pictures/photos/materials to express the identified items above. Magazines, newspapers, and images from the internet can help this process. For children who have often had the experience of not being kept in mind, the process of the therapist/supporting adult collecting the images that the child can then choose from can give a powerful message of being held and kept in mind.

5. The child should decorate and/or name the outside of their "box" with the identified images. If the therapist has collected the images, make sure the child has the opportunity to say which ones they like and/or which ones they do not want to include; it is also important to check if there are other images they have thought about since the initial discussions that they would like to add. Make sure you bring glue, scissors, and a range of resources to the session, as the majority of children like to decorate their boxes with additional materials, such as stickers, embellishments, fabrics, tissue paper, written messages, photographs, drawings, textured paper, glitter, etc.

It is a good idea to have several copies of the images in case some are lost/damaged and so that the child can cut them up and incorporate them into other strategies used during therapy, such as their safe calming place poster, a key ring with soothing images in it, an "All About Me"/life-story book, and/or laminated in the box.

6. Identified objects should be put in the sensory calming box (some may be suggested or contributed by the therapist and others by the child; see below for some commonly used items). Some young people may benefit from an extensive range of options, whilst others become over-stimulated and overwhelmed and would probably get more out of the process by having a small selection of items.

   The choice of items/objects will vary depending on the young person's unique needs, likes, choices, and safety requirements. Therefore, carrying out an assessment and getting to know the unique young person is key to this process. Ideally, many of the items will also match the child's responses to the questions about the things that make them feel happy and calm. For example, a child who says their favourite time of year is winter and when it snows may be supported to have or make a snow globe. Similarly, a child who likes stroking fluffy dogs may be supported to buy or be given some fluffy material resembling the hair of a dog.

7. When they are in their "thinking brain" and a regulated place, the child should be encouraged to practise/role-play using the items in the box during the session. Items and their usefulness should be explored and evaluated. The child should also be supported to think about a range of different scenarios/situations/feeling states where the box may or may not be helpful.

8. The child should be encouraged to use some of the items at home or in their school setting. With the child's agreement, the Team Around the Child should be told about the box, including the rationale behind it and how and when to use it. If this is done in the context of therapy (it can be adapted for use elsewhere), some children may like to keep the box with the therapist and have a mini version at home/school.

Some common items to include in the sensory box

This is not an exhaustive list and the items should not all be used at the same time. These suggestions are informed by theories about the impact of trauma and disrupted attachment on the body and brain.

Photo 3.13 Some items for a sensory box

Try and consider all of the different senses:

- tactile or somatosensory system – sense of touch

- visual – seeing system

- auditory – sense of hearing

- gustatory system – sense of taste

- olfactory system – sense of smell

- vestibular system – sense of balance

- proprioception system – sense of body position.

DISTRACTERS/SORTING/ORGANISING ITEMS

Examples of these include: fidget toys, such as a chewable item such as a chewy bracelet, puzzles, crosswords, brain teasers, stress balls, Rubik's cubes, colouring/drawing materials, colouring books, a kaleidoscope, and things to sort and organise such as different coloured buttons/badges/pebbles/stickers/ LEGO® pieces.

TACTILE/SOOTHING ITEMS

Examples of these include: soft materials (e.g. velvet, fluffy material, silk, and suede), feathers, bubble wrap, different coloured pipe cleaners, crystals/pebbles/precious stones, Play-Doh/aroma-doh/clay, bean bags, tangles, massage balls, and stress balls.

NURTURING ITEMS

Examples of these include: hand cream, lip balm, aromatherapy oils, a heat pad, face wipes, plasters, a self-hug cue card, a weighted blanket or pillow, and breathing and relaxation exercise reminders.

ORAL-MOTOR ITEMS

Examples of these include: sucking sweets, chewing gum/a chewy bracelet, sucking on straws, and blowing bubbles/ balloons/feathers.

OLFACTORY ITEMS (SMELL)

Examples of these include: comforting and down-regulating smells (e.g. lavender, camomile, rosemary, and vanilla), aromatherapy oil, perfume, candles, spray, and aroma-doh (smells, as with all senses, are very personal, so they need to be selected by the young person).

Auditory items (hearing)

Examples of these include: calming and smoothing music, drums, a rain stick, a shell that you can hear the sea from, wind chimes, white noise, and a voice recording from people who love and support the young person.

Reminders of support items

Examples of these include: letters, cards, recordings, and special items from the Team Around the Child (e.g. a "hand of safety", safety net, life cheerleaders, and a jar of coloured sand representing all those special people).

Coping tool reminder items

Examples of these include: pictures/photos/images/memories that are calming and have positive associations, positive affirmation self-talk cards, such as "I can do it", "I am OK", and "I am strong", and coping reminder cards, such as "When the difficult feelings take over I can calm myself by...".

Some other items that have been commonly selected by young people

Snow globes (these can be personalised), Guatemalan worry dolls, a calming glitter bottle, a weighted animal, a music maker, flowers, a heartbeat teddy bear, a dream catcher, a guardian angel, a wishing fairy, a mandala, and fairy dust.

Safe person/people

To enhance the concept of feeling safe and connecting with feelings of safety, a child can be supported to create, reflect on, or reconnect with a person or people who make them feel safe and protected. These exercises intend to support the child to feel more connected with that person, feel less alone, and have positive memories/ people to anchor to, internalise, and breathe and drink in. This can be done in multiple ways depending on the client, their unique experiences, the context, the relationship, and the overarching therapy aims. The following suggestions are some ways in which a safe person can be used, but the list is not exhaustive or prescriptive.

- The young person can be supported to think about someone in their life who makes them feel safe and protected. Discussions about this person can strengthen their presence and rich influence on the child's life. For example, the child may want to discuss, document, draw, sculpt, collage, or share stories of: 1) times when that person made them feel safe and protected; 2) qualities and skills that the person used to make them feel safe/protected/ listened to; 3) what that person was/is like; 4) what some of their most treasured memories with that person are/were. The child may also want to bring a picture of that person, make a drawing/painting/sculpt/key ring of them and/or of them together during a specific special memory, have a voice recording of their voice, or visualise them as being with and supporting them (see Photo 3.17).

- The young person may struggle to think of someone in their present or past who made them feel safe and protected. This can be a common challenge for children in a relational and developmental trauma context, especially amidst a particularly difficult time in their life. Instead, they may want to imagine and create a "person". This may be entirely from their imagination or they might want to take various parts/qualities/components from different people they have known and combine them to be one person/character (see Photo 3.14). This doesn't have to be a person; the young person may prefer it to be a being, a spirit, a creature, an item, a superhero, an animal, etc. (see Photos 3.15 and 3.16). The creative means of expressing and embedding these ideas described in the previous point can be applied to this imaginary person/item/object.

Photo 3.14 An imagined safe person made up of different parts and qualities

Photo 3.15 A safe person sculpture

Photo 3.16 Guardian angel and protector

Photo 3.17 Key ring of a special person

Photo 3.18 Paper dolls of the Team Around the Child

- The young person may want to think about famous people/celebrities/ historical figures and/or inspirational figures. These people can then be written down, sculpted, listed, or drawn. Discussions can be had about how to breathe in and internalise these people and how to hold them in their hearts and in heads.

Photo 3.19 Nelson Mandela inspired collage

- For some children, having a physical representation of all of the people around them who are in their team of life supporters can be very powerful (this needs to be done, as with all these exercises, with caution, as some children may be in a place where they feel very alone). This physical representation might be through making an eco-map or genogram; however, to make this more child-friendly, I prefer to use miniature figurines, stickers, materials, etc. (see Photos 3.22 and 3.23). This Team Around the Child/family can also be represented by using different layers of sand, with each colour representing a different person (see Photos 3.20 and 3.21) or by making support jewellery with each bead representing a different person. Sometimes I draw, make, or sculpt something like a safety net, blanket, team of cheerleaders, paper chain of people (see Photo 3.18), or lifeboat (see Photo 3.24) and get the child to draw/sculpt the different people who would fit into that category for them.

Photos 3.20 and 3.21 Sand art of a child's life cheerleaders

Photo 3.22 A representation using miniatures of the Team Around the Child

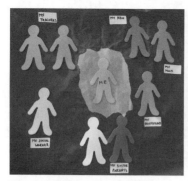

Photo 3.23 An anonymised recreation eco-map of the Team Around the Child

Photo 3.24 Lifeboat of supporters

Safety shield and protective items

Some children may like to create and make a safety shield of all of the things that will or do keep them safe (see Photo 3.25) or of all of the things that make them feel strong.

Others may prefer to represent this through making a safety/magic blanket, cape, jacket, hat, piece of jewellery, guardian angel (see Photo 3.16), or a lucky/magic item that supports them to feel safe and protected.

Photo 3.25 The beginning stages of a safety and strengths shield

Exploring our and others' multi-layered triggers

In order to increase children's feelings of safety and decrease their feelings of danger, it is important to really get to know the child and to identify and name their likes, dislikes, and multi-sensory triggers (e.g. environmental, sensory, autobiographical, physical, cognitive, relational, emotional, and situational) (see examples of each of these categories below). For example, what makes them up- or down-regulate? What makes them feel scared, for example, and how does this show itself on their face, or in their bodies, words, and behaviours? (Worksheets 3.2, 3.7, 3.8, and 3.9 can be used to support this process, as well as Worksheets 4.1 and 4.2 in Chapter 4.) Once some of these triggers (this is an ever-evolving process) have been identified and named, it is easier to spot them, understand them, plan for them, see common patterns and themes within them, reduce them, and intervene with them.

This decoding process is even more important, as these triggers within a relational and developmental trauma context are often difficult to decipher, have become hidden amongst layers of defences (see Worksheet 3.1), and/or are communicated in a different way. Some examples are listed below.

Riley learned to conceal his extreme feelings of fear by keeping others at a distance through his intense expressions of verbal and physical aggression.

Sacha, who had been described by carers as being a "tough cookie", as "bouncing back", and as being someone who was "nothing fazed", appeared on closer observation to respond to threat and dysregulation by zoning out, dissociating, or going into flight mode.

These triggers can span across spheres. Some examples of these spheres are given below.

Emotional/social/relational triggers

- A friend declining an invite to play, triggering past feelings of rejection.

- A therapist leaving to have a baby (feelings of abandonment, rejection, envy, or loss).

- Struggling with a task in class, which triggers their toxic sense of shame and reinforces their negative internal working model, e.g. "I'm stupid" or "I'm ineffective".

- A social worker's support being focused on another child, triggering feelings of being ignored and/or fears of being forgotten.

- An unpredictable situation or sudden change, such as having a substitute teacher or a fight breaking out in class, triggering feelings of being out of control, powerless, and unsafe.

Sensory/physical (auditory, olfactory, tactile, gustatory, and visual) triggers

- The feeling of being trapped amongst crowds of people on the tube, bringing back memories of being trapped during abusive situations.

- Doors slamming and bells ringing, reminiscent of the noises and sounds during witnessing domestic violence incidents.

- A teacher's raised voice echoing the angry voices of one's parents during a domestic violence incident.

- A neighbour's perfume being reminiscent of the perfume/scent of the person who carried out the abuse.

- Being at the back of the food queue at school and wondering whether there will be enough food to eat, triggering feelings of previously being deprived of food.

- The cold floor when going barefoot being reminiscent of the floor when one was locked in the bathroom for hours.

Autobiographical triggers

- Family tree assignments at school.

- "Bring in your dad" day at school or Mother's Day.

- Sex education classes or having to change in communal areas.

- The baby Jesus story in the nativity play.

- A newspaper article or news headline about domestic violence.

- When it snows (if it snowed the day they were removed from their birth parents), etc.

It is also worth mentioning that, as well as focusing on tricky triggers, it is important to have a balance and to identify happy/joyous/uplifting triggers and associations with the young person. Once these triggers have been identified, it can be helpful to represent, thicken, and externalise them. Some techniques that I find useful for recording triggers include using:

- insects to consider "What bugs me?" (see Worksheet 3.7 and Photos 3.26 and 3.28)

- using/drawing buttons to reflect on "What pushes my buttons?"

- using a remote control to think about "The things that make me lose control" (see Worksheet 3.8 and Photo 3.27)

- a lighter to reflect on "What lights my fuse?" (see Photos 3.26, 3.27, 3.28).

The identified triggers can then be drawn on, written, sculpted, collaged, or photographed and their origin, history, relationship, and function can be sensitively and non-judgementally explored. It is important that once these triggers have been identified and expressed to then explore with the young person what can be done to plan, respond, and reduce them, and to problem-solve around them. These can also be discussed creatively; for instance, in the remote-control example, discussions can be had around: *When are the times when things need to be put on pause? When does the channel need to get changed? When does the volume need to be put down?*

Or with the "What bugs me?" example, discussions can be had about: *What bugs need to be set free, to be squashed, to fly away, and which might turn into butterflies?*

Photos 3.26–3.28 "Things that bug me" or "Things that push my buttons" trigger sheets

It is also important to identify our own triggers as people, workers, and parents. Worksheet 3.2 can help you think about your own multi-layered triggers (these can be drawn, sculpted, photographed, or written down). See Chapter 7 for more strategies on supporting one's own self-care.

Self-regulation, centering, and grounding activities to increase feelings of safety

To support children to increase their feelings of safety, to decrease their feelings of danger, and to have some accessible and tangible coping strategies, it is helpful to identify, and to provide, some regulating, centring, and grounding tools. Some ideas are given here, which are mainly intended to fit with Bruce Perry's (2014) six Rs in trauma-informed work: Rhythmic, Repetitive, Relevant (developmentally matched), Rewarding (pleasurable), Respectful, and Relational.

They are intended as ideas and are not exhaustive or prescriptive. As with all the listed exercises, they need to be carefully thought about, planned, and individualised. These can be matched to some of the other tools discussed, such as the sensory box, the safe place exercise, and the identifying triggers worksheets (see Worksheets 3.2, 3.7, 3.8, and 3.9, as well as Worksheets 4.1 and 4.2 in Chapter 4). Several options are described, which are likely to be overwhelming for young people/parents, so it is important to use them as a guide rather than as a standalone list of strategies. It is also important to select a few and for these to be manageable and appealing to the young person. They should subsequently be reviewed, evaluated, and reflected on.

To support the child/carer/therapist to identify and select some regulating and soothing activities, there are also some accompanying regulating cards (see Worksheet 3.9) that can be cut out and used. These cards have intentionally been left without images so that the child/parent can select, design, or draw their own. This is likely to support the child in having more ownership and mastery over the process, as well as the end result being more tailored and individualised to them.

- Describe your environment and/or surroundings using all of your senses, e.g. What is around you? What can you hear? See? Touch? Smell? Feel? What shapes/textures/colours/noises are there? What is the room temperature?

- Support the child to enter into their *safe place*.

- Use the various grounding and regulating activities in the *sensory/calming box* such as: squeezing a stress ball, smelling a soothing scent, holding a grounding object such as a pebble, blowing bubbles, throwing feathers, and/or sorting a Rubik's cube.

- In line with theories of integration and connection, and supported by the dual stimulation exercises employed in therapies such as Eye Movement Desensitisation Reprocessing Therapy, it can be regulating to stimulate both sides of the brain and body. For example, by alternating hands to squeeze a stress ball or Play-Doh, by tracing a labyrinth picture, or by giving yourself a butterfly hug, ensuring that you are alternating the side of the body that is being tapped/hugged.

- Try and play a *brain-based game*, e.g. think of names/capitals of countries/ animals/food types that start with a letter of the alphabet, count backwards, do a crossword, make a puzzle, play I spy, etc. See Worksheet 8.11 for other cognitive and executive function activities.

- *Use humour, laughter, and/or distraction.* For example, watch a funny YouTube clip, flick through a magazine, listen to a funny podcast, or look at a funny image/photo.

- Do some *physical movement*, such as jumping, rocking, spinning, jogging, twisting, stamping, crawling, stretching, dancing, etc.

- *Play the drums, clap your hands, or rub your hands together* to feel the heat.

- *Run cold water or use a refreshing wipe* on your hands, neck, or face. Others might like to *drink a cold drink or suck an ice cube.*

- Do some *breathing and relaxing exercises.* For example: consciously and deliberately breathing in through your mouth and out through your nose; tensing and relaxing your muscles, starting from your feet and working all the way up to your head. Younger children might like to try more child-friendly relaxation exercises, such as: going from being a tall, stretched giraffe down to a tiny mouse, or being a stiff robot through to being a floppy teddy bear.

- *Listen to music/write a song/play an instrument.* Alternatively, *go through the words* (mentally or write them down) to an inspiring song, quotation, or poem.

- Do some *colouring in, trace the pictures from a colouring book, or follow a maze/ labyrinth with your fingers.*

- Do something creative, pampering, or that requires you to connect with nature. For example, massaging your hands, painting your nails, brushing your hair, going for a walk, cycling, running, doing some gardening, cooking, writing, making something, drawing, etc.

- Support the child to choose and then say/write/draw a *safety positive statement and a positive affirmation*, such as: "My name is... I am safe right now because... I am in the present, not the past. I am currently in...and the day and date is...", or something like: "I am OK, I will get through this, I am strong, I am safe, the feeling will pass, I can cope."

- Ask the child to *reflect on all of the things that are different now* compared with how they were before, for example: "I am now 15, I live in a different place that is..., I am stronger because..., I have people like...around me who care, I have coping strategies, which are...". To embed this further, the child could be supported to draw a *"Then, now, and future picture" or a dual portrait* (half representing their past and half representing their present) (see Chapter 4).

- *Use imagery to create a safer distance from the distressing feeling* (see Chapters 5 and 9 for a range of different examples around this). For example, skate/ run/swim away from the distressing thought/memory. The child could imagine that the image/memory is playing on a TV so that they can subsequently press it to pause or change it to black and white, a fuzzy image, or a different channel. Alternatively, they might think of a wall or piece of glass as a buffer between them and the distressing thought/image (these can be sculpted, drawn, or acted out).

- Some children might find it helpful to *imagine their difficulties floating away* at sea, going up in a hot air balloon, or drifting away in a message in a bottle. (These can be sculpted, drawn, or acted out.) See Chapter 5 for some examples of this.

- Some children might like to imagine their *safe person/item or superhero* of safety standing beside them. Others may like to look at *photos* of positive times, memories, and/or people (this might be in their treasure box).

Coping and option cards

Building on the above, it can be helpful to have a reminder of the child's/parent's coping strategies and go-to options for responding to difficult feelings/situations. An example of a coping card is given below, followed by a blank coping card template. Some children may prefer to use a creative alternative such as "my protective palm", where they write a coping strategy on each finger (see Photo 3.29) or an "octopus of options" with each coping strategy written on one of the octopus's tentacles (see Photo 3.30 and Worksheets 3.10, 3.11, and 3.12).

Other ideas to record coping options include: my treasure box of tools (see Worksheet 3.11), my coping cookbook, my chill skills, my bag of ideas, or my calm-down superpowers (see Photos 8.21–8.25 for more examples of these strategies brought to life).

Photo 3.29 Sample of "My protective palm"

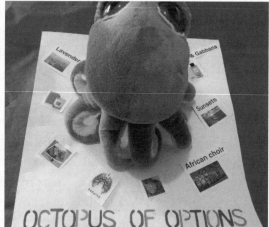

Photo 3.30 Octopus of options

Feeling unsafe/putting up defences

When I am feeling "unsafe" and need to protect myself I...

Surround myself with barbed wire	Go into attack mode like a hungry shark	Go into my own protective bubble	Put on my bulletproof vest	Retreat into my tortoise shell
Make myself small/invisible	Hide away in the fog	Freeze on the spot	Whizz around like a dart	Paint on a smile like a clown
Put up my spikes like a hedgehog	Zoom away like a speeding car	Push people away like an opposing magnet	Think in black and white	What else?

Copyright © Karen Treisman – *A Therapeutic Treasure Box for Working with Children and Adolescents with Developmental Trauma* – 2018

Worksheet 3.2
Multi-layered triggers

Sensory (auditory, olfactory, tactile/physical, gustatory, visual)	Autobiographical
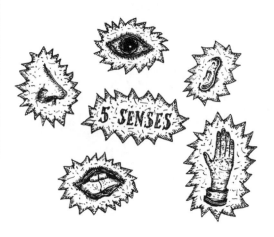	
Emotional/relational/core beliefs/life scripts	Other

Copyright © Karen Treisman – *A Therapeutic Treasure Box for Working with Children and Adolescents with Developmental Trauma – 2018*

Worksheet 3.3
Exploring the feeling of safety

Draw, collage, sculpt, write, or depict in sand your responses.

The feeling of "safety" is like…
If I gave the feeling of "safety" a name, I would call it…
If the feeling of "safety" was a colour, it would be…
If the feeling of "safety" was a shape, it would be…

Copyright © Karen Treisman – *A Therapeutic Treasure Box for Working with Children and Adolescents with Developmental Trauma* – 2018

If the feeling of "safety" was an animal, it would be…

If the feeling of "safety" was an object/item/metaphor, it would be…

If the feeling of "safety" could talk, it would say… What would its voice sound like?

Some examples of things young people have likened the feelings of safety to include: "a warm blanket", "a bubble", "a shield", "a guardian angel", "a deep breath", "floating on a cloud", "being rooted like a tree", "large loving hands", "candy floss", and "sunlight on my skin".

Copyright © Karen Treisman – *A Therapeutic Treasure Box for Working with Children and Adolescents with Developmental Trauma* – 2018

Worksheet 3.4
Exploring the feelings and meaning of safety further

Draw what feeling safe looks like/feels like to you…

Draw a specific time when you felt safe…

Copyright © Karen Treisman – *A Therapeutic Treasure Box for Working with Children and Adolescents with Developmental Trauma* – 2018

Exploring my different senses

I like to smell	I like to touch/feel
I like to hear	**I like to taste**
I like to see	**Other**

Copyright © Karen Treisman – *A Therapeutic Treasure Box for Working with Children and Adolescents with Developmental Trauma – 2018*

My sensory hand

In the space below, draw around your hand. If you prefer you can draw around someone else's hand or use a cut-out hand template. Write the categories below on each finger and thumb, and then decorate.

> » Something I like to touch.
>
> » Something I like to see.
>
> » Something I like to hear.
>
> » Something I like to taste.
>
> » Something I like to smell.

Copyright © Karen Treisman – *A Therapeutic Treasure Box for Working with Children and Adolescents with Developmental Trauma – 2018*

Things that bug me...

Copyright © Karen Treisman – *A Therapeutic Treasure Box for Working with Children and Adolescents with Developmental Trauma – 2018*

Things that push my buttons (make me lose control)

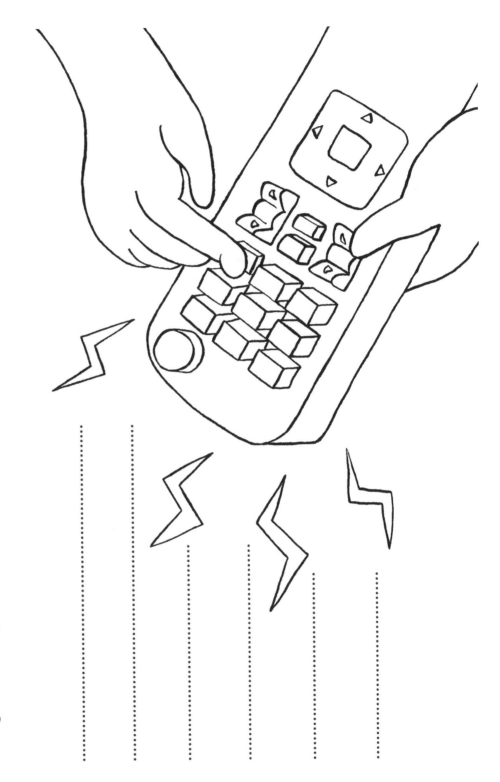

Copyright © Karen Treisman – *A Therapeutic Treasure Box for Working with Children and Adolescents with Developmental Trauma* – 2018

Worksheet 3.9
Grounding, soothing, and regulating cards

Describe my environment Think about all of the senses (see, feel, hear, taste, touch, balance)	**Go to my safe place (physical and imaginary) and use my safe place creative reminders** Name of my safe place: Safe place cue word: What can I see, smell, do, taste, hear? How do I feel emotionally and physically when in my safe place?
Use and explore my sensory regulating box	**Do a...** (e.g. puzzle, crossword, drawing) **Sort...** (e.g. Rubik's cube, papers, buttons)
Remind myself of my safe protective and supportive "person" Name: Description: Qualities:	**The things I can smell are...** (e.g. lavender, camomile, rosemary, vanilla, etc.) **The things I can touch are...** (e.g. fluffy material, velvet, silk, bubble wrap, etc.)
Listen to music/play an instrument/sing a song My go-to song is:	**Do something pampering** (e.g. painting nails, massaging hands, brushing hair/skin, having an aromatherapy bath, using a massaging chair, etc.) I will...

Copyright © Karen Treisman – *A Therapeutic Treasure Box for Working with Children and Adolescents with Developmental Trauma* – 2018

Do my breathing and relaxation exercises	Do my muscle tensing and releasing exercises
Step 1: Step 2: Step 3: Step 4:	Step 1: Step 2: Step 3: Step 4:
Do my mindfulness, meditation, yoga, and/or tai chi exercises	**Clean, organise, or tidy**
Rip, tear, or scrunch up some paper	**Give myself an alternating butterfly hug**
Blow bubbles, blow feathers, or blow a balloon	**Drink from a straw/have a hot drink with some spices like cinnamon and nutmeg**
Watch the movement of a lava lamp, a snow globe, fish in an aquarium, a rain stick, or glitter in a bottle	**Interact with water** (e.g. swimming water play, having a bath, playing with water)
Squeeze using alternating hands, a stress ball, clay, or some Play-Doh **Or stretch using a theraband or elastic**	**Do some physical exercise** (e.g. cycling, jogging, dancing, doing star jumps, shaking it out, etc.) I will…

Copyright © Karen Treisman – *A Therapeutic Treasure Box for Working with Children and Adolescents with Developmental Trauma – 2018*

Do some regulating exercises (e.g. drawing, putting weight on my back, swinging, twisting, rocking, crawling, climbing, wrapping myself in a blanket (weighted), etc.) I will...	**Make some rhythmic movement** (e.g. playing the drums, stamping my feet, dancing, or clapping my hands). I will...
Go for a walk/run/cycle in nature	**Interact with animals**
Chew or suck something like a sweet, dried fruit, chewing gum, or a chewy bracelet	**Wring out/twist/squeeze a wet towel**
Play a brain-based game such as...	**Do, listen, or watch something that will make me laugh...**
Look at positive memories such as photos, cards, or sentimental items (e.g. positive memory treasure box or sparkle moments diary)	**Let out a silent scream/find a quiet place to scream/bang a cushion**
Run cold water on my face	**Do something creative like...**

Copyright © Karen Treisman – *A Therapeutic Treasure Box for Working with Children and Adolescents with Developmental Trauma* – 2018

Count to ten or from ten backwards to zero	**Do some colouring in, trace a picture, or design a mandala**
Imagery and re-scripting When a difficult memory, thought, and/or feeling comes: I will imagine… I will remember… I will tell myself…	**My favourite inspirational quotes/sayings/ mottos/songs/movies are**
Name it to tame it (Siegel and Bryson, 2011) Name/say out loud how you feel. This feeling can also be drawn, acted out, danced, sculpted, depicted in sand, written about, etc.	**Positive self-talk** I am… I can… I will… I know… Things are different now because…
Speak to someone who I feel gets me That person is…	**???**

Copyright © Karen Treisman – *A Therapeutic Treasure Box for Working with Children and Adolescents with Developmental Trauma* – 2018

Octopus of
Options

Copyright © Karen Treisman – *A Therapeutic Treasure Box for Working with Children and Adolescents with Developmental Trauma – 2018*

Copyright © Karen Treisman – *A Therapeutic Treasure Box for Working with Children and Adolescents with Developmental Trauma – 2018*

A sample coping card

I will cope, calm, and soothe myself by...

1.  **Using my sensory box**

2.  **Listening to "Beautiful" by Christina Aguilera**

3.  **Giving myself butterfly hugs**

4.  **Going to my safe place: "breeze"**

I will tell myself: "I am strong", "I am not alone", and "I am in control"

 I will call...

I will go to... Nathan, Lara, Karen, or Julie

Copyright © Karen Treisman – *A Therapeutic Treasure Box for Working with Children and Adolescents with Developmental Trauma – 2018*

A blank template for creating a coping card

My Coping Card

1.

2.

3.

4.

I will tell myself:

I will call...

I will go to...

Copyright © Karen Treisman – *A Therapeutic Treasure Box for Working with Children and Adolescents with Developmental Trauma – 2018*

CHAPTER 4

Strategies for Supporting Children who have Experienced Relational and Developmental Trauma to Identify, Label, Express, and Regulate their Feelings

Introduction

Children use their caregiver and their surrounding adults as a mirror, a regulator, a guide, and an anchor to the outside world. Caregiver mind-mindedness, sensitivity, reflective function, and emotional availability are essential, as they contribute to interpersonal skills and resilience across multiple domains including supporting the development of secure attachment styles. Through caregivers' minds, facial expressions, tone of voice, and physical, sensory, and emotional responses, children are constantly discovering and developing their sense of selves and self-other separateness and information about themselves, others, and the world around them (through internalised Me, You and We Maps).

Therefore, in the context of sensitive, scaffolding, and meaningful relationships, children begin to learn how to read, signal, identify, understand, and express their emotions. These relationship-based communication loops, loving emotional exchanges, and co-regulation activities support children in developing the crucial life skills of modulating, regulating, and tolerating feelings such as frustration, anger, fear, disappointment, and stress.

Moreover, these moment-to-moment relational interactions between caregiver and child fill children's emotional tanks and treasure boxes up with positive relational experiences and memories; providing them with a secure base, safe haven, and strong platform from which to explore, play, engage, and learn from. These social exchanges and connections also teach children that relationships are rewarding, desirable, and worth investing in and trusting. They support children to develop a treasure box of ways for understanding and engaging with their social and emotional world.

Emotional regulation in the context of relational and developmental trauma

Having touched upon some of the positive effects of these parent–child interactions, let us consider the children who have had chronic disconnection, incongruent mirroring and absent-minded parenting, with very few emotionally rich and emotional-tank-filling experiences.

Within the context of relational and developmental trauma, many children will not have had their relationship ruptures and mismatches (we all have some) repaired. Children are likely to have had their experiences chronically mis-attuned to, or misattributed by dysregulated caregivers who have their own difficulties with self-regulating their levels of arousal; they struggle to step back from their own affective experience, and reflect on their child's internal experience.

Some of these children will not have experienced their feelings being noticed, labelled, and/or responded to. They might have learned that their feelings were not tolerable, important, or acceptable. Some examples are given below.

From when Dani was young, her parents were increasingly upset and distanced when she expressed anger in any form. So she concluded that anger was an emotion that could not be acknowledged or expressed. Instead, Dani developed a false self and buried her authentic self under protective layers of smiles and "Everything being wonderful".

Megan saw Carly's crying as a personal attack on her and as communication that she hated her and was purposely trying to upset her and make her life more difficult. Therefore, she tended to reply to Carly's distress by screaming, shouting, and being hostile and dysregulated.

Four-year-old Hayden told his father that he felt sick and had a headache, to which his father replied, "Stop complaining and grow a pair; I have headaches every day."

Additionally, some children will have been positioned as an extension of their caregiver. They may have learned that others' feelings take precedent over their own or they may not have been given the space to be a separate person with their own mind (i.e. mind-mindedness). Some examples are given below.

Nabil came home from school upset and disappointed that he had not been selected for a part in the school play. His mother, who was preoccupied and upset about his father forgetting her birthday the day before, assumed that Nabil's sadness was the same as her own. Therefore, she discussed her forgotten birthday at length but did not acknowledge the school play.

Caitlyn avoided telling her mum about being bullied at school for fear that her mum's own fragility would be evoked and that she would push her further into depression.

Following Luke's parents' frictional divorce, his mother assumed that he felt the same anger towards his father as she did. She was unable to see that their relationship and Luke's feelings towards his father might be separate or different to her own.

Six-month-old Matthew was playing happily with his trains when his father swiftly took the trains away and pushed the drum towards Matthew, whilst saying that Matthew was going to be a world-famous drummer and needed to practise. When Matthew became distressed and reached for the train, his father seemed preoccupied with his own desires and needs and responded by playing the drum louder and pushing the train further away.

When Nicky cried, Susan would become triggered and subsequently dysregulated herself. This left Nicky flooded in a storm of her own emotions and resulted in both of their arousal levels mutually escalating in intensity.

Blake's favourite toy (a free toy from a McDonald's Happy Meal) broke. His mother minimised his loss and told him to calm down, as it was only a freebie. In that moment, she struggled to see that the toy was very important to Blake, was giving him pleasure, and that it being broken felt like a big deal to him.

Some children might have had to find ways to survive in "shark-infested waters" (e.g. experiencing abuse and trauma – see Box 3.1) or to navigate their way through desolate islands (e.g. experiencing neglect and relational solitude – see Box 3.1) by hiding, dissociating, bottling up, avoiding, and/or shutting out their feelings (see Worksheet 3.1 for a visual representation of some common coping strategies). Having to endure relational poverty and absence of emotion means it is likely that some of these children's stress and arousal regulation systems will have become down-regulated and chronically suppressed. Some examples are given below.

Nelson excitedly performed a puppet show and his father responded by staring blankly with absent eyes, uttering a few monotone sounds, and shifting his head towards the TV.

Christina had not been played with as a child and had been under-socialised and relationally starved. When she became a mother herself, she met three-month-old Morgan's basic needs in a "robotic" manner, with her face and mood remaining unresponsive and flat in affect. When Morgan cried and appeared distressed, Christina would smile, laugh, and seem unaffected. At other times, Morgan would signal to Christina that she wanted to play and interact by putting her arms out, making a noise, or smiling, but these cues would largely go unnoticed. Sadly, Morgan quickly learned to manage this relational poverty by turning her head away, avoiding eye contact, losing herself in her own world, or going to sleep.

Penelope's fun and expressions of joy and excitement were restricted and dampened, as she was regularly told to be quiet or to stay still by her mother's side for fear of provoking her father's acts of violence when under the influence of alcohol.

Other children will have had to amplify their emotions and/or "Try to become or act like the sharks" to get their needs met and/or noticed (see Chapter 8). In certain cases, they will have been shown that their feelings were linked to terrifying responses. Some examples are given below.

Following falling over, Zach was burned by a cigarette for interrupting his parent's TV show and for "being a cry baby". On another occasion, despite walking on eggshells in an attempt to avoid "shark attacks", Zach accidently spilt Ribena on the floor and was subsequently made to lick it dry and to go without food for the remainder of the day.

Three-year-old Lucien was playing with his older brother, Niall. Niall took Lucien's ball away from him, and Lucien began flapping his arms and crying. Their dad swung off the sofa and hit and kicked Niall several times, whilst shouting, "Next time Lucien, you f*cking do this! You don't let no one push you around, boy."

As illustrated in the above examples, in the absence of a secure, regulating, caregiving system, and in the presence of complex and cumulative trauma, children like Zach and Lucien are at risk of living in a dysregulated state of arousal where they are soaked and trapped in chronic and cumulative toxic stress and exposed to a pendulum of rapid, high-intensity swings of emotions and flat, disconnected responses. This means that children are likely to trigger fight, flight, or freeze responses regularly and have few coping strategies available to them (i.e. fear with no solution). Bowlby (1980) described this phenomenon as the child either shrinking from the world or doing battle with it. See Chapter 3 for a further explanation on safety and regulation levels.

When these negative relational experiences occur on a chronic and cumulative basis, they are likely to have a host of consequences for the developing child's social, emotional, cognitive, and behavioural world.

For example, how can we expect children who have often missed out on a thinking adult, who connected with them in meaningful ways and supported them in co-regulating their emotions, to be able to self-regulate?

Think about the steps, support, and co-regulation that developing children ordinarily need to sleep in their own room, to potty train, to recover from a nightmare, or to calm down after their favourite toy goes missing, when they are told they cannot get chocolates at the supermarket, or when it is time to go home from a place they are enjoying. Imagine not having scaffolding, thoughtful, and co-regulatory support in mastering these skills.

Therefore, in the context of trauma, and in the absence of an attachment-facilitating environment, children have often not had the same opportunities and the fundamental building blocks that they need from a safe adult, to learn how to notice, modulate, tolerate, or recover from affect states and to develop their capacity to integrate the bottom-up influences of emotions with the top-down control of thoughts (Lilas and Turnball, 2009).

Recapping Chapter 3, children who have been raised in a developmental and relational trauma context often have a smaller window of tolerance (Siegel, 1999) and a sensitive defence system. They often present with a poor ability to self-regulate, process, and modulate affect and sensory stimuli (Koomar, 2009). This means that they regularly have a lower threshold for high-intensity emotions and can be slower to return to what is often a heightened baseline. Their defence systems can be like constantly beeping burglar alarms, meaning that a small drop of an emotion can feel to them like an all-consuming sea. These sensory processing and emotional regulation complications are further exacerbated by executive function and cognitive difficulties, such as struggling to problem-solve, control impulse, or filter information, which are all commonly associated within a relational and developmental trauma context (see Worksheet 8.11 for a range of strategies to support executive function skills).

Streeck-Fischer and van der Kolk (2000) discussed how children who have experienced complex trauma often lack the "internal maps to guide them", and therefore "act instead of plan" (p.905). Therefore, without the words, a facilitating environment, and regulating coping skills available and known to them, children can be driven by these pouring, cascading, emotions that can show themselves through a variety of behaviours (e.g. outbursts, aggression, attentional difficulties, etc.).

Moreover, many of these children have missed out on enriched environments, including having limited opportunities for relational talking, sharing stories, playing, singing, and reading time. This can also have a significant impact on children's speech and language skills and on their access to a rich, feeling-based vocabulary. For example, research has shown that children who have experienced complex trauma tend to struggle with differentiating facial expressions, are more likely to interpret events and faces as being negative, angry, and threatening, and subsequently have stronger emotional reactions to them (Perlman *et al.*, 2008). This is sometimes referred to as Hostile Attribution Bias, where a person will assume that another person has an intention to harm/wrong them, meaning that "normal/benign" behaviours can instead be perceived as hostile or aggressive. (See Chapter 8 for more information on understanding and responding to behavioural dysregulation.)

In addition, children and adolescents who have experienced complex trauma are more likely to have difficulty with their reflective-function capacities, cognitive flexibility, perspective-taking, ability to empathise, and ability to read emotional cues (e.g. connect with what goes on inside others' minds) (Cozolino, 2006). This is hugely significant, as these mentalisation and regulation skills are the cornerstone for guiding the child's relationships and their own ability to mentalise, sustain, and form attachments, to develop empathy, and to learn how to manage impulses and daily stressors (Grienenberger, Kelly, and Slade, 2005). An example is given below.

When Harry was developing, he was not held in safe hands and thinking minds and did not have skills such as empathy and perspective-taking sufficiently embodied, modelled, or shown to him. It is understandable that these skills may be less developed in him than in other children of his age. A moment that comes to mind that illustrates this further happened during a therapeutic assessment of the family for court: I saw five-year-old Harry fall over and bump his head on the corner of the kitchen table. His mother looked over, huffed in frustration, and rolled her eyes. After a few seconds, Harry started crying softly and rubbing his head. His mother minimised his felt pain and signals for support and told him, "It's nothing. You're so clumsy – stop being a stupid baby and get up. Maybe it will knock some sense into you – you sure need some." A few days later, during another observation of the family interactions, Simeon (Harry's younger brother from a different father) fell over and hit his head and his mother instantly leapt up, kissed his head better, and rocked him lovingly. Harry stared from the corner and then began frantically playing with a ball.

When we explored the different responses the children had received and how that might feel or be perceived by Harry, his mother struggled to perspective-take or get in touch with Harry's feelings. Imagine these sorts of misconnection experiences happening over and over again over a prolonged period of time.

Please see Chapters 1–3 in *Working with Relational and Developmental Trauma in Children and Adolescents* (Treisman, 2016) for more explanation and discussion on the foundations of emotional regulation and the impact of relational and developmental trauma on children's emotions, relationships, bodies, brains, and behaviours.

Implications for practice

To address some of the aforementioned difficulties, interventions and interactions within the context of relational and developmental trauma ideally will focus on supporting children and caregivers to be able to recognise, name, express, label, and regulate their feelings, as opposed to getting lost in a sea of emotions and overwhelming sensorial waves. Alongside multi-levelled safety (Chapter 3) and the relationship (Chapters 1, 6, and 7), this attention to feelings feels like the roots and anchor of any additional interventions or branches that will subsequently follow. The intention is that strengthening children's/caregivers' abilities to develop richer ways of describing emotion and modulating the duration, rhythm, and intensity of them will have a plethora of positive effects, including widening their window of arousal tolerance, developing skills such as perspective-taking, and guiding children out of their limbic system and back into their thinking brain. This also aims to increase the child's experience of meaningfully connected interactions to fill their emotional tank and treasure box up with new re-appraising positive experiences and to rebalance the negative tipping scale and the highly charged negative magnet. The strategies that follow aim to support children in learning that their feelings can be safe and build on the premise that the more we support children to have words to express themselves, to organise their feelings, and to make sense of their experiences, the less likely they are to come out through unprocessed emotions and tricky behaviours. These feelings foundations are fundamental and therefore often need to be laid down before the more complex talking and sense-making therapies can begin. Children need to learn and master how to roll and crawl before they can learn how to walk and run! *Within this, how can we expect a child to control their behaviour, or behave differently, if they don't understand what it is, why it is there, and how it can be and feel different?*

The following strategies offer the reader some practical creative and multi-sensory "feelings work" ideas to use with children and adolescents, either directly or indirectly via their key adults/therapists. These are not prescriptive or exhaustive and should be interwoven with existing tools and carried out within the context of a safe, positive, responsive, and containing relationship. Their suitability and appropriateness need to be considered carefully, whilst tailoring them for the unique child, provider, and context (see Chapter 1 for guiding principles and other factors to keep in mind when employing the described strategies).

It is also acknowledged that these ideas form a slither of one block of the feelings foundations, and some of the other blocks should be buffered through rich, moment-to-moment relational interactions, an overarching embodiment of an emotionally aware relationship/environment, and/or through emotional literacy programmes.

Practical strategies for supporting children to identify, express, name, and regulate their emotions

Role models and everyday naming of feelings

Children learn how to self-soothe, recognise, and manage their feelings through the people surrounding them. Therefore, the "thinking" adults play a pivotal role in verbally and non-verbally modelling, coaching, and scaffolding how to identify, express, and respond to high-intensity arousal and a range of feelings. Adults should endeavour, where appropriate, to put words to feelings, and to openly name the feelings in the child and in others in a tentative, attuned, and curious way. This fits with the saying: "The way we treat them teaches them."

How do we respond when a child's favourite toy breaks, in a frustrating situation (e.g. heavy traffic), or when managing difficult feelings (e.g. a bad day at work)? How do we show a child when we are feeling proud, happy, and excited? How openly are feelings named and acknowledged in front of and towards the child in an age-appropriate way?

Siegel and Bryson (2011) helpfully term this strategy in a catchy way as "Name it to tame it". Often, by acknowledging, validating, and naming feelings, we are finding ways to support the child in understanding, making sense of, and organising their feelings. Everyday opportunities should be used to identify and discuss a range of feelings. This might be in day-to-day interactions, on the TV, in a book/song/comic strip, or when playing. For example: "Wow, Peppa Pig has a big smile on her face; she looks so excited." "Lizzie the Lizard is feeling sick – what shall we do to make her feel better?" "If the dog could talk, I wonder what he would say to us?" "If I was in your shoes, I might feel…" "Why do you think the rabbit is looking a bit sad?"

Keeping in mind that children who have experienced relational and developmental trauma are more prone to misinterpreting emotional cues, it can also be helpful when naming emotions in a tentative, curious way to show the thinking and/or regulating process visually. For example, this could be done by visibly taking a purposeful, deep breath in, actively shaking out the tension, physically putting a finger to one's forehead, or commenting on the thinking cogs moving or the thinking clock ticking.

Ideally, children should also have desired skills modelled to them, such as showing kindness and empathy (e.g. showing concern when a neighbour is unwell, giving their old clothes or toys to others in need, picking up litter on the streets, volunteering at a soup kitchen, or offering an elderly person a seat on the train). These qualities have been positively linked to developing and enhancing prosocial tendencies (Masten *et al.*, 2011).

Practising and rehearsing

Role-playing, rehearsing, and practising feelings/scenarios/skills such as "Making new friends", "Asking for help", "Responding to the word no", or "Showing I feel upset" through using interactive and child-friendly puppets, masks, miniatures, or dolls can be very helpful. These scenarios, skills, and dilemmas can also be incorporated into games, like charades or Pictionary, or explored through writing a story, poem, rap, or comic strip (using photos) about the specific scenario or desired skill.

Self-reflection and self-care

When working/living with children who have experienced complex trauma, it is inevitable that a range of strong feelings will be evoked and triggered. Therefore, it is important to reflect and be aware of our own emotional reactions, triggers, unresolved traumas, and hotspots and to practise self-care and self-reflection (see Chapters 6 and 7). This is even more important, as we need to be able to model self-care and to stay as regulated as possible with the child (respond rather than react), as well as being able to offer them a containing space where they are and feel held in safe hands, thinking minds, and regulating bodies. Given that relational trauma requires relational repair, these relational responses and interactions need to be prioritised and fore-fronted. The child needs to experience a different way of doing and being in relationships and of having their feelings noticed, understood, valued, and responded to.

Getting to know the whole child

The more you really get to know a child, the more you can support them in identifying and learning about themselves and their feeling states. This is similar to a parent who, over time and with interest, and detective work, learns to decode and decipher the different types of their baby's cries, communications, and signals. For example, we need to be asking: *What triggers them and/or makes them feel scared/happy/angry/ sad/excited/embarrassed, etc.? How do they communicate this feeling through their body, face, words, or behaviours?* (See Worksheets 4.1 and 4.2 to expand on these questions and to visually represent the responses.)

We want to support children to explore, express, and be able to name what they feel (and why), what they think, and what they need at that particular time. This deciphering process can be increasingly difficult with children who have experienced complex trauma, as they often have their protective guard dogs surrounding them and their trauma jacket on. Therefore, we need to be able to look underneath the surface, their defences, and their survival strategies in order to see the hidden child and to hear and feel their unexpressed needs. This crystallises the significance of also looking beyond words, and attending to our own and others' unspoken communication, affect, and body language (see Chapters 6 and 8).

All feelings are accepted

It is important to show and communicate to the child emotionally, cognitively, and physically that it is safe, they have the right to experience a range of feelings (this is normalising, validating, and giving permissive messages), and these feelings can be sat with, tolerated, borne witness to, and accepted in containing and validating ways. This includes highlighting the difference between thoughts, feelings, and behaviours (see Worksheets 4.20 and 4.21), as well as acknowledging and exploring the usefulness of an emotion, such as how anger can help one fight for what one believes in or for protection.

It is also vital to remember that it can be very exposing for children to share their feelings, especially if they have not had positive experiences of doing this previously, so it is important to validate how difficult this can be and to show them actively that you are pleased that they came to/trusted you. It is also vital that surrounding adults are supported to really listen (using whole-body and active listening), hear, and join the children and avoid telling them how they should feel. Their feeling is their feeling, and they are entitled to feel it. *Put yourself in their shoes: how does it feel when someone tells you how you should feel or dismisses how you are feeling?*

Mixed and a melting pot of feelings

The child should also be supported in noticing the experience of having mixed feelings in varying levels of intensity. This is particularly significant for children who may have had to survive and cope by separating/splitting/oscillating feelings or been immersed in all-or-nothing and/or black-or-white ways of thinking. This can be through verbal statements, such as "I can imagine you are very excited about starting school, but also a bit worried about…" and "It was really nice to spend time with my mum, but it also made me feel sad about all the times that I am not with her."

Discussions around exploring mixed and blended feelings can also be enhanced through practical activities, such as the following.

- Designing/drawing children's mixed feelings in a rainbow, kaleidoscope, or melting pot.

- Designing/drawing children's mixed feelings in a pie, wheel, or cake (see Photo 4.18).

- Designing/drawing children's mixed feelings in a bag, jar (see Photo 4.4), or box (see Worksheet 4.6 and Photo 4.5).

- Designing/drawing children's mixed feelings in patchwork or in a puzzle (see Photo 4.1 and Worksheet 4.3) of feelings.

- Discussing the melting pot of feelings through mixing paints, cooking with various ingredients, making a kaleidoscope, designing inside/outside masks (see Photo 4.10), or using multiple layers of coloured sand (see Photo 4.3).

Where appropriate, the above ideas can also be extended to talking about different parts of one's identity, such as using a puzzle, a body puzzle/doll (see Worksheet 4.4), or a patchwork pattern (see Photo 4.2) to discuss the different pieces of me and/or my feelings (see Worksheets 4.3 and 4.5).

Photo 4.1 A patchwork of feelings using a puzzle

Photo 4.2 A patchwork of feelings using drawing

Photo 4.3 A sand art representation of different feelings

Photo 4.4 A jar of mixed feelings

Photo 4.5 A box of mixed feelings

Creative, expressive, and playful ways to discuss feelings

This section offers a range of creative, expressive, and playful ways to expand on children's understanding and emotion expression. The following is by no means a prescriptive or exhaustive list and should be used in conjunction with the strategies and concepts presented earlier in the chapter. Please read the factors to be mindful of in Chapter 1 to ensure that these are used with care.

- Make *biscuits, cakes, or pizzas* with different facial expressions on them (see Photo 4.6). As with all of the mentioned strategies, it is important to ensure that there is a range of positive, mixed, and negative expressions to demonstrate the whole spectrum and to open the space for rich and diverse feeling discussions.

Photo 4.6 Biscuits decorated with different facial expressions

- Make a *feelings of the day board* (e.g. Worry Wednesday) or a *feelings dictionary* (e.g. E is for Embarrassed, H is for Happy, and A is for Angry). These can be expanded on by using photos, collage, models, metaphors, and sensory materials. For example, for W is for Worry, one might use wiggly worms, jiggling jelly, a whirling-around washing machine in their head, or butterflies in their tummy to guide further discussions (see Worksheets 4.9, 4.10, 4.11, and 4.12). Materials can also be used; for example, to represent anger, items such as sandpaper, rocks, or red tissue paper could be used.

- Make or use a *feelings quiz or crossword* with questions such as: "What is a feeling word that has three letters?" "What feeling is often associated with red?" "What is another word for very warm?" Alternatively, one could use or make *sentence-completion tasks* with questions like "Think of a time when you felt...", "The things that make the anger come out are...", "The thing I need is...", "The thing I would change is...", "A thing that makes me smile is..." and "I'm happiest when..." (See Worksheet 2.7 for a series of sample sentence-completion questions and *A Therapeutic Treasure Deck of Sentence Completion and Feelings Cards*, Treisman, 2017).)

- Take *feeling photographs* (children often really enjoy using a disposable or digital camera) or use magazines to make a *feelings collage/scrapbook*, for example of "Positive body language", "Sad faces", "Things that make me happy are...", and "Fear is..." (see Photo 4.7).

Photo 4.7 "Fear is..." collage

- A fun way of talking about and exploring feelings can be through *painting or designing masks, plates, balloons, Play-Doh mats, or puppets* with different facial expressions or feelings about a particular person/situation/event (see Photos 4.8 an d 4.9). You can also use Worksheets 4.7, 4.8, and 4.13 to aid this process.

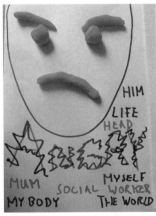

Photo 4.8 Feelings face made from Play-Doh

Photo 4.9 Balloon emotion faces

- Building on the above, using *inside/outside masks* can be a great way to explore different feelings. For example, the inside/outside masks in Photo 4.10 are a recreated version of masks completed by a young adolescent during the course of long-term attachment and trauma-based therapy. She was encouraged to name the masks and to give some narrative about them. She was supported in expressing on the left mask how she thought others and the world saw her, and on the right mask she shared some of the ways in which she felt inside and what people would be able to see if they could see inside her, like if they had an emotions X-ray. Subsequent sessions explored a range of avenues such as: *When were her different masks needed/worn/hidden/helpful/unhelpful? What made her put the different masks on or take them off? How did the different masks develop/grow/get responded to/perceived as? Which mask or parts of masks felt like her true self/authentic self? How did she think and feel (physically and emotionally) when she wore the different masks? Who, if anyone, saw her different masks?*

  This concept can also be expanded on by making dual portraits, where one side represents how one feels inside and the other side represents how one feels others see them (see Photo 4.11).

Photo 4.10 Inside/outside feelings masks

Photo 4.11 A dual portrait drawing

- Make a *feelings container* (bag, box, or jar) filled with *feelings cards*. The child/family/group can take it in turns to pick a feelings card (e.g. happy, sad, angry, scared, trapped, embarrassed, and proud). They can then choose to *describe the emotion, mould it, draw it, act it out, or tell a story about a time they had felt like that.* This is a bit like combining games, such as Pictionary and charades (Worksheets 4.7 and 4.8 can be used to help these exercises). I sometimes use different coloured pipe cleaners (see Photo 4.12), pebbles, buttons, or different coloured sweets to represent these feelings and to make the games more interactive and child-friendly.

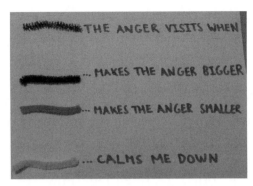

Photo 4.12 Pipe cleaner game using anger as an example

- Practise *making "faces in the mirror"* or *playing "Follow the leader with facial expressions"*. Another fun way of expanding this is by *playing "Guess the facial expression"*. The therapist/parent and child can take it in turns to cover their lower face (e.g. mouth) or upper face (e.g. eyes) with a scarf or a piece of paper and then the other guesses which emotion they are showing. If the therapist/parent is covering the part of the face with paper, the child can draw what they think the missing emotion is (see Photos 4.13 and 4.14).

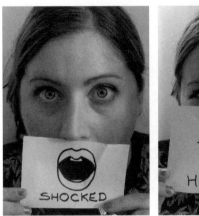

Photos 4.13 and 4.14 Guess the emotion game

- Most children enjoy pressing buttons, for example on lifts, remote controls, or toys. You can *use a PlayStation or TV control and choose different buttons to represent and label with different feelings*. Each time the child presses that button, they should describe that feeling, act it out, mould/sculpt it, draw it, or talk about a specific time they felt that way.

- *Head of thoughts and emotions exercise:* Draw a *blank head with speech bubbles* where the child can label different positive and negative thoughts and feelings (see Worksheet 4.15 for a paper version), as if we could see into our brains using an X-ray or through super vision. This might be exploring an overview of what thoughts and feelings the young person has in general or you might have a specific focus that you use this exercise for, such as: "The thoughts and feelings in your head when...happened", "Thoughts and feelings about your relationship with...", or "Thoughts and feelings about your forthcoming contact visit."

An even more interactive and engaging way of doing this exercise is by using *a sculpture of a head, a model of the brain, or a hat* to physically label the different feelings and thoughts (see Photos 4.15 and 4.16). This can be expanded on by using it as a tool for parents/teachers/carers and children to think about what is in each other's mind and to gain a different perspective/insight; for example: "If my foster carer was in the room she would say...", "When I hit my mum she might have felt...", etc.

This concept can be used in multiple ways, such as half of the head representing "then" and the other representing "now" or half of the head thinking about "negative thoughts" and the other about "positive thoughts". I generally encourage clients to combine positive and negative feelings to model a sense of integration, connection, and the notion that emotions can be mixed and multi-layered. It is helpful to have a range of shapes, colours, and sizes from which the young person can choose to represent the variety and diversity of feelings.

For older children, I often expand this by asking something like if you were going to write your social media status what would it say, what would you like it to say, what would you be worried to see, and so forth.

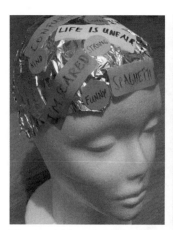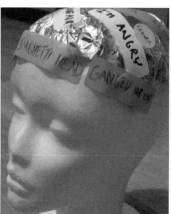

Photos 4.15 and 4.16 A 3D head model with some positive and negative thoughts and feelings (in progress): "If someone could look inside my head they would see or hear…"

- Make a *poster of all of the different types of feelings.* This can support children to learn about all of the different types of emotions and to increase their overall emotion vocabulary. To personalise and extend this exercise (see Photo 4.17), you can support the child to put *stickers, buttons, pebbles, or other materials* (use a range of shapes, colours, and sizes) by the emotions they feel and to show to what extent they feel them (you can use the list of feelings words in Worksheet 4.8 or the template cards provided in Worksheet 4.7, or you can make your own). These discussions can provide a useful springboard for future discussions, such as (using the emotion of fear as an example): *When do you notice the feelings of fear visiting? What makes the feeling of fear bigger/smaller/stronger/weaker/helpful/unhelpful? How do your face, body, words, and behaviour show and respond to the feeling of fear? On a scale from zero to ten, where would you place how strong the feelings of fear are? What made you choose that... (colour, shape, texture, size) to represent fear? Can you describe a specific time when the feeling of fear visited?*

This concept of exploring different feelings and/or the level and intensity at which they are felt can also be illustrated by using an emotion wheel/pie chart (see Photo 4.18 and Worksheet 4.14) and/or with a feelings LEGO® structure (see Photo 4.19).

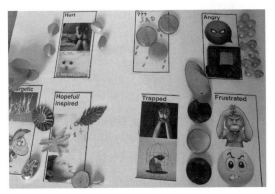

Photo 4.17 Feelings board with expressive materials

Photo 4.18 Feelings pie drawing with expressive materials

Photo 4.19 Feelings LEGO® sculpture with each colour representing a different feeling

- Make *feelings jewellery, brooches, and badges* using different beads and decoration. This can be a fun way of talking about emotions. For example, a child can choose a different coloured bead to represent the different emotions they feel or they may have a piece of jewellery to reflect a certain mood such as "happiness" or "worry". Alternatively, some children might like to collage or papier mâché a large bangle with images, colours, and words to represent different moods.

- Some children might like to get different shaped bars, bottles, and containers and fill them with *different coloured waters* or *different items*, such as rice, beans, and pasta, to represent different feelings and their intensity (see Photo 4.20).

Photo 4.20 Different coloured jars to represent different levels of intensity

- Some children might find it helpful to explore their feelings through thinking about, if they were to *look through the windows or open the doors* to different rooms in a house, what would one see in the: *happy room, sad room, angry room, scary room, fun room*, etc. (see Worksheet 4.16). Alternatively, children might think about what they would see if they were to *turn the channel on the TV to the happy, sad, angry, frustrated, lonely*, etc. (see Worksheet 4.17).

- Children or adolescents who are more physical might like some of the following ideas: *running* to different places in the room that represent different feelings; *design* a "feelings obstacles course"; *throw sticky hands* at a "feelings board" (see Photo 4.21); *throw balls* into "feelings buckets"; *choreograph* a "feelings dance"; *drum different feeling rhythms*; *write different feelings* on the "spots in a game of twister" (see Photo 4.22); make a "feelings hopscotch".

Photo 4.21 Throwing sticky hands at feeling cards game

Photo 4.22 Beginnings of making a feelings twister

The aforementioned feelings work ideas can be used as standalone activities or interwoven into the child's daily world and/or therapy session. For example, when the child tells you a story where they felt excited, you can connect it to their *feelings dictionary* or to a *feelings face*. In addition, *journaling, art, music, magazines, film, and dance* can be useful adaptations with older children. There are amazing resources available to complement these ideas that enhance and stimulate playful ways of talking about feelings, such as *feeling flashcards, emotion balls, feelings dice, feelings dolls, feelings books, emotion monsters, magnets, games (online and board), and stamps* (see the "Resources" tab at www.safehandsthinkingminds.co.uk for some suggestions and links).

Externalising and metaphors

Children should be supported in getting a stronger sense of what a feeling state is (this is nicely illustrated by the saying "Name it to tame it" (Siegel and Bryson, 2011). For example, children might like to name, describe, or externalise the feeling/"difficulty". For example, "worry" could be likened to a worry worm, a worry cloud, jiggling jelly, or a spinning wheel, or "anger" to a volcano (Photo 4.23), wave, tornado, lightning, or bubbling water (each child/caregiver/therapist will find different names that resonate and fit with them).

Worksheets 4.9, 4.10, 4.11, and 4.12 offer some ideas, metaphors, and questions around creatively exploring and externalising these feelings using the example of some of the core emotions of worry, sadness, happiness, and anger. This can lead to child-friendly conversations around, for example, how you can cool the volcano down, not let water bubble over, surf the angry wave, or calm down the whirling tornado. Some sample Narrative Therapy informed questions are listed below to build on these concepts and the idea of finding ways to explore, express, externalise, and expand on feelings.

What is... (the externalised character, object, or "thing" of a feeling) called? What does it look like? Sound like? Smell? Say? Do?

It can be very helpful for children to draw/paint/sculpt/mould/mosaic/depict in sand the character they create. Various therapeutic avenues that explore the influence and impact of "the difficulty" and respond to it are listed below (examples of names children have chosen for wetting the bed are used).

How did you manage to outsmart "Sneaky Wee"? How much bigger or stronger are you than "Dripping Derek"? What skills and strengths did you use to conquer "Lucy Liquid"? Who would you rather have in charge of your life – "Penelope Pee" or you? What is it like to share your life with "Raging River"? What plans does the "Worry Waterfall" have for your life? What is "The Trickling Terror" stopping you from doing?

Different names for difficulties and/or feelings are used here to show the breadth of possibilities.

How is "The Strangling Hand" affecting your life? When the voice of "The Crusher" is less strong, what will you be doing that you're not doing now? How is "The Cloud" attempting to prevent you from enjoying the self-confidence you were able to acknowledge before the trauma? What plans does the "Jittery Jelly" have for your life? When "The Volcano" is about to erupt, what can you do to lessen the effect of the lava?

Child-friendly weather or colour terms can also be useful, such as thunder or red for anger and blue, rain, or clouds for sadness. Some children may benefit from talking about different feelings in a more sensory way, for example using sandpaper for sad times, a rock for hard times, and fluffy material for calming times.

Photo 4.23 A Play-Doh and puppet volcano to explore externalising "the anger": "Livid Lava" and "Eric the Eruption"

Mind–body links

Where possible, support the child in making links between their feelings and their bodily sensations. This is especially important given the relationship between trauma and the body (see Chapter 3 in *Working with Relational and Developmental Trauma in Children and Adolescents* (Treisman, 2016) for a detailed account of the impact of trauma on children's bodies and some body-based therapeutic interventions). For example, it can be helpful to say mind–body statements such as: "I wonder if you are feeling butterflies in your tummy." "I have noticed that your hands are tensing and you're breathing fast." "Sometimes when I'm scared, my heart beats like a runaway train." "I think I am feeling a bit anxious about my meeting at work today, as my body is telling me. My stomach feels like it is at the circus."

Some children might want to make a visual representation (to draw, sculpt, or write) of these types of body-based feelings. For example, they may like to cut out or draw the butterflies and then write a worry on each one and let them fly away.

Other children might find *body-mapping exercises* a helpful tool for exploring their relationships with their bodies (see Photo 4.24). Where appropriate and agreed by the child (being mindful of the child's comfort level, their relationship to touch, the person doing the exercise with them, and their body), you can draw around the child's body or vice versa on a large sheet of paper. Alternatively, a ready-made body cut-out, teddy bear, or a doll can be used.

There are endless avenues of using body-mapping; however, some useful lines of enquiry include: *Put a sticker where you feel...? Where do you feel the feelings of... in your body? Which bits are for example tense/hot? How do we look after...part? What shape/colour/size is the feeling of...in your chest? When the...took over when...how did your body feel? What is the story and journey of your body? If your body that part could talk, what would it say? What is your body trying to tell you? How does your body feel now or when you were... (a regulated happy time)?*

Worksheet 4.18 offers a template of a body that can be used to represent different feeling states through using colour, size, and shape. Sample examples are also shown in Photos 4.25 and 4.26.

These feelings and sensations can also be pictorially/physically represented (e.g. by drawing a brick on their chest or by placing a miniature drum figurine to symbolise their beating heart). For example, the child in Photo 4.24 discussed and explored his emotional and physical pain by choosing to place butterflies in his tummy, plasters on some of the places where he had been physically hurt, and a lock on his heart, and he said, "I've closed my heart now; it is tightly shut." He also represented the confusion and full-up nature of his thoughts as what he called "Messy tangled spaghetti in my head" with twisted pipe cleaners.

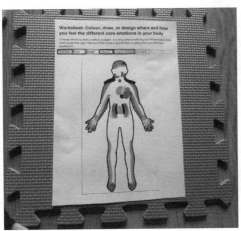

Photo 4.24 A body-map exercise

Photo 4.25 Representing where and how the core emotions are felt in the body

Photo 4.26 Body sensations being expressed with fabric pens on a doll

Monitoring arousal levels

Adults need to be as vigilant and responsive as possible to the child's arousal and regulation level when they are under- or over-aroused and, subsequently, to support them in increasing their awareness and monitoring of these processes. This can be through using scales and metaphors (Photos 4.27 and 4.28), such as a "feelings thermometer, volcano, engine, or ladder" (see Worksheet 4.19), a "traffic-light system", or "a pot of bubbling feelings" (see Worksheet 8.9). The child can then be supported in learning how to recognise these patterns and to chart where on the scale they are/were, how intense the feeling was (big, small, or medium; the engine was too fast (Photo 4.29), just right, or too slow; strong, medium, or mild), what helped bring them to a different feeling state, and what being in a different feeling state felt like. Day-to-day examples can help bring these to life, such as down-regulating at bedtime, or up-regulating when getting ready to play sports. To bring these concepts to life, using 3D examples can sometimes be helpful. Examples are given below.

One young person I worked with would show the level and intensity of his mood by pouring dye into bottles of water: the darker it was the more intense he felt.

Another young girl I supported would make a circle out of Play-Doh, or a small tower out of LEGO®, to demonstrate where she was at and how small or big her feeling was of certain emotions.

Photo 4.27 Using scaling questions to mark intensity through different sized LEGO®

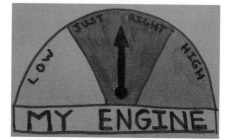

Photo 4.28 Using scaling questions to mark intensity through different sized Play-Doh shapes

Photo 4.29 Using scaling questions to mark intensity on a feelings engine

Young people can also be supported in learning more about their arousal state and monitoring their feelings through keeping a "thoughts, feelings, actions, and sensations diary" (see Worksheet 4.22) or using computer games and apps like HeartMath and StressEraser.

Adults also need to be the child's memory bank and support them in creating links and consequential thinking between events, behaviours, and feelings; for example: "Do you remember when...?" "When you felt...then...?" "What would happen if...?" Using the head-heart-hand concept (see Worksheet 4.21) can be a child-friendly way of discussing these connections, as can physically making a paper chain or a domino trail (see Chapters 2 and 8 for examples of this).

Once children are more aware of what is happening and what feelings they are experiencing, particularly in emotionally charged situations, grounding and coping strategies can be introduced (see Worksheet 3.9 for a range of regulating and soothing exercise cards).

Regulation skills should be practised and evaluated within a safe relationship and then transformed into a realistic and achievable plan (e.g. my coping card, my treasure box of tools, my coping cookbook, my chill skills, my bag of ideas, my calm-down superpowers, my protective palm, or my octopus of options – see Chapters 3 and 8 for a range of examples and worksheets on these option tools). Identified strategies aim to maintain the child's arousal-equilibrium and to reduce the intensity and duration of future dysregulation. These might include relaxation exercises, a sensory box, safe place imagery, verbal affirmations, scent/smell box, and distraction techniques (see Chapter 3 and in particular Worksheet 3.9).

I recognise when...is feeling...because they show me through their...

Draw/sculpt/write/collage/depict in sand your responses.

Body	**Words**
Facial expressions	**Behaviours**

Copyright © Karen Treisman – *A Therapeutic Treasure Box for Working with Children and Adolescents with Developmental Trauma – 2018*

Worksheet 4.2
I recognise when I am feeling...because I show it through my...

Draw, sculpt, write, collage, or depict in sand your responses.

Body	Words
Facial expressions	**Behaviours**

Copyright © Karen Treisman – *A Therapeutic Treasure Box for Working with Children and Adolescents with Developmental Trauma – 2018*

Copyright © Karen Treisman – *A Therapeutic Treasure Box for Working with Children and Adolescents with Developmental Trauma – 2018*

Puzzle person of different feelings

Copyright © Karen Treisman – *A Therapeutic Treasure Box for Working with Children and Adolescents with Developmental Trauma* – 2018

My patchwork of ...

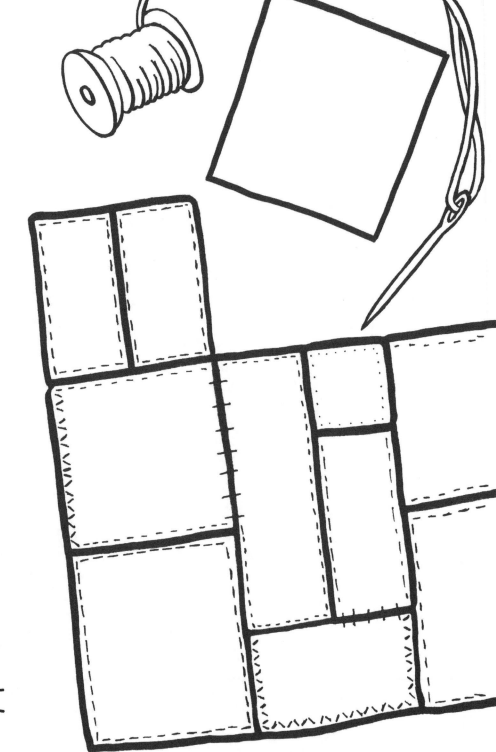

Copyright © Karen Treisman – *A Therapeutic Treasure Box for Working with Children and Adolescents with Developmental Trauma – 2018*

Copyright © Karen Treisman – *A Therapeutic Treasure Box for Working with Children and Adolescents with Developmental Trauma – 2018*

Sad/Upset	Confused
Bored	Happy
Lost	Disappointed

Copyright © Karen Treisman – *A Therapeutic Treasure Box for Working with Children and Adolescents with Developmental Trauma – 2018*

Copyright © Karen Treisman – *A Therapeutic Treasure Box for Working with Children and Adolescents with Developmental Trauma* – 2018

Copyright © Karen Treisman – *A Therapeutic Treasure Box for Working with Children and Adolescents with Developmental Trauma – 2018*

Copyright © Karen Treisman – *A Therapeutic Treasure Box for Working with Children and Adolescents with Developmental Trauma* – 2018

Copyright © Karen Treisman – *A Therapeutic Treasure Box for Working with Children and Adolescents with Developmental Trauma* – 2018

Table of feelings words

Describe, draw, act out, paint, sculpt, make, or collage the different feelings and emotions.

Sad/Upset	Confused	Bored
Happy	Lost	Disappointed
Scared/Fearful	Hurt	Surprised
Embarrassed	Helpless	Hopeless
Loved	Appreciated	Proud
Excited	Hopeful	Inspired

Copyright © Karen Treisman – *A Therapeutic Treasure Box for Working with Children and Adolescents with Developmental Trauma – 2018*

Energetic	Shocked	Angry
Confident	Safe	Secure
Jealous	Frustrated	Alone
Tired	Lucky	Disgusted
Relaxed	On edge	Trapped
Worried	Betrayed	Low
???	???	???

Copyright © Karen Treisman – *A Therapeutic Treasure Box for Working with Children and Adolescents with Developmental Trauma – 2018*

Anger is (using metaphors)...

Anger

The feeling of "anger" is like...

If I gave the "anger" a name I would call it...

I would describe the "anger" as being like...

Avalanche	Volcano	Fire	Shark	Lion hunting
Boiling blood	Banging drum	Tidal wave	Monster	Dragon
Thunder & lightning	Adrenaline rush	Spiked ball	Red mist	What else?

Copyright © Karen Treisman – *A Therapeutic Treasure Box for Working with Children and Adolescents with Developmental Trauma – 2018*

About the "anger" (replace "anger" with your own choice of name)

» If the "anger" was a colour, it would be...

» If the "anger" was a shape, it would be...

» If the "anger" was an animal, it would be...

» If the "anger" was an object/item/metaphor, it would be...

» If the "anger" was a flower, a tree, or something from nature, it would be...

» If the "anger" could talk, it would say... (What would its voice sound like?)

» The "anger" stops me from...

» The "anger" helps me...

» Without the "anger", I would...

» If the "anger" disappeared, I would miss...

» ...makes the "anger" much bigger.

» ...makes the "anger" smaller.

» I am stronger and bigger than the "anger" when...

Expanding creatively on the metaphor

Once a metaphor/name/item/object has been chosen and discussed in detail, it can be helpfully embedded and expanded on by carrying out related expressive and creative activities.

For example, if a child says that their feeling of "anger" is like a shark, they might sculpt, mould, draw, paint, or make "the shark". Similarly, the child might be encouraged to act as if they are "the shark" or fleeing from "the shark"; they may be supported in using physical movement, puppets, masks, or a sand-tray exercise to explore this metaphor further.

The above questions can be used to bring the metaphor to life; for example, What is "the shark's" name? What does "the shark" sound like? If "the shark" could talk, what would it say? What makes "the shark" stronger? What scares "the shark"?

Additionally, the metaphor can be played with according to the need. For example, the ocean, other sharks, boats, dolphins, divers, fish, seaweed, and waves can be discussed as being symbolic.

Photo 4.30 Anger externalised as a "Spike the Snappy Shark"

Copyright © Karen Treisman – *A Therapeutic Treasure Box for Working with Children and Adolescents with Developmental Trauma* – 2018

Sadness is (using metaphors)...

Sadness and Low Mood

The feeling of "sadness/low mood" is like...

If I gave the "sadness/low mood" a name I would call it...

I would describe the "sadness/low mood" as being like...

Clipped wings	Flat battery	Deflated balloon	Empty glass	River of tears
Deserted island (alone)	Invisible	Heavy heart	Fog	Falling
Ball & chain	Trapped	Black hole	What else?	What else?

Copyright © Karen Treisman – *A Therapeutic Treasure Box for Working with Children and Adolescents with Developmental Trauma* – 2018

About the "sadness/low mood" (replace "sadness/low mood" with your own choice of name)

» If the "sadness/low mood" was a colour, it would be…

» If the "sadness/low mood" was a shape, it would be…

» If the "sadness/low mood" was an animal, it would be…

» If the "sadness/low mood" was a tree, flower, or something from nature, it would be…

» If the "sadness/low mood" was an object/item/metaphor, it would be…

» If the "sadness/low mood" could talk, it would say… (What would its voice sound like?)

» The "sadness/low mood" stops me from…

» The "sadness/low mood" helps me…

» Without the "sadness/low mood" I would…

» If the "sadness/low mood" disappeared I would miss…

» …makes the "sadness/low mood" much bigger.

» …makes the "sadness/low mood" smaller.

» I am stronger and bigger than the "sadness/low mood" when…

Expanding creatively on the metaphor

Once a metaphor/name/item/object has been chosen and discussed in detail, it can be helpfully embedded and expanded on by carrying out related expressive and creative activities.

For example, if a child says that their feeling of "sadness" is like a "dark cloud", they might sculpt, mould, draw, paint, or make "the dark cloud". Similarly, the child might be encouraged to act using physical movement, puppets, masks, or a sand-tray exercise to explore "the dark cloud" further.

The above questions can be used to bring the metaphor to life; for example: What is "the dark cloud's" name? What does "the dark cloud" sound like? If "the dark cloud" could talk, what would it say? What makes "the dark cloud" stronger? What overshadows or moves "the dark cloud"?

The metaphor can also be played with according to the need. For example, the rain, other clouds, wind, sun, storms, rainbows, and thunder can be discussed as being symbolic.

Copyright © Karen Treisman – *A Therapeutic Treasure Box for Working with Children and Adolescents with Developmental Trauma* – 2018

Happiness is (using metaphors)...

Happiness, Joy, and Excitement

The feeling of "happiness/joy/excitement" is like...

If I gave the "happiness/joy/excitement" a name I would call it...

I would describe the "happiness/joy/excitement" as being like...

Rainbow	Sunshine	Fireworks	Hugs	Warm glow
Cosy blanket	Rollercoaster	Flying high	Music	King of the world
Opening a present	Warm bath	Carnival	Scoring a goal	What else?

Copyright © Karen Treisman – *A Therapeutic Treasure Box for Working with Children and Adolescents with Developmental Trauma – 2018*

About the "happiness/joy/excitement" (replace "happiness/joy/excitement" with your own choice of name)

- » If the "happiness/joy/excitement" was a colour, it would be…
- » If the "happiness/joy/excitement" was a shape, it would be…
- » If the "happiness/joy/excitement" was an animal, it would be…
- » If the "happiness/joy/excitement" was a tree, flower, or something from nature, it would be…
- » If the "happiness/joy/excitement" was an object/item/person/metaphor, it would be…
- » If the "happiness/joy/excitement" could talk, it would say… (What would its voice sound like?)
- » The "happiness/joy/excitement" stops me from…
- » The "happiness/joy/excitement" helps me…
- » Without the "happiness/joy/excitement" I would…
- » If the "happiness/joy/excitement" disappeared I would miss…
- » …makes the "happiness/joy/excitement" much bigger.
- » …makes the "happiness/joy/excitement" smaller.

Expanding creatively on the metaphor

Once a metaphor/name/item/object has been chosen and discussed in detail, it can be helpfully embedded and expanded on by carrying out related expressive and creative activities.

For example, if a child says that their feeling of "happiness" is like "fireworks dancing and exploding", they might sculpt, mould, draw, paint, or make "the fireworks". Similarly, the child might be encouraged to act using physical movement, puppets, masks, or a sand-tray exercise to explore "the fireworks" further.

The above questions can be used to bring the metaphor to life; for example: What are "the fireworks" called? What do "the fireworks" sound like? If "the fireworks" could talk, what would they say? What makes "the fireworks" stronger? What overshadows or dampens "the fireworks"? Who lights "the fireworks"? Who else can see and appreciate "the fireworks"? What are the different colours in "the fireworks"? What would make "the fireworks" visit more and become brighter?

Photo 4.31 Externalising happiness as fireworks using magic scratch paper

Copyright © Karen Treisman – *A Therapeutic Treasure Box for Working with Children and Adolescents with Developmental Trauma* – 2018

Worry is (using metaphors)...

Worry and Fear

The feeling of "worry/fear" is like...

If I gave the "worry/fear" a name I would call it...

I would describe the "worry/fear" as being like...

Butterflies in stomach	Wobbly jelly	Tornado	Thoughts whirling like a washing machine	Bursting pipe (under pressure)
Being strangled	Ant on somebody's shoe	Racing heart	Runaway train	Lost in a maze
Trapped	Feeling tiny	Heavy load	Mr Stretchy (pulled in different directions)	What else?

Copyright © Karen Treisman – *A Therapeutic Treasure Box for Working with Children and Adolescents with Developmental Trauma – 2018*

About the "worry/fear" (replace "worry/fear" with your own choice of name)

- » If the "worry/fear" was a colour, it would be…
- » If the "worry/fear" was a shape, it would be…
- » If the "worry/fear" was an animal, it would be…
- » If the "worry/fear" was a flower, a tree, or something from nature, it would be…
- » If the "worry/fear" was an object/item/metaphor, it would be…
- » If the "worry/fear" could talk, it would say… (What would its voice sound like?)
- » The "worry/fear" stops me from…
- » The "worry/fear" helps me…
- » Without the "worry/fear" I would…
- » If the "worry/fear" disappeared I would miss…
- » …makes the "worry/fear" much bigger.
- » …makes the "worry/fear" smaller.
- » I am stronger and bigger than the "worry/fear" when…

Expanding creatively on the metaphor

Once a metaphor/name/item/object has been chosen and discussed in detail, it can be helpfully embedded and expanded on by carrying out related expressive and creative activities.

For example, if a child says that their feeling of "worry/fear" is like "butterflies in their tummy", they might sculpt, mould, draw, collage, paint, or make "butterflies in their tummy". Similarly, the child might be encouraged to act using physical movement, puppets, masks, or a sand-tray exercise to explore "the butterflies in their tummy" further.

The above questions can be used to bring the metaphor to life; for example: What are the different butterflies' names? What do "the butterflies" sound like? If "the butterflies" could talk, what would they say? What makes "the butterflies" stronger and flitter more? What would make "the butterflies" fly away? When do "the butterflies" sleep and rest?

Additionally, the metaphor can be played with according to the need. For example, caterpillars, flying, wings, butterfly hugs, and butterfly kisses can be symbolically discussed as being symbolic.

Photo 4.32 Butterflies in my tummy artwork

Copyright © Karen Treisman – *A Therapeutic Treasure Box for Working with Children and Adolescents with Developmental Trauma* – 2018

Draw or use Play-Doh to show the different emotions on the blank faces

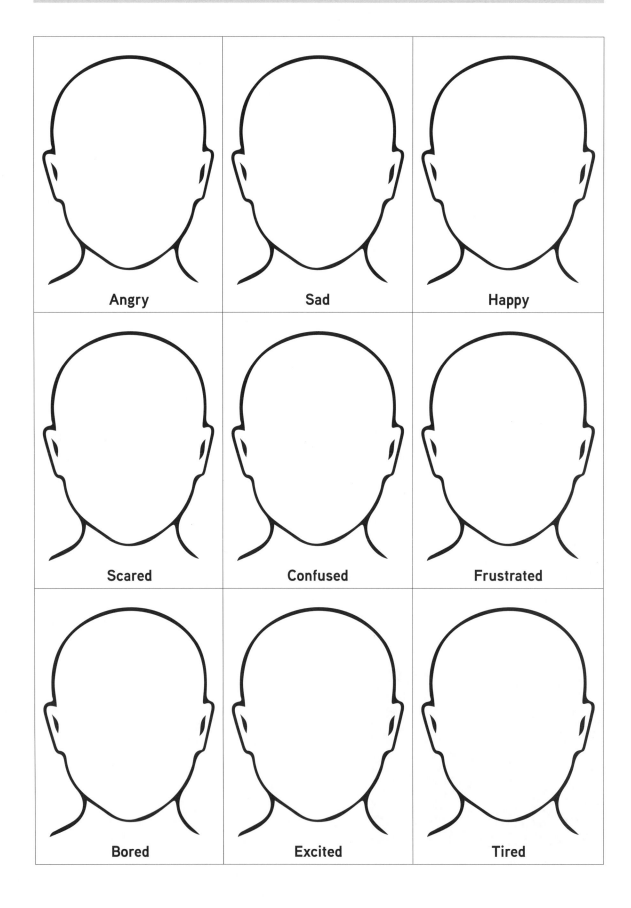

Angry

Sad

Happy

Scared

Confused

Frustrated

Bored

Excited

Tired

Copyright © Karen Treisman – *A Therapeutic Treasure Box for Working with Children and Adolescents with Developmental Trauma* – 2018

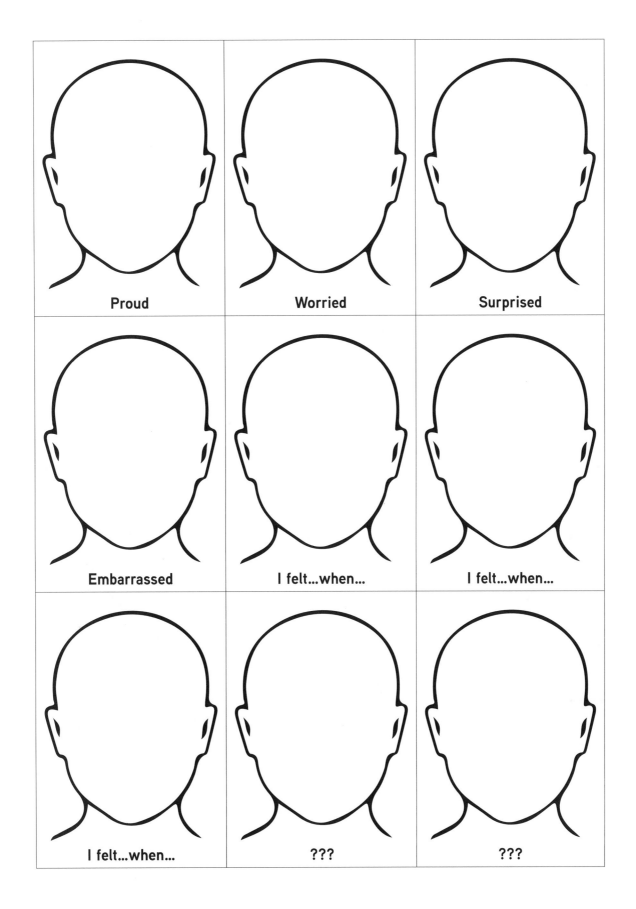

Proud

Worried

Surprised

Embarrassed

I felt...when...

I felt...when...

I felt...when...

???

???

Copyright © Karen Treisman – *A Therapeutic Treasure Box for Working with Children and Adolescents with Developmental Trauma* – 2018

Feelings wheel

(Some may prefer to call it a feelings pie, pizza, or cake.)

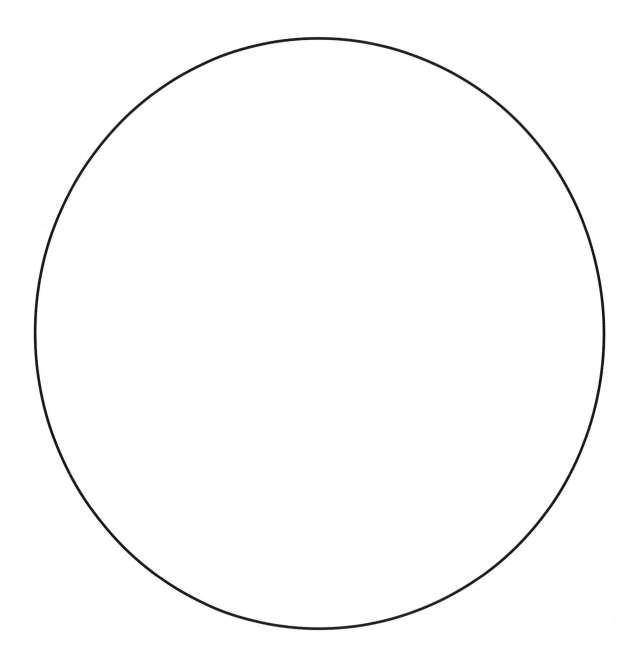

Copyright © Karen Treisman – *A Therapeutic Treasure Box for Working with Children and Adolescents with Developmental Trauma – 2018*

Head of thoughts and feelings

Draw or write in or around the head.

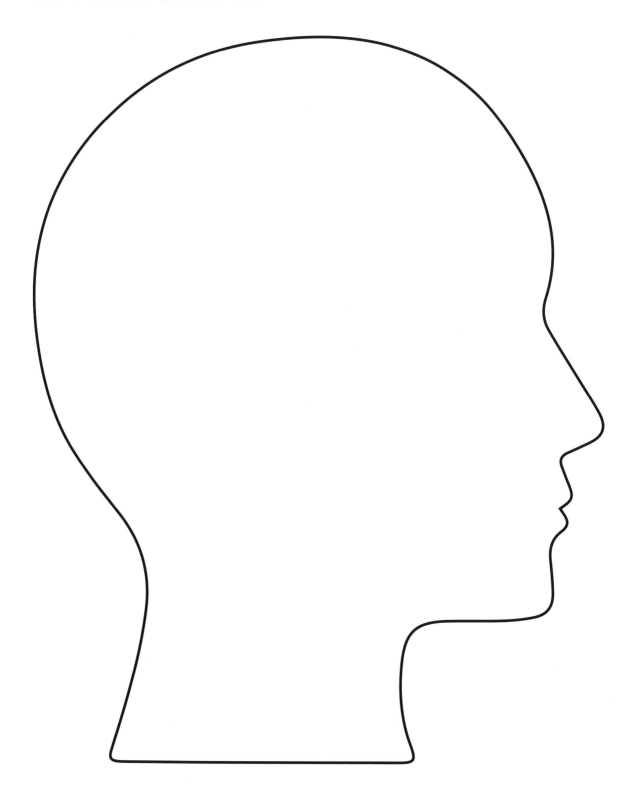

Copyright © Karen Treisman – *A Therapeutic Treasure Box for Working with Children and Adolescents with Developmental Trauma – 2018*

Worksheet 4.16
House of feelings

Draw or make a house.

If you were to look through the windows or open the doors to the different rooms, what would you see in the happy room, sad room, angry room, scary room, fun room, etc.?

Copyright © Karen Treisman – *A Therapeutic Treasure Box for Working with Children and Adolescents with Developmental Trauma* – 2018

Feelings TV and feelings channels

If I turned the TV on to the... (angry, sad, happy, scared, fun, etc.) channel, what would I see?

Copyright © Karen Treisman – *A Therapeutic Treasure Box for Working with Children and Adolescents with Developmental Trauma* – 2018

Worksheet 4.18

Colour, draw, or design where and how you feel the different core emotions in your body

If these emotions were a colour, a shape, or a thing, what would they be? If they had a voice, what would they say? Can you think about a specific time or story when you felt these emotions?

Sadness	Fear	Anger	Shame	Joy/ excitement	Curiosity	?	?

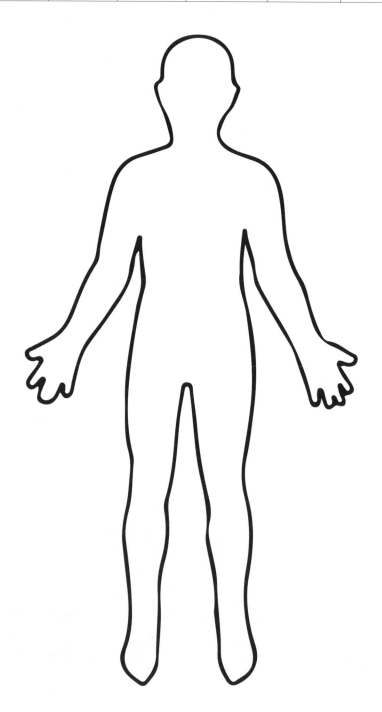

Copyright © Karen Treisman – *A Therapeutic Treasure Box for Working with Children and Adolescents with Developmental Trauma – 2018*

Worksheet 4.19
Feelings thermometer

Choose a different word or statement to represent the feelings for each colour. For example, green could be calm and cool as a cucumber and black could be raging like an exploding volcano. Then colour them in and choose which colour you would place yourself in at different times.

Black
Red
Orange
Yellow
Blue
Green

Copyright © Karen Treisman – *A Therapeutic Treasure Box for Working with Children and Adolescents with Developmental Trauma* – 2018

Worksheet 4.20
Thoughts, feelings, physical sensations, and behaviours

 What is a thought?

 What is a feeling?

 What is a physical sensation?

 **What is a behaviour?**

 **How are thoughts, feelings, physical sensations, and behaviours different and separate to each other? How are thoughts, feelings, physical sensations, and behaviours connected to each other?**

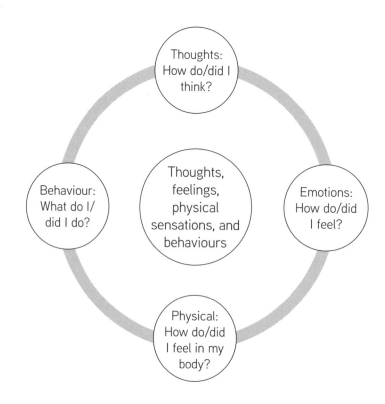

Copyright © Karen Treisman – *A Therapeutic Treasure Box for Working with Children and Adolescents with Developmental Trauma* – 2018

Head, heart, and hands

Draw, collage, act, or write your responses.

Head (What was I/am I thinking?)	Heart (How did I/do I feel emotionally and physically?)	Hands (What was I/am I doing?)

Copyright © Karen Treisman – *A Therapeutic Treasure Box for Working with Children and Adolescents with Developmental Trauma – 2018*

Worksheet 4.22

Thoughts, feelings, actions, and sensations diary

What was going on around me at the time?	How was I feeling emotionally and in my body?	What was I thinking?	What did I do?	What happened?	If I could go back in time, what would I do differently?

Copyright © Karen Treisman – A Therapeutic Treasure Box for Working with Children and Adolescents with Developmental Trauma – 2018

CHAPTER 5

Strength, Resilience, and Hope-Based Practices

Finding Ways to Identify, Notice, Celebrate, and Build on Children's Strengths, Skills, Resilience, and Positive Qualities

Why is focusing on building children's self-esteem so important?

Children who have experienced relational and developmental trauma are more likely to have been exposed to harsh and repeated forms of verbal abuse, including criticism, humiliation, and negative attributions, often from the people who were supposed to be their biggest supporters and cheerleaders in life; for example: "You're a waste of space", "You ruined my life", "I wish you hadn't been born", "No wonder no one likes you, you're ugly", "You're so stupid", and "You'll never amount to anything".

In the context of chronic and cumulative trauma, children may also have been rejected, neglected, and/or had their emotions, presence, and needs minimised or ignored (see Chapter 4). In many cases, these children's opportunities to experience being and/or feeling appreciated and cherished will have been limited and/or conditional. Therefore, it is likely that children raised in relational poverty will not have had the same opportunities to develop positive internal cheerleaders or a chain of built-in memories of people who were there for them – unconditionally and consistently rooting for them, believing in them, and supporting them. Thus, in the context of relational and developmental trauma, children's internal treasure boxes are likely to have been left much emptier, less richly decorated, and less well looked after (see Photos 5.1 and 5.2).

Photos 5.1 and 5.2 Richly filled and emptier treasure boxes

A range of case examples that capture some of the experiences that are likely to influence children's self-esteem and self-worth are given below.

Four-year-old Bailey splattered some soup on the floor. His father responded by pushing him and shouting, "What the hell is wrong with you? Why are you so incompetent and pathetic? Everything you do ends in a mess. You make my life hell. I wish you had never been born."

Nine-year-old Suzy excitedly ran home to show her mother the certificate she was awarded in school that day. Her mother glanced over, sighed, and said, "Everyone gets those", and then turned her head back to the TV programme she was watching.

Seventeen-year-old Fatima had learned that love and acceptance were conditional, could easily be lost, and were used as a play of power. When she agreed and "obeyed" her parents, they praised and embraced her. However, when she asserted her own independence, or shared her own opinions that differed from her parents' religious and cultural beliefs, she was "outcast and shamed". She described this by saying, "If I'm what they want me to be then I'm OK but still constantly having to prove myself, but if I'm me, I'm nothing, and a disgrace, it's a lose–lose situation."

Seven-month-old Hugo signalled to his mother to play with him and to join him in his excitement and exploration of a shiny object (smiling, babbling, opening his eyes widely, and pointing). His mother looked blankly at him with little affect and no verbal acknowledgement. Instead, she placed Hugo down beside her and told him to "Shhh, calm down, it's just a balloon", and moved it away.

Bianca was asked to describe her 18-month-old daughter Poppy's personality in three words. She shrugged and said, "I don't know – she's the same as all babies, she's a baby." She was then asked what parts of parenting Poppy she enjoyed, and she responded, "I can't think of any, when she's asleep I guess."

Two-year-old Romeo excitedly entered the room for his weekly contact with his birth mother. She made minimal eye contact, did not acknowledge his entrance, and went into a long story about her journey to the contact centre and the stressful day that she had had. Eventually she leaned over and gave Romeo a hug and for the rest of the session talked and texted on her mobile phone, with minimal interaction with Romeo. When it was time to leave, she casually and quietly with little affect uttered, "Bye, see you later."

These examples shed some light on why it is commonly reported that such children go on to develop a negative sense of self, negative internal working models, poor self-esteem, poor self-efficacy, and low self-worth. Imagine these types of scenarios and moment-to-moment interactions happening over and over again to developing and impressionable children, who are dependent on and shaped by the adults surrounding them. These children often present with negative self-perceptions, core beliefs (such as "Me", "You," and "The world" maps), labels, problem-saturated stories, and negative discourses, such as, "I'm bad and dirty", "I am unlovable", "I am worthless", "I am disposable", "I am a mistake", and "I am invisible". Worksheet 5.1 builds on these core beliefs and life scripts with some common, but by no means exhaustive, examples of core beliefs in the context of relational and developmental trauma.

In line with the above, children's interpretative lens and trauma-tinted glasses (see Photo 5.3) can become internalised and can contribute to young people self-stigmatising, self-blaming, and/or feeling stuck in a learned helplessness position (e.g. "I don't deserve good things", "I know he hurts me, but I'm lucky he loves me", "I should have been better", "I wasn't good enough", "I have nothing to add", "What is the point in even trying?", "Everything I touch turns into dirt", and "I make things worse").

This can also lead to self-defeating attitudes and the "difficulty" becoming the child's way of defining themselves and becoming their master identity: "I've always been depressed", "I am a liar", "I am a waste of space", "Everyone I know ends up dead or in prison, so why would I be any different?", "I'm damaged", "I'm broken", "I always screw up", and "I am a horrible person". These can be further exacerbated and reinforced by negative dominant discourses in popular media, communities, and wider society. These wider influences will be discussed later in this chapter and in Box 5.1.

These belief systems and guiding maps are likely to make children more vulnerable to cognitive errors, such as all-or-nothing thinking ("I'm stupid, so there is no point in even trying"), mental filtering (where they only pay attention to certain evidence, in this case to negative information, e.g. "Who cares if I got a C? The teacher went on and on about my grammar, I can't do it" or "My presentation was rubbish, did you see Jacob rolling his eyes and laughing?"), mind-reading ("I know no one will like me", "I am going to fail the test anyway", or "She thinks I am stupid"), and self-labelling ("I'm a loser", "I am weak", or "I am nothing"). Having this negative lens and negative attentional bias means that children are more likely to have diminished self-appreciation, disqualify the positive incoming information, and hold on to the negative information as if it were true, like a highly charged negative magnet. Negative comments stick like superglue and can be pulled to strengthen the negative magnet (see Photo 5.4 and Worksheet 5.2).

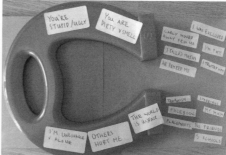

Photo 5.3 Looking through the world with a unique lens   **Photo 5.4** Negative thoughts magnet

This is further supported by research on attribution and locus of control theories, which have suggested that individuals classified as having high self-esteem are more likely to make global internal attributions for positive events (e.g. passing a maths test and attributing it to internal factors such as their intelligence or their hard work), leading to the reinforcement of their positive self-image ("I am quite smart", "I'm actually quite good at maths", and "My hard work has paid off").

However, individuals classified as having low self-esteem are more likely to associate negative events to internal attributions ("It's my fault, I should have done more, I'm so stupid") and positive events to external factors and luck (e.g. attributing the success of a maths test to an easy paper or to pure luck). This gives further weight to the importance of understanding and widening children's conceptualisations and attributions around both positive and negative situations when addressing self-esteem.

This is significant, as the power of positive self-esteem and positive self-belief should not be underestimated. Positive self-esteem is highly correlated with resilience and other wellbeing factors, such as positive social behaviour, quality of life, happiness, confidence, and more effective coping strategies (Mann *et al.*, 2004). In many ways, positive self-esteem and self-worth serve a motivational function and can significantly impact children's and adolescents' lives and daily choices, decisions, hopes, and visions. It can influence every sphere of interactions, including how a child sees themselves and how they approach different life scenarios. For example, self-esteem and self-worth can influence how capable, worthy, and/or deserving of good things, including love, the child feels. *Imagine the difference between a child with high levels of self-esteem and self-belief engaging in a school play, asking another child to be their friend, doing their first job application, or making intimate relational choices compared with a child who feels negative about themselves, others, and themselves within relationships. Moreover, consider the difference between a child who has been enveloped in love and encouragement and has several internalised nurturers and cheerleaders being told that they are "ugly" by a child at school and that they can't join in with the game compared with a child who for their whole life has been told that they are ugly and that no one will like them.*

Negative self-beliefs reinforced by the wider systems (the power of language)

As previously discussed, the negative discourses, negative labels, and problem-saturated narratives that children have developed are, unfortunately, often further embedded and reinforced by the wider systems, services, and contexts around them. For example, this happens through expressed and held statements, beliefs, and values, such as "He is damaged like his father", "She has bad blood, there is only one way this is going", "He is always rude and will never change", "He doesn't want to learn", "She purposely pushes my buttons", "She's a thief", "She doesn't have any empathy, she's cold", "He's defiant and a trouble-maker", and "He's just attention-seeking".

These children are often reduced to and defined by some of their presenting behaviours instead of there being an acknowledgement and understanding of the experiences that have shaped them or of the child who lies hidden behind the behaviours (e.g. "What's wrong with you?" as opposed to "What happened to you?" or "What are you trying to tell us?"). Thus, people often fall into the trap (it is easy to do) of labelling, stereotyping, or "placing a child into a box", particularly when faced with distressing behaviours over a long period of time and/or if their own self-care is being restricted and/or emotional hotspots are being triggered.

The negative labels that are assigned to these children are often married with definitive terms such as "always" and "never" (e.g. "He's always nasty" or "She is never kind"). It is important to hold in mind that language shapes reality, judgement, conceptualities, and subsequent responses; and so need to be used with care and intention. Labels and boxes can be so powerful and can stick throughout a child's journey. They can feel like they are inked tattoos or scars etched onto one's body. Box 5.1 explores the power of labels and bias further.

These labels, stereotypes, and negative discourses can be hazardous for several reasons. They can:

- lead to self-fulfilling prophecies (e.g. if a teacher has poor expectations of a student and communicates this implicitly or explicitly to the student, the student may not perform as well in school as they otherwise would)

- contribute and reinforce children's already formed sense of hopelessness, negative self-esteem, and internal working models

- affect people's responses to, expectations of, and management styles of them, which can create a vicious cycle

- place blame on the child as opposed to thinking about the wider context and other influencing variables

- define a child purely by their behaviour and/or coping strategies, rather than seeing the whole child, the hidden child, and all of their different parts

- impede hope and block ideas and thinking on different ways to move forward.

> ## Box 5.1 **Reflective exercise and practical activity the power of labels**
>
> What emotions, labels, images, and attributions do you think of and feel in association with the words "looked after child", "foster care", "gangs", "antisocial behaviour", "young offenders", and "adopted child"? (Make a drawing, list, or collage to reflect these associations, labels, and images.)
>
> Imagine how it would feel to be labelled as, for example, "damaged", or for your child or family member to be positioned as "a lost cause" or "bad blood". How would it feel to be defined by purely your behaviour or by your "worst" quality?
>
> Are there labels that you were given as a child and that have stuck? Did you agree with these labels? How do you feel if you are reminded of these labels now? What labels, if any, would you prefer to have? How do you/would you like to be described?
>
> Descriptions are powerful and colour responses. For example, would you describe someone by saying "She's cancer" or "He's HIV"? If not, why would you say "He's ADHD"? Is a child who has been deprived of affection, support, and relational riches "attention-seeking" or are they, thankfully, "attention-needing" and "attachment-seeking"?
>
> What do you think are some of the underlying reasons for why a child may be part of a gang, engage in antisocial behaviour, or end up in an offending unit? Do these reasons/understandings/perspectives differ if considering this question for a child, adolescent, or adult?
>
> What feelings and thoughts might you have when hearing about a four-year-old boy who has been physically abused and neglected? What happens to these thoughts/feelings when you hear about that same boy aged 17, who has just been arrested for a school stabbing?
>
> What discourses and perceptions might there be around a girl who is dressed in revealing clothing? How might receiving different information about this girl adjust those perceptions, worries, and conceptualisations (e.g. she was abused, she was eight years old, she has had sex with 30 men, she was 19 years old, she was raped, she was a politician's daughter, she was an A* student, and so on)?

Strengths-based language and storying

With the above in mind, it feels essential that we consciously and deliberately consider our choice of words and the way in which we speak and story young people. This feels like an overarching way of being that should underpin all of our interactions with young people/parents/colleagues and inform the rest of the strengths-based strategies described in this chapter. Some of the ways in which we can re-story include the following.

- Using the Narrative Therapy technique of identifying the unique exceptions (e.g. times when the children/parent have overcome a particular problem or when the problem was absent, less noticeable, or less stressful). This supports young people to be able to begin to notice and connect with the less told parts of their identities, rather than focusing on just the behaviour or on the trickier parts. For example, if in a session a parent describes the difficult experiences that she has during the mealtimes, after hearing, listening to, and empathising with the difficulty and getting a strong sense of what the problem is, one might explore and thicken the unique exception by asking questions such as: *What would mealtimes look like if they didn't end in screaming and shouting? What is your ideal mealtime and why are good mealtimes important to you? Can you tell me about a time when a mealtime was calm/fun/ran smoothly? How did you manage to not let a mealtime turn to "chaos" on that day? Where and with whom is the "chaos" at least likely to appear? What did that calm mealtime feel like/look like/achieve/lead to? What would the ideal mealtime be like/feel/look like? What difference would that make to your life, to you as a person, and to your relationship with your child?*

- Using the Narrative Therapy technique of externalisation. This advocates for not seeing the problem as intrinsic to the person and therefore supporting the young person/parent/family to externalise the problem and see that they are not the problem: the problem is the problem (White, 2007). It feels as if this is important, so the young person doesn't feel that it is their personality that is fundamentally flawed or wrong or that they as a person are being criticised. This is the difference between saying "You're such a naughty boy" (positioning the difficulty within the whole child) compared with "It is not OK to hit your sister; hands are not for hitting" (positioning the difficulty within the behaviour, not the child). One way of working towards externalisation is by supporting the child/family to label or personify the problem as a character/being/creature/object, which aims to allow the problem to be seen as a separate entity. Examples of externalisation techniques will be interspersed throughout this chapter and throughout the entire book.

- Finding ways to positively reframe and re-story the behaviour, which positions it in a more positive and less pejorative way. For example, instead of labelling a child as being "hyperactive", one might say she is "energetic" or "spirited", or instead of storying a child as "attention-seeking", one might say he is "attention-needing" or "attachment-seeking". (See Worksheet 5.3 for several other examples of positive reframing and alternative phrasing suggestions.)

- Finding ways to communicate to the child what you want them to do and what behaviours you want to see, rather than what you want them to stop doing. For example, instead of "Don't run", you might say "Walk by my side", or instead of "Stop shouting", you might say "Speak quietly" or "Please use your indoor voice". (See Worksheet 5.3 for other examples of alternative phrasing, and for space to try your own statements.)

- Reclaiming the balance and shifting the focus onto the child's positive strengths, skills, qualities, and resiliencies. The more we look for the positives, and take stock of what the child can do, the more we will appreciate, notice them, and find an "in" that hooks onto the child's uniqueness. We often find that the more we look for positives, the more we find them, like on an archaeological dig. This also fits with the premise that the more we pay attention to the positives, the more they grow, a bit like nurturing and nourishing a plant. *For instance, how often do we comment when the toilet is not flushed or the toothpaste lid is left off but not acknowledge when the toilet is flushed or the toothpaste lid is put back on? Or how differently do we respond to someone who annoys us or who we dislike compared with someone we like and enjoy if they do exactly the same thing? Or how differently do you respond to the same thing, such as getting a flat tyre or losing your credit card, when you are having a bad day and are in a bad head space compared with when you are in a calm, positive place?*

The above strengths-based philosophies and techniques will be expanded on throughout this chapter and are peppered throughout this book. However, before going on to present a variety of creative and expressive strategies for building, celebrating, and noticing strengths and positive qualities, it feels important to consider our own relationship to praise, encouragement, and self-esteem, as this can have a significant impact on the appropriateness, effectiveness, and delivery of these strategies.

In addition, a common apprehension around strengths-based practice expressed by caregivers/professionals is shown by statements such as "My child can't accept praise", "My child can't think of any positives" or "Things are so difficult at the moment that I am finding it hard to like my child". This will be explored and some ideas will be offered, whilst acknowledging the individual differences of each child/parent/family, before proceeding to the sections on creative and practical strategies for building strengths, resilience, and self-esteem.

Our own relationship with praise, encouragement, and positive feedback

The task of giving or receiving praise and encouragement is further complicated by all of us having our own history, values, experiences, relationship with praise, encouragement, positive feedback, and self-esteem. It feels important to reflect on and consider the influence of these before implementing the following strategies in a genuine and natural way or finding a way that fits and feels as comfortable as possible. Keep in mind that it can be difficult to model giving and accepting praise and encouragement if this was not something that one received/receives themselves. Box 5.2 offers some questions to explore this further.

Box 5.2 **Self-reflection on your own experience of praise and positive feedback**

Was praise, encouragement, affection, or positive feedback shown to you as a child? If so, how was it given and communicated? When was it given and how often, and what was it given for? (Try to think of specific examples.)

What were the messages, sayings, stories, values, and actions about praise, self-esteem, self-worth, and positive feedback in your home environment?

Did you know when your "caregivers" were pleased/impressed/proud of you? If so, how? Can you think of examples of when you were praised or when you knew you had done something that was positively received?

How do these experiences link to your current relationship with praise, positive self-esteem, and self-worth feedback?

How do you feel physically and emotionally when someone praises you or gives you positive feedback? What factors and variables influence your feelings and responses to praise and positive feedback? (Try to think of specific examples.)

How have these been shaped and influenced throughout your life? How easy or difficult is it now to show, give, and/or receive praise and positive feedback? What factors make giving and receiving praise easier or more difficult?

Finding it difficult and/or uncomfortable to hear and receive praise and positive feedback

In addition to vast cultural, familial, and generational differences around praise and encouragement that could constitute a book in themselves, it feels important to acknowledge that some children and adults can find it harder than others to hear, and even more to believe, positive comments, encouragement, or praise (see Box 5.2). Within a relational and developmental trauma context, praise and positive feedback can feel alien, fake, conditional, or loaded. This is particularly the case for many children who have been soaked and drowned in discourses that have been filled with criticism, humiliation, and negativity, who have rarely had the experience of being praised, encouraged, or celebrated.

For instance, before Leelah's maths test (a subject she had said that she was struggling with, but despite this she was persisting and working hard at it), I had texted her to say good luck and that I was thinking of her. After the test, I texted again to check in and see how she had found it, and then in the session we debriefed and discussed the experience of the test. A few months later, Leelah shared that this exchange had been shocking to her, as she felt that it had been the first memorable time that someone in her life had remembered and acknowledged something like that or, in her words, "cared enough to bother to check in".

Moreover, in some cases, children will have learned that praise and gratefulness can be associated with abuse and power.

For example, each time Kara was made to perform sexual acts on her uncle, she was "rewarded" with verbal praise, less punitive responses, and desired items, such as clothes.

Leighton's only experience of praise from his father was when social services would visit. When they left, if he had behaved in a way his father had coached him to, then he would receive positive feedback.

Therefore, praise, encouragement, and positive feedback can evoke questions, worries, and thoughts such as "Why is he being nice to me – what does he want in return", "If I let myself believe it, I will only have it taken away, taken advantage of, or ruined?", "They are just saying that because they feel sorry for me", "I've been told good things a million times before and it has never helped or made a difference", "They don't really know me; if they did truly know me then they wouldn't think that", or "My last foster carer told me nice things every day and then it all fell apart, so it's bulls*it".

Every child/parent is unique and responds differently to different strategies and, unfortunately, there are no magic bullets for getting around this difficult relationship with praise and positive feedback, so this often requires large amounts of patience, time, understanding, and creativity. However, some of the things that I have found helpful in gradually addressing this are presented below.

- Telling the young person what you would like to say if you could but that you know you can't because they would not like it. For example: "Nelly, I know you don't like compliments, so I won't say anything, but I wish I could tell you how impressed I was today with your confidence during the class presentation", or "Ged, I am going to be quiet, as I know you told me you can't stand praise, but it is so frustrating because I wish I could tell you about…".

- Sharing some of the positives about the young person with someone else whilst they are within earshot.

- Using non-verbal, positive feedback, such as giving a thumbs-up, clapping, giving high-fives, winking, or smiling.

- Using praise and positive feedback very sparingly and slowly drip feeding it at key times. This is, in essence, reserving it for genuine occasions and communicating it in a toned-down way that the young person can manage.

- Writing thank you or appreciative post-it notes, sending text messages, or sending care parcels, "a compliment in the post", "a hug in a box", postcards, or letters instead of saying it out loud or having a face-to-face conversation. These non-face-to-face interactions can also be used when in the car, doing household chores, or playing a game.

- As the surrounding adults, modelling the ability to receive and hear praise and positive feedback.

- Making a positive treasure box or a sparkle moments diary that the child is aware of but they have the choice over if and when they would like to look at it.

- Making a treasure hunt where they have to look really hard and at each stage they discover a clue/treasure about something positive about them.

- Asking the child to support you in or teach you something that they feel confident doing.

- Asking the young person what ideas they have for how you could let them know when things are going well or when you have noticed something positive. It can also be helpful to reflect on a time they can think of when this happened with someone and what they liked about it and also to explore how they show their appreciation to a friend, teacher, etc.

Children who find it harder to identify positives about themselves

The following strategies might be helpful in facilitating the process of identifying positives. However, it should be emphasised that, with all of these tools, it is important to assess, formulate, and reflect on whether this is the appropriate time and approach for each particular child or whether there are other steps that need to be put in place before the strategies in this chapter can be worked on. The examples below should be complemented and enhanced by the other tools in this chapter.

- Some children may not have access to an emotional and strengths-based vocabulary, particularly if these are alien and/or unfamiliar terms for them. They might need to do some of the feelings work described in Chapter 4 before being able to translate these to themselves.

- Some children may find it easier to practise by labelling their friends', toys', or families' strengths, skills, and positive qualities before identifying their own. Others might find it more manageable to discuss positives from a distance, such as talking about them through a third-person narrative story or role-playing and/or talking about them through dolls, masks, miniatures, and puppets.

- Talking with children about how you see them through your positive eyes and lens can be helpful. This can be enhanced by putting on magic glasses or a magic mask (e.g. asking them what they would look like through a positive mask) (see Photo 5.5) or looking through a kaleidoscope or a special magnified glass.

Photo 5.5 Positive lens masks

- It can also be useful for the surrounding adults to be the child's memory bank and connector. For example: "Remember the time when you really helped Suzy with her homework – that was so kind, caring, and thoughtful", "Didn't Mrs Beech give you a sticker for great attendance last Wednesday?", and "Lisa comes round to visit you a lot and seems to really enjoy it – what do you think she enjoys? What do you think she would miss if she didn't come round?"

- Some children may find it more difficult to think of their own positive qualities. (This is a common difficulty for many people, let alone children who have experienced relational and developmental trauma.) Therefore, providing some form of scaffolding and prompting can be helpful, for example having a ready-made list of positive-qualities words that they can circle (see Worksheet 5.4) or the surrounding adults can use as a guide. These positive qualities can also be written/drawn/collaged by their team of supporters (e.g. teacher, parents, carers, friends, social care professionals, health professionals).

    In addition, using sentence-completion cards can be great in assisting this process, for example "My favourite thing about myself is…", "It's a great day when…", "I'm happiest when…", "The thing that always puts a smile on my face is…", "My dream for myself is…", "If I had to give myself an award it would be…", or "If I wasn't myself I would miss…" (see Worksheet 2.7).

    Questions that can aid these conversations are interspersed throughout this chapter; however, examples include: *If you became a different person tomorrow, or life changed as you know it, what would you miss, even if it is the tiniest thing? If you could go back and replay one happy special moment over and over again, what would it be? If you were to give yourself an award, what would it be for?* (See Worksheets 5.5 and 5.16 for ways to expand on these questions.)

- Providing psychoeducation around self-esteem and confidence can be important in supporting children to understand why these conversations may be beneficial and why they might find them tricky. I often talk about the cognitive thinking styles of mental filtering, self-labelling, mind-reading, or all-or-nothing thinking. I also use a range of metaphors, such as positive and negative powered-up magnets, quicksand, a negative-thoughts suction/sticking paper, and/or positive and negative scales. The use of metaphors and other examples will be presented throughout this chapter.

- It also can be helpful to think with the child about the influence of their perspective and perception. This can be embedded by cognitive therapy conversations around the thoughts, feelings, behaviours, and sensations cycle. These can be supportive in reflecting on how differently we can all see and interpret situations and some of the reasons why this might be the case.

For example, in a session after a difficult day at school, 13-year-old Jacob said, "Everyone hates me." He then went on to say, "I hate myself, so I don't blame them for hating me." Through using the thoughts, feelings, physical sensations, and behaviours cycle (see Worksheet 4.20 and some of the questions in Worksheets 8.6, 8.7, and 8.8] in Chapter 8), Jacob was able to identify that he was making a sweeping generalisation that "everyone" hated him and that he was discounting and minimising several parts of the positive evidence. He also could reflect on how thinking that no one liked him was having a ripple effect on how he was behaving towards his peers, such as either being rude to them or distancing himself, which in turn fed into the cycle of people staying away from him, which subsequently reinforced his negative beliefs that no one liked him and so forth.

Props such as optical illusions and kaleidoscopes can be used playfully to illustrate the power of taking multiple perspectives and seeing various angles of a situation. Other ways to demonstrate these concepts, in line with the notion that, like treasures, the more we look for something, the more we find it, are to hide treats/treasures in a sand tray for the young person to find, to play games such as find-it tubes (a portable game which is a combination of treasure hunt and hide-and-seek in a container) and hide-and-seek, or to design a treasure hunt for them to take part in.

The sense of hopelessness can be contagious and pervasive, particularly when things are feeling stuck, cyclical, and/or overwhelming. At these times, it feels important, although incredibly difficult and, that the Team Around the Child holds on and conveys confidence and hope for a better future for the child and recognises the complex processes and dynamics that are at play. We need to try and hold children at their very core in unconditional positive regard (Rogers, 1961); this fits nicely with the saying: "Treat a child as though he is already the person he's capable of becoming" (Ginott, 1972). This is where a take-back practice letter (see Worksheet 5.17) can be helpful, as are self-care, reflective practice, and supervision (see Chapter 7). It is helpful to ask, amongst others, the following questions.

What is the caregiver's/child's/therapist's relationship to change? How does the child look through my positive, hopeful, and confident lens? What part of themselves is the child not seeing? What do I admire, appreciate, and respect about them? What would I miss about them if they were not in my life? What skill would be invaluable and appreciated if we were stranded on a desert island?

Practical and creative strategies for building on children's self-esteem and positive sense of self

(Some of these strategies may be implemented directly in therapy sessions, whereas others may be tools that can be supported therapeutically but delivered by carers/teachers/other trusted adults.)

Modelling verbally and non-verbally positive self-esteem

The Team Around the Child/family should aim to model and to teach, verbally and non-verbally, self-esteem, pride, and self-confidence. This might include self-care practices, such as pampering, little self-treats, and looking after themselves, through to saying self-statements out loud, such as "I'm really proud of myself today because…". This also includes modelling positive body language, body positioning, and eye contact.

Naming, validating, and acknowledging a child's emotions and lived experiences

See Chapter 4 for more discussion on naming and acknowledging children's feelings. This feels like it is an essential part of communicating to a child that their feelings matter, are important, are acknowledged, and are heard. This is also an important step in communicating to the child that they are worthy and that they deserve to be loved, happy, and cared for.

Quality time together and really getting to know the young person

Use a variety of relational treasures and positive relational experiences on a regular basis to stack the positive side of the child's scale, and to power up their positive magnet with positive emotions, memories, and experiences. Try and spend time together doing enjoyable activities and communicate verbally and non-verbally how much you look forward to, value, and enjoy this time with them. This can symbolically, verbally, and/or creatively add to their positive treasure box or sparkle moments diary (see the following sections). See Chapter 6 for a variety of ways of optimising these tools.

Show the child that they are valued as an individual and really get to know them as a unique person. This can be extended through active means, such as using sentence-completion cards, designing a getting-to-know-each-other quiz/game (see Photo 5.6), making an "All About Me" or "My Life-Story" book, or doing some getting-to-know-each-other artwork such as "Katie's World" (on a picture of the globe) or "Peter's Puzzle" (next to a body-shaped puzzle). (See Chapter 2 for a range of "All About Me" ideas and examples.)

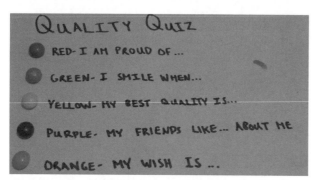

Photo 5.6 Positive-themed game using sweets

Confidence-boosting and curiosity-enhancing activities

It can also be helpful to find age-appropriate activities that a child enjoys and is good at. It is even better if these are confidence-boosting experiences from which they get a sense of achievement, such as drama, circus skills, finding their way through mazes, conquering an obstacle course, answering clues on a positive/strength-themed treasure hunt, mountain climbing, and/or zip-lining (individual-dependent and variable). Children who have had to invest more energy into their survival have often not had the same opportunities for fostering their sense of curiosity and adventure. Therefore, encouraging opportunities where the child can explore, be curious, and play should be harnessed.

Providing opportunities for mastery and agency

Find ways to show the child that they can effect change and that their opinion is important, listened to, and valued. Given that many children who have experienced trauma will have been in situations where they felt powerless and out of control, this is crucial. It is likely that their voice was often silenced or minimised, and they may have been left with a sense of things being done to them.

This sense of mastery and agency can be worked towards in a variety of ways from day-to-day things, like asking what they would like for dinner or getting them to teach you something that they know about, through to involvement in larger things, such as fundraising, social action, and/or youth-led projects. This can filter down to showing the child that you trust them by giving them some age-appropriate responsibility (which should be selected according to their social and emotional age rather than their chronological age).

Maximising opportunities for success

It is important to understand that these children require a stepped approach that appreciates that there are multiple footprints and routes on a long journey. This can be likened to having a young baby, where most parents expect the steps to be slow and difficult, and yet they are still able to marvel at each new milestone, whether it be a gargle, a turn, or a smile. It needs to be acknowledged and respected that these children have had to put up certain barriers and protective strategies for good reasons, such as their survival. Therefore a helpful starting point is an expectation and a level of acceptance that a child will need lots of support, preparation, repetition, and time to master each step.

It is unfair and reinforcing of negative discourses if we set children up to fail or put them in situations that they are not prepared or ready for; this is likely to have the opposite effect and to add to their negative self-esteem.

How fair is it for a child who is so dysregulated, living in survival mode, and full up with fear, who is regularly being excluded and sent out of class, and who barely manages to function for a half-hour lesson to be expected to go through a whole day of school without incidents? How realistic is it to expect a four-year-old child who is socially and emotionally much younger to manage unsupported and unsupervised time in the playground? How fair is it to expect a newly adopted child who has had multiple placements to bond with and trust their adoptive parents in a short time period? How easy is it to measure and achieve a broad, undefined goal, such as when a young person says their goal is to "be happy"?

Steps and goals ideally should be in line with the acronym SMART (Specific, Measurable, Achievable, Realistic, and Timely) (see Worksheet 5.6) in order to maximise the child's opportunities to succeed, have a sense of achievement, and eventually master the desired skill. We want children to have a far greater likelihood of experiences of things going well for them and we want them to move forward in a positive way. This doesn't mean having low expectations or wrapping children up in cotton wool, but rather finding a balance that allows them to explore and develop from a place of safety and to aim for realistic and manageable expectations that they can achieve, have a sense of success and accomplishment from, and then continue to move forward from.

To work towards these opportunities of success, we can also support children by anticipating potential obstacles and identifying skills that need to be prepared for and developed. An example is given below.

> If a child is finding it difficult to demonstrate the skill of sharing with others, strategies need to be put in place to support them in learning how to share before a goal of them managing to share effectively and regularly can be realistically set. This might be through: 1) practising sharing in fun and engaging ways; 2) role-playing sharing scenarios by using puppets, dolls, and masks; 3) having discussions around sharing (what sharing is, why sharing is important, pros and cons of sharing, consequences of not sharing, and the rewards of sharing); 4) praising and magnifying the times when the child did share; 5) having a comic strip/social story made about sharing; 6) reading stories and watching programmes where characters show skills, including sharing, that are subsequently pointed out and praised; 7) rewarding and incentivising sharing; 8) discussing why sharing is difficult and/or acknowledging and empathising with the feeling around wanting things for themselves and not having things taken away from them; 9) modelling sharing yourself; and 10) ensuring that they have some things that are special and just for them that they do not have to share.

The steps taken and distance travelled need to be punctuated, noticed, and celebrated. Some concrete ways of celebrating steps forward and positive qualities shown will be expanded on in the following suggested strategies.

Normalising and owning mistakes

It feels crucial, particularly in a context where children have often learned that mistakes have catastrophic consequences and for children who have high levels of shame and toxic stress, to acknowledge that mistakes do happen and that they are a normal and expected part of life and can be moved on from. This includes the surrounding adults owning, acknowledging, naming, and apologising for their mistakes if they make them. This is in line with rupture-repair principles. Mistakes can also helpfully be framed as learning opportunities.

Keeping the young person in mind and showing them this

Where possible, show the child that they are important and that you have actively kept them in mind (e.g. having daily check ins, remembering things that they said to you, noticing when they are absent, naming and labelling their feelings) (see Chapter 6 for a range of examples). This might extend into supporting them to feel like they belong through things like having an allocated seat at the table, making a name sign for their door, designing a family crest, labelling their items, and so on.

Non-verbal and verbal praise

Some children might respond better to non-verbal expressions of praise, such as giving a thumbs-up, clapping, giving a high-five, or positive facial expressions. For others, framing, magnifying, and saying the positives out loud can be beneficial.

Where possible, this praise should be specific so that the child knows what the praise is for and so that it feels more genuine and purposeful. For example, instead of "Good boy" or "Well done", the child might be told "Wow, thank you so much for tidying up your toys – that is so helpful and kind". Also, the praise and encouragement should acknowledge effort and trying, not focus purely on the outcome. For example, "Goodness, that was tough – I can see you worked really hard on it" or "Look how much you have done, you are getting better and better".

Tangible, creative, and expressive ways of noticing, celebrating, praising, and expanding on the child's positive skills, strengths, talents, qualities, and attributes

Please note that the strategies that follow can be enhanced by readily available (or making your own) strengths-identifying games and resources such as a self-esteem ball, self-esteem Jenga, self-esteem bingo, strengths board games, strengths cards, strengths magnets, and strengths dominoes. See www.safehandsthinkingminds.co.uk for a range of helpful resources.

Praise boards, strengths cards, and celebration walls

Make or design praise boards, positive work portfolios, strengths cards, certificates, and celebration walls that are regularly added to. I have seen some schools or homes having a "praise pod", a "strengths sign", a "positive poster", or a "celebration corner". It can be nice to link the skill to the reward, such as the child being a star in their school play by having a star named after them or a star-shaped cuddly toy given to them.

Maximising on everyday items and routines

It can be useful to integrate positive and happy memories and items into everyday routines, for example selecting an uplifting song for the child's alarm clock sound, eating from their special cereal bowl (which they made or a special adult made for them), having a diary that they have decorated or has positive photos in it, having a special chair or wearing a positive-themed badge.

Sparkle moments diary, treasure box, journey/ jewel jar, and bottled brilliance

Strengths can be further acknowledged, magnified, and celebrated by making a "positive me" or "sparkle moments" diary (see Photo 5.7), sticker book, or scrapbook that celebrates all of the child's progress, positive qualities, happy memories, and special moments. These can be decorated with gems, jewels, glitter, collage, and/or images and photos of positive-themed aspects of the child's life.

In addition, celebrating the multiple moments and taking a purposeful focus on positives can also be worked towards through filling up a treasure box (see Photos 5.1 and 5.8) with written/drawn reminders and memorabilia or a jar with precious stones, which represents the child's positive qualities, progress, and special memories. A template for "my treasure box diary" designed for older children and adolescents can be found in Worksheet 5.7.

Building on the above, it can also be fun to fill a jar/container up (and call it "my journey jar" or "my jewel jar") with post-it notes of positive things every day (or use stickers or drawings instead) (see Photo 5.9) and then to find a time to read and review the contents (e.g. once a month, on their birthday, or on New Year's Day).

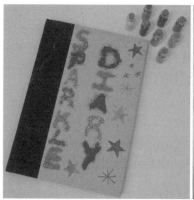  

Photo 5.7 A sparkle moments diary

Photo 5.8 A memory box

Photo 5.9 A memory jar

I also like the idea of bottling up special moments (and calling them bottle of brilliance). This could be done by actually filling bottles up and labelling them or drawing the bottles with the associated contents drawn in (see Worksheet 5.9 for a template).

One young person really enjoyed this concept and extended it herself by getting little jars and boxes, which she wrapped up like they were gifts. When she was having a bad day she could unwrap one and then would add a new one to the collection.

See Worksheet 5.8 for information on expanding on this gift concept.

Positive affirmations

Identify some positive self-mottos and affirmations with the child, for example "I am strong", "I am loved", "Every day I get better at...", "I am safe", "I deserve to be happy", "I did the best I could", and "I am someone and meant to be here". To expand on these positive affirmations, sometimes I ask a young person the following questions.

If you looked up in the sky and there was a feel-good message guaranteed to put a smile on your face written on the clouds, being led by an aeroplane, or carved in the rocks, what would it be? If you opened a fortune cookie, what message would you like to be inside it that would put a smile on your face? (See Worksheet 5.5.)

For younger children, these positive affirmations and positive self-talk mottos can be made into poems or catchy rhymes, for example "I am as strong as could be, like a lion and a tall rooted tree" or "I did the best I could, like any special princess would".

These positive self-mottos can be written down, drawn, sculpted, or collaged; they also can be added to other related items such as their treasure box or a patchwork of positives (described below). Some children might also like making a positive self-talk shield, cape, or teddy.

Tower of strengths, skyscraper of strengths, patchwork of positives, shield of strengths, blanket of bravery, pillow of positives, and quilt of qualities

It can be helpful to find ways to write down, draw, or visually represent the child's many strengths, positive qualities, and skills. There are lots of variations I find useful in supporting children to identify their strengths, such as:

- simply writing/drawing a list of all of their different strengths and positive skills

- sculpting or collaging all of their different strengths and skills

- making a poster, flag, or sign of all of their different strengths and skills

- writing a story, song, poem, or rap about their strengths and skills

- making a "patchwork of positives" (see Photo 5.10)

- making a "tower of strengths" or a "skyscraper of strengths" (using LEGO®, building blocks, or pillows) (see Photo 5.11)

- making or decorating a "quilt of qualities" or a "pillow of positives" (see Photo 5.12)

- designing a "shield of strengths"

- creating a "blanket of bravery" (using transferred photos or fabric pens).

Photo 5.10 Patchwork of positives

Photo 5.11 Tower of strengths (skyscraper of strengths)

Photo 5.12 Pillow of positives

Rainbow of resources, puzzle of positives, brilliant beautiful body, and star of strengths

Other extensions to identifying and representing children's strengths and positive qualities include:

- writing down/drawing/collaging all of the child's strengths on different colours of the rainbow (to make a rainbow of resources – you can use Worksheet 2.5 in Chapter 2)

- writing down/drawing/collaging all of the child's strengths on different pieces of a puzzle (to make a puzzle of positives) (see Photo 5.13)

- writing down/drawing/collaging all of the child's strengths on different parts of the body (to make a brilliant beautiful body) (see Worksheet 5.10 and Photo 5.14)

- writing down/drawing/collaging all of the child's strengths on different corners of a star (to make a star of strengths) (see Worksheet 5.12 and Photo 5.15).

Photo 5.13 Puzzle of positives

Photo 5.14 A body-map of strengths and positive qualities

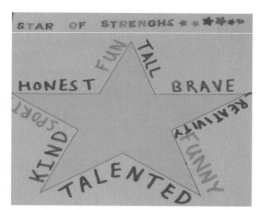

Photo 5.15 Star of strengths

Strengths doodle bear, blanket, T-shirt, pillow, and scarf

Support the child to decorate a T-shirt, a doodle bear (see Photos 5.16 and 5.17), a pillow, a blanket, or a scarf using fabric pens, transferred photos, or badges.

They can list or draw all of the positive things that they feel about themselves and that they have in their life. You can also contribute all the positive things their Team Around the Child has expressed about them. This can also have positive self-talk statements, affirmations, and inspirational quotes added, as well as any special mementos and items.

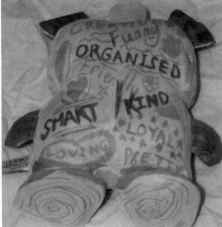

Photos 5.16 and 5.17 Front and back of a positive doodle bear

Chocolate box of positive qualities, positive pearls, and strength shells/stars

Caregivers/surrounding adults/children can be supported to label and decorate items, such as shells, stars (see Photo 5.18), stones, chocolates (see Photo 5.19), or hearts, with all of the things that they like/love/appreciate/respect about the young person. I find using a clam puppet is helpful for talking about identifying children's pearls (see Photo 5.20).

Photo 5.18 Stars of strength   **Photo 5.19** A chocolate box of positive qualities   **Photo 5.20** A clam and pearl puppet

Positive name acronym, positive self-portrait, picture of positives, and strengths snowflake

Other ways of expressing these strengths include: 1) making a positive quality list using a name acronym (see Photo 5.21) – for example, for Kate: Kind, Affectionate, Trustworthy, Enthusiastic; 2) the child drawing a positive self-portrait, for example themselves as a superhero; or 3) sticking a photograph of themselves on a piece of paper and writing or drawing all the positive qualities and adjectives around the picture (see Photo 5.22).

It can also be fun to reflect with a child on their uniqueness. I often use either snowflakes (see Photo 5.23), shells, or fingerprints as examples, as each of these are unique and different in their own way. Children can then be supported to make their own snowflakes, shells, and/or fingerprints and write, draw, or collage around them all of the things that make them the person they are.

Photo 5.21 Positive name acronym

Photo 5.22 Positive portrait

Photo 5.23 Snowflake of strengths

Strengths-based jewellery

It can be fun to make or decorate "strengths"-inspired jewellery (see Photos 5.24 and 5.25). For example, the child can decorate plain/wood jewellery by adding a collage of positive and strengths-based words or they can make a necklace/bracelet/anklet with each coloured or shaped bead representing a strength/skill/positive quality/supportive person. Others might like making a charm bracelet, with each charm representing a particular strength, special memory, adversity survived, etc.

Photo 5.24 Strengths-focused jewellery with each colour representing a different strength

Photo 5.25 Strengths-focused jewellery with fabric pens

Self-esteem and sensory hand

A useful tool to bring some of the above together is to make a self-esteem and sensory hand (this is an extension of Worksheet 3.5 in Chapter 3). The child draws around their own hands or the supporting adult draws around their hands (if the child prefers to not be touched then you can use cut-out hands or foam hands). The categories (one for each finger/thumb) can be individualised and tailored, but might include the following:

- Something I am proud of.

- Something I like about myself.

- Something other people like about me.

- Something that makes me uniquely me.

- Something I bring to other people (See Photo 5.26.)

The other hand might use the same categories to encourage more than one response or be a sensory hand to support the child in reflecting on things that make them feel happy and calm (this can be helpful for identifying tailor-made grounding and regulating ideas) – for example: something I like to touch; something I like to see; something I like to hear; something I like to taste; something I like to smell.

The child's responses can be pictorially and visually represented (see Photo 5.27). For example, if a child says they like to touch dogs, there can be a picture of dogs and a piece of material that resembles how touching a dog feels.

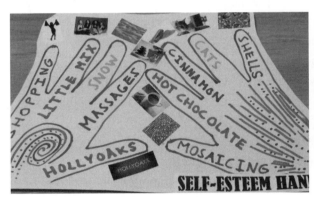

Photo 5.26 Self-esteem hand

Photo 5.27 Bringing responses to life

Expanding and embedding each identified positive trait

With all of the described creative tools, each of the identified traits (i.e. being brave, being funny, showing courage, and being talented at singing) should then be magnified and thickened through additional questioning and creative means. This is an important way of embedding, expanding, and enriching the concepts (see Chapter 1 for more on this). The experience of making and expanding on these creations can itself add to a positive relational experience. Some examples of expanding and enriching the identified traits are given below.

Alice regularly showed the skill of being brave, which she likened to the qualities shown by a lion. So, in therapy sessions, Alice made a list and drawing of all of the times she had been brave, strong, and courageous; she was also asked several questions about how these positive qualities developed and who she had known in her life who had shown these qualities or taught her them. Alice was also encouraged to tell some stories about these specific times and to write them down and place them in a special memory treasure box. Alice was supported to make and draw her very own lion shield of strength, which was filled with symbolic pictures, patterns, and photos of her showing strength and bravery. Subsequently, stories were shared about lions and bravery and a diary recording all of her "lion moments" was kept. Alice also made a lion and bravery collage decorated with inspiring images and quotes. In addition, she was supported to make a portable miniature version of this collage in the form of a lion key ring so that she could take it with her to school and other places. This metaphor also became part of the vocabulary of the house, so each time Alice showed bravery and courage, she was reminded by her surrounding adults; for example: "Wow, the lion is in full force today", "That sounds a bit scary, we might need some help from your lion part", etc.

Joan identified that when her foster child Jasmine was kind, she had a "heart of gold" and that she wished that she saw this side more often (at the time there were numerous incidents of physical and verbal aggression). So, to magnify this "heart of gold", we made a life-size drawing of Jasmine and gold hearts were added to it each time this part showed itself. Each time Jasmine used "helping hands and kind words", Joan gave lots of specific praise and encouragement and rewarded Jasmine by adding "kindness points" (pebbles) to her special jar, which earned Jasmine a heart-shaped certificate when it contained a certain number of pebbles. Joan and Jasmine practised these skills by playing a game called "Adventures into Kindness Kingdom", which included helping pack up her toys, brushing the dog, and looking after a "sick" cuddly toy. Joan was also supported to make a heart-shaped poster, which was decorated with all the things she loved and appreciated about Jasmine. This was contributed to by Jasmine's teacher, tutor, LAC (Looked After Child) nurse, babysitter, best friend, and social worker.

Debbie (adoptive mother) expressed to me how proud she felt about the progress and journey of her daughter Remi. Debbie used a catchphrase for this: "Proud as a peacock" (a common saying in their household). To enrich this image, lots of creative photos, sculpts, stickers, and drawings were used to help think about peacocks and the feeling of being proud. In addition, thickening discussions were had around this, such as: "Can you think of a time when you felt proud as a peacock?" "Can you describe this time?" "What did you think and how did you feel at that time?" "When else has the proud peacock visited?" "What makes the peacock's feathers glow brightly?" "What would you miss if the proud peacock went away?" Debbie and Remi enjoyed these discussions so much that they decided to make peacock-themed cards, which they regularly swapped with each other when they felt proud of one another. A few years later, Debbie shared with me that upon Remi's graduation they had decided to have a peacock-themed party to celebrate.

Reflecting on past challenges, what skills the young person has overcome, and what journey they have travelled

Children who have overcome adversity are often positioned as passive victims; however, in line with a strengths-based approach, and with the intention of reducing feelings of powerlessness and helplessness, I prefer to think of these children as active survivors who have used various survival strategies and qualities to respond to the traumas they faced and to survive them. Therefore, it can be powerful to reflect on times when children have overcome something, been brave, been strong, felt confident, been successful, and felt proud. After identifying some of these times where they overcame obstacles, challenges, and adversities and showed strength, bravery, survivorship, etc., the following questions can be used to expand on these qualities (the wording of the questions must be tailored to the individual).

What does this mean and say about you? What did you learn about yourself? What contributed to this learning? How did others respond to you at these times? What supported you in getting through these times? Where did you learn that skill from (e.g. being brave)? What is your relationship to... (the skill and quality used)? Who would be the least surprised to hear you talking about this? Who has acknowledged this in the past? What, because of your experience, do you now have to teach and offer to others?

It can be helpful to try these questions on yourself too.

To bring the above questions alive young people can subsequently be supported to write a list, story, poem, or song, draw a picture, depict in sand, or make a sculpture of, for example, "A scene that describes a time when I...", "All of my achievements", "The good choices I have already made", "All of the things I have already done", or "All of the times that I have felt proud" (see Photo 5.28). Sometimes I zoom in even further and ask the young person to draw/sculpt/write to a part of themselves that they are proud of or to the part that they feel is their best part, for example "To my sense of humour" or "To my brown eyes".

I also support young people to reflect/draw/sculpt/write about something that they have recently learned about themselves or to illustrate the way in which they overcame a particular difficulty. These discussions fit with Solution-Focused and Narrative Therapy models, which are based on the premise that young people possess the skills and the key to support them to get to their own solutions. This can be visually represented by drawing, making, or giving the young person a key.

In addition, metaphors can be useful embedding tools for thinking about conquering challenges or travelling on vast journeys, such as climbing over a mountain, navigating a maze, or surviving a storm. These can also be enhanced through inspirational books, films, and documentaries.

Photo 5.28 I can do it art

The distance that the child/family have already travelled and the steps that they have taken can be extended further by verbally discussing and expanding on them and by visually drawing/making/sculpting a path, timeline, or ladder. This can also be thickened by supporting the young person/family to make "a then, now, and future" picture, portrait, or collage (see Photo 5.43). Grotberg (1995) uses the helpful guidance of "I am, I can, and I have", which young people can draw or make a story or a collage around.

Externalising confidence and self-esteem

In line with previous discussions about the power of language and the importance of externalising the problem from the person, it can be useful to have discussions around: What does confidence/self-esteem look like, sound like, say, and do? For example, to ask questions such as the following (the example name of Mr Mirror is used – this would be supplemented with the child's choice of name).

If you were to name the part of you that is confident, what would it be called? What does Mr Mirror look like, sound like, do? Who supported Mr Mirror to grow and exist? When does Mr Mirror show himself? If Mr Mirror could speak, what would he say? What makes Mr Mirror stronger and brighter? How do others respond when Mr Mirror visits? What is different when Mr Mirror visits?

Some children might like to imagine that the character representing confidence, such as Mr Mirror, is there with them, helping them, and cheerleading them on. They might want to draw, sculpt, collage, or write about Mr Mirror (see Photo 5.29). They might like to imagine or visually represent various scenarios and how they might be different with Mr Mirror by their side.

Photo 5.29 Mr Mirror (externalised confidence)

Confidence and positive self-esteem can also be linked to different body language on the TV, in magazines, and/or through role-playing body positions and day-to-day scenarios (illustrated in Photo 5.30). I often find it useful to walk in and out of the room by role-playing the same scenario but using different body language, tone of voice, and eye contact and asking the child to comment and reflect on the similarities and differences.

Photo 5.30 Confident body language collage

Role models and inspirers

It feels important to find ways to build and connect with role models and inspirers, as this can have an extremely positive influence on young people including supporting them in finding and connecting with the meaning, value, and purpose of their lives and having concrete representations of how things can be and look different. Therefore, it can be useful to ask the young person about whether they have any heroes/role models/inspirers and, if so, who they are and why. This might be through finding a mentor or connecting with other people who have lived through similar experiences or experienced adversity. Popular examples include (although this will hold different meanings for the individual depending on their age, values, culture, gender, political leaning, interests, wider exposure, etc.): Nelson Mandela, Martin Luther King, Maya Angelou, Malala Yousafzai, Viktor Frankl, Aung San Suu Kyi, Rosa Parks, Mother Teresa, Mahatma Gandhi, Desmond Tutu, Helen Keller, Oprah Winfrey, Katie Piper, Louis Zamperini, J. K. Rowling, Stephen Hawking, Bethany Hamilton, etc. Younger children may prefer to think about these concepts using superheroes, fairies, mystical creatures, and magical power.

Identifying these sources of inspiration can also be supported by drawing from poems, quotes, films, books, music, and plays. Young people might, for example, make a positive song playlist, choose a positive song to be their ringtone on their phone, make a collage centred on an inspirational quote (see Photo 5.31), and/or write out the words to an inspiring song and then frame them. Some examples are given below.

Seventeen-year-old Jonah made a collage around the Nelson Mandela quote: "Do not judge me by my successes, judge me by how many times I fell down and got back up again." He then reflected on why this quote resonated with him, what it meant to him, and how it related to his life, hopes, and dreams.

> Fifteen-year-old Cece was inspired by Christina Aguilera's song "Beautiful", and so in the session she wrote out the words to "Beautiful", made it her phone and alarm ringtone, and made a painting titled "Beauty is…". She also made some positive affirmation statements that started with: "I am beautiful because…".

The influence of these inspirers can be expanded on in several ways, including through some of the following questions.

What can you learn from…about life and living? What images, quotes, and mottos come to mind when you think of…? What strengths, positive qualities, and skills can you draw, learn, and build from…? What and how did…overcome adversity? How does…show confidence? What strengths and skills do you have that are similar to…? What advice might…give to you if they were here? What would…be proud of or impressed by if they heard about or met you? What would you like…to see you doing and achieving? Who would you like to be a role model for?

Photo 5.31 A Nelson Mandela inspired poster collage

Tree of Life (Ncube, 2007)

The Tree of Life is a wonderful and powerful Narrative Therapy tool that uses the tree as a metaphor to discuss children's lives, experiences, identity, connections, resiliencies, and skills. Worksheet 5.13 offers more guidance on the different steps of the Tree of Life.

Re-shaping ideas and metaphors of negativity and criticism

Many children will have experienced repeated negativity and criticism about themselves, which probably will have contributed to their negative sense of self. In the context of a safe, therapeutic relationship, it can be powerful to think about who or what these negative words, feelings, or actions looked and felt like. For example, common metaphors used included bars on a bird cage, weights, spongers, crushers, hammers, squeezers, hoovers, and drainers. These can be visually represented through drawing, sculpting, or using an item in the session (e.g. drawing or sculpting one's inner critic or doubter). (They need to be adapted depending on the individual's age, needs, and language), such as a ball and chain (see Photo 5.32), worry stones (see Photo 5.33), a hammer, a bird cage (see Photo 5.34), a crusher (see Photo 5.35), a straitjacket, a tall wall, a spiked fence, a hoover, a sponge, a backpack full of bricks, tattoos, bullets, glass shards, etc. Discussions can be had around these. For example, when using the straitjacket metaphor, some of the types of questions that may be used include the following.

How did the straitjacket get put on and by whom? How long have you been wearing the straitjacket for? What does the straitjacket feel like when it's on? What makes the straitjacket tighter and more restrictive? What makes the straitjacket looser and easier to slip out from? What does it feel like when you are free from the straitjacket? What can you do differently when you are not in the straitjacket? What other types of jackets can you and do you wear? Who else notices when you are straitjacket free? What ways have you learned to outsmart the straitjacket? Can you show me some ways how you can get out of the straitjacket? Can you draw yourself getting out of the straitjacket and then draw yourself straitjacket free?

Photo 5.32 A child depicting being held down by a ball and chain

Photo 5.33 Representing through stones what worries are weighing the young person down

Photo 5.34 A girl being restricted in a bird cage and trapped by words on the bars

Photo 5.35 A young person feeling like they have been trampled on by someone's shoe

Some children and adolescents, where appropriate and within a safe, therapeutic relationship, might want to identify and externalise these "hurtful words" through writing down/drawing/sculpting some of these negative and restricting thoughts, for example "You're stupid", "You are a waste of space", "You are ugly and no one will love you", and "You'll never amount to anything". For some, it can be useful to explore the negative self-statements in a more Cognitive Behavioural way, such as by using the following example questions.

What evidence is there for and against the statement "I'm stupid"? What would you say to your best friend if they said "I'm stupid"? What hazards are there of holding on to the thought "I'm stupid"? If you hold on to thinking "I'm stupid", how does this impact your decisions, actions, situations, etc.? Is there a kinder alternative way of thinking about yourself than "I'm stupid"?

Additional possible lines of enquiry might include.

What is the worst thing that you fear will/can happen when you, for example, speak in class? What is the best thing that can happen when you, for example, speak in class? If the worst did happen, what skills could you use to cope with that? Do you think this situation will be important in five years' time? When you have had this feeling in the past that "I can't do it", what did you tell yourself or think to help yourself feel better?

Building on the above, a diary drawing on these Cognitive Behavioural concepts can be found in Worksheet 4.22 in Chapter 4. This can be a useful platform for older children and adolescents to begin reflecting on their thinking styles and to start developing fairer and more balanced statements towards themselves. This may also lead to some helpful experiments; however, these exercises should only be carried out by those trained and comfortable in Cognitive Behavioural Therapy for self-esteem.

These responses can be expanded on and embedded further by drawing/sculpting/collaging them, for example visually representing the situation in five years' time or drawing the best thing that could happen. Alternatively, as in Photo 5.36, the young person could represent the harsh and critical words versus other more nurturing, supportive, and comfortable words.

Photo 5.36 A visual representation of a girl tattooed with negative words compared with a more confident, positive-messaged version of herself

After some support and discussion about these thoughts and the weight of them, the young person may actually get rid of, or imagine getting rid of, them. This might be by putting the negative thoughts:

- inside a bottle and watching them float away

- inside or written on a rising balloon (see Photo 5.37)

- inside a rubbish bag

- on a piece of paper that is then burned, ripped up, or buried

- on a tissue and watching them fade away when dipped in water or when they are flushed down the toilet

- on stickers and then ripping them up/off and replacing them with positive-worded stickers (see Photo 5.38)

- on a piece of paper and physically cutting them out.

Others might like to write the words down on sand, clay, or an Etch a Sketch and then have the power to remove them, make them fade, or blur them out. It can be helpful to reflect out loud with the child during this process on how much stronger and bigger they are than the words on the paper.

Photo 5.37 Negative words floating away in a balloon

Photo 5.38 Ripping off labels

Imagery re-scripting

In the context of a safe, therapeutic relationship, children might find using imagery re-scripting techniques helpful. This is where a negative mental image is transformed into a more benign image. For example, imagining the person who said the hurtful comments:

- with a funny face on

- with a small head

- on mute or in black and white

- stuck behind a screen or wall.

In addition, some children may want to imagine or design a protective shield, a bulletproof jacket, a safety bubble (see Photo 5.39), a guardian angel (see Photo 5.40), or a magic blanket that can protect them from the hurtful comments.

Photo 5.39 Being protected by a safety bubble

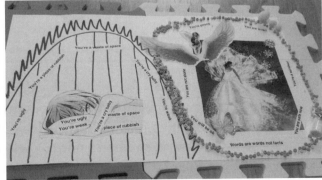

Photo 5.40 A guardian angel and mystical creature protecting and countering the negative words that a young girl felt trapped in

Future-oriented thinking and reconnecting with dreams

Many children have had to invest so much time and energy in their survival and the present moment that they have not had the same opportunities as others to think about their future and their dreams. This is particularly the case for children who have been marinated in hopelessness, powerlessness, and negative discourses about what they are worth and what they can achieve. This can also be exacerbated through having limited access to positive role models or to visions of a better future. Therefore, it can be useful to create a future-oriented approach. For example, reflecting with children on how they see their future self: how they would like to be, feel, think, act, believe, and achieve, and what their various hopes, goals, dreams, and wishes are.

This can be extended using exercises such as writing a letter from their future to their current self, making a time capsule (see Worksheet 5.14 and Photo 5.41), creating a bridge of them getting to their future, or drawing a then, now, and future picture/portrait. This can be supported by asking the solution-focused miracle question (De Shazer, 2012); there are lots of different variations of this but an example of one version is given below.

If you woke up tomorrow and a miracle had happened and your key difficulties had disappeared, what would be different about the way you act, feel, and think? Walk me through what your day would look like after the difficulties had vanished.

The miracle question and wider discussions about wishes, hopes, dreams, and aspirations can be complemented by using actual props (see Photo 5.42), such as making or drawing things like magic wands, genies, fortune-teller balls, dream catchers, a wishing well, and/or wishing dandelions.

Photo 5.41 A time capsule and letters to my future self

Photo 5.42 Dreams, hopes, and wishes props

You may like to use the templates provided on Worksheets 5.14 and 5.15 or you may prefer to make your own. Sometimes I introduce a character, such as a "wishing wizard", a "dreaming dragon", or a "dreaming dandelion", to support this process (ideally, it is best if children choose their own names for their characters) (see Worksheet 5.16); other times, I ask adolescents to write a bucket list (e.g. things I'd like to try/do/see/achieve) or ask younger children to make a "Things I want to do when I am bigger" list. Other strengths-based wish questions might include the following.

When we come to the end of therapy, what, if anything, would you like to be different? If you could fast forward time, or travel into the future, what would you like to see/notice/have happened? What news from the future would you like a fortune teller to tell you? What are you hoping will have changed? What would you like to be doing/to see that you are not doing, or seeing, at the moment? What are your wishes for yourself, for your relationships, and for the world around you? If you could ask your wishing wizard/genie/dreaming dragon for some wishes, or some dreams to come true, what would they be?

It is recommended that you thicken the discussions of each identified wish or goal so that they become and feel richer and more energised. An example is given below.

Eleven-year-old Saskia, who presented with very low self-esteem after experiencing chronic emotional abuse, struggled to prioritise herself, have dreams for herself, or have the self-belief that she could achieve them or deserved them. Eventually, after some time and some of the aforementioned strategies, she was able to come up with several hopes. One was to finish school and to become a teacher. To embed this further, I supported Saskia to write a story about her becoming and being a teacher. I encouraged her to draw a picture of her future self as a teacher. I asked her to write what type of teacher she would like to be and the reasons why she wanted to be a teacher. I also asked her to write and draw what she hoped her future students would say about her. I got her to reflect on her favourite teacher, to draw their portrait, and to share what skills and qualities they had that made them her favourite teacher and so forth.

Photo 5.43 A then, now, and future drawing

Worksheet 5.1
Common core beliefs worksheet

Copyright © Karen Treisman – *A Therapeutic Treasure Box for Working with Children and Adolescents with Developmental Trauma – 2018*

Worksheet 5.2
Magnetic thoughts and feelings worksheet

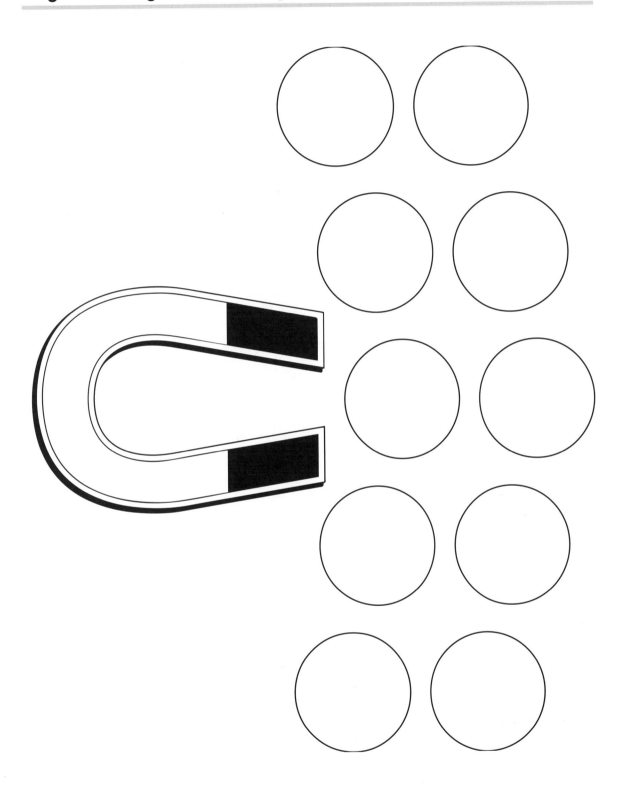

Copyright © Karen Treisman – *A Therapeutic Treasure Box for Working with Children and Adolescents with Developmental Trauma* – 2018

Worksheet 5.3
Positive reframing and alternatives to "don't", "stop", and "no"

State what you want the child to do. Say what you want, and what behaviours you want to see more of, as opposed to what you don't want to see.

The table below gives some examples of "no" and "don't" statements and some possible corresponding positive reframes. There are blank rows left at the end for you to complete and to individualise.

Some commands and disciplinary statements using don't, stop, and no, and negative descriptors	Some ways of reframing these to communicate to the child what behaviours we do want to see and positively reframing the child's behaviours
Don't shout	Please speak quietly/Use your indoor voice
Stop running	Please walk beside me/Walk slowly
Don't hit	Please use your kind hands/Keep your hands to yourself
Stop stealing	I need you to leave the items where you found them/Ask before taking something
Don't snatch the toys from…	Share your toys with…
Don't lie	Please tell me the truth
Stop being late	I need you to come home on time
Stop ignoring me	I would really appreciate it if you could listen to me/Please use your listening ears
Stop misbehaving	I need you to behave by…
He is so attention-seeking	He is attention-needing and attachment-seeking
She is so resistant	She is understandably cautious and hesitant
He is so hyperactive	He is spirited and energetic
She is manipulative	She has had to learn lots of different ways to get her needs met
He is so easily distracted	He is very easily fascinated, curious, and/or interested
He doesn't want to try	He must be so exhausted by trying
She refuses to sit still	She seems overstimulated

Copyright © Karen Treisman – A Therapeutic Treasure Box for Working with Children and Adolescents with Developmental Trauma – 2018

List of positive descriptors and adjectives

(These can be used to guide all of the strengths-based exercises and the writing of a take-back practice letter or can be directly circled, underlined, or highlighted by the young person/worker/surrounding adults.)

Fun	Enthusiastic	Passionate
Funny	Organised	Spiritual
Helpful	Reliable	Practical
Kind	Interesting	Decisive
Thoughtful	Interested	Assertive
Loyal	Relaxed	Adaptable
Caring	Adventurous	Survivor
Honest	Open	Friendly

Copyright © Karen Treisman – *A Therapeutic Treasure Box for Working with Children and Adolescents with Developmental Trauma – 2018*

Strong	Trustworthy	Warm
Brave	Sporty	Unique
Creative	Attractive	Calm
Clever	Confident	Compassionate
Persistent	Resourceful	Sensible
Responsible	Analytical	Energetic
Smart	Talkative	Empathetic
Artistic	Affectionate	Considerate
Musical	Witty	Courageous
Charming	Dynamic	Determined

Copyright © Karen Treisman – *A Therapeutic Treasure Box for Working with Children and Adolescents with Developmental Trauma* – 2018

Logical	Frank	Gentle
Sociable	Generous	Hardworking
Imaginative	Independent	Inventive
Intuitive/strong gut instinct	Neat/tidy	Loving
Humble	Down to earth	Optimistic
Proactive	Polite	Patient
Dreamer	Balanced	Content
Hopeful	Reflective	Curious
Excitable	Diplomatic	Active
Ambitious	Grateful	Appreciative

Copyright © Karen Treisman – *A Therapeutic Treasure Box for Working with Children and Adolescents with Developmental Trauma* – 2018

Articulate	Authentic	Open-minded
Cultured	Daring	Direct
Eager	Enchanting	Ethical
Elegant	Fashionable	Forgiving
Inquisitive	Knowledgeable	Likeable
Loveable	Lucky	Mature
Motivated	Nurturing	Perceptive
Problem-solver	Realistic	Resilient
Spontaneous	Thorough	Understanding
Wise		

Copyright © Karen Treisman – *A Therapeutic Treasure Box for Working with Children and Adolescents with Developmental Trauma* – 2018

Worksheet 5.5
Reflecting on my strengths and positive qualities

If you became a different person tomorrow, or life changed as you know it, what would you miss about yourself and your life, even if it is the tiniest thing? (Draw, write down, sculpt, collage, tell a story, or use photos.)

If you could go back and replay one happy and special moment over and over again, what would it be? (Draw, write down, sculpt, collage, tell a story, or use photos.)

Copyright © Karen Treisman – *A Therapeutic Treasure Box for Working with Children and Adolescents with Developmental Trauma* – 2018

If you were to give yourself an award, what would it be for? (Draw, write down, sculpt, collage, tell a story, or use photos.)

If you looked up in the sky and there was a feel-good message (guaranteed to put a smile on your face) written on the clouds, being led by an aeroplane, or carved in the rocks, what would that be? (Draw, write down, sculpt, collage, tell a story, or use photos.)

Copyright © Karen Treisman – *A Therapeutic Treasure Box for Working with Children and Adolescents with Developmental Trauma* – 2018

SMART goals: think SMART

Specific Be very clear and concrete in what you want to achieve. It needs to be defined. Ask yourself: what specific behaviour do we want to see more of? Consider breaking the goal down into smaller steps.

For example, instead of "being good" or "good behaviour", what specifically do we want to work on or to see? What does "being good" look like and mean? This might be tweaked to be something more specific, like staying close to me when we go to the park or brushing your teeth in the morning, and at night time.

Measurable How will you know when you have achieved your goal? How will you be able to measure and monitor this goal/change? What will you be doing at that time? What will others notice you are doing? What will be different? What will you have started or be doing regularly? What will you have stopped or be doing less of?

Achievable/Attainable Ensure that the goals are not too high or unattainable. Don't set yourself up to fail! Consider setting smaller goals on your way up to the big one. Celebrate your successes. If you don't achieve what you set out to, then ask: What could you do differently and what would make it more likely to succeed next time or to get closer to the goal?

Realistic Is this goal realistic? Are there any measures that need to be put in place to make this more realistic and manageable? Again, think about breaking it down, one step at a time.

Copyright © Karen Treisman – *A Therapeutic Treasure Box for Working with Children and Adolescents with Developmental Trauma* – 2018

For example, if a child is struggling to behave in class, and is having several incidents a day in school, is expecting and setting a goal to behave all day or all week realistic? Consider the young person's emotional, developmental, and social age/needs versus their chronological age/needs. Also, reflect on their journey so far and the skills that they need to learn in order to meet the goal.

Time-limited Set a reasonable and realistic time limit to achieve the goal. When will your goal be re-evaluated/adjusted? When will behaviour change be measured? When will rewards be given?

Some suggestions for turning a wide goal into something more achievable

If a young person/parent/carer says something wide, vague, and non-specific such as "I want to be happy", try to break this down into more manageable, achievable, and specific steps. We want to frame the goal, define it, and get a good grasp on what it actually is. It is very difficult to target something or to make measurable change if it is open and large.

For example: *What does happiness look like? How will you know you are happy? How will I know you are happy? What would you be doing differently if you were happy? What would be different from now? Talk me through a day-to-day account of what "doing happiness" or "being happy" would look like. What things make you feel a bit happy now? Can you describe an example of when you felt happy? What stops you from feeling happy? What makes you feel less happy? How will you know when you are happy enough?*

Use scaling questions can also be helpful in narrowing this down. *For example, on a scale where zero is extremely unhappy and things could not get worse and ten is extremely happy where things are at the best place that they could be, where would you place yourself? If the young person says three, you might explore what is keeping them at a three, instead of a zero, one, or two. Following this, you may want to reflect with them on what they think would support them to move to a five, six, or seven and what different numbers felt like and looked like at different times.*

This is similar to if a young person lists several different things that they would like to work on all in one go: it is important to prioritise these things and to think about which ones are best to work on first, which ones are interconnected, and which ones can wait. It is far easier to make effective change when focusing on one thing at a time, which it is hoped will have a ripple effect rather than getting muddled with lots of different complex avenues.

Copyright © Karen Treisman – *A Therapeutic Treasure Box for Working with Children and Adolescents with Developmental Trauma* – 2018

Obstacles/barriers

Consider, reflect, and anticipate any obstacles and barriers that may impact on the success of achieving the proposed goal (these can be drawn, sculpted, or likened to metaphors). Plan and problem-solve around how these may be reduced, minimised, or managed.

Creative ways of goal-setting

(See Chapter 2 and earlier in Chapter 5.)

» Discuss children's/family's wishes. Props such as a wand, magic ball, genie, dream catcher, fortune teller, fairy, and angel can be helpful in bringing this process alive.

» Support the child to think about what things they want to be different and how. Using props or metaphors, such as a time machine, a magic door, or a time capsule, can aid these conversations.

» Pictorially, represent different steps and journeys, for example by using images of ladders, steps, a path, a road, snakes and ladders, pieces of LEGO®, and/or pieces of a puzzle (see Chapters 6 and 10).

Reward charts

Sometimes, if appropriate and done in an attachment and trauma-informed way that is focused on enhancing strengths and pro-social behaviour, SMART goals can be used to support the creation and implementation of a reward chart. The following ideas offer some top tips on making and administering reward charts.

Introducing the reward chart

Once you have gone through the above SMART goal steps and feel clear about the purpose and goals of the reward chart, you can go on to introduce it to your child in a friendly, non-punitive, and playful way. Where possible, link the reward chart to something the child will be interested in, for example their favourite hobby/TV character/place.

Children often need some practice and role-playing about how and when to use the reward chart; this can be supported by using teddies, dolls, and puppets. Try and introduce the concept of the reward chart when the child is regulated and in a "thinking brain" moment and a "learning head space". They might need lots of repetition and reminders whilst making sense of the reward chart.

Copyright © Karen Treisman – A Therapeutic Treasure Box for Working with Children and Adolescents with Developmental Trauma – 2018

Common traps to be mindful of when designing and implementing a reward chart

Giving up or changing tack too early: Sometimes, the smallest tweak or rethink to a reward chart can make a world of difference. Like with all techniques, they are generally slow burners and need some time, practice, repetition, consistency, and persistence before the effectiveness can be seen.

Expecting failure: We need to go on believing on the ability of change and in the rationale for the technique. Half the battle is believing; this significantly impacts how we subsequently implement the tool.

Magnifying the negative: Try and think about the positive behaviour. What do we want to see more of? What will be rewarded? Remember, the more we focus on the positive behaviours, the more often they are likely to occur and grow. For example, instead of a chart targeted at "No shouting", you can reframe this by giving a sticker for every time the child "Speaks quietly" or "Uses their indoor voice".

Too broad: This means trying to have a reward chart that encapsulates everything. The most effective reward charts are small and specific. For example, instead of a reward chart for being good, one might make a reward chart for packing up toys. Remember to think SMART.

Taking away rewards: Rewards are to be given and earned when the positive behaviours are shown; they are not to be taken away or lost. Reward charts are not to be used as a form of punishment. For example, if a child brushes their teeth, they earn a sticker; however, if they refuse to brush their teeth, they don't earn a sticker that time but the previous one is not removed. If the child does not do as they are told, other consequences and parenting strategies can be put in place, but it is important not to remove previously earned rewards.

Reward charts are not the only tool: Reward charts can be an effective way to manage tricky behaviours and/or increase positive behaviours. However, they should be used in the context of other parenting strategies. For example, if a child has a reward chart for brushing their teeth, then this should be the focus, but when they do other "good" behaviours these can be rewarded in other ways. Generally, reward charts work most effectively when they are as specific and as narrow as possible. Some children can manage a higher number of target behaviours or multiple reward charts but, in most cases, starting simple and working up is more likely to achieve successful outcomes.

Fixed and constant: As we know, children are constantly developing and changing, so we need to review and evaluate the reward chart. Do they need another reward chart targeting a different behaviour? Do they need to stick with this behaviour for a bit longer to embed it? Is the reward chart still effective? Is it proving too difficult to gain a reward? Do they need it broken down into smaller steps?

Consistency: If there are multiple people in the household, it is important that everyone is aware of how the reward chart works and is coordinated and consistent in using it.

Incentives: Where possible, make sure you select an incentive that the child is interested in and has some ownership over. Also, ensure that it is manageable, for example promising a child a trip to a theme park after ten reward stickers is likely to prove expensive and unrealistic on a long-term basis, especially if they are getting several stickers a day.

Copyright © Karen Treisman – *A Therapeutic Treasure Box for Working with Children and Adolescents with Developmental Trauma* – 2018

Worksheet 5.7
My treasure box diary

Days of the week and date	Things to ask myself (draw, collage, record, sculpt, or write my thoughts): What was a positive thing that I did today? What positive qualities does that say about me? What is a positive thing in others or the world that I saw, noticed, or heard about today? What was my favourite thing about today (a thing that made me smile or a moment that if I could I would bottle up)? When was a time today when I felt good about myself/proud of myself/had fun?
Monday	
Tuesday	
Wednesday	

Copyright © Karen Treisman – *A Therapeutic Treasure Box for Working with Children and Adolescents with Developmental Trauma – 2018*

Thursday	
Friday	
Saturday	
Sunday	
Other thoughts and things to remember	

Copyright © Karen Treisman – *A Therapeutic Treasure Box for Working with Children and Adolescents with Developmental Trauma – 2018*

Gifts I have been given and gifts that I have to give...

Gifts I have been given

Gifts I already have myself that I can give to others

Copyright © Karen Treisman – *A Therapeutic Treasure Box for Working with Children and Adolescents with Developmental Trauma* – 2018

Bottling up special moments

This is like taking a mental snapshot or soaking in a special moment. Which moments would you bottle up and why? Write or draw on the bottles below and try to give each one a label. If you prefer, you can label and fill actual bottles.

Try and remember and hold on to all the details, the smells, the sounds, the tastes, the feelings, the movements, and more of each memory and moment...

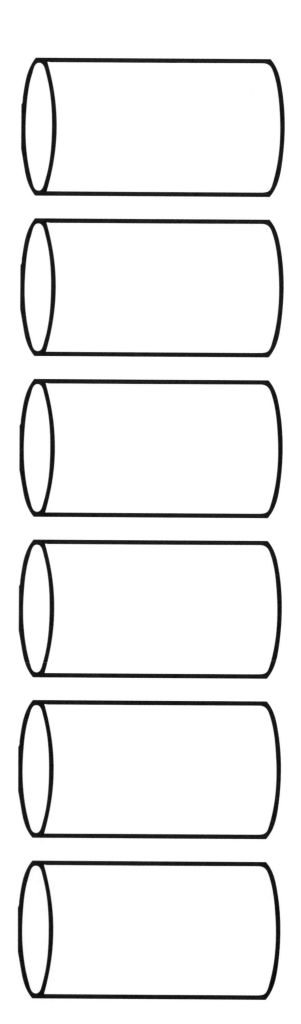

Copyright © Karen Treisman – A Therapeutic Treasure Box for Working with Children and Adolescents with Developmental Trauma – 2018

Puzzle of positives

Copyright © Karen Treisman – *A Therapeutic Treasure Box for Working with Children and Adolescents with Developmental Trauma* – 2018

My patchwork of ...

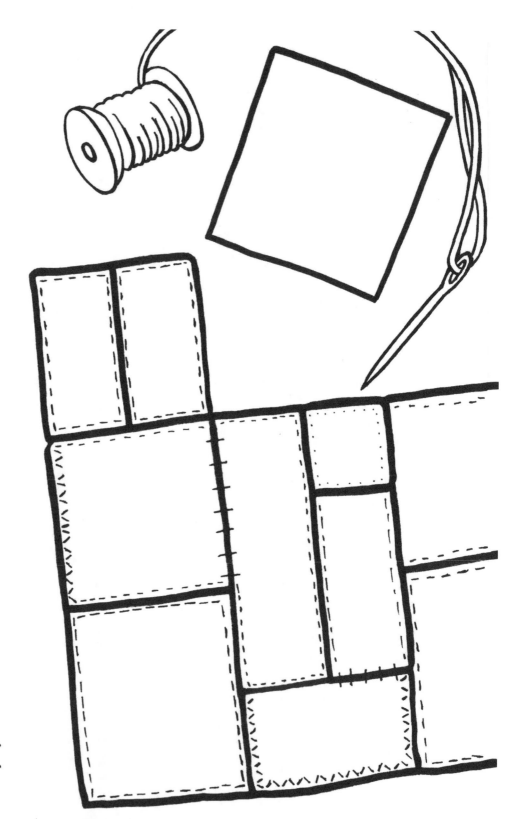

Copyright © Karen Treisman – *A Therapeutic Treasure Box for Working with Children and Adolescents with Developmental Trauma – 2018*

Star of strengths

Copyright © Karen Treisman – *A Therapeutic Treasure Box for Working with Children and Adolescents with Developmental Trauma – 2018*

Worksheet 5.13
Tree of Life Narrative Therapy technique

(This tool should only be carried out/supported by trained professionals and those who are familiar with Narrative Therapy philosophies, techniques, and ideas, as well as models of trauma, resilience, and attachment.)

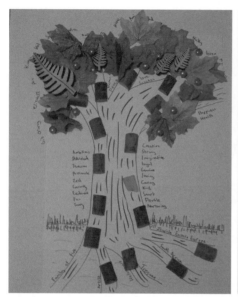 

Photos 5.44 and 5.45 Creative representations of the Tree of Life

The Tree of Life (ToL) is a Narrative Therapy tool originally developed by Ncazelo Ncube, a Zimbabwean psychologist, for children who had been orphaned by HIV/AIDS. However, the ToL has since been extended to working with numerous age groups and in wide-reaching areas. The ToL aims to support people to strengthen their relationships with their history, culture, and significant relationships.

In this technique, children use a tree as a metaphor for their lives. Often, these representations are in pictorial form. Children can express their ideas in whichever way they choose, including using objects, pictures, paints, collage, sculpture, etc.

Step 1 Discussion about trees

Children are supported to have discussions about trees, for example about their favourite tree, their feelings about trees, the variety of trees in the world, and the characteristics, purpose, and function of trees.

Step 2 Making and creating the trees

This can be over a prolonged period to allow for richness, discussion, and creativity. A range of expressive modalities and methods can be used.

The tree consists of six parts:

» The roots (these represent where the child came from, their family life, their family name, stories/songs/quotes/sayings from their past, and their ancestry).

Copyright © Karen Treisman – *A Therapeutic Treasure Box for Working with Children and Adolescents with Developmental Trauma – 2018*

- » The ground (this represents the child's present world, and their everyday activities/hobbies/interests/likes).

- » The trunk (this represents the child's strengths, resiliencies, positive qualities, and skills).

- » The branches (these represent the child's hopes, wishes, goals, and dreams).

- » The leaves (these represent important people in the child's life; these can be people who are real, imagined, or dead, inspirational people, pets, etc.).

- » The fruits (these represent the physical, psychological, and social gifts that the child has been given by others).

Step 3 Forest and community of trees

If the tree has been created in a group, this is where they can be displayed together to create a forest of trees – a community. This can support children in feeling part of something and being listened to. The group may choose to reflect on what they have been struck by/learned from/been inspired by/impressed with in others' trees. If the tree has been created in individual sessions, this concept can be applied to the Team Around the Child if appropriate.

Step 4 The hazards and storms that trees/children/families face

After being rooted and creating one's tree, the group/individual then discusses the storms and dangers faced by trees and can use this as a metaphor for thinking of ways of weathering their own life storms. Sample questions might include: *What hazards do trees and forests sometimes face? Are trees free from danger? Are the dangers the tree's fault? How do animals and children respond to storms that come into their lives? How do animals and children try to protect themselves? Are storms always present in their lives? Are lives sometimes free of storms? What can be done when the storms have passed?*

Step 5 Celebration ceremony and certificate

The ToL process is usually completed with a certificate and ceremony celebration.

Extensions and adaptation of the ToL

Since development, the ToL has been extended and creatively applied in a range of contexts. For example, through using a football pitch metaphor with former child soldiers (Denborough, 2008) or a kite of life, focusing on moving people from intergenerational conflict to intergenerational alliance (Denborough, 2010).

More examples of and information on the ToL are available from:

- » http://dulwichcentre.com.au/the-tree-of-life

- » Denborough, D. (2008). *Collective Narrative Practice: Responding to Individuals, Groups, and Communities who have Experienced Trauma*. Adelaide: Dulwich Centre Publications.

Copyright © Karen Treisman – *A Therapeutic Treasure Box for Working with Children and Adolescents with Developmental Trauma* – 2018

Inside the time capsule I/we would put ...

DO NOT OPEN UNTIL

2050

Copyright © Karen Treisman – *A Therapeutic Treasure Box for Working with Children and Adolescents with Developmental Trauma – 2018*

My wishes for...
are...

Copyright © Karen Treisman – *A Therapeutic Treasure Box for Working with Children and Adolescents with Developmental Trauma – 2018*

Worksheet 5.16
Wishing wizard or dreaming dragon

What does my wishing wizard or dreaming dragon look like? (Draw, sculpt, write, collage, or depict your responses.)

What does my wishing wizard or dreaming dragon sound like/smell like?

What does my wishing wizard or dreaming dragon do and help me with? (Draw, sculpt, write, collage, or depict your responses.)

What messages do I have to give my wishing wizard or dreaming dragon?

Copyright © Karen Treisman – *A Therapeutic Treasure Box for Working with Children and Adolescents with Developmental Trauma – 2018*

Worksheet 5.17
Strengths-based approach: writing a take-back practice letter

Guidance on how to use these questions

The following questions offer some possibilities and options for reflecting on and identifying young people's/carers'/families'/parents'/colleagues' strengths, skills, and positive qualities. These can be powerfully pulled together and documented in a letter, email, poem, story, or card. Alternatively, these can be recorded on a video camera or phone. They can also be used as inspiration to complement some of the previous tools, such as writing them on a pillow case, adding them into the child's treasure box, putting them in the sparkle moments diary, or making a collage of them.

You may also want to use Worksheet 5.4 for inspiration for positive descriptive words. It can also be helpful to draw on responses and input from the Team Around the Child.

This list is not prescriptive or exhaustive. Each question can be expanded on by asking thickening questions and embedding them through creative means.

Think about a young person/parent/colleague/client:

» What has gone well? What has been achieved so far? What steps have been taken? What can they do already? (Think about their journey and the distance already travelled.)

» What hobbies and activities does the person engage in, enjoy, and excel in? What makes them sparkle/get excited/feel proud/be happy?

» What skills, strengths, successes, and positive qualities of theirs have you been struck by/inspired by/impressed by? What are their superpowers?

» If you were writing a review or recommendation about this person, what positive things would you say to others about them? If you had to give them an award for something positive, what would it be for?

» If you were stranded on an island with them, what skills of theirs would you appreciate?

» If they became a different person or life as you know it changed, what would you miss about them?

» If you were no longer with them/seeing them, what parts of their personality would you miss?

» How has knowing them made an impression on you? What have you learned from them?

» What will you take forward from what you have learned from them?

» What are your wishes, hopes, and dreams for them?

» How can these skills, strengths, successes, and positive qualities be recognised, acknowledged, noticed, celebrated, and built on?

Copyright © Karen Treisman – A Therapeutic Treasure Box for Working with Children and Adolescents with Developmental Trauma – 2018

Strengthening and Supporting "Parent–Child" Relationships, Relational Trust, and Interpersonal Connections

Who is this chapter for?

This chapter has a focus on strengthening and supporting the parent–child relationship, which, in the context of relational and developmental trauma, is the fundamental core of the majority of subsequent interventions. It should be noted that this chapter uses the word "parent" in the broader sense – this may be a foster carer, a kinship carer, a special guardian, a residential worker, and so forth – and recognises that the parenting task and role can be in many different constellations (e.g. single-parent households, same-sex households, a step-parent arrangement, therapeutic re-parenting, "corporate parenting", etc.).

The concepts and strategies that follow have relevance and applicability to a range of other subgroups that are focused on relationship-based practice, including social workers, early years workers, family support workers, teachers, therapists, etc. This said, it is essential to acknowledge that it is neither helpful nor accurate to lump all types of "parents" (e.g. adoptive, foster, kinship, special guardians, residential workers, etc.) together in one category, as they are a heterogeneous group of individuals within unique contexts, each with their own needs, journeys, experiences, and motivations.

It is also important to recognise that the task of parenting is complex, dynamic, and evolving. It does not take place in a vacuum and is influenced and shaped by wider systems, cultures, and contexts. Therefore, each relationship, and the interaction between them, is unique and multi-layered. The following questions might be helpful in widening these discussions and reflective processes.

What are some of the factors and variables that you feel might influence the a) parenting role, b) parenting capacity, c) nature and quality of the parent–child relationship, and d) parenting task itself? How are these similar or different? How do they interplay, overlap, or conflict with each other? How might your own experience of parenting, and/or being parented, influence these identified factors and your associated values/attributes/conceptualisations of parenting? How might the context you are in, including societal discourses/culture, influence these ideas of, and about, parenting?

Positioning these strategies within the context of parent–child therapies and factors to be mindful of

This chapter should be read in conjunction with Chapter 1, which discusses some of the underpinning principles and the factors to be mindful of when implementing the described strategies. It is important to note that this chapter offers some ideas and strategies to enhance and increase connections and to strengthen parent–child relationships; however, the ideas are not intended to be standalone techniques or a replacement/substitute for existing parent–child relationship therapy and intervention models. The strategies described in this chapter offer some ideas to be interwoven with and to complement these types of approaches.

Some of these therapies and models might include:

- Video Interaction Guidance (VIG)

- the Attachment and Biobehavioral Catch-up (ABC) intervention

- Attachment, Self-Regulation, and Competency (ARC)

- Dyadic Developmental Psychotherapy (DDP)

- Child–Parent Psychotherapy (CPP)

- Mentalisation-based treatment

- Child-Relationship Enhancement Family Therapy

- Theraplay

- The Parent–Child Game.

This is not an exhaustive or prescriptive list. Please see Chapter 7 in *Working with Relational and Developmental Trauma in Children and Adolescents* (Treisman, 2016) for more detail on these interventions.

As with all interventions, their timing and appropriateness need to be carefully considered and reflected on. It is important to ensure that it is safe and appropriate to focus on the parent–child relationship or to carry out joint activities/sessions. In some cases, risk factors, practical/social factors, parental motivation/engagement levels, parental capacity to change, and/or the parental emotional and behavioural regulation skills may need to be assessed, prioritised, and supported before being able to take a more relational focus.

Why is it important to focus on parent/caregiver–child relationships in the context of relational and developmental trauma?

In the context of relational and developmental trauma, children are more likely to have been soaked in negative relational patterns and interactions. Parenting experiences have often been characterised by emotional unavailability, incongruent mirroring, and dyadic dysregulation, meaning that access to relational riches or relational anchors are more likely to have been limited and fractured. Developing children are likely to have experienced multiple toxic ruptures and repeated misconnections within the context of their relationships. They have probably been exposed to fear and power-based relationships and relational interactions that may have been the source of pain/danger/fear, rather than of comfort, security, trust, and safety.

Therefore, these children need more than love; they need to be kept in the mind and heart of another in a meaningful and genuine way. They need environments and relationships that are going to provide them with a reparative, second-chance, secure base and safe haven and relational experiences that will support them in developing a learned/earned secure attachment style (Saunders *et al.*, 2011). Fundamentally, and put into one simple phrase: "Relational trauma requires relational repair" (Treisman, 2016). In essence, the magic is in the relationship, the interactions, and the human connections. This is also powerfully captured by a quote from an online podcast by Jesse Hanson: "Let's invite ourselves to see trauma not as a noun, but as a relationship."

Children need a relationship where they feel that they can trust and can believe that they are safe; they need to start to feel safe to explore from, and able and safe to return to, that relationship. They need a trusting relationship where they feel physically, emotionally, and cognitively safe (see Chapter 3) and to be meaningfully connected with another, where they feel they are noticed, belong, and are appreciated.

In order for children to revise, refine, and re-evaluate their previous relationship templates and maps, they need to have repeated, genuine, and rewarding positive relational experiences. These children need to learn new ways of doing and being in relationships. This is crucial in creating the map and path for their future relationships, as one's way of doing and being in relationships permeates all spheres of life and relationships. This includes considering relationships in their wider sense, such as one's intimate relationships and relationships with one's peers, self, body, community, and broader society. We want children to be able to have a (and ideally multiple) positive, embodied meaningfully connected relationships that they can subsequently internalise and transfer to future relationships and to future interaction blueprints.

Another rationale for why relationships should be central and prioritised is because they are paramount in supporting healthy brain development and increasing the richness and strength of brain connections and functions. This is partly because the brain is an experience-dependent, developing, live organ, which, promisingly, is at its most plastic and flexible during the critical sensitive periods of childhood. Therefore, the window for brain organisation and reorganisation is even wider and more open to new possibilities (Lupien *et al.*, 2009) during these developing times. This experience-dependent property also means that it is possible for the brain and its neural pathways to be positively shaped, rewired, and sculpted through repeated positive and reparative life experiences and relational interactions (Glaser, 2000). This is because, although children are born with a surplus of cells, it is predominantly the parenting and the surrounding environment (like in a draw-by-numbers game) that connects, integrates, thickens, and strengthens these links, gives birth to new neurons (neurogenesis), and can bring different parts of children's brains online. Moreover, positive safe human exchanges and social interactions recruit neural circuits which promisingly support one's brain health, growth, and restoration (Porges, 2014). Therefore, to some extent, parents are the architects and sculptors of children's brains; they are some of their most important teachers in children's lives and provide them with foundational and impactful lessons, skills, and a starting platform from which to take off. As with a house, care and attention needs to start at the foundations, as everything else, such as the internal structure, the wiring, the decorating, and so forth, is reliant on and supported by the foundations.

The focus of an intervention is often around symptom reduction and/or behavioural change; however, we know that behavioural change is far more effective and long-lasting when it is anchored to, and supported by, relationships through attachment-based learning.

> For example, an adolescent who has internalised their parent's voice, developed a moral compass, and would be mindful of, and impacted by, their parent's disappointment is more likely to make prosocial choices. Similarly, a toddler can be guided away from an unsafe activity by looking back and seeing their caregiver's cautionary facial expressions. The same toddler is likely to increase their positive behaviour based on the incentive of pleasing their caregiver or getting to spend more time with them.

Therefore, prioritising relationships and connections is likely to have a ripple effect on reducing problematic behaviour and/or parent–child conflict, as well as supporting the co-learning of key skills. For example, a child learns self-regulation through co-regulation, and empathy through being empathised with.

Last, but by no means least, in support of the emphasis being on relationships and supporting and strengthening the Team Around the Child and their key relationships, the potential for change and new possibilities is far greater in a 24-hour relationship (e.g. a caregiving relationship), which takes place over a longer timespan across multiple contexts with thousands of everyday moment-to-moment learning opportunities available, than in a standalone, one-hour-a-week therapy arrangement.

These relationships are even more important in the context of relational and developmental trauma given the cumulative experiences of relational trauma and relational misconnections. Therefore, in considering the mammoth task of therapeutically re-parenting a child who has experienced relational and developmental trauma some of these complexities and tasks will be built on further in the following section using the metaphor of a parenting orchestra/choir. Some of the key components and qualities of therapeutic re-parenting are detailed, followed by some creative and practical strategies and ideas for strengthening parent–child relationships and connections.

Some of the complexities of therapeutically re-parenting a child: the parenting orchestra/choir (adapted from *Working with Relational and Developmental Trauma in Children and Adolescents*–Treisman, 2016)

The task of parenting a child is huge and demanding, especially a hurt child who has experienced relational and developmental trauma and loss. Therapeutic re-parenting involves massive amounts of time, skill, and energy. These parents often have to juggle multiple balls, some of which are heavier, quicker, and slippier than usual; some are even camouflaged or magic balls that rapidly change. This juggling is often done in the spotlight in an arena of people watching, judging, and assessing (social workers, court, school, family members, therapists, etc.).

In order to manage these competing balls, therapeutic re-parents have to employ various roles and skills (e.g. being the child's external brain/thinking mind, teacher, safe hands, detective, translator, advocate, moral compass, nurturer, and co-regulator). These parenting roles and skills can be likened to the complexity of an orchestra/choir: *a parenting orchestra/choir*. Like parents, musicians have generally been guided and taught on their musical journey and their skills have been refined and practised repeatedly over time. Each instrument requires different skills, timing, physical strength, care, and maintenance. The successful coming together as a choir requires structure, order, and organisation. This might need to evolve and adapt depending on newcomers, people departing, change of venue, injuries, securing permission to use the music, etc. Imagine an orchestra playing relentlessly for hours on end with little or no re-energising time or a guitar being played for years without having its strings changed or tuned.

The instruments are reliant on the person playing them, and the performance is influenced by multiple factors (e.g. the health of the instrument, the audience, the conductor, the environment, and the other players). Similarly, the love and enjoyment of the musicians will have an impact on their feelings about being part of the orchestra, as will the energy of the audience and of their fellow musicians. The music can also affect and be interpreted differently by different people at different times.

There can be times of absolute musical union and harmony and others when it is, or feels, out of sync and disconnected. Sometimes the orchestra plays together as a team and at other times it might be dependent on a soloist or the conductor. The music's pace, volume, tone, and feelings can be adjusted and shaped. When the music isn't sounding quite right, thought, reflection, experience, problem-solving, support, practice, and gut instinct are needed to consider how to improve the performance and what should be added, taken away, or tweaked. See Box 6.1 to continue building on this metaphor. Following this, some underpinning positions and guiding frameworks for strengthening parent–child relationships and for therapeutically re-parenting in the context of relational trauma will be discussed.

Box 6.1 **Reflective practice parenting orchestra/choir**

Think about your own experience of being parented and/or when you are parenting. What did/does your parenting orchestra/choir look/sound/feel like? What skills, roles, and qualities are needed to play effectively in your orchestra/choir? What did/does it feel like when it's in unison or when it's out of sync? What changes, influences, or factors make/made its performance better or worse?

When parenting a child who has experienced relational and developmental trauma, how might the orchestra/choir/audience/performance feel or be different?

Consider how these different roles (e.g. the child's external brain, teacher, detective, translator, safe hands, advocate, nurturer, moral compass, and co-regulator) relate to therapeutically re-parenting a child who has experienced relational and developmental trauma. What skills, support, and qualities do these roles require and what skills and qualities do they teach children?

What roles or skills do you anticipate might be the trickiest/easiest for you? Why might this be? What is your relationship to, history with, and experience of that role/skill/quality/task?

If the parenting orchestra/choir does not resonate with you, what other metaphors can you think of that fit with your experiences more accurately?

Some underpinning positions and frameworks for promoting positive parent–child relationships in the context of relational and developmental trauma

This section will detail some of the different key components and frameworks for underpinning positive parent–child relationships within the context of relational and developmental trauma. This is not an exhaustive or prescriptive list. Different elements will probably have different weightings, depending on the particular context and the uniqueness of the dyad/triad. These elements are also captured in Figure 6.1 (please note these are not positioned in order of importance).

Understanding the impact of relational and developmental trauma/loss and the role of relational repair

Providing a secure base, safe haven, and multi-levelled safety/trust (recognising and reducing triggers)

Staying regulated and grounded as parents (mindful parenting)

Noticing, acknowledging, validating, and responding to a range of emotions (including co-regulation)

Viewing behaviours as communication and within a wider context and responding accordingly

Developmentally sequenced and whole-brain-body parenting (multi-sensory)

A warm, nurturing, playful, consistent, and predictable parenting style

Spending positive, quality time together/taking a deep interest in each other

Thinking SMART (picking battles, SMART goals and expectations)

Routines, limits, discipline, and structure – logical, fair, predictable, and trauma-informed

Normalising and owning mistakes – relational rupture repair

Providing children with a sense of mastery and agency

Keeping children in mind and showing them that they are kept in mind

Identifying, celebrating, and building on children's strengths, uniqueness, and positive qualities

Figure 6.1 Components of positive parent–child relationships in the context of trauma

Some of the above components will now be discussed, before presenting some creative and expressive ways of strengthening parent–child relationships.

Awareness, sensitivity, and knowledge around the multi-layered impact of developmental and relational trauma and how this requires relational repair

Enhanced parenting/therapeutic re-parenting includes having an increased awareness, sensitivity, and knowledge around the multi-layered impact that developmental and relational trauma, loss, and toxic stress can have on the child, caregivers, and surrounding systems and vice versa. Therapeutic re-parenting also requires the acknowledgement and commitment that, due to the trauma having occurred within the context of the child's relationships, the primary focus needs to be on relational repair (break-reconnect). This means that the magic is in the relationship and the meaningful connections.

Therefore, like in the parenting orchestra/choir, the caregiver ideally will go into the relationship expecting it to be challenging at times, a journey, and something that needs to be worked on, nourished, and nurtured (see Worksheet 6.11 for some activities around this). This includes the therapist/parent and child working through difficult conflicting times and relational ruptures to ensure that there is relational repair, relational growth, and relational connection.

Box 6.2 **Reflective exercise therapeutically re-parenting a child who has experienced relational and developmental trauma**

What does the caregiver know (or what would they benefit from knowing) about the impact of trauma on babies'/children's/adolescents' bodies, brains, emotions, relationships, and behaviours? What does the caregiver know (or what would they benefit from knowing) about the impact of the trauma on themselves, as people with their own childhood and relational experiences and as caregivers, and around the interplay between these various layers and relationships?

What is the caregiver's greatest hope/joy/fear/expectation about parenting that particular child/of being a parent?

Second-chance secure base and safe haven

Children who have experienced relational and developmental trauma need to be held within a physical, metaphorical, and psychological secure base and safe haven. This is a relationship where the child can eventually feel that they belong, are adored, are held, can trust, and are contained and knows that they have someone who is available, responsive, and sensitive to whom they can turn in difficult times and to celebrate with in joyous times. This is a person who takes a deep interest in them, who is emotionally invested in them, who holds them in their mind and in their heart, who acts as their co-regulator, who sees the best in them, and who supports them in making sense of their inner world. This fits with the idea: "To the world you may be just one person, but to that one person, you are their world." This relationship should feel like the child's anchor, safety net, protective vest, and/or lifeboat, particularly when in stormy weather, choppy seas, and changing landscapes and when faced with overwhelming emotional, sensorial, and physiological waves. (An additional explanation and specific strategies for promoting multi-level relational safety and trust are detailed in Chapter 3.)

Staying regulated and in one's thinking mind

Building on the above, it is important to acknowledge that being those safe hands, thinking minds, and regulating bodies can be challenging. This is particularly so when supporting children who bring with them complex trauma, powerful relational scripts, embedded survival/defence strategies, and immensely strong feelings and body sensations. These feelings are, at times, likely to push and trigger surrounding people's buttons and emotional hotspots (including one's own relational and developmental trauma). This is heightened when these traumas and losses remain unresolved, raw, and unprocessed. For example, when the hotspots of a "caregiver" (this refers to all of us) are pushed, they too can become dysregulated, re-triggered, preoccupied, and/or absorbed in their own trauma and own loss experiences. They too can go into fight, flight, or freeze survival mode and can have their attachment/relational history rather than their caregiving/parenting mode activated. In those moments, when lost in a sea of emotions, feeling full up, running on empty, or having fallen through a "timehole" (Hobday, 2001), caregivers may struggle to read, connect, and respond appropriately to their children's emotional states. They are more likely to, for example, be hyper-vigilant, overreact, respond disproportionately, feel threatened, feel criticised, and/or to interpret and read into things more negatively and as a personal attack.

This can be a significant block to being able to parent mindfully, and can expand situations and feelings, and create further barriers to connecting and strengthening parent–child relationships rather than defusing them. Therefore, it feels crucial to support caregivers/therapists/surrounding adults to recognise which patterns are being evoked or triggered, sucking them in like quicksand, or overwhelming them like an emotional avalanche. After all, one of the greatest ways to teach and support children to learn about how to express and regulate their emotions (see Chapter 4) is through them watching and observing how their surrounding adults identify, process, and respond to their own emotions. Additionally, it becomes increasingly difficult for parents to tune in to their children's emotions, thoughts, and sensations; or to support them to learn how to tune in, if they themselves are not able to tune in to their own emotions, thoughts, and sensations. Please see Chapter 7 for more strategies and activities around self-care and caring for the carer.

With this in mind, it is important, although difficult, for surrounding adults to, as much as possible, exercise and model positive emotional regulation skills themselves (to respond rather than react), to stay grounded and centred, and to operate in their thinking brains. This, in a simple phrase, is: "Being mindful, instead of mind full." This thinking and regulated position communicates to the child that they are in safe hands, thinking minds, and regulating bodies, and supports them to organise and put words to their feelings, rather than being caught up in their caregiver's feelings or in a mutually escalating arousal situation (e.g. anger being met with anger or a tug-of-war power battle). Therefore, it is hoped that this parenting position will reduce parent–child conflict situations and power battles, and increase positive parent–child interactions, whilst also teaching and showing children a different way of being and doing relationships. It is also anticipated that parenting mindfully will make it more likely that actions, such as discipline and consequences, will be implemented as more rational, thought-out, and logical learning opportunities, rather than being disproportionate, emotionally driven, and/or coming from a place of punishment/anger/fear.

Box 6.3 **Reflective exercise staying regulated and response styles during conflict**

These questions can be applied in relation to yourself or a caregiver, teacher, etc. For simplicity, and in line with the target audience of this chapter, the term "caregiver" is used. They are just starting-point questions and can be adapted and expanded on depending on the situation and relationship.

How does a caregiver respond when they are in a conflict situation with their child (consider fight, flight, or freeze coping strategies, their body language, sensations, voice tone, words, and behaviours)? How able are they to stay regulated and mindful in the moment/after the event/in retrospect?

Is this a patterned and common way of responding, or is this a representation of them at their worst and when feeling depleted? How do they respond when they are in their best place? What factors, triggers, and emotional hotspots might contribute to these different responses? Are they able, with support, to reflect on the difference between acting from a place of anger/fear/being emotionally driven compared with being in a calm and thinking place? What do they know about the importance of, and rationale behind, staying regulated?

How would they like their child to be able to respond in a time of conflict/threat to them/with others/at school? How similar or different is this to their actual way of responding to conflict? How does this marry up with how, as a caregiver, they respond to their child during a conflict situation?

What was their own experience as a child of having their emotions managed and regulated? (See Worksheet 6.2 for expanding on these experiences.) How did their own caregivers respond to conflict/stay regulated? What skills and support might they need to be able to stay regulated for more of the time?

If they are able to stay regulated most of the time, where did these skills come from? What skills, strengths, knowledge, resiliencies, and abilities help them to do this, despite all they are facing?

Acknowledging, naming, and validating emotions and lived experiences

A key part of strengthening parent–child relationships, and of increasing relational connections, is for parents to be able to identify, name, validate, make links with, and acknowledge their child's wide range of feelings (without overwhelming or flooding them) and to offer them connection, reflection, empathy, and understanding around these emotions, rather than telling them what to do or how to feel (see Chapters 4 and 8). This includes supporting the child to be able to co-regulate so that they can eventually self-regulate using active whole-brain-body listening (see Worksheet 6.3) and really showing the child that what they say is important and is heard. Daniel Siegel helpfully terms this strategy of identifying and labelling feelings as "naming it to tame it" (Siegel and Bryson, 2011). This can involve parents taking the role of being a feelings detective, where they decipher and decode messages and try to see children's behaviours as forms of communication, clues, and as a map to the child's inner world.

Within the importance of meeting the child where they are at and seeing the behaviours as communication, Daniel Hughes (2011) speaks of the powerful parenting strategy of "connecting before correcting". This parenting position is also crucial in being able to take perspective, see the world through the child's eyes, and honour their lived experience (in the context of relational and developmental trauma, this is often something that has not been done as much as for other children). These perspective-taking and reflective function skills (which are interlinked with being able to stay regulated) are important in helping the development and strengthening of the child's sense of mind, identity, and own reflective self. This also fits with the importance of seeing that the child is a separate, valued individual with their own thoughts, choices, and feelings, rather than minimising their needs and/or positioning them as an extension of their parent (see the case examples illustrating this in Chapter 4).

Viewing behaviour as a form of communication and as being within a context

This section builds on the above skills of staying regulated, identifying feelings, and seeing the world through the child's eyes (perspective-taking and connection before correction – Hughes, 2011). Therapeutic re-parents also need to be able to use their reflective function and detective skills to recognise, deconstruct, respond, and respect the emotional needs underlying their child's behaviours, survival strategies, and/or defences (see Worksheet 6.1 for some creative representations on common defences and survival strategies). This looking-beyond-the-layers-to-a-deeper-level technique is often likened to an iceberg, where one can just see the tip and the surface levels of the iceberg; however, all of the other hidden layers and levels are underneath. Similarly, this can also be likened to a set of Russian dolls, where we see the outer layer but can be unaware of all of the other smaller dolls that are within the larger one.

Therefore, carers should be supported to view their child's behaviour as multi-layered and as being within and part of a broader context and to see the child (who is often hurt and vulnerable) behind the behaviour and beyond the survival modes/defences. This has the intention of supporting caregivers to try to stick with their caring part and to try to decipher what function the behaviour might be serving, what story it might be telling, and what it might be communicating. This process of connecting the dots can also support caregivers to see the behaviours as windows into the child's inner world and to keep the child's mind in mind.

This is an important part of being a thinking mind – making sense of the behaviours and disentangling and organising them rather than simply taking them at face value or conceptualising them in black-and-white terms. It is striking that behaviours are powerful, can get under people's skin, and can trigger a range of difficult feelings, sensations, memories, and thoughts. The complexity and dynamics within behaviours are further contributed to by the experiences, history, meaning-making, and attributions of the person who is receiving the behaviours. These behaviours will be conceptualised, interpreted, and responded to differently depending on the lens that they are viewed through. Examples are given below.

Consider a foster carer whose foster child refuses to eat. Now bring into the mix the foster carer's possible: history of having an eating disorder; belief that food is the vehicle for giving love; experience of being raised in a war-torn country where food was limited.

Consider a birth mother whose eight-year-old child repeatedly kicks and hits her. Now bring into the melting pot the birth mother's possible: history herself of harsh punishment; experience of domestic violence and feeling attacked, targeted, and powerless by the child's father; years of struggling to get pregnant and of having multiple miscarriages.

Box 6.4 contains some recommended questions and reflective exercises around thinking in more detail about behaviour as a form of communication. Examples of looking beyond the surface are sprinkled throughout this entire book.

Box 6.4 **Practical activity and reflection behaviour as communication**

1. Think about a child/parent who is presenting with a behaviour you would like to understand in more depth. What are the behaviour patterns/triggers/hotspots? What fuels, amplifies, changes, and calms it? What is the history of the behaviour, and how and why might it have developed?

2. What function/meaning/purpose might the behaviour be having for the child/parent/their relationships? What might be the meaning and intention of the behaviour? What might the child/parent be communicating and why? What is the story behind the behaviour and underneath the surface? If we think about a painting, we often only see the "finished" product, but what are all the different colours, layers, techniques within it? What different interpretations and feelings does the behaviour evoke in different people? What clue does the way we feel when we are at the receiving end of this behaviour give us about the child's/parent's/colleague's feelings?

3. If the behaviour could talk or had a voice, what would it say? If the behaviour was a puzzle, what pieces would it be made up of, and what picture would it form when put together? If the behaviour was a map, where would it have started from, what direction does it travel in, and where might it be heading?

4. How does knowing a bit more about what the behaviour might be communicating shape your feelings/thoughts about the child/parent and the behaviour? How does the behaviour change when viewed from a different angle? How might this impact on your way of responding and supporting the behavioural and relational change?

5. Is there a particular behaviour/difficulty that really pushes your buttons or gets under your skin? What is your relationship to that difficulty/theme? What values are being challenged by the presenting behaviour? What is being triggered in you? (See Chapter 7.)

6. What are some of your own emotional, cognitive, sensory, and physical responses to the behaviour/difficulty/person/situation? Which of your own stories, values, and experiences are influencing you? How are these interacting with your meaning-making, conceptualisation, and responses to the behaviour/situation/person?

Developmentally sequenced parenting

Therapeutic re-parents will also require knowledge around child development and an enhanced awareness of the potential impact that trauma and disrupted attachments can have on children's developmental skills, stages, and competencies (see Box 6.5). This includes understanding and connecting with the child's social, developmental, and emotional age versus their chronological age and how this can change and move depending on certain factors, including triggers and perceived threat. (For more information, please refer to the "Parenting Patchwork Exercise" in Chapter 1 of *Working with Relational and Developmental Trauma in Children and Adolescents* (Treisman, 2016).) Examples are given below.

Six-year-old Kacey was relatively settled in her foster placement. However, when her foster carer became pregnant, Kacey appeared to regress and requested that she was dressed, held, and fed by her foster carers.

Milo's adoptive parents described how they often felt as if they were around a four-year-old. Ten-year-old Milo's attention span was short-lived, he struggled with any form of separation from his adoptive mother, and he had to be supervised constantly to ensure that he was safe.

Nineteen-year-old Kayla became weepy when she got a small scratch and said that she wanted a magic kiss and a special plaster.

On the other end of the spectrum, as a "parentified" child, five-year-old Jax felt responsible for his younger sister. Once placed in foster care, he would continue to take it upon himself to bath and feed her and found it difficult to share these duties or pass them over to his carers.

Understanding the differing ages and stages that a child presents with has important implications for ensuring that expectations are developmentally appropriate and that caregivers and other surrounding adults can meet the child where they are at. This includes the ability to be able to scaffold the child's learning, find their zone of proximal development, maximise their opportunities for success, and find a balance between autonomy and dependence.

Within this, a key and ever-changing component of parenting is seeing that different skills are required at different stages of the child's development. For example, a new-born baby will require different skills from their parents to a toddler, adolescent, and so forth.

Box 6.5 **Practical activity and reflection social, emotional, and developmental age/stage/skill versus chronological age/stage/skill**

Some questions to consider are listed below. (The example of "caregiver" is used; however, these questions can be applied to any surrounding adult.)

How aware is the caregiver of the developmental stages of childhood and of what is required and expected at the different stages? Are they aware of what skills, parenting qualities, and experiences do children need for optimal development?

How aware is the caregiver of the impact of relational and developmental trauma and toxic stress on child development and on their specific child?

Reflecting on their early experiences, what key developmental opportunities, skills, and experiences did the child miss out on?

What factors, situations, and triggers have been observed to create a "different age" response for the child?

How do the caregiver's expectations and goals fit with the child's social, emotional, and developmental age and stage compared with their chronological age and stage? (For information about SMART goals, see Chapter 5.)

Is there a particular stage of parenting that the caregiver feels most confident in, finds most difficult, enjoys, etc.?

Whole-brain-body approach

Considering the sensory and body-based impact and disintegration of relational and developmental trauma, and trauma being a whole-body, whole-brain experience, it is vital that this is matched by attachment-facilitating parents promoting a whole-brain, head, hand, and heart approach. This multifaceted, sensory approach contributes to making integral connections between the mind and body, hemispheres and functions of the brain, internal and external experience, and thoughts, feelings, and physical sensations. This also allows for consideration of the child's age/stage, different learning/communication styles, and possible cognitive difficulties, which are more common within this client group.

For instance, caregivers should aim to bring concepts, rules, feelings, and desired behaviours alive by communicating them verbally and non-verbally using an array of senses, such as through kinaesthetic (role-plays, games, physical movement, and cooking), auditory (discussions, music, and stories), and visual (worksheets, diagrams, and pictures) means. They need to think on a wider level than simply using words.

When one is communicating or conveying a concept, expectation, goal, hope, or rule, how much is this based on talking and left-brain dominance? Are there ways to embed this further by taking a multi-sensory, creative, and whole-brain approach? Similarly, how can a child be supported to respond to their feelings and to regulate their emotions and behaviours through multi-layered, multi-sensory, creative, and whole-brain approaches?

Examples of using creative and expressive means are peppered throughout this book, however, a couple of specific examples follow.

When explaining the concept of a safe place to a child, one might embed this through a range of creative ways (see Chapter 3 for examples of some of these techniques), including:

- drawing the safe place

- making a sculpture, collage, or sand tray representation of the safe place

- writing a song, poem, story, or rap about the safe place

- recording the story of the safe place

- choosing a smell or cooking a meal associated with the safe place

- physically moving, role-playing entering, and being in the safe place (for more information see Chapter 3).

When conveying the house rules, one might:

- discuss the house rules

- think of a fun name for them, such as "peacemakers and peace breakers"

- make a rules poster or a piece of art

- role-play the different rules

- draw or collage the rules

- find a way to agree the rules, such as using handprints or making a special handshake.

Consistent and predictable parenting

The majority of the time, children should have a general sense of how their caregivers will respond to a range of situations/feelings and what they are likely to do. This extends to knowing that the caregiver will be there for them physically and emotionally, that they will be a reliable and available presence in their life, and that they have strong sticking power. This feels even more important in the context of trauma, where so many children will have experienced inconsistency, unavailability, unpredictability, chaos, and broken promises from surrounding adults. Within this, it is vital that parents do what they say and implement strategies in a consistent, logical, and fair way whilst having clear and predictable rules, routines, and structure (see Chapter 8).

Picking battles and setting limits

To optimise parent–child relationships, it is helpful to focus on reducing conflict and for caregivers to pick their battles wisely and carefully. It can be exhausting, draining, and depleting to live continuously in a battlefield and for one's home to feel like a warzone or an ice block. Moreover, this only continues to push caregivers/ children into survival mode and for unhealthy relational patterns to be further reinforced. Therefore, although it is a complex area, it feels important to focus on what battles can be reduced, avoided, or given less weight (see Box 6.6 and Chapter 8) and which are pressing and need to be prioritised and addressed.

This might include, alongside many other strategies, setting limits but also offering alternatives and telling children what they can do instead of what they can't do. This also fits with the "connection before correction" (Hughes, 2011) concept. Some examples are given below.

When Lace goes to paint on the wall with her brushes, her attachment-friendly teacher says, "I'm sorry, I know you want to paint on the walls, I can see why but walls are not for painting – canvases are though. Why don't we put up a big canvas or a white board and then you can paint on those?"

Sloane really wanted to go to the park, but instead of her dad simply saying "No", which previously had escalated into outbursts and arguments, he said, "I know you love the park, and really want to go to the park, and I'm sorry because I want to take you, but it is getting dark and almost bedtime, and the night fairies are waiting for you, but let's eat earlier tomorrow and then we can go to the park then. How about today we read…"

It is important to hold in mind that parenting tasks such as implementing boundaries, setting limits, and so forth will mean different things to different caregivers, depending on their own experiences, values, and relationships. Some possible questions to consider around this are given here. *What are the caregiver's values, beliefs, attitudes around, for example, rearing, discipline, boundaries, limit-setting? Where did these develop from, what is their history with them, and how have they since been reinforced? How does the caregiver feel when these are questioned or in conflict with someone else's values, beliefs, attitudes? Are there any blocks or barriers making certain strategies more difficult to implement safely and consistently? If so, what are these, and what is the caregiver's relationship to them?*

These parenting experiences, values, scripts, and beliefs are important to acknowledge, respect, explore, and reflect on, as they can create barriers to implementing strategies safely and being able to deliver them in a confident and efficacious way. Parents need to believe in the strategies, or in the underlying rationale for them, and feel confident and efficacious in consistently implementing them (examples of common barriers and beliefs which need to be reflected on include: "She's been through too much, I just can't say no", "I want her to like me", "My step-father was so strict and militant. I hated him, so I will never be anything like him", "I was hit when I was naughty, and it didn't do me any harm").

Box 6.6 **Practical activity and reflection picking one's battles**

What does the conflict/distance with your child feel like emotionally, physically, and cognitively? (Draw, sculpt, collage, or externalise your responses.)

What does the conflict/distance do to the nature and quality of the relationship?

If the conflict was externalised as an item/thing/creature/type of weather, what would it be/look like/sound like/say? (See Worksheet 6.4 to expand on these ideas.)

How is the relationship different when there is a sense of calm/fun/understanding? How can these times be celebrated and expanded on?

Could any of the battles be lessened? Will the point of contention matter in a month, in a year, or in five years?

Is the parenting response to the presenting difficulty proportionate? If not, why? What is that caregiver responding to or fighting for? Why is that issue getting under their skin? What is their relationship to that theme? (See Box 6.4.)

Is there another tactic that could be used to avoid escalation and to minimise conflict?

Warm, playful, and nurturing parenting

Throughout the literature, being able to express warmth, affection, and love has been associated with closer parent–child relationships (Zeanah, Berlin, and Boris, 2011). In the context of relational and developmental trauma, many children will have experienced more power, fear, and conditional and control-based relational interactions; therefore they need reparative relationships that are kind, authentic, warm, nurturing, and affectionate. Positive, playful interactions also stimulate the production of chemicals such as dopamine and opioids (the feel-good chemicals) (Panksepp, 2004). Nurturing parenting may show itself in many forms, ranging from holding, feeding, tickling, laughing, and pampering, to paying special attention to any hurts. Some examples are given below.

Each time Andrea hurt herself, Janice would give her a getting-better ritual, which included three big breaths, three kisses, three puffs of magic dust, some healing cream, and a special plaster.

Brendan found touch and intimacy difficult and re-triggering, so we made him a blanket of love and a doodle bear filled with loving messages.

Patrick brought in a slug from the garden. Instead of saying "Get that dirty thing out now!" his adoptive mother said, "Oh my goodness, look at that. What is the slug's name?" Patrick answered, "Mr Slimy." So, setting limits but being mindful of Patrick's perspective and of the power of playful parenting, Janice said, "Great name – shall we go and play outside with Mr Slimy? That's where slugs are happiest – they need to live outdoors near the ground and the trees. They don't like being inside houses. After that, maybe we could draw a picture of Mr Slimy and take some photos of him. How does that sound?"

Catherine found getting dressed in the morning difficult and often would be late for school because of this. So, with support, her foster carer made and recorded her a fun song about getting dressed in the morning, which, in a playful rhythmic way, went through all the different steps and stages of getting dressed.

Similarly, the ability to be humorous, fun, and child-centred (this is called playful parenting) is key for diffusing power battles, pushing on parents' and children's reward buttons, and increasing positive parent–child interactions. This can be anything from making a treasure hunt to going on a camping adventure in the garden, having a race to the bus stop, playing I spy in the car, making faces with food, making mundane routines into games, playing supermarket sweep, and so on.

Spending quality time together

Caregivers need to find ways to get to know and communicate, spend quality time, and connect with their children as valued, unique individuals and to make space for and maximise times where they can experience mutual enjoyment, reciprocal exchanges, and have both of their reward buttons pushed. This might include trying to find common interests with their child/ren and the time to do something together. Chapter 5 contains some suggested activities and more discussion around this.

Really getting to know each other

Building on the above, the notion of seeing each child as a valued, unique individual includes aiming to see, accept, tolerate, and appreciate all of the child's different parts, like the different layers of Russian dolls, patches in a patchwork, strokes in a painting, or pieces in a puzzle. This is particularly important given that many of these children have low self-esteem and a toxic sense of shame, self-loathing, and humiliation (e.g. "I'm a mistake" and "I'm unlovable") and because many children will not have had opportunities to identify, build, and celebrate their identities and life stories. See Chapters 2 and 5 for various strategies that support this getting-to-know-the-child process and magnifying their strengths.

It also feels important to make connections and links and share stories with children. I have worked with many families who rarely speak about their own lives or own experiences. Often, this is because it has been clouded by their own trauma and/or because they didn't have someone who shared stories and named feelings with them. Generally, children enjoy hearing stories (in an age-appropriate way) about their parent's first day in school or their birth story or funny stories of what they got up to when they were younger. Using stories to strengthen parent–child relationships can also be enhanced by narrative-based therapies such as: Narrative Therapy, Bibliotherapy, Attachment Narrative Therapy, and Family Attachment Narrative Therapy.

Normalising and owning mistakes

It feels crucial, particularly in a context where children have often learned that mistakes have catastrophic consequences and for children who have high levels of shame and toxic stress, to acknowledge that mistakes do happen and that they are a normal and expected part of life and can be moved on from. This includes the surrounding adults owning, acknowledging, naming, and apologising for their mistakes if they make them. This is in line with rupture-repair principles. This can be a difficult skill or action to take for some people, so it is useful to reflect a bit more on one's relationship to mistakes or apologising (see Box 6.7).

Box 6.7 Practical activity and reflection apologising, mistakes, and relational repair

Some possible lines of enquiry include the following questions. How easy or difficult is it to own mistakes and/or to apologise? What factors, values, or beliefs make this easier or more difficult?

What are one's beliefs and values around saying sorry to a child or around owning one's mistakes? What might be one's fear around saying sorry or admitting one's mistakes?

How are/were mistakes or errors responded to? How is this similar or different to one's experience of making mistakes or receiving or giving apologies as a child?

What do caregivers want their children to learn about making mistakes or what making mistakes means about them as a person?

What is the caregiver's/child's relationship to change?

Keeping the young person in mind and showing them that they have been kept in mind

Where possible, show the child that they are important and have actively been kept in mind (e.g. having daily check ins, remembering things that they said to you, being their memory bank, noticing when they are absent, making an intentional effort to see things from their perspective or through their eyes, being attuned and sensitive to their signals and cues, and naming, labelling, and responding to their feelings, etc.).

There are also some lovely symbols and items that can convey some powerful messages, such as giving a child some string or a golden thread to represent that you are always connected and tied together; giving them a mini brain to convey the message that "you are always on my mind"; writing loving post-it notes and putting them in the child's school box/sticking them on their mirror; and sending them a "hug" or "positive vibes" in the post (see Chapters 9 and 10 for additional ideas around this).

Providing opportunities for mastery and agency

It is important to find ways to show the child that they can effect and be an agent of change, and their opinion is important, listened to, and valued. Many children in the context of trauma will have often been in situations where they felt powerless and out of control, so this is very important. Their voice will probably have been silenced, misinterpreted, or minimised, and they may have been left with a sense of things being done to them. Therefore, supporting children to have a sense of autonomy (at a level that is right for them as an individual) and to be in the driving seat of their own car and the author of their own story can be transformative.

This sense of mastery and agency can be worked towards in a variety of ways, including day-to-day things like asking what they would like for dinner, engaging in child-led play, getting them to come up with their own solutions to an identified problem, validating and respecting them when there is a difference of opinion, getting them to teach you something that they know about, being the leader in follow-the-leader games, and involvement in larger things, such as fundraising, social action, and/or youth-led projects. This can filter down to showing the child that you trust them by giving them some age-appropriate responsibility (this needs to be selected according to their social and emotional age/stage/skills rather than their chronological age/stage/skills).

Strengths, resiliency, and hope

Carers should provide children with high levels of hope, future-oriented thinking, encouragement, and praise. The following messages, in line with holding children in unconditional positive regard (Rogers, 1961), are important to convey explicitly and implicitly: "I will believe in you, even if you don't believe in yourself", "I see the best in you", "I want the best for you", "I will be there with you", "We are in this together", and "I am rooting for you". This also means maximising opportunities for children's success and cultivating their positive affect, strengths, and resiliencies. These sparkle moments, mutual joy, and positive connections are fundamental for both parents and children to experience reciprocal, meaningfully connected relationships and to fill their and their children's treasure boxes up with positive relational experiences and memories. The fuller this treasure box is, the more it can be anchored to when the child is feeling depleted. This also aims to power up the child and carer's positive magnets and to push their reward system buttons. Caregivers need to identify and magnify what keeps them going and what parenting rewards and gifts they receive. This is especially useful when in problem-saturated and/or crisis situations. The following sections will offer some strengths-based ideas (also see Chapter 5 for a range of ideas and strategies for celebrating, noticing, and building on children's strengths and Chapter 7 for ideas around self-care and caring for the carer).

Box 6.8 **Practical activity and reflection type of parent and relationship**

How do you want your child to talk about you/to describe you/to remember you/to write about you – now, as an adult, or when you die?

What do you want them to learn from you? What do you want them to do/have and how do you want them to be similar or different to you? (See Worksheets 6.2 and 6.4 for additional exercises around this.)

What type of parent/partner do you want to teach them to be when they grow up?

Practical and creative strategies for building and improving parent–child relationships

Please note that these should be used in line with Chapter 1 and the underpinning frameworks, strategies, and positions described in the previous sections of this chapter. They also go hand-in-hand with the strategies described in Chapters 3, 4, and 5.

Magnifying positives and being strengths-focused

It feels important to notice, celebrate, and build on the child's unique qualities and positive attributes, as well as the strengths of the actual parent–child relationship. In order to have the energy and motivation to invest and to hold the hope, a priority needs to be made around finding ways for caregivers' and children's reward buttons to be pushed and for their emotional, physical, and spiritual tanks to be refuelled (see Chapter 7 for some specific ideas on prioritising and supporting one's self-care). The strengths-based strategies in Chapter 5 can be adapted and applied to these aims. Some other ideas around enhancing the strengths within the parent–child relationship are listed below.

- Using positive video clips and photos of the child–caregiver interactions, and incorporating feedback of the relational exchanges.

- Supporting caregivers and children to keep/make a sparkle moments diary or fill a jar or a treasure box with cherished relational memories/moments/photos (see Photos 6.1–6.3).

Photo 6.1 Special moments and memory box

Photo 6.2 Relational treasure box

Photo 6.3 Sparkle moments diary

- Making a family collage/scrapbook/photo album of memorable and happy times.

- Creatively displaying the strengths and positive memories in the relationship through activities such as making a patchwork of relational positives (see Photo 6.4), tower of relational strengths (see Photo 6.5), skyscraper of strengths, shield of strengths, pillow of positives, quilt of qualities, rainbow of resources, puzzle of positives, and/or star of strengths (see Chapter 5 for an explanation and examples of using these tools for the individual, which can be adapted to illustrate the strengths of the relationship).

Photo 6.4 Patchwork of relational positives

Photo 6.5 Tower of relational strengths

- Finding creative ways of depicting various relational moments and positive relational qualities and attributes, such as: in a chocolate box (see Photo 6.6) or in a picture of, or wrapped up as actual, gifts/presents (see Worksheet 5.8). An example is given below.

Fifteen-year-old Jayda gave her mother a box of chocolates, but she removed the chocolates and wrote messages about each of the things she loved about her mother instead. (This could have been done on stars (see Photo 6.7), shells, hearts, pearls, beads, etc.)

Photo 6.6 A chocolate box of strengths

Photo 6.7 Stars of relational strengths

- These strengths and appreciated parts can also be written down in alphabet form (see Photo 6.8).

For example, Nate and his foster carer made an alphabet list of all of the things they appreciated about each other, such as "A" for "Artistic", "B" for "Great at baking", "C" for "Caring", and so on.

Photo 6.8 An alphabet list of appreciated parts of another

- Making a picture or a sculpt of a positive parent–child relationship moment and/or of doing something/an activity together. These relational treasure moments might also be enhanced by reflecting on the moments that the caregiver/child wants to keep and preserve in a time capsule (see Photo 6.9) or wants to keep safe and bottled up (see Worksheets 6.7 and 6.8 for templates). Examples are given below.

Carla and Trisha chose the time they went horse riding together on the beach whilst they were on holiday as a special memory of their time together. They were supported to tell stories about this time and to connect with the sounds, smells, images, and feelings that were associated with that moment and then guided to make a creative representation of this memory.

Gilly and Tom said they were at their best and enjoyed each other when they were baking, as they both enjoyed this activity and would do it whilst listening to music. They too were encouraged to reflect and magnify this moment and then to think about how they could bring more baking, and the feeling that bakery facilitated, into their lives and how they could make a visual reminder of this time. They chose to decorate aprons for each other and to take a series of photos of them baking, which were placed on the family fridge.

Photo 6.9 Time capsule of memories and special moments

- Celebrating positive moments, such as birthdays, a positive day in school, and festivities (it is acknowledged that these times can also trigger autobiographical memories, so they need to be planned and thought about carefully).

Building on the above aim of identifying, magnifying, expanding on, and celebrating each other's appreciated, liked, and admired parts (see Photo 6.10), it can be helpful to reflect on and explore the following questions taken from the take-back practice letter format (see Worksheet 6.10). Some options for different ways to thicken and creatively embed these responses will be discussed afterwards.

If you were stranded on a desert island, what would you appreciate about…? If you woke up, and that person was no longer there, or had disappeared, what would you miss about them? If you were writing a review or recommendation about this person, what positive things would you say to others about them? If you had to give them an award for something positive, what would it be for? Can you think of one time or moment where you enjoyed each other – what was this and what did it look like, feel like, and mean to you?

These responses will, ideally, be discussed for all parties and from each other's perspective to emphasise the reciprocal nature of relationships. The responses can then be creatively extended by writing, collaging, sculpting, or drawing them, for example a collage, sculpt, or drawing of: "My mum's best parts", "My dad at his best", "Twenty reasons why I love you" (see Photo 6.11), "The things I would miss if my grandma was no longer in my life", or "I love/appreciate my foster carer, because…".

The responses can also be added to previously mentioned strategies, such as a sparkle moments diary, or be used to fill a treasure box. They can also be recorded as a voice recording or filmed to be played back at different times, or they can be transformed into a written letter/card/book. These concepts can also be extended by supporting children/caregivers to write a letter to their "best part" of the other person, for example to their eyes, loyalty, resilience, etc. Some examples of creatively expanding on family members' best parts are given below.

Despite there being a high level of conflict within the family, after some explorative questions, Layla was able to identify that she appreciated her foster mother's eyes, heart, and confidence, her foster father's sense of humour, organisation skills, and enthusiasm, her foster brother's goofiness, ability to do maths, and patience, and her dog's energy and playfulness. She then went on to draw a "person" that combined all of these positive attributes (see Photo 6.10) and was supported to have discussions that enhanced these qualities, as well as thinking what parts she appreciated about herself and what parts other members of her family appreciated about her.

Ali identified that his favourite part of his foster carer was her passion, so he was supported to write a letter to that part of her, i.e. "Dear Passion". He went on to write about when "Passion" visited, what influence and effect "Passion" had, what it felt like when "Passion" was not there, and so forth.

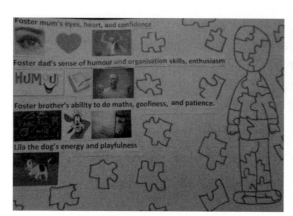

Photo 6.10 Parts of the family I appreciate

Photo 6.11 Twenty reasons why I love you poster

Solution-focused ideas and expanding on the unique exceptions

In line with taking a strengths-focused framework, and as discussed in more detail in Chapter 5, it can be helpful to use the solution-focused miracle question to re-story some of the difficulties, shift away from being purely problem-saturated, and bring some different threads and underrepresented stories into the situation/relationship. There are lots of variations of asking the solution-focused miracle question (De Shazer, 2012), but some examples include: *If you woke up tomorrow and a miracle had happened and the main difficulties within your relationship had disappeared, what would be different about the way you both act, feel, and think? Walk me through what your day would look like after the main difficulties within your relationship had vanished or significantly reduced.*

These questions and discussions can be extended through drawing or visually representing their responses, such as through depicting them in a collage, sand tray, or sculpt, for example a "difficulty-free day" (see Photo 6.12) or drawing a dual picture of "us battling the…" and "us having conquered the…".

Photo 6.12 A difficulty-free day together as a family battling the violence

This can also be worked towards by using Narrative Therapy techniques, such as identifying the unique exceptions (e.g. times when children/parents have overcome a particular difficulty or when the difficulty was absent, less noticeable, or less stressful). For example, if in a session a parent describes the difficult experiences that she has during the morning school run, after hearing, listening to, and empathising with the difficulty and getting a strong sense of what the difficulty is, one might explore and thicken the unique exception by asking questions such as: *What would the school run look like if it didn't end in screaming and shouting? Can you tell me about a time when the school run was calm/fun/ran smoothly? How did you manage to not let the school run turn to "chaos" on that day? Where and with whom is the "chaos" on the school run least likely to appear? What did that calm school run feel like/look like/achieve/lead to? What would the ideal school run be like/feel/look like? What difference would that make to your life, to you as a person, and to your relationship with your child?*

These responses should be thickened and creatively represented to embed the concepts further. For example, children and parents may be encouraged to show in a sand tray, drawing, or sculpt what their life would be like without, for example, the stressful school run. Once these have been identified, discussions can be had around what factors and work are needed to feed, water, build on, strengthen, and improve the parent–child relationship. This can be discussed in different ways, including using the metaphor of feeding, watering, and looking after a flower/garden (see Photo 6.13) or of building a strong and sturdy relationship tower (see Worksheet 6.11).

Photo 6.13 Ways to look after the relationship garden/flower

Reflecting on what a positive relationship is, exploring each other's meaning-making around relationships, and using inspirational quotes

It can be helpful to reflect with parents/children on what a "good", "positive", and "healthy" relationship looks like/is/feels like, particularly as many children/parents will have experienced a range of negative and challenging relational styles, templates, and maps. This can also be extended to discussing and exploring what each other thinks it means to be, for example, a "good daughter" or a "good mother". This is a helpful way of understanding different people's perspectives, wishes, opinions, values, and relational experiences/templates. This also gives a starting point to identify and acknowledge similarities and differences, as well as opening up an opportunity to create some mutual goals (Worksheets 6.4–6.6 and 6.9 can help these discussions). It can also be helpful to consider where they have seen a "good relationship" (e.g. getting them to describe a specific example of a good relationship and define what specific ingredients and attributes they feel this relationship has) and exploring what benefits they think there are of being in a "good" relationship. These concepts of a "good father", "close relationship", or "healthy relationship" can be expanded on further creatively, for example by depicting this type of relationship in a sand tray, through collage, or in a sculpt using miniature figurines.

It can also be useful to draw on and explore some positive relational quotes and sayings (ideally the child will select their own, but it can be helpful to have a selection to choose from). Examples include: "A snowflake is one of the most fragile creations, but look what it can become when it sticks together with other snowflakes" (Vista M. Kelly), "Sticks in a bundle cannot be broken" (African proverb), "I can do things that you can't, and you can do things that I can't, so together we can do great things" (Mother Teresa), or "Individually we are one drop, but together we are a whole ocean" (Ryunosuke Satoro).

Can you think of any other inspirational quotes about togetherness or relationships? How could these be expanded on, connected with, drawn on, creatively embedded, and visually represented? (See Photo 6.14.)

Photo 6.14 A visual representation of a relational quote: "No relationship is all sunshine, but two people can share one umbrella, and survive the storm" (Unknown)

Understanding the roots and the feeders of some relationship difficulties

Building on the above notion of defining what a positive, healthy relationship is, it is also important, in the context of a safe, therapeutic relationship, to reflect on and explore one's own history and relationship with relationships and connections. This can be explored in numerous ways; some of the following questions may be a helpful guide.

In the context of "their" experiences and history, why might relationships be more difficult for the child/caregiver? What have "their" relational experiences, styles, maps, and templates been? What fears, expectations, assumptions, and hopes might "they" have around relationships as a result of these experiences? What might relationships and connections represent and mean to them? What might they have learned about relationships, trust, closeness, and intimacy?

Following this, it can also be helpful to reflect together on what it looks/feels like when they are "at their relationship best" and when they are "at their relationship worst" or what their "relationship peaks and pits" are. These can be usefully sculpted, drawn, collaged, or written about and then placed beside each other to reflect on the differences, similarities, themes, and links between them (see Photos 6.15 and 6.16).

Photo 6.15 Our relationship at its best and at its worst sculpt

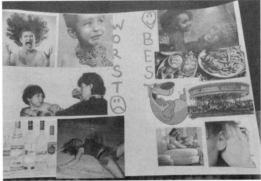

Photo 6.16 Our relationship at its best and at its worst collage

When discussing "us at our worst", it feels important also to reflect on what the consequences are of "the conflict", for example. This line of enquiry is built on further in Box 6.3 earlier. The questions below are examples.

What does "the conflict" feel like? What does "the conflict" do to the relationship? What does "the conflict" stop you from being able to do or keep you from doing? What makes "the conflict" bigger or smaller? What can you learn from "the conflict"? What have you learned from the times when you have been able to work through, overcome, or conquer "the conflict"? Sometimes "the conflict" can enhance connection – how might this happen? What does it say about both of you as people, and about your wishes, that you are both here fighting for your relationship and trying to find a solution?

These questions and responses can subsequently be expanded on by using the externalisation techniques discussed throughout the book and the questions presented on Worksheet 6.4. For example: If the conflict/closeness was an item, object, person, or thing, what would it be? I find that visually representing the "conflict/difficulties/barriers/blocks" can be helpful. Some examples are given below.

Rachel and her dad, Simon, labelled the conflict/alcoholism as being a "giant bottle of vodka". They were encouraged to draw the bottle between them and to reflect on the impact and influence of this (see Photo 6.17).

An adoptive mother, Hayley, and her adopted adolescent, Emily, spoke of "the wall" that separated them, so they were encouraged to use LEGO® to make their relationship wall and to reflect on what each brick represented, what the wall felt like, what the wall kept them from, when the wall had cracks in it, etc. Following this, Hayley and Emily were encouraged to draw/sculpt themselves next to each other, closer to each other with "the wall", and further apart, and to reflect on the emotional, relational, cognitive, and physical differences (see Photo 6.18).

Foster carer Debra spoke of how the conflict to her felt like "deathly silence, a closed door, and being able to cut the atmosphere with a knife" – whereas her foster child, Ace, likened it to a "loud constant sounding horn/bell". These metaphors were expanded on creatively and played with.

Step-father Callum described how he often felt stuck between "a rock and a hard place", and his step-daughter, Lizzie, described how she felt that within their relationship she was being "sucked by an emotional hoover". Callum was able to describe that when their relationship was at its best he felt that it was like "glue", and Lizzie described it as a "fairground". These metaphors were expanded on, creatively depicted, and explored further.

Residential worker Gloria described how she experienced the negativity and low mood of a resident, Andre, as a "negative magnet and negative bubble" and said that in response she could be taken over by anger, which she entitled "a red mist" (see Photo 6.19).

Photo 6.17 The vodka bottle between parent and child

Photo 6.18 The wall between parent and child

Photo 6.19 The conflict and red mist externalised

The journey of one's relationship

It feels important to reflect on and mark the journey and distance already travelled within the relationship, particularly in the context of lots of ups and downs, changes, conflicts, new beginnings, and so on. This should be done whilst making sure that there is both physical and metaphorical space for the future and that further development is left blank. Some ways that can be helpful to reflect on the journey, depending on the dyad/triad, include:

- a "then, now, and future" or a "dual portrait" picture, sculpt, sand-tray representation, or collage

- a visual path, road, track, board of snakes and ladders (see Photo 6.20), and/ or a fairground that marks the relational journey

- a story, poem, rap, or song of the relational journey

- a visual representation of some of the challenges and obstacles faced and overcome within the relationship, such as making or drawing these challenges as a maze, a labyrinth (see Photo 6.21), an obstacle course (see Photo 6.22), a jungle, or a rollercoaster

- making a sand tray, sculpt, or drawing of a representation of the journey.

The above ideas can be optimised by supporting the child/parent to think of a word, sentence, song, poem, or film to represent and describe their journey and then to represent this visually.

Photo 6.20 Snakes and ladders of the relationship

Photo 6.21 Labyrinth/maze of the relational journey

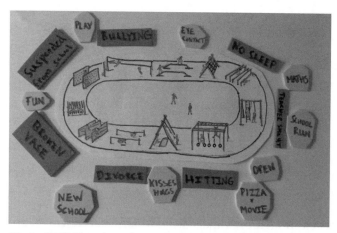

Photo 6.22 The obstacle course of the relationship

Reflecting on wishes and hopes for one's relationship

Building on the above, once the journey has been reflected on, the child/parent can be guided to think about where they hope their relationship will be in the future and what this might look like and feel like. This can be complemented by the solution-focused miracle question. This can also lead to positive conversations about what children's/parents' wishes, dreams, and hopes are, for example "My wish for myself is…" (see Photo 6.23), "My wish for my child/parent is…", and "My wish for our relationship is…" (see Worksheets 5.14, 5.15 and 6.9 for a range of interactive ideas around supporting these discussions).

The parent–child dyad/triad can then be supported to imagine themselves getting to those future relationship hopes and goals and can even draw or make a bridge or a magic gateway (see Photo 6.24) of them getting there.

Photo 6.23 Wishes for self

Photo 6.24 Magic gateway to goals, hopes, and a better tomorrow

Perspective-taking and role reversal

In a therapeutic context and a safe relationship it can be helpful to reflect with both the child and the parent/s on what the world may look like from each other's eyes.

This can be supported by "swapping seats", physical role-plays where the parent takes the role of being the child and vice versa, and/or using masks and puppets. Other ways of exploring what the other may be thinking in a tentative, curious way are through using the "head of thoughts and emotions" exercise from Chapter 4 or reflecting on what they think the other might answer to a series of questions/sentence-completion cards. Another supportive exercise around this is for each of them to have a disposable camera and to capture what their world looks like, or what the other's world may look like, and then to share observations and reflections. These, as with all of the strategies in this book, need to be informed by a thorough assessment and formulation and done with care, pacing, sensitivity, and reflection.

Sense of belonging and connectedness

It can be helpful to verbally and non-verbally support the child to feel that they are appreciated and that they belong and to do some tangible activities that support this. The activities are described in the context of a family, but they could be carefully applied to other communities, teams, groups, and so on. Activities might include:

- creating a family shield, badge, or crest

- drawing/making/sculpting a family portrait or having a family portrait photo taken

- making a family scene in sand

- making a family mural, family montage, shared picture, family patchwork, family tree, or family mosaic

- making a pillow, soft toy mascot, or blanket with photos of the family (see Photo 6.26)

- writing a story, rap, song, or poem about the family

- making a reciprocal family rules poster or canvas

- making a family door sign or designing a welcome door mat for the family house

- having designated seats at the meal table or labelling their items with the family name

- recording a joint family message on the answering phone

- making family home movies, a family album, or a family scrapbook

- everyone having the same item, such as a key ring, a badge, or a piece of jewellery

- making things together and for each other. This can create lots of positive memories and relational experiences whilst also having fun. Some options and ideas include: making jewellery for each other; making something out of pipe cleaners or other household/craft materials for each other to wear; painting a mug/cereal bowl for each other; drawing and decorating around each other's hand outlines; making handprints within each other's handprints (see Photo 6.25); making relational moulds (see Photo 6.29); drawing a portrait of each other; making a family tree; making a tree of everyone's hands (see Photo 6.27); making or decorating dolls of the family; making key rings of each other (see Photo 6.28); making different pieces of a puzzle that represent each other and the family putting the pieces together, etc.

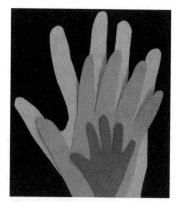

Photo 6.25 Family set of handprints

Photo 6.26 Cushion of family photos and memories

Photo 6.27 Family tree of hands

Photo 6.28 Key rings of each other

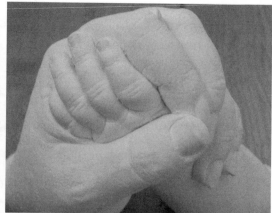

Photo 6.29 Relational moulds

Turn-taking, building trust, and safe ways of having agency

Games that support parents and children to take turns, listen to each other, and share feelings of control can be helpful, particularly in the context of trauma, where children will often have experienced power and fear-based interactions or have had to function predominantly in their survival brain (Chapter 3) and had less time and space to invest in other relational and social life skills, such as sharing. Due to previous experiences of feeling powerless, trapped, and out of control, and often living in unpredictable, ever-changing environments, the concept or feeling of relinquishing control or trusting others to hold that position may feel overwhelming or dangerous. Therefore, alongside working towards multi-levelled safety (see Chapter 3), children need to be supported in gentle, paced, and playful ways to begin experimenting with these concepts.

These skills might be worked towards through activities such as playing follow the leader or Simon Says (this might be through following the leader's physical movements, clapping or drumming sequences, or tongue-twister sentences or through the squiggle exercise in Chapter 2). This can also be done through making obstacle courses or mazes and/or giving directions to each other through special codes, such as directing a child to go to the left by looking to the left with one's eyes or when touching your nose to indicate they should turn right. This can also be enhanced through making treasure hunts where each person holds a different clue, so each member has to find ways of working and problem-solving together.

Other games that can also promote the concept of serve and return, and of reciprocal and turn-taking play, include activities such as: blowing bubbles or feathers back and forth to each other (see Photo 6.30); throwing a ball/beanbag/balloon back and forward; making hand towers; playing board games; and starting a story/picture and letting the child add to it (see Photo 6.31).

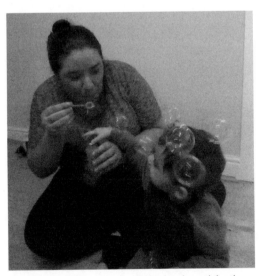

Photo 6.30 Blowing bubbles back and forth

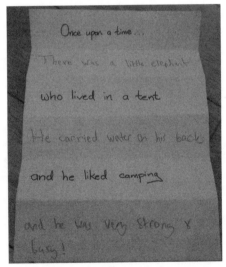

Photo 6.31 Completing a story together

Promoting safe and positive touch

The concept and extent of touch varies and needs to be thought about carefully, due to relationships, cultural factors, and children's previous experience of touch and how their bodies were treated. There are specific body-based and sensory-based therapies that focus on the body such as: Sensorimotor Psychotherapy, Sensory Motor Arousal Regulation Treatment, Sensory Attachment Intervention, Yoga-Based Therapy, and Theraplay (these are described in *Working with Relational and*

Developmental Trauma in Children and Adolescents – Treisman, 2016). However, it can be bonding to find different ways to show and encourage safe touching within the context of a positive relationship. This might be through activities such as dancing, hand palm dancing, massaging hands, painting each other's faces, finger painting, hand printing, tracing each other's hands, plaiting each other's hair, painting each other's nails, playing games such as Twister, making shapes on each other's backs, cooking or baking together, or playing games like "This little piggy", "Head, shoulders, knees, and toes", "Popping cheeks", or "Pat-a-cake".

Rituals and routines

As well as ensuring that there are clear, predictable, and consistent daily routines that are communicated implicitly and explicitly (see Chapter 8 for more on this), it is also enhancing for the parent–child relationship to create special rituals, in-house jokes, and/or routines. These can be a great way of marking and individualising the relationship whilst working towards a sense of familiarity and predictability. This could include having a special handshake, a regular special night such as movie night or pizza time, creating a unique type of kiss, or writing a joint song or quote that is said at particular times of the day such as when the child is being dropped off at school or going to bed.

Feeling Unsafe/Putting Up Defences

When I am feeling "unsafe" and need to protect myself I ...

Surround myself with barbed wire	Go into attack mode like a hungry shark	Go into my own protective bubble	Put on my bulletproof vest	Retreat into my tortoise shell
Make myself small/invisible	Hide away in the fog	Freeze on the spot	Whizz around like a dart	Paint on a smile like a clown
Put up my spikes like a hedgehog	Zoom away like a speeding car	Push people away like an opposing magnet	Think in black and white	What else?

Copyright © Karen Treisman – *A Therapeutic Treasure Box for Working with Children and Adolescents with Developmental Trauma – 2018*

Worksheet 6.2
Core emotions and history of emotions exercise

Be mindful: this can be a powerful exercise to do yourself or with parents/carers; however, as with all the activities, it can be triggering and evoke a range of feelings and memories. It therefore needs to be done within a safe and secure therapeutic relationship and space.

» Draw/paint/make a circle.

Inside the circle, using colour, shape, and size, represent how much your primary caregiver gave to you the core emotions of sadness, fear, joy, anger, shame, and curiosity.

Copyright © Karen Treisman – *A Therapeutic Treasure Box for Working with Children and Adolescents with Developmental Trauma – 2018*

Reflect on and explore what is interesting/surprising about this. Consider if and how this has had an influence on your current relationship with sadness, fear, joy, anger, shame, and curiosity.

Reflect on and consider the following: When you experienced… (anger, sadness, fear, and shame) as a child, how did you calm or comfort yourself? How did or didn't your parents/carers support you with these feelings?

When you experienced… (joy, excitement, or curiosity) as a child, how was this responded to/fostered/encouraged by your parents/carers?

How similar or different is this now in your adult relationships and/or parenting of your own children?

Copyright © Karen Treisman – *A Therapeutic Treasure Box for Working with Children and Adolescents with Developmental Trauma – 2018*

Worksheet 6.3

Listening with my whole body and brain: attending to the multiple layers and different shades of communication

	My eyes: making eye contact and showing that I am engaged, present, interested, and compassionate through my eyes
	My mouth: being quiet when necessary, listening, and speaking kindly, calmly, and thoughtfully
	My body: being actively engaged, calm, welcoming, regulated, and open
	My brain: being present, regulated, reflective, and focused
	My hands: being open, still, inviting, and/ or mirroring the conversation
	My heart: feeling and connecting with what the other person is saying
	My ears: actively listening and hearing what is said
	?????

Copyright © Karen Treisman – *A Therapeutic Treasure Box for Working with Children and Adolescents with Developmental Trauma – 2018*

Worksheet 6.4
Exploring the nature and quality of the parent–child relationship

What is the current parent–child relationship like? What three words could be used to describe the relationship? What specific examples can be given to describe each of the three words? How are these words different or similar and depending on whose perspective?

What are the strengths and positive qualities within the relationship? What is it like when it is at its best? (Draw, collage, sculpt, or depict in sand the responses.)

Copyright © Karen Treisman – *A Therapeutic Treasure Box for Working with Children and Adolescents with Developmental Trauma* – 2018

Where are the tensions within the relationship? What is it like when it is at its worst? (Draw, collage, sculpt, or depict in sand the responses.)

What name or title would the parent/child give their relationship at its best and at its worst? What does it look like when it is at its best/at its worst? (Draw, collage, sculpt, or depict in sand the responses.)

If the relationship/difficulty/conflict was described as an item, object, thing, colour, shape, animal, or person, what would it be and why? What would it look like/be like/sound like? If it could talk, what would it say? (Draw, collage, sculpt, or depict in sand the responses.)

Copyright © Karen Treisman – *A Therapeutic Treasure Box for Working with Children and Adolescents with Developmental Trauma* – 2018

What does the… (e.g. the conflict) stop you both from doing? How does the…help you both? If the…disappeared, what would you both miss/what would you gain? What makes the…bigger/smaller/stronger/weaker? (Draw, collage, sculpt, or depict in sand the responses.) (The term "conflict" can be replaced with a range of other concepts/terms.)

Who would you rather have in charge of their life – … (e.g. the conflict) or both of you? What is it like to share your life with…? What plans does the…have on your life? Have you ever managed to deal with…in a different way, without "the…" (externalised name)? If so, how? (Draw, collage, sculpt, or depict in sand the responses.)

Copyright © Karen Treisman – A Therapeutic Treasure Box for Working with Children and Adolescents with Developmental Trauma – 2018

Worksheet 6.5

Similarities, differences, and commonalities

What would be in the "Me" section? What would be in the "You" section? What would be in the "Us" section in the middle? What do you notice? What are you surprised by/interested in?

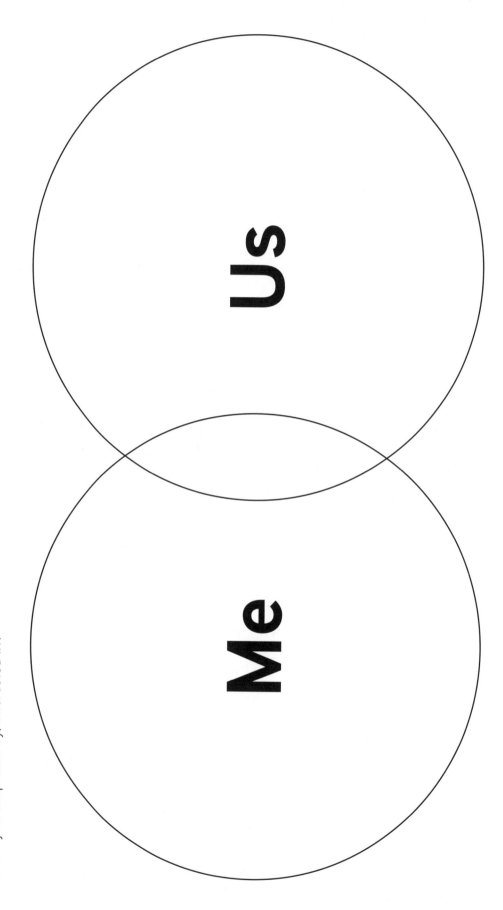

Copyright © Karen Treisman – *A Therapeutic Treasure Box for Working with Children and Adolescents with Developmental Trauma – 2018*

Our relationship then, now, and in the future

Write, draw, collage, depict in a sand tray, or sculpt the responses.

Our relationship then	Our relationship now	Our relationship in the future

Copyright © Karen Treisman – *A Therapeutic Treasure Box for Working with Children and Adolescents with Developmental Trauma – 2018*

Worksheet 6.7
Bottling up special moments

This is like taking a mental snapshot or soaking in a special moment. Which moments would you bottle up and why? Write or draw on the bottles below and try to give each one a label. If you prefer, you can label and fill actual bottles.

Try and remember and hold on to all the details, the smells, the sounds, the tastes, the feelings, the movements, and more of each memory and moment...

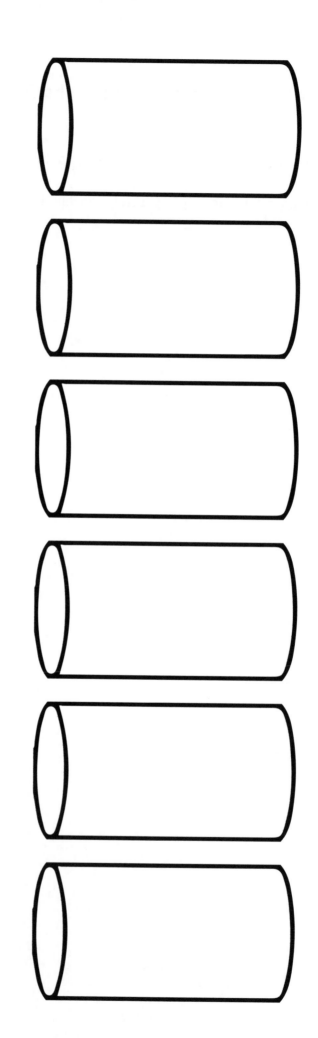

Copyright © Karen Treisman – A Therapeutic Treasure Box for Working with Children and Adolescents with Developmental Trauma – 2018

Inside the time capsule I/we would put ...

DO NOT OPEN UNTIL

2050

Copyright © Karen Treisman – *A Therapeutic Treasure Box for Working with Children and Adolescents with Developmental Trauma – 2018*

Worksheet 6.9
Wishes for myself, you, and our relationship

My wish for myself is... (Draw, sculpt, depict in sand tray, or collage the responses.)

My wish for you is... (Draw, sculpt, depict in sand tray, or collage the responses.)

My wish for our relationship is... (Draw, sculpt, depict in sand tray, or collage the responses.)

Copyright © Karen Treisman – *A Therapeutic Treasure Box for Working with Children and Adolescents with Developmental Trauma* – 2018

Strengths-based approach: writing a take-back practice letter with a relational focus

Guidance on how to use these questions

The following questions offer some possibilities and options for reflecting on and identifying young people's/carers'/families'/parents'/colleagues' strengths, skills, and positive qualities. These can be powerfully pulled together and documented in a letter, email, poem, story, or card. Alternatively, these can be recorded on a video camera or phone. They can also be used as inspiration to complement some of the previous tools, such as writing them on a pillow case, adding them into the child's treasure box, putting them in the sparkle moments diary, or making a collage of them.

It can also be helpful to draw on responses and input from the Team around the Family. This list is not prescriptive or exhaustive. Each question can be expanded on by asking thickening questions and embedding them through creative means.

Support a young person to think about their "caregiver" and vice versa. The focus can be on each other as people or on the parent–child relationship itself:

» What has gone/is going well? What has been achieved so far? What steps have been already taken? (Think about the journey and the distance already travelled.)

» Can you think of one time or moment where you enjoyed each other? What was this and what did it look like, feel like, and mean to you? How could you share this feeling and memory with them?

» What hobbies and activities does…engage, enjoy, and excel in? What about shared and joint activities within the parent–child relationship that you do together? What makes them sparkle/get excited/feel proud/be happy?

» What skills, strengths, successes, and positive qualities of theirs have you been struck/inspired/impressed by? What are their superpowers? What are the relational superpowers?

» If you were writing a review or recommendation about this person/the relationship, what positive things would you say to others about them? If you had to give them/the relationship an award for something positive, what would it be for?

» If you were stranded on an island with them, what skills of theirs or properties of the relationship would you appreciate?

» If they became a different person or life changed as you know it, what would you miss about them and the relationship?

» If you were no longer with them/seeing them, what parts of their personality and of the relationship would you miss?

Copyright © Karen Treisman – *A Therapeutic Treasure Box for Working with Children and Adolescents with Developmental Trauma* – 2018

» How has knowing them and being in a relationship with them made an impression on you? What have you learned from them?

» What will you take forward from what you have learned from them/from the relationship?

» What are your wishes, hopes, and dreams for them, and for the relationship?

» How can these skills, strengths, successes, and positive qualities be recognised, acknowledged, noticed, celebrated, and built on?

Copyright © Karen Treisman – *A Therapeutic Treasure Box for Working with Children and Adolescents with Developmental Trauma* – 2018

Feeding and strengthening our relationship

What can we do to nurture and nourish our relationship? What feeds, waters, strengthens, and protects our "relationship flower"? (Draw, sculpt, collage, write, or depict in sand your responses.)

What can we do to make our relationship tower stronger? What bricks need to be celebrated and noticed? Which bricks need to be added? How can the tower be looked after and maintained? (Draw, sculpt, collage, write, or depict in a sand tray your responses or build your relationship tower and label the different bricks.)

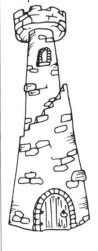

Copyright © Karen Treisman – *A Therapeutic Treasure Box for Working with Children and Adolescents with Developmental Trauma* – 2018

CHAPTER 7

Team Around the Family: Caring for the Caring

Holding Carers in Safe Hands, Thinking Minds, and Regulating Bodies

Who is this chapter aimed at?

Self-care and positive emotional wellbeing applies to everyone. They are a fundamental part of any situation, relationship, and/or intervention, and therefore should be prioritised. When self-care and personal wellbeing are weakened, there is likely to be little ability, energy, motivation, confidence, or belief to implement the necessary strategies safely or consistently or for them to be sustained and done in an intentional, regulated, and meaningful way. Self-care (caring and nurturing onself) ideally would be as routine as brushing one's teeth!

This chapter is written with parents, carers, and caregivers in mind (these terms are used interchangeably) and offers ideas and strategies that therapists can use to support caregivers in this area. The majority of strategies detailed are applicable and adaptable to therapists, wider systems such as teacher and residential workers, and, of course, to the young people themselves. Therefore, I hope the reader will consider reflecting on and applying some of the presented ideas to the Team Around the Child/family/worker and themselves. For more specific strategies focused on the self-care of therapists and on some of the complexities of working within traumatised organisations and within complex systems, see Chapter 8 of *Working with Relational and Developmental Trauma in Children and Adolescents* (Treisman, 2016).

Why is self-care so important in the context of relational and developmental trauma?

In the context of supporting/living with children who bring with them complex trauma, relational scripts, and immensely powerful feelings, it can be challenging to consistently be those much-needed nurturing and nourishing safe hands, thinking minds, and regulating bodies. At the core, what children need is relational repair and empathic engagement, which in itself means getting in touch with and feeling, to an extent, their experience and their pain. This can be challenging, as trauma and loss can be pervasive, can be absorbed and can seep out. It can be a tricky tightrope walking between empathic care and empathic distress.

The complex feelings evoked by trauma can be contagious, and the ripple effects and permeation can be felt throughout multiple layers of the surrounding systems. Britton (1994) uses a theatre metaphor to discuss how family dynamics can move through the audience: "The cast changes, but the plot remains the same" (pp.79–80). This proposes that surrounding adults/organisations can often be the containers for children's intolerable feelings (and vice versa) and can, in turn, unintentionally mirror the child's early experiences and family dynamics. This can also lead to surrounding adults being caught in an emotional cyclone or in an emotional swamp of quicksand and subsequently having to function in their own fight, flight, or freeze survival modes (see Box 7.1 and Worksheet 7.1). This, in turn, is likely to weaken surrounding adults' coping resources, buffers, and protective factors and to make their ability to think and respond effectively, and in a regulated and grounded way, more challenging.

These powerful and complex feelings, responses, and relational interactions can at times push and trigger surrounding people's survival modes, own buttons, hotspots, and vulnerabilities. This is heightened when these experiences, feelings, and memories remain raw, unresolved, and unprocessed (e.g. themes of abandonment, rejection, feeling like a failure or not good enough, secrecy, abuse, powerlessness, fear, injustice, vulnerability, and helplessness) and if as a child/adult you have not had, or are not having, that experience yourself of being nurtured and contained. Additionally, these become even more powerful when caregiver's own feelings, rituals, routines, guiding principles, and/or core values are affected, intruded on, shaken-up, violated, or challenged. These concepts have been sprinkled throughout the book and will also be expanded on below. This is important, as past experiences and relational patterns are inevitably brought into current relationships to some degree and can subsequently colour and shape people's perceptions, attributions, conceptualisations, and responses.

For example, when a caregiver's hotspots are pushed, they too can become dysregulated, re-triggered, preoccupied, and/or absorbed in their own trauma and loss experiences. In these moments, when lost in a sea of emotions or having fallen through a "timehole" (Hobday, 2001), caregivers may struggle to read, connect, and respond appropriately to their children's emotional states and needs. At these moments, their own attachment and relationship history is often being triggered, rather than their caregiving and parenting modes being activated. This can pose a significant block to being able to parent mindfully. *How can a parent respond mindfully and reflectively when they are full up, burnt out, feeling underappreciated, and/or are in survival mode?* Examples of the relationships and interplay between triggers and one's parenting role are given below.

Kayden's rejecting and distancing behaviour towards her adoptive father, Jay, triggered his own long relationship with rejection. Kayden shouted at Jay, "You're disgusting, I don't love you", and refused his invitations: "I don't want to go to the cinema with you, I'd prefer to eat poo." For him, it was like looking through a corridor of past mirrors. Once again, he was haunted by his ghosts from the past (Fraiberg *et al.*, 1975), and felt the rawness of his own experiences of feeling "unlovable" and "not good enough" that came from his critical mother. His feelings of being "a failure" as a father were echoed and entangled with his feelings of being a failure of a son.

When faced with her four-year-old son Kai's rage, Julie would see her ex-partner's anger during a domestic violence incident, rather than the hurt little boy standing in front of her. Feelings of powerlessness and helplessness resurfaced. In order to manage these terrifying feelings, she had learned to emotionally distance herself and position Kai as a threat: "He's just like his father – bad blood."

Cate was described by her health visitor as being barely able to look at her baby. Each time he cried, she physically recoiled or retreated into a "bubble". Being in touch with his distress and dependence was too painful for Cate and triggered her own vulnerability and earlier unmet needs.

Adding to the weight of the importance of emotional wellbeing and self-care, we also know that working/living with complex trauma can evoke hugely powerful feelings (Maslach, 2003; Rothschild, 2006). Studies have shown that, within this client group (people who have experienced complex trauma and disrupted attachments), there are higher occurrences of secondary trauma (ST) (Stamm, 1999), vicarious trauma (VT) (McCann and Pearlman, 1990), compassionate fatigue (CF) (Figley, 1995), and burnout. The presence of ST, VT, and CF is likely to permeate various areas of one's spiritual, physical, emotional, and cognitive life and subsequently impact on the ability to do and be one's best. The effects of ST, VT, and CF can be far reaching and may include: a loss of interest, weakened empathy, anxiety, low mood, withdrawal, anger, hopelessness, helplessness, detachment, reliving symptoms such as nightmares and flashbacks, and physical responses such as headaches and heart palpitations. Surrounding adults also can experience shifts in the way they perceive themselves, others, and the world, including an erosion of one's self-esteem and decreased sense of efficacy.

Therefore, to protect oneself from these powerful and painful feelings, common ways of surviving, coping, and responding include: shutting down (dissociating), having crushed empathy, emotionally withdrawing/disconnecting, splitting (them and us), attacking others, objectifying or depersonalising people, and putting one's walls up (see Worksheet 7.1 for a range of illustrated survival modes). At the other end of the spectrum, being in touch with and connecting to these powerful feelings might also push people's rescue valency into overdrive and/or they might also have an overwhelming sense of responsibility and accountability. Illustrative examples of some of the ways in which trauma can permeate through systems and can have a wider influence are given below.

Edith, a mum, presented with symptoms of depression, her child presented with low mood, their social worker felt hopeless and depleted, and the overarching organisation was deflated with a collective sense of helplessness. Within this case, the arousal states and feelings of hopelessness and sadness were flowing through and permeating the multiple layers of the system.

The fragmented, warring nature of Evan's birth family became echoed in the warring and fragmented interactions within his adoptive family. Powerful divides occurred amongst usually united family members, and they found themselves playing out the reciprocal role of Evan's transference of, for example, his birth parents, who themselves were experiencing lots of feelings of anger, fear, and chaos.

Noah, who was living in foster care with three other foster children, had experienced significant neglect within his birth family and presented with an insecure avoidant attachment style. He internalised his difficulties and often seemed to fade into the background and fall through the net. In therapy consultation meetings, the three other foster children were all discussed in detail, yet on numerous occasions the session would end and myself and the foster carers would discover that we had forgotten to discuss Noah. As a system, we were unintentionally mirroring what had happened to Noah in his birth family: we were not keeping him in mind and he was once again becoming invisible.

Leah was repeatedly told and shown that she was unlovable and disgusting by her parents. This "repelling bubble" seemed to be replayed through the system that subsequently labelled Leah as "unlikable and troubled" and located several difficulties within her as a person.

Sophie shared how she was usually a calm and relaxed person and described how as a parent to her own birth children she had been a very laid-back, go-with-the-flow parent. However, since fostering Adam, Sophie described how she was a "ball of nerves" and felt constantly "on edge and anxious".

Taylor presented with beliefs that included: "I'm bad, unlovable, and a failure." These were then reflected in her carer reporting similar thoughts about her role and herself: "I am not enough. She needs more than I can give her. I can't do it. She doesn't even like me"; consequently, the social worker also picked up and absorbed these feelings: "I'm ineffective. I'm helpless to change things. I don't think I am the right fit for them."

Talia was allocated a new case and, upon reading graphic details of neglect, said: "It's not that bad; I've seen worse." Her threshold had become so high and, for a range of reasons including having to almost retreat into a position of protective dissociation, she had become desensitised and hardened to the work.

David had become so emotionally full up, exhausted, and depleted by his work that he defended against these difficult feelings by making fun of the clients, distancing himself emotionally from them, seeing things in very black-and-white terms, and widening the "them and us" gap.

Box 7.1 **Reflective exercise on fight, flight, or freeze responses**

These questions can be asked or reflected on about oneself or with the Team Around the Child, such as with caregivers.

How and when do you show your survival, fight, flight, or freeze responses? What do these look/feel like? Can you think of examples of when these fight, flight, or freeze modes were/are activated? How similar or different are these modes now compared with when you were younger? How similar or different are these to your family members'/friends'/colleagues' ways of responding to threat, fear, etc.? Is there a collective family/organisational way of responding to threat/danger/pain? (See Worksheet 7.1.)

With this complexity and multi-layered nature in mind, there needs to be an acknowledgement and awareness of the emotional, physical, social, financial, spiritual, and cognitive impact that parenting/supporting/caring for a hurt child can have, alongside a validation of the lived and felt experience of supporting/caring for these children.

Imagine what it's like to be left black and blue by your five-year-old child when you are pouring all your energy into caring for them. Or a child who regularly bites you when you go to kiss them goodnight. Or to be excluded from birthday parties and other previously treasured social events due to your child's behaviour. Or to have the appreciation letter you spent hours writing to a child ripped up in front of you. Or to find out the young person you have been working with intensively after the removal of their baby is pregnant again. And so forth... These examples offer further weight as to why self-care and caring for the carer is so crucial (see Box 7.2).

Box 7.2 **Reflective exercise on the importance of self-care and caring for the carer**

If we keep filling children's glasses up with water, or their bowl up with fruit, who is going to replenish ours and how? What can we offer to others if our glass of water or fruit bowl is depleted or expired?

What do they say on an aeroplane about putting your own oxygen mask on before putting on a child's mask?

How can you be there for others without leaving yourself behind?

How can we light other peoples fires if ours has burned or faded out?

Some examples are given below that build on the above, further highlight the importance of self-care in the context of relational and developmental trauma, and identify some of the hazards of not caring for oneself or of not recognising one's triggers and emotional hotspots.

Lucy had had years of trying to manage Emily's "challenging" behaviour with relatively little movement or change, despite endless service involvement and employed strategies. She was exhausted and feeling hopeless. When a new social worker began, and in the first couple of sessions introduced a reward chart and subsequently expressed frustration at Lucy's response, Lucy felt even more hopeless and judged. This social worker had unintentionally underestimated the huge emotional toll Lucy was experiencing and how depleted and exhausted she was feeling.

Lucy needed time to recharge before she could engage with something like a reward chart. She needed to reconnect with lost hope, motivation that things could change and improve, and the belief that she could be an agent and part of this change. She also needed validation and an acknowledgement of the distance she had already travelled and the difficulties she was facing, as well as recognition for the effort, skills, and time she had already put in. She needed to feel held in safe hands and thinking minds herself so that she could continue to provide this for Emily.

Cara and Simon's home had become a battlefield; they were regularly punched, kicked, hit, and spat at. Their furniture, including much-loved sentimental items from their parents who had passed away, had been damaged and broken. They were both at the point where they dreaded putting the key in the door and were already on edge and expecting disaster before entering the house. They were walking on eggshells and functioning in fight, flight, or freeze survival mode themselves. Understandably, they were struggling to remain regulated or to use their thinking part of their brains. Their minds were full rather than being mindful.

Juliet had been in a 12-year relationship characterised by domestic violence and dominated by fear. She had been told over and over again that she was "ugly, fat, and a waste of space", was deserving of such treatment, and was "unlovable". This echoed the words of her own father, who had treated her in a similar way. She was then expected by services, and the court, to implement effective behavioural strategies and boundaries and to show her twin girls how to love and respect themselves. Given that she felt that she had "nothing to offer", was a "waste of space", and a "failure at everything" she did, this was a mammoth task and expectation.

The examples above show that it is imperative that we focus on and facilitate relational repair in order to address relational trauma. Our ability to make and model healthy relationships, and to show children different ways of doing and being in relationships, is the superglue ingredient. Therefore, our own self-care, emotional wellbeing, ability to stay regulated and have a mentalising stance, and ability to continue to hold the hope and to believe that things can move forward are paramount to enabling this relational process.

This chapter will therefore present a variety of different strategies to support areas around self-care, self-reflection, and stress management. These are not standalone strategies; they should be anchored to and interwoven with existing coping strategies and tools. However, before proceeding to these ideas, it feels important to reflect on different ways of exploring one's relationship to self-care and what might be preventing or acting as a barrier to taking a focus on oneself. The exercises and questions in Boxes 7.3 and 7.4 should be informed by a thorough assessment and the unique context. They should also be carried out within the safety of a positive and containing relationship. Ideally, each question response should span several sessions and should be thickened through creative means. They are not intended to be a list of endless questions, but rather a springboard for rich and meaningful exploration and discussion. Please note that this chapter should be complemented by Chapter 5 on strengths, hope, and resilience-based practice.

Box 7.3 **Practical activities and reflective exercises on self-care, empathy, and hotspots (part 1)**

Blocks and barriers

What does self-care mean to you? Why is self-care important? What are some of the hazards of cumulative, stacked-up stress? What do you look like, feel like, and act like when you are stressed or depleted? (See Worksheets 7.2 and 7.3.) How do others know when this is the case? What do you look like, feel like, and act like when you are at your best? (See Worksheets 7.2 and 7.3.) How do others know when this is the case? What could you do today that your future self would thank you for? (Write down, sculpt, collage, or draw your responses.)

How did/does it feel to care for yourself? Do you experience any guilt over taking time to care for yourself? What does "the guilt" say to you? Where on a scale from zero to ten, with zero being very poor and almost non-existent to ten being excellent all the time, would you place yourself on how well you take care of yourself? What makes this easier and facilitates this time? What blocks and barriers are there for you taking this time? If you were to describe these blocks and barriers, what would they look like/feel like? If the blocks and barriers were an item/type of weather/creature, etc., what would they be? How does it feel when the blocks and barriers are there compared with when they are less visible? What do the blocks and barriers stop you from doing/achieving/feeling. (Write down, sculpt, collage, or draw your responses.)

Multifaceted identity and all your different parts

What makes you uniquely you? What lens do you like to be seen through? What are the different layers and parts of your identity and fabric? Which layers and parts are really important to you? What is the meaning, relationship, and story behind each layer and each part? You might like to draw, make a list of, or collage these different layers or parts. As illustrated in Chapters 2–5, this can be done using pieces of a puzzle (see Photo 7.1), sections of a pie (see Photo 7.2), patterns on a patchwork, different masks, LEGO® pieces, a Rubik's cube, Russian dolls, layers of coloured sand, or corners of a shield to represent these different parts (see Photo 7.3). How are these different layers currently being used/acknowledged/built on/pushed aside? If they were on a pie chart, which layer would be a large chunk or a little slither? How have these changed over time? Are there any parts you miss or wish could become bigger?

Motivation and satisfaction

Remind yourself why you do what you do (be mindful that this can have very different responses and triggers, e.g. adoptive parenting versus kinship carer). What motivated you in the first place? What are the values underlying and informing it? What parts do you enjoy and get satisfaction from? What parts are you learning and developing from? Which elements do you feel valued in? Which do you feel you make a difference in? What parts are you proud of? Which would you miss if you were no longer doing what you are doing or living the life that you are living?

Box 7.4 **Practical activities and reflective exercises on self-care, empathy, and hotspots (part 2)**

Hotspots and triggers

Is there a particular behaviour/difficulty/theme/person that is currently worrying you/distressing you/getting under your skin? What is your relationship, connection, and history to that theme/issue/experience/difficulty? Let's take food refusal as an example of something that really gets under your skin. What is your relationship to food or the deprivation of it? What does the refusal of food and significant weight loss mean to you? What issues does it stir up in you? What ideas/values/themes/beliefs/hotspots do you have that are being evoked/triggered/challenged by the food refusal?

Identify and reflect on your own triggers, hotspots, and vulnerabilities, and try to apply the above questions to that particular issue. This may shed some light on why you may be reacting the way you are. The more we understand about why, the more it makes sense and subsequently the less personal and the more manageable it can become. How can you reduce/notice/respond to/understand these? How can you find ways to stay regulated and grounded when a hotspot is pushed?

Empathy

How do you show empathy to the young person/caregiver? What makes it easier or trickier to show empathy? How do you know when your empathy levels are depleted? What are the hazards and consequences of weakened empathy?

How does this impact on your thinking and decision-making? What helps you reconnect with feelings of empathy? Where and how did you learn those reconnecting and empathising skills?

Reflect on an experience where you felt deeply empathised with and vice versa. How did this leave you feeling emotionally, cognitively, and physically?

Photo 7.1 Puzzle pieces of my identity

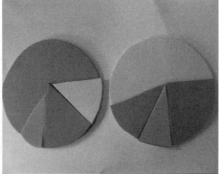

Photo 7.2 A visual representation of identity and priorities before and after my fostering role

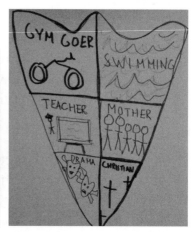

Photo 7.3 An identity shield

Practical strategies for addressing and improving self-care

Below are some examples of strategies to support parents to look after and care for themselves. They are based on the premise that working and supporting children who have experienced relational and developmental trauma and loss, and the systems around them, inevitably evokes a range of multi-layered conflicting and complex feelings. Careful selection and thought around their timing, introduction, and delivery, and how to tailor them suitably, is strongly recommended (see Chapter 1 for underpinning principles and factors to be mindful of when implementing the described strategies).

The following strategies are also complemented by those found in Chapters 5 and 6, and in the reflective exercises described in Boxes 7.3 and 7.4. A case example is presented at the end of the chapter that illustrates how several of these strategies can be intertwined and brought to life (see Box 7.7).

Triggers and hotspots

As discussed in the introduction section, and demonstrated through the case examples, it feels integral to this process to continually reflect on our and others' triggers, hotspots, and vulnerabilities. It is also important to subsequently identify how these developed, what our relationship is to them, what theme they play/played in our lives, what pushes them, and how we can relieve, reduce, and respond to them. In essence, this includes recognising which patterns are being evoked, being triggered, sucking one in like quicksand, or overwhelming one like an emotional avalanche. This is especially important, given that research strongly suggests that the processing and integration of childhood experiences is an integral variable in a parent's ability to be a safe haven for their children (Cozolino, 2002). This builds on the idea that if we are not tuned into ourselves, it becomes much harder to tune into others, or to support them in enhancing this "tuning-in" skill. The following question returns to the shark-infested waters metaphor (see Chapter 3): *How can you avoid becoming one of the sharks but also not drowning in the fear, whilst learning about which waters scare them, and who are/were their own sharks, choppy waves, dolphins, and lifeboats?*

Within this, it can be helpful to externalise these triggers and to separate them from the person in order to be examined, processed, and explored. Some strategies from Chapters 3 and 8, such as "Behaviour as communication", Narrative Therapy externalising techniques, and "Connection before correction", can be helpfully translated here to apply to supporting adults. Worksheets 7.6 and 7.7 can also aid this process of identifying and expanding on triggers, as can keeping a diary and closely monitoring one's own responses and reactions. This process of identifying and bringing triggers to one's awareness also positively models to children the importance of self-awareness and reflectivity. Once these triggers have been identified (it is an ongoing work in progress and a dynamic process), subsequent coping strategies can be sought that aim to identify some ways to stay regulated and empathetic, to manage high levels of affect, and to regain emotional equilibrium, rather than getting hooked in or engaging in mutually escalating arousal patterns. Some common regulating, soothing, and grounding exercises are listed on

Worksheet 7.9; however, as with all these strategies, these are likely to be more effective and meaningful when individualised.

Being informed and supported

Having access to high-quality and relevant information and psychoeducation feels as if it is an important part of feeling informed and having some sort of cognitive framework to anchor to, whilst also feeling part of something and having a sense of wider universality. It can be helpful to have a nurturing safe space to meet like-minded non-judgemental people who get it and who understand the complex nature and impact of relational and developmental trauma. This can include supervision, reflective practice, support groups, online forums, one-to-one sessions, training, workshop opportunities, reading materials, plays, and so on. Ideally (although it is likely to be in multiple different spaces) this would offer the opportunity to express the good, the bad, and the ugly, whilst also being able to get practical advice and emotional support (e.g. "My child is rejecting me", "Why is my child behaving like...?", "He is hitting me", "I'm so full up and burnt out", and "I feel so guilty as I am struggling to like my child").

Having the space and opportunities to have these types of discussions and to voice these feelings and dilemmas feels so important, as the deeper one's understanding of disrupted attachment and relational and developmental trauma is, the more able people are to decipher and connect with what the child may be communicating through their behaviour (see Box 6.4 in Chapter 6 and "Behaviour as communication" in Chapter 8). This can also make it feel a bit less overwhelming, confusing, frustrating, and personal.

Personal and professional team of support

It is important to have a supportive network around the parent – in essence, a "team around the parent/family". The increased sense of isolation felt by carers and, conversely, the buffering and protective factor that a positive support system can create are consistent findings in the literature. This is brought to life by the African proverbs "It takes a village to raise a child" and "Sticks in a bundle cannot be broken".

Strengthening current ties and seeking out new social support opportunities can include online forums, therapy, spiritual/religious support, and family and friends. The suggestions below offer some other ideas for strengthening one's sense of belonging and connectedness (these are expanded on with examples in Chapter 6).

- The parent can be supported to think about someone in their life who makes them/made them feel safe, cared for, appreciated by, and protected. Discussions about this person can strengthen their presence and rich influence on the parent's life. For example, the parent may want to discuss, document, draw, collage, or share stories of 1) times when that person made them feel safe and protected, 2) qualities and skills that the person had that made them feel safe/protected/listened to/appreciated, 3) what that person was/is like, and 4) what some of their most treasured memories with that person are/were, etc. Other sample questions to strengthen this connection (in line with the concept of "re-membering" conversations from Narrative Therapy) are detailed in Box 7.5. To creatively express this further, the parent may also want to bring a picture of that person, make a drawing/painting/sculpt of them, have a voice recording of their voice, or visualise them as being with them, supporting them, and cheering them on.

- The parent (particularly in the context of their own relational and developmental trauma) may struggle to think of someone present, or past, in their life who made or makes them feel safe, appreciated, and protected, so instead they may want to imagine and create a person/item/object/spirit. This may be entirely from their desires and imagination, or they might want to take different parts/qualities from different people they have known and combine them together to form one person/character (see examples and photos in the "Safe person/people" section in Chapter 3). The creative means of expressing and embedding these ideas described in the previous point can be applied to this imaginary person/item/object.

- The parent may want to think about famous people/positive role models/celebrities/inspirational figures who they have been inspired by/impressed by. These people can then be written down, sculpted, collaged, listed, or drawn (see examples and photos in the "Safe person/people" section in Chapter 3). Discussions can be had about how to breathe and internalise these people and times in; and hold them in their hearts and heads. Example questions can be asked, such as:

  Who are your role models, inspirers, feeders, and life cheerleaders? How can you utilise and expand on these? How can you draw on their positivity, strength, and encouragement? How can you drink them in and internalise them? How can you see yourself through their eyes? What do you think they would say to you about...? What do they or do you think they would admire/notice/appreciate in you? What qualities of theirs can you try and aspire to?

- For some people, having a physical and visual representation of all of the people around them who are in their team and are their supporters can be very powerful. (This needs to be done, as with all these exercises, with caution, as some people may be in a place where they feel very alone and isolated.) This physical representation might be through using an eco-map or genogram (see examples and photos of these tools in the "Safe person/people" section in Chapter 3). This can also be represented by using different layers of sand, with each colour representing a different person, or by making support jewellery, with each bead representing a different person. Sometimes I might draw or sculpt something like a parachute, a blanket (see Photo 7.4), a circle of friends (see Photo 7.5), a team of cheerleaders, a lifeboat (see Photo 7.6), or a safety net (see Photo 7.7) and get them to draw/label/sculpt the different people who would fit into that category for them (other examples of these tools are found in Chapter 3). It can also be helpful to collect/display photos, sentimental items, and/or meaningful letters/cards from these people.

Photo 7.4 Blanket of supportive people

Photo 7.5 Circle of friends

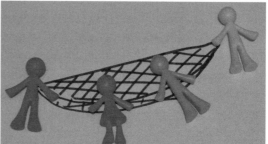

Photo 7.6 Lifeboat of supporters

Photo 7.7 Safety net of friends

Box 7.5 Re-membering conversations Narrative Therapy inspired questions

In pairs try and have, and reflect on, the below conversation.

Can you remember a person who you felt understood, valued, and appreciated by?

What was it that they brought to your life? What is it/was it that they helped you with? What did they see that others missed?

If that person was sitting here, what do you think they would say that they appreciated/enjoyed/admired about you?

How did their hopes and positive view of you contribute to or shape your life?

How did they influence what you felt about yourself? What do you think it meant to them to be connected to you? How might their life have been different for knowing you?

How might the way you saw them, and the way you were when you were with them, have contributed to how they saw themselves?

Are there times when your connection with this person feels stronger?

What strengths did they have that you would want to keep close?

How are they still able to be present, in varying forms, in your life?

What differences could you make in your life to remember/honour them?

Expectations and setting yourself up to fail (SMART goals)

Caregivers need to be supported to reflect on, and if appropriate review, their expectations of themselves and of their young person/people and to take one step at a time, as well as being kind, fair, and compassionate towards themselves. If expectations are too high or unrealistic, it is more likely that there will be feelings of disappointment, frustration, and not feeling good enough. For example, *if a child is extremely dysregulated and getting repeatedly removed from the classroom, is it fair or realistic to expect them to manage without incident all day? Or if a child is emotionally and socially more like a three-year-old, is it fair that they are left unsupervised at playtime? Or is it fair for a new adoptive parent to expect themselves to bond instantly with the child and to know exactly how to parent them?*

These expectations are helpfully framed within the acronym SMART (Specific, Measurable, Achievable, Realistic, and Timely). See Worksheet 5.6 for more detail on thinking SMART and making SMART goals. Some useful discussions and reflections around expectations and picking one's battles are detailed in Box 7.6. These are also complemented by Box 6.6.

Box 7.6 Practical activities and reflective exercises (expectations, SMART goals, and picking battles wisely)

1. Which tasks can be achieved? (Think SMART goals (see Worksheet 5.6); for example, are your expectations realistic and manageable?)

2. Which can you make a difference to and are manageable? Which need to be put aside for a bit or shared with others? What can wait, and what needs to be done now? Which can be broken down into smaller steps?

3. Are you holding on to too much worry and/or other people's worries? Which ones are out of your control?

4. How can you pick your battles wisely and make decisions when you're not feeling too overwhelmed and/or depleted? Is there a different system of organisation and time management that you could employ?

5. What is the worst thing that can happen if...? What is the best thing that can happen if...? If the worst did happen, what skills could you use to cope with that? It can be useful to link these to some of the common cognitive errors, for example overgeneralising, catastrophising, using all-or-nothing thinking, filtering, and mind-reading.

6. Do you think this situation will be important in five years' time? Is the situation being dominated by emotional thinking? When you have had this feeling in the past (e.g. "I can't do it"), what did you tell yourself or think to help yourself feel better?

Integrating feel-good factors into daily routines

It can be helpful to support caregivers to incorporate some feel-good factors and items into their everyday routine (these will be different for everyone). Examples of what this might be include: having a positive memory mug, having a regulating and nurturing chair (e.g. a rocking or spinning chair) having a positive key ring on their keys, having a positive door sign or door mat that they see when they enter their house, having a calming positive-associated scent, candle, hand wash or room spray, having a positive photo or motto as their screensaver, having a positive photo or an uplifting phone cover on their phone, and/or making a feel-good music playlist to listen to on their journey.

Self-care plan/pledge and regulating activities

As illustrated in Photos 7.8 and 7.9, it can be helpful, if appropriate and well paced, to support parents to reflect on, write down, draw, sculpt, or make a collage about the following: *What feeds them? What helps them to feel happy/calm/at their best/ relaxed/recharged? What pushes their "parenting" reward and feel-good buttons? What fills their emotional, spiritual, cognitive, social, and physical containers up? What makes them feel the opposite? What happens when their feel-good buttons are not pushed, are ignored, or are rusty? What happens when their emotional, spiritual, physical, social, cognitive, and spiritual containers are running on empty?* (See Worksheets 7.4 and 7.5 for ways to support these discussions and visual representations of these concepts.)

Photo 7.8 Self-care collage

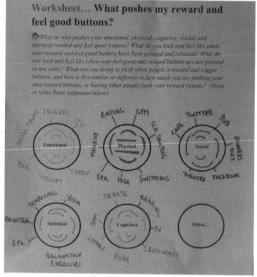

Photo 7.9 The things that push my reward and feel-good buttons

It can be helpful to try and support parents in thinking about these soothing, calming, refilling, and regulating things/activities from a multisensory perspective (e.g. visual, kinaesthetic, tactile, olfactory, affective, and auditory) and taking a multipronged approach (physical, emotional, spiritual, cognitive, social, personal, and professional). Thinking in a multisensory and multi-layered way also models how we hope parents will respond to their children. Keep in mind that trauma is a multisensory, whole-body-brain experience and therefore requires multisensory, whole-brain-body responses. Additionally, parents have often had to use their social engagement system so much, that moving towards a different type of stimulation and interaction can be important.

Everyone is different, and so each individual will need to find out what works for them, but some possible regulating activities are detailed in Worksheet 7.9. These activities "model the model" and are based around Bruce Perry's (2014) six Rs in trauma-informed work: rhythmic, repetitive, relevant, rewarding (pleasurable), respectful, and relational.

Once these strategies have been identified and trialled, it can be useful to also make a self-care plan or pledge that details how carers can increase and strengthen these tools on a daily, weekly, monthly, and yearly basis (see Worksheet 7.11 for a self-care pledge template; however, carers may prefer to make their own one).

It is important to encourage carers to start small and at a place that feels manageable and achievable, but also to give themselves permission and time to try at least one of their identified things on a daily basis. This can be something as small as listening to their favourite song before picking the children up from school. It is helpful, as with the SMART goals, to try to be specific, so, for example, if a parent says watching TV helps them to relax, try to think about what specific programmes help them to do this, how they feel when they watch these programmes, how often they actually get to do this, what enables this to happen, whether there is any way of bringing more of this into their life, etc.

In order to embed these activities further, and to thicken their effect, it is helpful to monitor and evaluate the effectiveness of these activities.

How were they able to protect this time? What did it feel like during and after the strategy was employed? Did it make a difference, and, if so, what difference did it make? If it did make a difference, how can they bring this activity into their life more? By taking this time, what are they saying to themselves and what are they teaching to their children?

De-roleing and going to one's safe place

Following a tricky day/situation/period of time, after having a space to debrief to have it acknowledged, validated, and reflected on (which is very important and foundational), it can be helpful, alongside some of the regulating, grounding, and soothing activities described in Worksheet 7.9, to physically shake the day off, write down the difficulties in a diary or box, and/or lock them away, rip them up, flush them down the toilet, etc. In addition, going to one's safe place cognitively or physically can also be a powerful way of recharging and having a brain break (see Chapter 3 for a description on connecting with one's own safe place, alongside creative extensions of embedding the safe place).

Strengths-based reflection and positive affirmations

Carers may also find it helpful to use positive self-talk or positive self-mottos or to draw on inspirational movies, people, books, plays, quotes (see Photos 7.10 and 7.11), or affirmations.

In addition, after having a chance to voice concerns, explore them, and have them received in a listening and empathetic way (it is important that there is a chance to share the difficulties and have them validated and acknowledged before moving on to a strengths-based focus), one can support parents to consider the following questions:

Can you remember other times when you have been through difficult situations that have been/felt worse and how they improved or changed? How did you get through those times? What skills, strengths, resiliencies, and positive qualities did you use? What is your history/relationship to that skill/value/positive quality? Who did you learn it from, and how did you learn it? Who would be least surprised to hear you talking about that skill/strength/positive quality? How can you build, strengthen, celebrate, and reconnect with these qualities, skills, and strengths?

It can also be helpful to support the parent to revisit these positive times verbally, for example "Remember the time when...", and to find ways to hold on to and magnify the positive times, for example keeping a "positive moments" journal (see Worksheet 7.8), filling a treasure box up with positive memories, making a "sparkle moments" box, and/or drawing/sculpting/writing stories of these times and moments (see Chapters 5 and 6 for more ways of noticing and celebrating positives and for some photographed examples of these techniques).

Photos 7.10 and 7.11 Collage of inspirational quotes

Strengths-based strategies

An integral part of supporting parents to feel good about themselves is building, noticing, and identifying their strengths and resiliency and fostering their sense of hope. This can go a long way towards pushing parents' reward systems and refuelling their emotional tanks, as well as boosting morale and offering them a chance to feel appreciated and valued, which in turn can support them in being able to provide the same for their young people. This includes using techniques such as externalising, imagery re-scripting, tangible and creative ways of building strengths, and making a Tree of Life. See Chapter 5 for ideas on how to use these techniques.

Strengths-based, take-back practice letter

Sometimes I find writing take-back practice letters (informed by Narrative Therapy techniques) to a colleague/parent/carer/child a helpful and powerful way of taking a strengths-based appreciative perspective (see Worksheets 5.17 and 6.10 for some guidance on writing one of these letters). The questions are just a guide; you can be as creative and tailored as you wish. I try and write these types of letters, or some variation of them, to each person (e.g. colleague, child, social worker, foster carer, adoptive parent, etc.) I have had a meaningful piece of work with to celebrate the journey travelled and them as a person. Receiving and giving them has given me some of my most remarkable moments in therapeutic interactions.

Box 7.7 **Shoshana a case example of integrating some of these self-care techniques**

Shoshana, alongside her husband, was a foster carer of a sibling group of two. Both children had experienced multiple relational and developmental traumas and losses. The children each presented with complex difficulties and, at the same time, Shoshana was faced with managing complex contact arrangements, supporting her elderly father who was transitioning to a care home, and working a part-time "stressful" job. Shoshana was, understandably, feeling full up and depleted. She said she felt that she was "losing herself" and that she felt she was always the "giver". Through exploration, it also came to the surface that throughout her childhood Shoshana had been a young carer for her mother, who had been struggling with a physical condition and with episodes of clinical depression. This experience and role was a key part of the subsequent work.

With the above in mind, it was mutually decided that before going on to address the presenting difficulties of the children (although some brief strategies and discussion were had, as these were interlinked with her current stress levels), the focus would be on supporting Shoshana, on her wellbeing, and on filling her own emotional tank. It should be noted that the work stated below is a snapshot to give a flavour and is not a comprehensive, step-by-step version. Also, the focus of this case example is on Shoshana; however, it should be mentioned that there was a lot of work done to coordinate, support, and link up with Shoshana's husband, the children's school, and her supervising social worker.

We explored using some of the exercises described in Boxes 7.1–7.4 to identify and reflect on what fed Shoshana, what she was like at her best/worst, what obstacles there were around caring for herself, what filled her emotional tank, what depleted it, and why this was important, etc.

To embed these, the majority of her responses were then creatively expressed. For example, she shared that, when she was at her best, she felt as if she was the life and soul of the party and people labelled her as "Little Miss Sunshine", but when she was at her worst, she felt as if she was a deflating, grey balloon. She was supported to sculpt and draw these descriptors side by side and then we had conversations around these metaphors/feelings/experiences. Another example is when she shared that swimming was one of the activities that fed her and refuelled her but this had been side-lined amidst all her current stressors. So we made a collage of her swimming, drew a picture of her "doing" swimming, and made a body-map of how different she felt within her body and her mind during and after swimming.

We then went on to explore the barriers and obstacles (actual and perceived) to caring for herself, and depicted these as walls and balls and chains (her chosen metaphors). We then explored where these came from and linked them to a range of areas, including to her lifelong role as both a young and an adult carer and her own self-esteem/self-belief. We then emotionally and practically problem-solved around these. We also actively and creatively presented how she could conquer, move, or reduce these barriers and obstacles (the walls and balls and chains).

We also reflected on the journey that she had already travelled with the children and punctuated and magnified through creative means the successes and progresses that they had all made already. We drew these, wrote them down, and filled her treasure box of memories (the children decorated this box). We also (using Worksheets 7.4 and 7.5) filled her treasure box up with the things that pushed her reward buttons and the moments that she would like to bottle up.

We then went on to identify a range of activities that she could do, including swimming, coffee with friends, listening to a particular uplifting song, and other ideas taken from the regulating cards on Worksheet 7.9. We also problem-solved around how and when she could integrate these things into her life and why they were important and had a rippled effect on her, her husband, and the children. These were then translated into a self-care pledge and plan.

We also took several weeks to create her Tree of Life, which emphasised her own strengths, skills, and resiliencies, and then, from a place of strength, we went on to discuss the storms of her life and how she could survive and overcome them. Shoshana was also supported to write a take-back practice letter (Worksheet 10.10) to both of the children and to a close friend who she had found very supportive during difficult times. I also wrote a take-back practice letter to her and to her husband.

Having done this crucial ground work to nurture and support Shoshona, this led us to go on to explore the children's behaviour and the interaction of their behaviour with her own triggers. Once we had moved to a place where she had felt re-energised and supported, and had had her experiences validated, made sense of, and acknowledged, we were able to share the focus on the children, and the work continued.

When I feel unsafe and need to protect myself

Feeling Unsafe/Putting Up Defences

When I am feeling "unsafe" and need to protect myself I ...

Surround myself with barbed wire	Go into attack mode like a hungry shark	Go into my own protective bubble	Put on my bulletproof vest	Retreat into my tortoise shell
Make myself small/invisible	Hide away in the fog	Freeze on the spot	Whizz around like a dart	Paint on a smile like a clown
Put up my spikes like a hedgehog	Zoom away like a speeding car	Push people away like an opposing magnet	Think in black and white	What else?

Copyright © Karen Treisman – *A Therapeutic Treasure Box for Working with Children and Adolescents with Developmental Trauma* – 2018

Worksheet 7.2
Reflecting on my best and worst self visually

Draw, write, collage, or depict in sand your responses.

What do I look like and feel when I am at my worst? What does my world look and feel like when I am at my worst?	What do I look like and feel when I am at my best? What does my world look and feel like when I am at my best?

Copyright © Karen Treisman – *A Therapeutic Treasure Box for Working with Children and Adolescents with Developmental Trauma* – 2018

I recognise when I am feeling depleted/
stressed because I show it through my…

Draw, sculpt, or write your responses.

Body

Words

Facial expressions

Behaviours

Copyright © Karen Treisman – *A Therapeutic Treasure Box for Working with Children and Adolescents with Developmental Trauma – 2018*

Worksheet 7.4

Filling my emotional, physical, cognitive, and spiritual containers

What or who fills your emotional, physical, cognitive, and spiritual containers up? What do your containers look and feel like when they are full up and energised? What do your emotional containers look and feel like when they are depleted and running on empty? What are you doing to fill others' emotional, physical, cognitive, and spiritual containers up, and how is this similar or different to what you are doing for your own or receiving for your own containers?

Draw or write these responses below.

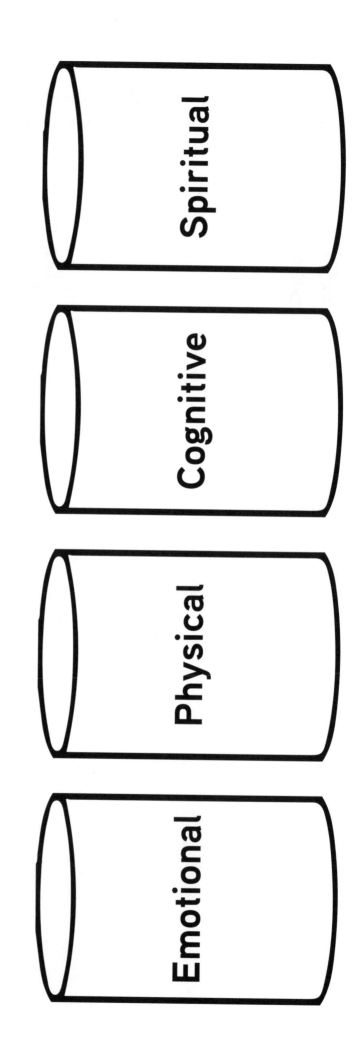

Copyright © Karen Treisman – A Therapeutic Treasure Box for Working with Children and Adolescents with Developmental Trauma – 2018

Worksheet 7.5
What pushes my reward and feel-good buttons?

What or who pushes your emotional, physical, cognitive, social, and spiritual reward and feel-good buttons? What do you look and feel like when your reward and feel-good buttons have been pressed and released? What do you look and feel like when your feel-good and reward buttons are not pressed or are rusty? What are you doing to push other people's reward and trigger buttons, and how is this similar or different to how much you are pushing your own reward buttons or having other people push your reward buttons?

Draw or write your responses below.

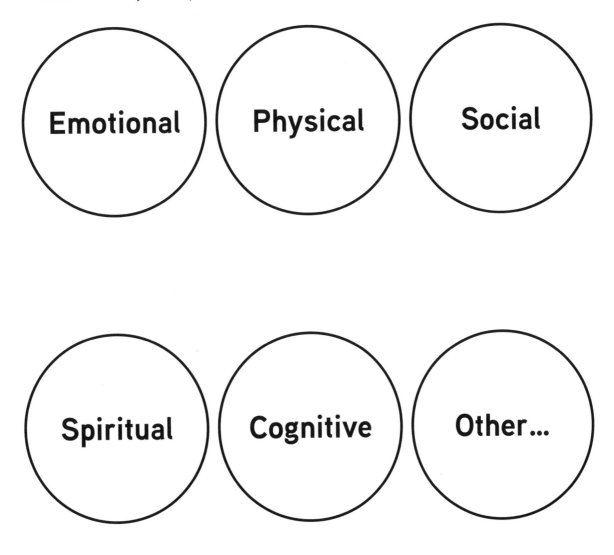

Copyright © Karen Treisman – *A Therapeutic Treasure Box for Working with Children and Adolescents with Developmental Trauma – 2018*

Worksheet 7.6
Multi-layered triggers

Draw or write your triggers for each heading below.

Sensory (auditory, olfactory, tactile/ physical, gustatory, visual)	Autobiographical
Emotional/relational/core beliefs/life scripts	Other

Copyright © Karen Treisman – *A Therapeutic Treasure Box for Working with Children and Adolescents with Developmental Trauma* – 2018

Hotspots and triggers with regard to a specific behaviour/situation

Write, draw, collage, or sculpt your responses.

Is there a particular behaviour/difficulty/theme/person that is currently worrying and/or distressing you? What is it? Describe and define it.

What is your relationship to... (that specific behaviour/situation/theme)? What is your history with/of...?

Copyright © Karen Treisman – *A Therapeutic Treasure Box for Working with Children and Adolescents with Developmental Trauma* – 2018

What does…mean to you?

What issues does it stir up in you? What feelings/memories/experiences are associated with it?

What ideas/values/beliefs/hotspots do you have that are being evoked/triggered/challenged by the…?

Copyright © Karen Treisman – *A Therapeutic Treasure Box for Working with Children and Adolescents with Developmental Trauma* – 2018

What, if any, impact does having a deeper understanding of why this pushes your buttons have?

How can you reduce/notice/manage this trigger? How can you find ways to stay regulated and grounded when this hotspot is pushed?

Copyright © Karen Treisman – *A Therapeutic Treasure Box for Working with Children and Adolescents with Developmental Trauma* – 2018

Worksheet 7.8
My treasure box diary

Days of the week and date	Things to ask myself
	Draw, collage, record, sculpt, or write the responses.
	What was a positive thing I did today? What positive qualities does that say about me?
	What is a positive thing in others or the world that I saw, noticed, or heard about today?
	What was my favourite thing about today (a thing that made me smile, or a moment that if I could I would bottle up)?
	When was there a time today when I felt good about myself/proud of myself/had fun?
Monday	
Tuesday	
Wednesday	

Copyright © Karen Treisman – *A Therapeutic Treasure Box for Working with Children and Adolescents with Developmental Trauma* – 2018

Thursday	
Friday	
Saturday	
Sunday	
Other thoughts and things to remember	

Copyright © Karen Treisman – *A Therapeutic Treasure Box for Working with Children and Adolescents with Developmental Trauma – 2018*

Worksheet 7.9
Grounding, soothing, and regulating idea cards

Describe my environment Think about all of the senses (see, feel, hear, taste, touch, balance)	**Go to my safe place (physical and imaginary) and use my safe place creative reminders** Name of my safe place: Safe place cue word: What can I see, smell, do, taste, hear? How do I feel emotionally and physically when in my safe place?
Use and explore my sensory regulating box	**Do a...** (e.g. puzzle, crossword, drawing) **Sort...** (e.g. Rubik's cube, papers, buttons)
Remind myself of my safe protective and supportive "person" Name: Description: Qualities:	**The things I can smell are...** (e.g. lavender, camomile, rosemary, vanilla, etc.) **The things I can touch are...** (e.g. fluffy material, velvet, silk, bubble wrap, etc.)
Listen to music/play an instrument/sing a song My go-to song is:	**Do something pampering** (e.g. painting nails, massaging hands, brushing hair/skin, having an aromatherapy bath, using a massaging chair, etc.) I will...

Copyright © Karen Treisman – A Therapeutic Treasure Box for Working with Children and Adolescents with Developmental Trauma – 2018

Do my breathing and relaxation exercises	Do my muscle tensing and releasing exercises
Step 1: Step 2: Step 3: Step 4:	Step 1: Step 2: Step 3: Step 4:
Do my mindfulness, meditation, yoga, and/or tai chi exercises	Clean, organise, or tidy
Rip, tear, or scrunch up some paper	Give myself an alternating butterfly hug
Blow bubbles, blow feathers, or blow a balloon	Drink from a straw/have a hot drink with some spices like cinnamon and nutmeg
Watch the movement of a lava lamp, a snow globe, fish in an aquarium, a rain stick, or glitter in a bottle	Interact with water (e.g. swimming water play, having a bath, playing with water)
Squeeze using alternating hands, a stress ball, clay, or some Play-Doh Or stretch using a theraband or elastic	Do some physical exercise (e.g. cycling, jogging, dancing, doing star jumps, shaking it out, etc.) I will…

Copyright © Karen Treisman – *A Therapeutic Treasure Box for Working with Children and Adolescents with Developmental Trauma* – 2018

Do some regulating exercises (e.g. drawing, putting weight on my back, swinging, twisting, rocking, crawling, climbing, wrapping myself in a blanket (weighted), etc.) I will…	**Make some rhythmic movement** (e.g. playing the drums, stamping my feet, dancing, or clapping my hands) I will…
Go for a walk/run/cycle in nature	**Interact with animals**
Chew or suck something like a sweet, dried fruit, chewing gum, or a chewy bracelet	**Wring out/twist/squeeze a wet towel**
Play a brain-based game such as…	**Do, listen, or watch something that will make me laugh…**
Look at positive memories such as photos, cards, or sentimental items (e.g. positive memory treasure box or sparkle moments diary)	**Let out a silent scream/find a quiet place to scream/bang a cushion**
Run cold water on my face	**Do something creative like…**

Copyright © Karen Treisman – *A Therapeutic Treasure Box for Working with Children and Adolescents with Developmental Trauma* – 2018

Count to ten or from ten backwards to zero	**Do some colouring in, trace a picture, or design a mandala**
Imagery and re-scripting When a difficult memory, thought, and/or feeling comes: I will imagine… I will remember… I will tell myself…	**My favourite inspirational quotes/sayings/ mottos/songs/movies are**
Name it to tame it (Siegel and Bryson, 2011) Name/say out loud how you feel. This feeling can also be drawn, acted out, danced, sculpted, depicted in sand, written about, etc.	**Positive self-talk** I am… I can… I will… I know… Things are different now because…
Speak to someone who I feel gets me That person is…	**???**

Copyright © Karen Treisman – *A Therapeutic Treasure Box for Working with Children and Adolescents with Developmental Trauma – 2018*

Coping card template

My Coping Card

I will cope, calm, and soothe myself by...

1.

2.

3.

I will tell myself:

I will call...

I will go to...

Copyright © Karen Treisman – *A Therapeutic Treasure Box for Working with Children and Adolescents with Developmental Trauma – 2018*

Worksheet 7.11
My self-care pledge and plan

Write, collage, or draw the responses below.

Why taking care of myself is important (including what I look like and the advantages of when I am at my best, and what I look like and the hazards of when I am depleted)…

I am committed to taking care of myself because…

I know I need to really do this when…

The things that make me feel happy, calm, relaxed, and fed are…

Copyright © Karen Treisman – *A Therapeutic Treasure Box for Working with Children and Adolescents with Developmental Trauma – 2018*

The things that support my mind are…

The things that support my body are…

The things that support my spirit are…

The things that support my relationships are…

Every day I will…

Copyright © Karen Treisman – *A Therapeutic Treasure Box for Working with Children and Adolescents with Developmental Trauma* – 2018

Every week I will...

Every...I will...

People I can see and places that I can go to remind me of the importance of this and to help are...

Barriers and obstacles to doing the above are...

Ways I will address these are...

Signature...

Copyright © Karen Treisman – *A Therapeutic Treasure Box for Working with Children and Adolescents with Developmental Trauma* – 2018

Strategies for Understanding, Reducing, and Responding to Outbursts, Tantrums, Rage, and Expressions of Dysregulation

Introduction

Before going on to explore some tangible and practical strategies for responding to expressions of dysregulation, it feels integral to reflect on and understand how and why these expressions might occur (although there are vast individual differences and many more factors than it is possible to detail in this chapter). This deeper understanding often supports children to organise their feelings and can support surrounding adults to connect with children's unexpressed feelings and see the behaviour as a form of communication. This can also support surrounding adults to receive the behaviour as less of a personal attack and to get less hooked into or stuck on the feeling, survival strategies, or defences. In essence, the more understandable a behaviour is, the less overwhelming it becomes and the more "thinking" can occur in creatively responding to it.

Multi-layered difficulties, such as regular and intense expressions of anger and rage, require multi-levelled and layered approaches (this will be discussed in the following sections). This chapter links to and is supported by several other chapters in this book. It draws on lots of the ideas and pulls many of the other chapters' threads together, so it should be read in conjunction with them. Issues to consider include attending to: children's identification, expression, and regulation of their feelings (Chapter 4); establishing their sense of safety (Chapter 3); celebrating their strengths and promoting their self-esteem (Chapter 5); and strengthening the parent–child relationships (Chapter 6).

Understanding further outbursts, rage, and expressions of dysregulation in the context of relational and developmental trauma

Experience and relationship to toxic stress and dysregulation

Children who experienced chronic and cumulative relational and developmental trauma, including toxic stress and chronic states of fear, have often not had the opportunities to learn healthy ways of expressing themselves, including ways of managing high arousal and of tolerating a wide range of emotions. Examples are given below; however, it is helpful (whilst looking after yourself and your wellbeing) to put yourselves in the shoes of three-year-old Teddy, two-year-old Nancy, or four-year-old Bailey (and their parents, who themselves are struggling and hurt). Keep in mind that these case examples are a snapshot of information rather than a full-length film. Imagine these types of experiences and toxic stress happening over and over again to developing and impressionable children, who are dependent on the adults and the world around them.

Three-year-old Teddy felt physically uncomfortable and was sore from a soiled nappy, being stuck in a cold room, and the bruising on his left arm, which was as a result of being pushed and grabbed days earlier. He was left in charge of his two-month-old baby sister, Jenna, who was hungry, crying, and distressed. Teddy didn't know how to soothe her, so he was left bearing witness to her distress and being overwhelmed by her shrieking cries. Teddy also had hunger pains; his mum and step-dad had gone out the night before to a party and left him unsupervised and without sufficient food or water. To him, it felt like forever since he last ate. He couldn't leave to find food, as he was locked in the room, but even if he could have left, he would have been scared about what response he might have received if he had been caught. He recalled that when his mum and step-dad had got back, they were walking all wonky and in a funny way, laughing hysterically, and talking very loudly and quickly, and their eyes had looked big and scary. After their arrival home, bar a brief check in, his mum and step-dad slept for the whole of the next day and locked the door of the room he and Jenna were in so that they could not get out to "annoy" them. At different points of the day, Teddy could hear the voices of strangers and the footsteps of people's shoes. Later that night, he hid in the corner, worried that the events of the night before would happen again. This time, he heard an extreme argument between his mum and step-dad. His mum was screaming and crying loudly, his step-dad was swearing and shouting, and Teddy could hear various thuds, stomps, and smashes around the house. Then all of the noises disappeared, and there was silence. Teddy did not know what awaited him, or what had happened. He stayed in his room, as still as possible, with his hands covering Jenna's ears.

Two-year-old Nancy had been given a toy from her grandmother. This had become her favourite toy. A few days later, a part broke off it and Nancy started sobbing. Her mother, unable to connect with the big emotions she was facing and the loss she felt, hit her firmly, took her other favourite toy away, and told her: "Stop being a baby, and get over it. It's your fault – you should have been more careful." Later in the day, Nancy spilt a drop of cola on the sofa and her mother responded in an explosion of emotions and verbal abuse.

Four-year-old Bailey's father returned home from a football match. His team had lost the game, and he responded by telling Bailey, using a range of swear words and high affect, what had happened. He then proceeded to punch the wall and bark orders at Bailey. The next week, Bailey had to go to the doctor's for a vaccination. Bailey's father became increasingly aggressive and threatening towards the receptionist as the waiting time got longer. Once in the room with the doctor, Bailey's father swore at the doctor, firmly positioned an anxious Bailey on the chair, and told the doctor: "Hurry up and get it done."

Children in a relational and developmental trauma context, like Teddy, Nancy, and Bailey, are often left without the presence of a safe, regulating adult in an overwhelming sea of emotional, sensorial, and physiological waves, including cortisol and adrenaline-driven waves. Therefore, their children's rage and fear systems will probably have been highly activated on a regular basis, without the necessary coping strategies or the responsive adult needed to calm their systems down. They often will have been trapped in a state of persistent fear without a solution or a way out and will have been dependent on the adults around them (who themselves are often struggling with regulating their emotions and/or being a consistent source of comfort). (See Chapter 3 to read about these situations being likened to the metaphor of shark-infested waters and/or desolate islands.) Some studies have shown that children exposed to traumas, such as family violence, show a similar pattern of activity in their brains as soldiers who have been exposed to combat. However, these are not soldiers; they are children who haven't developed fully, don't have a formed cognitive framework, haven't consented and chosen to join the army, haven't been trained, don't have a team of soldiers around them, don't have a guiding motivator or purpose in the same way, and don't have the weaponry, armour, and tanks to protect them.

Living in shark-infested waters, battlefields, or deserted islands, such as those experienced by Teddy, Nancy, and Bailey, can result in children having to find ways to survive, protect themselves, and develop the ability to quickly identify potential threats (see Worksheet 3.1 on different types of survival strategies). Bowlby (1980) described this fight, flight, or freeze phenomenon by stating that children learn to shrink from the world or to do battle with it (i.e. rage, outbursts, verbal abuse, etc.).

Therefore, in the context of cumulative and chronic trauma and toxic stress, children who have had to function in survival mode have often developed sensitive defence systems. Due to lots of practice and frequent activation, their fight, flight, or freeze responses (from the reptilian and survival brain) have probably been overused, like an extremely well-exercised strengthened muscle or a burglar alarm with the trigger constantly taped down. Their survival brain has been taken to the gym many times! This offers one of many explanations as to why children like Teddy often have a preoccupation with detecting and surviving threats and are more easily triggered and dysregulated (e.g. having outbursts) than many other children. They are often on high alert and have had to develop an amazingly attuned "trauma and danger" antenna, which has evolved through their experiences to constantly scan the environment for potential threat and danger.

This means that, in the context of trauma and toxic stress, children have often spent more time in their survival mode (in the lower building blocks of the brain). This can make this survival, primal part of the brain (the lower building blocks) highly activated and strengthened, but this survival mode dominance can also result in the other higher-level brain parts/functions, such as the thinking, rational, and learning parts of the brain, being underutilised, under-mastered, and less integrated. This explains one of the reasons why children who have lived in sensory disintegration and regularly felt unsafe/under threat often present with reflective function, cognitive, and executive function difficulties. This is problematic as it can impact a range of complex skills (e.g. managing impulses, thinking about the cause and effect of a situation, conflict-resolution/problem-solving skills, cognitive flexibility, perspective-taking skills, theory of mind, the ability to read others' emotional cues, mentalisation skills, reasoning, planning, showing empathy, and regulating one's own emotions).

Reflect on why and how a skill, such as perspective-taking or thinking of the cause and effect of a situation, might impact one's regulation of emotions/responding to conflict, etc. *What might happen, or what would it be like or look like, to have less developed skills, for example skills for problem-solving, reading others' emotions, or impulse control?* (See Worksheet 8.11 for some strategies for supporting and strengthening children's executive function skills.)

These difficulties can be exacerbated, as described in Chapter 3, because children who have experienced complex trauma are more likely to already have raised adrenaline and cortisol levels and to have a narrower window of tolerance (Siegel, 1999). The complex trauma and toxic stress these children have experienced means they are often over-sensitised and hyper-vigilant to threat and can have an out-of-sync emotional equilibrium system. These children often have a lower threshold for high-intensity emotions (so things can escalate faster and they can be more easily triggered) and are slower to return to what is often a heightened baseline of arousal (they can take longer to ground and soothe themselves and to restore their equilibrium). Because of these experiences, children can also present with a poor ability to self-regulate, process, integrate, and modulate affect and sensory stimuli (Warner and Koomar, 2009). For example, they might show changes in the way in which they regulate their stress systems, with their systems being either chronically elevated, over-expressed, and up-regulated (e.g. verbal and physical aggression, hyperactivity, hyper-vigilance, etc.), or chronically suppressed, under-expressed, and under-regulated (e.g. shutting off, blocking out, dissociating, etc.) (Gunnar and Fisher, 2006). This makes sense as many of these children have had to function more in hyper-aroused or hypo-aroused states; and/or more commonly oscillate between the two. These difficulties can also extend to children struggling with alternating between or transitioning smoothly from one arousal state to another (see Chapter 10), for example moving from playtime to a structured lesson or from being alert to needing to down-regulate in order to be able to sleep. These difficulties can often trigger and/or exacerbate behavioural dysregulation.

This is crystallised further by the multi-sensory aspect of trauma. For example, in the context of relational and developmental trauma, children often experience numerous sensory overloads (too much touching, intrusive eye contact, physical aggression, loud bangs, slamming of doors, the smell of alcohol, screaming, etc.) and/or sensory deprivation (too little touching, neglect, lack of stimulation, avoidance of eye contact, etc.), which can make the world around them feel too loud, too big, and too bright. Therefore, one drop of emotion to them can feel like a vast, all-consuming ocean that overrides their inhibitory systems. This is heightened when this ocean is experienced in the absence of a regulating and grounded responsive adult or when the ocean is being fuelled and the waves made more intense by the very adult who is supposed to be the source of comfort and calmness. Some case examples are given below.

During a maths lesson, a parked car's alarm went off outside the school. All of the children became unsettled and curious but were easily brought back to the task by the teacher, whereas Samantha remained on edge and distracted for the remainder of the day.

Cameron, aged 12, would have extreme physical outbursts lasting for up to two hours. His foster carers described him as being like "Jekyll and Hyde" and shared how they had to "walk on eggshells" to avoid a fiery rage. Due to earlier experiences of violence, abuse, unpredictability, and feeling utterly powerless, Cameron had developed a highly attuned antenna for danger. This meant he often misread incoming cues (e.g. a neutral face) as threats, and "small" triggers, such as a stare or the sound of the doorbell, could easily catapult him into a primitive "over-reactive" state.

Jamie had experienced numerous disrupted attachment relationships and traumatic endings and goodbyes. He had been moved through several foster placements. Each time Jamie's current foster carer dropped him off at school, or left the room, Jamie would become extremely distressed. His abandonment and rejection triggers would be pushed and he would fall through a "time hole" (Hobday, 2001) to a chain of negative and scary memories. He was unable to express this fear and instead communicated it through kicking, hitting, and shouting at his foster carer.

Anger as a form of communication and as a protective survival strategy

In line with the above points, it is essential to keep in mind that behaviour is a form of communication (see the "Behaviour as communication" section below and Box 6.4 for more explanation of this concept). Many young people who have had traumatic early experiences would have not experienced their feelings being noticed, labelled, and/or responded to, so this can be something more difficult for them to do. This is significant, as several outbursts are caused by limited emotional-regulation skills and/or from children's emotions spilling and cascading out through behaviours. Particularly, as children might not have developed or have access to the internal maps to guide them, the cognitive framework to structure them and to anchor to, or the words to make sense of their feelings.

For instance, some children who have experienced relational trauma are likely to have often felt powerless, used, abused, and vulnerable. Showing anger might give them a temporary sense of power and invulnerability, which in those moments can combat the intolerable feelings of powerlessness and being out of control again (the case example in Box 8.1 brings this to life). Within this, anger is usefully seen as a bodyguard emotion and as a mask emotion. It is often protecting and/or married to other emotions, such as guarding or masking underlying or unexpressed pain, hurt, sadness, fear, or shame. Therefore, the rage that surrounding adults can be faced with (e.g. shouting, slamming doors, punching, threatening, or swearing) is often a shield and a defence that the child has learned to put up in order to keep themselves protected, alive, and away from the shame, fear, pain, sadness, etc. For example, to survive shark-infested waters, some children might have to pretend to be or to take on the role of being a shark themselves. Thus, it is helpful, in addition to seeing the behaviour as communication, to keep in mind that it is often the hurt, trauma, pain, fear, or vulnerability that one is arguing with or facing, rather than the child.

Many of these children have learned that their vulnerability and needs won't be responded to in an attuned and sensitive way or met sufficiently, or that they will be met by pain, control, or fear, so they have had to develop different ways of communicating, expressing, regulating, or concealing these feelings (see Chapter 4 and Worksheet 6.1). This can also fit with the internalised notions that some children have learned and had reinforced over long periods of time and multiple relational situations that it is better to "attack than be attacked", "hate than be hated", "push away than be rejected", "shut out positivity and love than to have it taken away or result in pain", and "be feared than to be fearful". See Box 8.1 for a case example illustrating some of these concepts.

Box 8.1 **Case example Ethan**

Ethan, aged 15, had stacked up experiences of "anger" modelled to him in unhealthy ways through witnessing domestic violence from his father to his mother and being the recipient of regular harsh parental discipline. These expressions of rage and dysregulation started from being in the womb, which was essentially a warzone due to the frequent domestic violence and verbal hostility. Ethan's mother was so often frozen in her own fear and preoccupied with her own survival that she was unable to provide Ethan with the level of safety, stimulation, and positive interaction that he needed. Ethan's father also placed blame on him for taking away his wife's emotional and sexual attention and for "draining" him financially. At age six, Ethan witnessed his father stab his mother repeatedly, which resulted in her death and his father's imprisonment. Ethan was subsequently placed in foster care and unfortunately had placements.

At age 12, Ethan would often respond to others with a "tornado of rage", shouting and showing behaviour that had been described as being physically aggressive. He was described as having an "extremely short fuse and as enjoying arguing". Ethan was frequently in trouble with the police and had been excluded from two different schools. Although it was difficult to decipher and to see past the power of these spiky defences that Ethan had learned to put up to protect himself, it seemed that Ethan responded in this way when he felt threatened and/or vulnerable. Due to past unsafe, dysregulated experiences, Ethan's baseline of danger and safety seemed skewed; he had also learned to survive by cutting himself off from his feelings. He depersonalised and switched off from others' pain. Ethan found connecting with others' vulnerability and neediness too painful and re-triggering of his own vulnerability, so he responded by going into fight mode and hurting other vulnerable people or by finding other ways, such as taking drugs, to forget the past and attempt to get rid of intolerable feelings. For Ethan, being "mad rather than sad" and "feared rather than fearful" was preferable to feeling vulnerable and hurt. In order to survive the shark-infested waters, he had learned to act like a shark himself. He had learned that being in control made more sense than having meaningful, connected relationships, because closeness and connection equalled pain and danger. The ongoing warfare in his mind was reflected outwardly and externalised into his conflict with others. His rage seemed to be playing the role of guard dogs with spiked chains, which successfully kept others at bay and reinforced his belief that "I am not good enough" and "I am unlovable" (see illustration 8.1). Unlike the painful feelings Ethan had repeatedly experienced of being helpless, invisible, and powerless, these expressions of rage gave him temporary "adrenaline buzzes" and "kicks of energy" that made him feel alive, potent, and strong.

Illustration 8.1 Inner child beyond the defences and survival strategies

Dysregulation and the interplay with past experiences

For some children, an outburst of emotion may mean that they are responding to something that has been triggered in their past and, in that moment, they are back in a distressing place, reliving the experience, or contending with a trauma reminder. Unresolved, disintegrated, and unprocessed trauma experiences can have a powerful way of disorientating time. They often have no time stamp and can be fragmented, so the past can feel very alive and as if it is occurring in the present. One association or memory can stimulate a whole chain of memories and/or associations, a bit like a domino effect or a chain reaction. Examples of the interplay between triggers, trauma, and the expression through outbursts are given below.

Nadia was told by her foster carer that dinner was going to be 15 minutes late and that instead of the shepherd's pie they'd planned, they were going to share a pizza. In that moment, Nadia became increasingly distressed and dysregulated and spiralled into a rage (screaming, shouting, slamming doors, and punching the walls). After some exploring in later weeks, it emerged that when Nadia heard that dinner was delayed and they would have to share, she had fallen through a "time hole" (Hobday, 2001) back to past and painful experiences where she had felt deprived and starved of food and her needs had been forgotten and minimised. This had catapulted her into fight mode and extreme panic.

Ryder was playing football on a Saturday when one of the boys pushed him out of the way. Ryder responded by tripping the boy up and kicking him. In that moment, Ryder had feelings of being bullied, pushed around, hurt, and taken advantage of. These were all feelings he'd experienced repeatedly during the trauma he faced from his uncle. His body remembered many times where he had been hit, shoved, and pushed, and when he could not physically fight back, so he responded accordingly.

Kayla brought a stray dog back to her new foster placement. The foster carers told Kayla that she could not keep the dog but that they could take it to an animal shelter. Kayla became increasingly distressed, shouted verbal abuse at them, and ran out of the house. For Kayla, this dog symbolised so much more. It was about taking care of something and rescuing something, like she had tried to look after and rescue her siblings before they had been removed and she had been separated from them. It was about seeing the good in the dog, not giving up on it, and giving it a home, like she wished people could do for her.

Social learning theory – learned behaviour

It is helpful to consider the influence of learned patterns of behaviour and the power of role models and learning through watching and imitating. For example, for some young people, anger, aggression, and violence will have been weaved strongly into their family fabric and will have set the emotional tone of the house. Children could have often been reared in situations where violence and anger were the common language/economy, regularly witnessed and absorbed, and the normed and internalised way of managing situations and communicating feelings. These children probably had limited access to consistent, positive role models, demonstrations of positive conflict-resolution/problem-solving skills, and the modelling of prosocial behaviours and codes of conduct. They will have been exposed to antisocial behaviour and unhealthy messages, which may have been reinforced or rewarded through repeated experiences. Some examples of these are described below.

Whilst reading these cases, it is helpful to consider the following questions: *What would these children/caregivers have learned about expressing, communicating, and regulating their feelings? What would these children/caregivers have learned about consequences, behaviours, boundaries, and rules? What would these children/caregivers have learned about how to respond to situations of frustration, sadness, anger, and/or disappointment? What would these children/caregivers have learned about regulating their emotions and about skills such as perspective-taking, reflecting, problem-solving, and showing empathy?*

Jonah came home from school and shared a story of another boy pushing him. His father responded by pushing him against a wall and saying, "Next time you fight back, you weak little girl." The next day, when Jonah's brother reported getting into a fight at football practice and winning the fight, their father beamed with pride and gave him a high five.

Jessica's mother was disconnected, preoccupied, and emotionally unavailable. She generally left Jessica alone and rarely interacted with her. Jessica had learned that the only way she could get her mother's attention was when she upped the ante and magnified her behaviour, for example throwing items, smashing doors, and screaming.

Manny's father, David, got a verbal police warning for getting into a physical altercation in a pub. Later that night, when Manny and his father walked home, David spotted a police car, and, in front of Manny, he keyed the car in retaliation for the warning whilst shouting verbal abuse about the police.

Mason watched from the back seat of the car as his dad stole an 83-year-old lady's handbag. Later, Mason witnessed his dad retelling and celebrating the day's success with a group of friends.

George's mother took him to A&E after he broke his arm at the playground. She became increasingly frustrated about the long wait and expressed her frustration by shouting at the nurse and throwing a piece of medical equipment at the wall.

Within this, many of these children will also have been raised with a lack of age-appropriate boundaries and parental supervision, limit-setting, and monitoring.

The discipline they received will often have been inconsistent, disproportionate, of harsh nature, or given in an emotionally driven, non-thinking place from a dysregulated/triggered caregiver. Examples are given below.

Harry hit his brother repeatedly with a frying pan and his mother said nothing and looked away. The next day, Harry accidentally spilled some milk, which resulted in his mother "violently beating him" with a chair.

Maia went uncorrected by her uncle after shouting racial abuse at a bus driver and was given permission to go to a friend's party that night.

Liora came home with a paint stain on her new dress and one of her plaits loosened and was repeatedly kicked and hit because of presenting a "poor, dirty, and lazy" appearance to the outside world.

Ten-year-old Drew would walk home from school unescorted and would subsequently have three hours wandering around the estate, known for gang-related activities, until his mother would return home from work.

Hostile attribution bias

Research has shown that children who have experienced complex trauma tend to struggle with differentiating facial experiences and are therefore more likely to interpret events and faces as being angry and threatening and subsequently have stronger emotional reactions to negative facial expressions (e.g. negativity and/or attentional bias and negative mind-reading) (Perlman *et al.*, 2008). This is sometimes referred to as the Hostile Attribution Bias phenomenon. This is where a person will assume that another person has an intention to harm/wrong them, meaning that "normal/benign" behaviours can be perceived as "hostile or aggressive".

This adds another layer in further understanding why young people may be more easily triggered and misinterpret others' behaviours/facial expressions/tone of voice. This type of thinking has also been referred to in the literature as hyper-mentalisation (Sharp *et al.*, 2011) – where someone misattributes another person's intention and responds with epistemic hyper-vigilance. An example is given below.

On the way to college, Fiona was accidently pushed by an elderly man due to the busy, rush-hour streets. Fiona saw this as being deliberate and attacking and responded as such. Similarly, when I was travelling on the tube in London with Fiona, she would comment on how other passengers (who were listening to their music or reading their newspapers) were staring at her in a provocative, goading way. She shared that she felt they were thinking negative thoughts about and judging her.

These situations seemed to trigger and switch on Fiona's learned way of seeing herself, others, and the world (e.g. her core beliefs and life scripts), her narrower window of tolerance, higher baseline for arousal, and tendency to read hostile/threatening intentions in others. These difficulties can be intensified by emotional regulation, reflective function, and cognitive difficulties, which are more common in a relational and developmental trauma context.

Having presented some of the reasons why children may express themselves through rage, anger, and/or dysregulation, some key messages to hold in mind about these arousal states will now be discussed. Following this, there will be discussion on assessing behaviours and viewing them as forms of communication before presenting some practical and creative strategies for responding to and supporting outbursts.

Some key messages and principles about anger, rage, dysregulation, and outbursts

These principles and messages should inform subsequent interventions, responses, and strategies.

The feeling is OK and understandable

We all feel and experience different types of emotions at different times, including emotions such as anger. It is vital to hold in mind that anger is a valid and important emotion. It can have a lot of useful purposes, such as ensuring our survival, fighting for our rights, relieving us of pent-up feelings, and helping us to protect the things that we value the most.

When has anger been a useful emotion or effective form of communication for you? What other benefits and advantages are there to expressing one's anger? Are there times when you wish you could have shared the feelings of frustration and anger and were not able to?

With this in mind, it is advocated that there should be an overarching message and acceptance explicitly and implicitly shared with children/parents that the feeling of anger is OK, healthy, needed, understandable, and can be useful but that the action of being aggressive and/or of hurting others is not. This should clearly distinguish the difference between a thought, a feeling, and an action/behaviour (see Worksheets 4.20 and 4.21). For example, a child has every right to feel angry/wronged/hurt, but taking this out in unhealthy and/or hurtful ways is not the optimal way of expressing and responding to these feelings.

This is in line with the concept of externalising, which advocates for the child to be positioned as separate to their difficulties and not to be defined by them. (The problem is the problem, not the person) For example, rather than saying "Stop being a naughty boy", one would say "I understand you are feeling frustrated that your sister took your ball but it is not OK to show your frustration through kicking your sister"; or instead of "What a good boy", one might say something more specific, such as: "Wow, well done for tidying up – that was so kind and thoughtful of you."

Early intervention and prevention

Another key message is that early intervention and prevention is the best form of behavioural change. In essence, we want to try and catch behaviours early and to put in place strategies that reduce triggers, crises, and/or escalations. This is under the premise that it is far easier to prevent a fire than to put it out or to stop it from spreading. This can be likened to a tornado, which builds and gets bigger the more it moves forward, travels, and is fuelled. For example, if a child is starting to become triggered or dysregulated, it is far easier to support them during the run up to that moment than once they are so caught up in the sea of emotions that they are no longer in their thinking, reflecting, and learning brain. Similarly, if a child is occasionally pushing other children, this behaviour and their underlying feelings are likely to be much more easily shifted if it is acknowledged and addressed at that time, rather than at the point of a more serious incident or when there has been an increase in its frequency and severity.

Behavioural change within the context of a relationship

In addition to the above key messages, the best anchor for behavioural change is through a safe, positive, containing, responsive, and containing relationship (e.g. attachment-based learning). Therefore, building on one's relationship is a key part of making shifts in behavioural patterns and expressions (see Chapter 6 for expansion of this concept and for ideas on strengthening the parent–child relationship). The more positive the relationship is, the more likely it is that the child will be able to allow themselves to be supported during a time of dysregulation and to find other ways to communicate their distress, rather than through outbursts. Within this, behavioural change through relationships frames these behaviours as not only occurrences that cause conflict and tension within a relationship, but rather as opportunities for reconnection, growth, and learning. The child needs to learn to respond to big feelings through co-regulation; and to know that they have the safety and consistency of that relationship unconditionally. This also fits with the concept of doing things relationally and together in a supported way, for example, "for" and "with"; rather than "to" and "on".

Where possible, avoid assumptions

Another key principle is that, where possible (I know it is easier said than done), it is important to be curious, understanding, and not make assumptions or take things for granted. For example, one might say loaded statements to a child, such as "Calm down", "You're safe", or "Don't exaggerate", but, for a child who has experienced relational and developmental trauma, these might be completely alien concepts and huge asks. They are responding to the world and to others from their relationship lens and from their attachment mirror, which might look and feel very different to our own. They might never have experienced calm, know what calm is, feel or trust that they are safe enough to be calm, or have the actual skills to calm themselves down. Telling children who have been raised in shark-infested waters to, for example, calm down may be the equivalent of telling them not to swim, to do aqua aerobics, or to try out synchronised swimming whilst they are surrounded by sharks!

The cycle of anger being reinforced: negative discourses

Many children who have experienced relational and developmental trauma have developed a fragile sense of self and have a toxic amount of shame, for example

"I am bad, unlovable, a mistake". Therefore, it is important that we are mindful of the power of language and/or the choice of words/descriptors. This includes avoiding statements and joking threats such as "It's in her blood", "He is just like his father", "Pack your bags, you're out of here", and "Nah, I never liked you much anyway". Labels stick, they can be restrictive, they are powerful (see Chapter 5), and they can travel with children on their journey.

Before presenting suggested strategies, some ideas around assessment and viewing behaviour within its context will be discussed.

Assessment of the behaviours

Taking the above into account, it feels important that, before embarking on introducing or offering any strategies, a thorough and informed assessment is carried out to understand the presenting behaviour in more detail and to see and to try to understand the behaviour within a wider context and in an attachment and trauma framework. Behaviours are generally on a continuum and can show themselves in multiple ways and to varying degrees in diverse contexts and with different people. They can also be coloured significantly by the impact of the behaviour and how stressful the behaviour is perceived to be. The child's "age" (social, emotional, and developmental versus chronological) and associated expectations will also hold some bearing. For example, a two-year-old who spits at their nursery school teacher when frustrated would be viewed differently to a 17-year-old who spits at their boss at work.

Box 8.2 supports this assessment process with possible questions to ask about a specific behaviour. This is in addition and not a replacement for a wider attachment and trauma assessment (see Table 2.1 and Chapter 5 in *Working with Relational and Developmental Trauma in Children and Adolescents* – Treisman, 2016).

Box 8.2 **Behaviour kaleidoscope**

1. What is the behaviour? What does it look like? Can you give an example of when the behaviour happened? It is important to use specific descriptions that clearly *define* the behaviour, rather than vague descriptions such as "He's naughty" or "She has a temper".

2. Can you describe a typical day in your household, and how the behaviour shows itself?

3. How does this behaviour look in relation to other children of their age?

4. When did the behaviour start and how frequently does the behaviour occur? Why might the behaviour have started at that time?

5. What is the child's relationship with the behaviour? Where might they have seen, learned, developed, and needed it?

6. Where does the behaviour occur? Are there differences depending on the context?

7. What other variables impact the behaviour? Are there particular patterns of behaviour? It can be helpful to track, map, chart, and/or diarise the behaviour's patterns. Consider what happened before, during, and after the behaviour.

8. What triggers, hotspots, and variables (e.g. environmental, sensory, autobiographical, physical, cognitive, relational, emotional, and situational) make the presenting difficulty bigger, smaller, absent, present, etc.? What happens when these triggers occur? What do they look like? What is the impact of them? What is the young person's relationship to the triggers? Are there ways in which they could reduce and take control over the triggers? How can others support them to reduce and manage the triggers?

9. What other strategies does the child use to regulate their arousal, to keep themselves safe, and to function?

10. What happens in the times when the behaviour is absent or less? What is different and why? How can these times be increased and celebrated?

11. What is the impact of the behaviour on the child and those around them (e.g. on their self-care, self-presentation, sleep, eating, mood, school life, relationships, learning, hobbies, daily living skills, and self-esteem)? What is the presenting difficulty making trickier or stopping the child/caregiver from doing?

12. What different interpretations and feelings does the behaviour evoke in different people? What clue does the way others feel when at the receiving end of this behaviour give us about the child's feelings?

13. What do we think the behaviour is communicating? What functions is it serving? What might the story be behind the behaviour and underneath the surface? (See Box 6.4.)

14. If the behaviour could talk/had a voice, what might it say?

15. What might it look/feel like (the advantages and disadvantages) if the behaviour disappeared or was absent?

16. What is the child's sense-making and meaning-making and what are their attributions and explanations about the behaviour? How are these similar or different to other people's conceptualisations of the behaviour? How stressful and/or manageable is the behaviour to the child and/or Team Around the Child?

17. What strategies/interventions have been tried already? What bits of these were helpful or less helpful and why?

18. What responses/reactions from others has the child had when showing the behaviour?

19. What skills are needed to modify the behaviour? (Think about the child's experience of relational and developmental trauma, their survival strategies, their developmental stages, their executive function skills, etc.)

If there are multiple concerning behaviours, this process may need to be done several times; however, also consider whether there are any linking threads and themes between the behaviours.

Behaviour as communication

As demonstrated in the previous sections, it is important that we look beyond the presenting behaviour, defences, or survival strategies, i.e. the rage, the hitting, or the verbal abuse. This can be likened to a set of Russian dolls, where we see the outer layer but can be unaware of all of the other parts within the larger doll. Such as in Photo 8.1, the child felt that others saw their outer layer of "anger", but not the more hidden and internalised layers of sadness and fear.

Photo 8.1 Using Russian dolls to represent the different feelings underneath the anger/defence

It is helpful to view behaviours as forms of communication. Behaviours are multi-layered, they tell a story, and they often provide us with a map of and clues about the child's inner worlds and unexpressed needs. We need to try to take the role of detectives, translators, and archaeologists in order to uncover, decode, and discover what the child/parent's behaviour might be communicating and what the behaviour might be trying to tell us.

If the behaviour could talk or had a voice, what might it say? If the behaviour was a puzzle, what pieces might it be made up out of and what picture might it form when put together? If the behaviour was a map, where would it have started from, what direction does it travel in, and where is it heading?

This is an important part of making sense of the behaviours, of disentangling them, and of organising them. See Box 8.2 for some recommended questions and reflective exercises around thinking about behaviour as a form of communication.

The questions presented in Boxes 6.4 and 8.2 are crucial, as the more we know why something might be happening, the more we can support the young person to become aware of the why and in organising their feelings, and the less alien, personal, and confusing they can feel. This deciphering and decoding of behaviours, and viewing them as communication and from multiple angles, is also important, as it influences our meaning-making, sense-making, and attributions about a behaviour, which inevitably have an impact on how we receive, make sense of, label, conceptualise, and respond to a behaviour (see Chapter 6 for examples of this). Examples of the helpfulness of looking beyond the presenting behaviour are given below.

Christopher's special guardians, Helga and Brian, were becoming increasingly concerned about his behaviour. They shared that he regularly "lied". This included "lying" about large life facts, things that were done in front of them (such as taking the biscuits from the cupboard in their presence and then denying he took them), and things like telling the class he had visited Disneyland on the weekend when he hadn't. This was extremely difficult, as two of Helga and Brian's strongest values were around honesty and truth-telling, and in both of their families lying was seen as deceptive and disrespectful. Through meaning-making, detective work, and seeing the multiple layers of the behaviour iceberg and wider behavioural landscape, Helga and Brian were able to make links with why this behaviour got under their skin and triggered them.

They were also able to reflect, with support, on some of the reasons why Christopher might stretch the truth, such as: his fantasy world felt better and safer to him than his reality; the stories he told to his peers were an attempt to build himself up in others' eyes and to address his low self-esteem; his previous experience of truth-telling had resulted in extreme punishment and catastrophic consequences; he stretched the truth for fear of relational rejection. Moreover, his previous experience of relational and developmental trauma had been intertwined with deception, secrecy, and a conspiracy of silence; therefore this way of relating had become the common place language and emotional tone. This also was exacerbated by Christopher being socially and emotionally much younger than his chronological age, which meant that some of the behaviours he presented with would be considered a "normal" part of child development. These increased understandings supported Helga and Brian to understand what function the stretching of the truth was serving and to subsequently find responses to match these rationales.

Nelly's foster carer reported that she frequently took items of food from the cupboards. This had been framed as saying she was "dishonest, a hoarder, a thief, ungrateful, and greedy". However, when viewed in context and considered as a form of communication, it was conceptualised that Nelly took items of food because she had previously experienced deprivation and had been raised in an environment where food was often absent, conditional, and unpredictable. She had also developed a pattern of soothing herself and filling her "emotional void" with food. This different framing inevitably influenced the foster carer's response and understanding of Nelly.

Points to be mindful of/tips around the following strategies

Readers should refer to Chapter 1 for some factors to consider when implementing the described techniques; however, some extra tips and points to be mindful of in relation to outbursts and rage are presented below.

The chosen strategies should be informed by a thorough assessment and formulation process, so that an appropriate, matched intervention can be selected. This should include attention to the theories presented previously about why outbursts, rage, or dysregulation might occur (see Box 6.4 and the "Behaviour as communication" section). As with all the strategies presented in the book, these should be guided and anchored to a safe, trusting, containing, and positive relationship. Holding at the heart of all interventions that relational trauma requires relational repair.

In addition, for those who have experienced relational and developmental trauma and who have a diagnosis of a neurodevelopmental disorder such as autism, have a foetal alcohol spectrum disorder diagnosis, and/or a learning disability, it is likely that more specialist and adapted techniques will be needed than those presented in this chapter. It is also worth mentioning that there is a whole school of thought around diet and nutrition with regards to reducing and responding to certain behaviours, which is an area that may be helpful to consider and to integrate with the strategies that follow (however, these will not be detailed here).

It is also recognised that tantrums and expressions of anger are normal and an expected part of child development and human nature. Therefore, the appropriate tool will also differ depending on the type of outburst and/or dysregulation and whether it is one of distress and fear. Often, if it is not one of distress, then distracting, ignoring, humour, and/or walking away may be the best options. This is why getting to know the young person you are supporting and the way they communicate their distress is so important.

Additionally, it is important to hold in mind that it is normal and expected that developing children explore their boundaries and have moments of dysregulation. Although these strategies are intended for the more extreme end, they may have some use for the "average" moments, but I am not suggesting that a wealth of tools be tried and tested for every child exhibiting tantrums. The strategies in this chapter are aimed at children who are having regular, frequent, and intense expressions of dysregulation that are having a significant impact on them and their surrounding adults.

Practical and creative strategies for reducing and responding to outbursts and dysregulation

Role-modelling, self-care, and self-regulation

Children need to be surrounded by positive role models. Children are like sponges, are very impressionable, and, in the context of relational trauma, have often been exposed to unhealthy ways of communicating and responding. This means they need different and more positive ways of expressing, communicating, and responding to emotions and arousal states taught and modelled to them. This fits with the saying "The way we treat them teaches them". The positive thing to hold in mind from a social learning perspective is that if these behaviours were learned, therefore, they can also be relearned. However, because these behaviours took a long time to learn and had endless reinforcement and repetition at an impressionable age, it is likely that it will also take a lot of time, trust, repetition, and safety for the child to relearn them or to learn different ways of responding.

In the context of relational and developmental trauma, children will probably have had anger met with anger, had their anger fed or fuelled further, or had a dysregulated, triggered caregiver respond disproportionately and/or engage in mutually escalating behaviours that inevitably reinforce and perpetuate the cycle of anger and dysregulation (see Box 8.3). Therefore, many children's expected responses would have been based on their chain necklace and memory bank of receiving angry, punitive, and non-connected responses from their surrounding adults. They are less likely to have had a safe, secure adult who could support them in effectively co-regulating big emotions, which is an essential process in being able to go on to master the skill of self-regulation. This means that children need positive role-modelling from regulated, attuned, and thinking adults to show them a different way of doing and being in relationships, to offer them a different and reparative relational experience, and to fill their memory banks up with thoughtful and positive experiences. See Chapters 6 and 7 on different ways for working towards being these safe hands, thinking minds, regulating bodies, and positive role models.

Box 8.3 **Practical activity and reflection my own relationship to anger/aggression/frustration**

What is your relationship to anger/aggression/frustration/outbursts? What was your experience as a child of anger/aggression/frustration/outbursts? How much was anger/frustration/aggression given to you by your caregivers? How was anger/aggression/frustration responded to by others when you were younger? How is this similar or different now? How able are you to respond rather than react? What factors make this more or less possible?

How does it make you feel when someone responds to you now in an angry/hostile/frightening way? (Also consider the questions in Box 6.4.) How do you tend to respond or protect yourself?

How do you show your feelings of anger/frustration, if at all? How would people around you know you were experiencing this feeling (e.g. through your body, face, words, or actions)? (See Worksheets 4.1 and 4.2.) How would it feel if others responded to you in this way? When in a place of "anger", what skills and coping strategies support you to move out of this place or to stay centred? Where did you learn these skills and coping strategies from? How have they developed and been reinforced? How similarly or differently do you think the children you are supporting/living with would respond to these questions?

Labelling, identifying, and expressing emotions

Outbursts are often a result of underdeveloped emotion regulation skills, of children not having the words to make sense and name their emotions, and of children showing surrounding adults how they feel through communicating these feelings through their behaviours. The key building blocks and foundations of emotions have often not been provided for children in the context of relational and developmental trauma and therefore have not been mastered or had opportunities to be practised and positively reinforced over long periods of time. Therefore, children need to be supported to recognise, notice, identify, manage, organise, modulate, and self-regulate their emotions (see Chapter 4 for a range of different strategies on feelings development, as well as an explanation of linked concepts such as "connection before correction" (Hughes, 2011) and "name it to tame it" (Siegel and Bryson, 2011), which are key concepts when responding to dysregulation).

The correction and discipline part should be anchored to connection with the child and to the relationship and to a place where they feel heard, seen, validated, acknowledged, and understood. This fits with trying to get alongside the child, see the world from their perspective, decode what they are trying to say through their behaviour, and responding in an empathetic, connected way that reduces shame rather than triggering it. Some examples are given here.

"I can imagine that you might be feeling angry because your mum is not here to play with you. It is OK and understandable that you are feeling angry, and I am really sorry that this has happened to you, but it is not OK to let the anger out by hitting your sister – you can let the anger out by…"

"I am sorry that you learned that…but in this house, we do… We know it will take time, but we are going to work with you to feel differently about…"

"I can see you feel very cross with me, and I get it. What you are feeling is really important and is understandable, and I want to hear what you are saying to me. So, I need you to use your words instead of your hands."

"I just noticed how frustrated you felt when I corrected your homework. I think you might have thought that I thought you were stupid or that you couldn't do it – no wonder you would feel angry. I am so sorry – that wasn't my intention."

"I know that when I get angry, you might think I do not love you, but I love you lots because… I tell you these things because I care and want to keep you and us safe."

It is unfair to expect a child to respond and adjust their expressions of anger if they don't understand what it is, how it feels, why it is there, what impact it has, and what different ways there are to respond to it. This includes prioritising the expression and identification of feelings and supporting children to understand and to make distinctions between their own and others' thoughts, feelings, and actions. The head, hand, and heart metaphor, the chain of sequences model, or the Cognitive Behavioural thoughts, feelings, and actions cycle can be useful ways of exploring these differences (see Worksheets 4.20 and 4.21 to support these discussions). Within this, it is also important to remember that we cannot take away a vehicle of expression and a coping strategy without replacing it with another solution and a coping strategy. For example, if Luca normally releases his frustration by throwing items and banging doors and can no longer do this, where will this frustration go, and what can he do instead?

Monitoring and recording emotions

Children who have experienced relational and developmental trauma and toxic stress can understandably struggle to transition smoothly from gear to gear or to go gently from accelerate to brake; instead they can jolt from one to another. Surrounding adults often describe feeling that a young person can go from "zero to hundred within seconds" or that they are like "Jekyll and Hyde". Surrounding and supporting adults need to be vigilant and responsive to the child's arousal level – when they are both under- or over-aroused – and support them in increasing their awareness of these different feeling states and in monitoring these processes as opposed to being overwhelmed by an intense avalanche of emotions (Chapters 3 and 4 provide a range of strategies to support this).

Exploring multi-layered triggers

As previously discussed, behaviour is a form of communication, and outbursts, rage, and dysregulation are often caused and/or fuelled by multi-layered triggers being pushed. Therefore, it is important to really get to know the individual child and to identify their unique likes, dislikes, cues, and multi-sensory triggers (e.g. environmental, sensory, autobiographical, physical, cognitive, relational, emotional, and situational) (see Chapter 3 and Worksheets 7.6 and 7.7 for more on identifying and supporting triggers). Identifying these triggers can make it easier to find ways to reduce them and subsequently to increase feelings of safety, which is crucial as behavioural dysregulation often comes from a place of feeling unsafe, threatened, and/or in survival mode. Identifying triggers is also important, as it can provide greater opportunities for catching situations early and de-escalating them before they cascade; as well as increasing one's ability to make sense of and decode tricky responses and behaviours. This meaning-making and sense-making process not only helps the responses to feel less overwhelming, but also means that the more surrounding adults have a deeper understanding of the underlying message of the behaviour, the better equipped they are to support the children in enhancing their own understanding, and to offer genuine connection and empathy to the child. Examples are given below.

India had had repeated experiences in her early childhood of learning that her feelings were not important and that it was safer to leave them buried and concealed. She rarely shared her feelings, and instead would often have what appeared to be an inauthentic smile plastered across her face. Her response to being asked if she was alright would generally be "Yes, I am fine" or a nod. This was even the case if she fell over and hurt herself or was physically sick. Through close observation, whole-body listening, and purposeful effort, India's foster carers began to notice that when she was feeling distressed there were subtle signs that she communicated. This included her twirling her hair, skin changing colour, putting her hands in her pocket, biting the left side of her lip, becoming quieter, and turning her head away. Identifying these triggers significantly increased opportunities for connecting with India and offering her attuned, sensitive, and reflective responses. This also gave her foster carers a platform from which to begin to support India in learning other ways of expressing herself and having more relational interactions of experiencing her feelings being noticed and kept in mind.

Eleven-year-old Sophie was having difficulty in maths class. She showed her distress in a variety of ways including fidgeting, distracting her classmates, and at times shouting and throwing the papers and chairs around the classroom. This was described by one of her teachers as being "naughty, lazy, and showing off". Sophie's adoptive parents were also upset by this behaviour, and she was repeatedly told off and reminded of the importance of maths. In response, Sophie's teacher paid more attention to her and put in place some additional practice sessions. This seemed to exacerbate the difficulty. After some exploration in therapy, it emerged that Sophie was having intrusive images and body memories during the maths class and her behaviour was her way of trying to ward off and avoid these feelings. Her maths teacher wore glasses and had a beard. These were two of the prominent features that her uncle, who had repeatedly sexually and emotionally abused her, had. Once this connection was made for Sophie, her adoptive parents, and the school, the attributions and conceptualisations made around Sophie's behaviour shifted, as did their responses.

These triggers can be helpfully embedded by expressing them creatively, such as through using metaphors of bugs, a remote control, a fuse, etc. Chapter 3 contains a range of ideas, photographed examples, and worksheets on these creative strategies.

Emphasising the helpfulness of talking and sharing

There are numerous ways of talking about the hazards of children holding things in or of the chain of events that can occur from expressing oneself in certain ways, including:

- writing down/drawing an advantages and hazards list

- making a physical paper chain of events (see Photo 8.2)

- labelling domino pieces to illustrate the domino effect (see Photo 8.3)

- drawing a bag, wall, ball and chain, or an obstacle course that illustrates the difficulties and what they might be stopping the young person from being able to do.

Photo 8.2 Paper chain of events

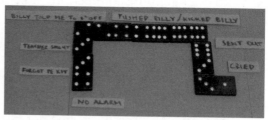

Photo 8.3 Domino chain of events

Another technique I have found useful in therapy is to give young people a balloon and ask them to think of a time that they have felt "the Anger" (an externalised character name can be used) take over and then to blow into the balloon. I then support them to continue to reflect on additional situations when "the anger" took over/visited/got in their way. Each time they are encouraged to keep blowing into the balloon. Inevitably, the balloon eventually pops. This can provide a helpful platform to explore what happens when feelings are held on to for a long time, when there is a build up of feelings, when a pop happens, and so on. One can also explore, if appropriate, what they felt like physically when they were blowing into the balloon and how they felt and imagined others might feel when it popped. It can then be useful to encourage them to try again, but this time to support them to talk about the feeling, name it, draw it, write it down, and so forth, and to subsequently let some of the air out each time. They can then reflect on the similarities, differences, and lessons learned. It is also worth holding in mind that some young people might find this easier and more distancing to talk about this from the perspective of a friend or in an imaginary scenario. This concept can also be illustrated by pouring water into a cup and talking about how it can spill over (see Photo 8.4), or filling a box with items that are eventually too heavy to lift or tip over.

Photo 8.4 Water spilling over

Expectations and goals

Often, outbursts can occur or situations can escalate due to poor communication, frustration, and unrealistic and unmanageable expectations. The following sections will offer some tips for addressing these, with the overarching aim of reducing outbursts and optimising children's opportunities for success.

First, it is generally useful for surrounding adults to tell the young person clearly and calmly what is expected from them before the proposed action takes place. This has the intention of preparing them for what is to come, reducing anxieties, and increasing their chances of success. This also fits with the notion of not making assumptions or taking for granted what the child had previously been shown or had learned. This aims to be transparent, improve communication, and alleviate some of the unknowns and anxieties that children may have around uncertainty and feeling out of control. This is important, as many young people find transitions particularly difficult and triggering (see Chapter 10). For example, one might say: "We are going shopping, and I want you to walk next to me and hold on to the trolley, then we will…"

This can also be enhanced by giving the child regular warnings, prompts, and anchors, including using words like before, after, next, when, and then, and/or using props such as egg timers, alarms, and visual calendars; for example: "We are going to play two more rounds of Connect 4 and then we will finish and pack it away in your games box so that we can get ready for dinner" or "At the end of Peppa Pig, which is in five minutes, we will be…"

Within this, expectations need to be delivered and set in a child-friendly, age-appropriate, clear, specific, and consistent way. For example, think how many potential things we ask children to do for something as seemingly simple as brushing their teeth (e.g. go into the bathroom, pick up the toothpaste, take the lid off, put the water on, put toothpaste on the toothbrush, etc.). It becomes a huge ask, especially for children who have less developed executive function and cognitive skills (see Worksheet 8.11).

Instructions should be kept as simple, short, and straightforward as possible, with the different steps supported, scaffolded, and, if necessary, repeated multiple times. Some children may benefit from having extra reminders for certain routines, such as through making a social story, a comic strip of the steps, or a visual prompt card or role-playing/rehearsing the steps themselves or through a teddy (see Worksheet 8.11 for additional ideas and strategies for supporting and strengthening executive function skills).

Expectations vary and should be appropriate to the context and to the child's individual abilities and differences. This may include reviewing and adjusting expectations accordingly. For example, children do not have the same cognitive abilities as adults, which means that their brains are likely to need more processing and thinking time. They also do not have the same ability to control and regulate themselves as most adults. Children who have experienced chronic and cumulative trauma can present as socially and emotionally much younger than their chronological age and therefore require expectations and goals to be adjusted accordingly (this also needs to take into consideration cultural and societal expectations and conceptualisations of children/childhood). See Chapter 5 for more ideas and accompanying worksheets on creating SMART goals.

Behavioural contracts, house rules, and consequences

In line with the above, it feels important to ensure that children have as structured, consistent, and predictable environments as possible, especially as this is not likely to have been experienced previously. The rules and expectations may be alien or extremely different to rules and expectations that the children experienced previously, so they can find them more difficult to understand and to follow. This is heightened if a child is living in survival mode, is struggling to regulate their emotions, and/or has sensory processing, cognitive, and executive function difficulties (see Chapter 3 and Worksheet 8.11). Ideally, expectations and rules should be as clear, logical, defined, and specific as possible to support this process. For example, instead of "Be good", it is helpful to try to state what being good looks like or what specific behaviours are deemed as being "good". To build on this, certain behaviours can be linked to SMART goals and to associated reward charts (see Worksheet 5.6) when done in a trauma-informed and attachment–aware framework.

It can also be useful to write down or draw the house rules and the expectations of the house. This is important, as so often we expect children to do something without them actually knowing what to do, what doing it looks like, what is expected of them, or what skills are needed to do the task. These rules and expectations should, ideally, be as collaborative as possible and reciprocal so that it is not a one-way street or something that is only being done to children. There should also be rules for the teachers/caregivers/therapist too; for example: "We will read to you every night" or "We will ask you about your day and listen to what you say." Discussing the rules should be done in as child friendly, playful, humorous, and engaging a way as possible. An example is given below.

Six-year-old Hazel was repeatedly hitting her foster carers. No one technique tends to work in isolation, so her foster carers used many of the previously described techniques. They were also supported in exploring with Hazel, in a creative, relational, and playful way, other things that hands can be used for instead of hitting by making a poster (see Photo 8.5).

It can also be nice to get everyone involved in creating the rules, for example, in addition to choosing the rules together, children might like to decorate and sign the document, younger children might like to sign using their hand or footprint.

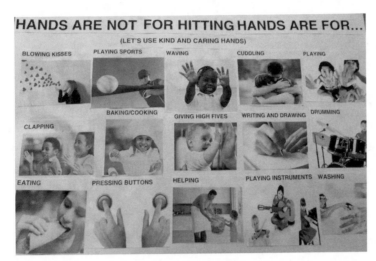

Photo 8.5 Hands are not for hitting, hands are for… poster

Keeping and breaking rules

Where possible, rules should be explicitly linked to predictable, consistent, logical, and fair consequences. These identified consequences should be given as a learning experience, as a discipline strategy, and as a way of learning a new skill and having prosocial behaviour modelled, and not as a punishment, a shaming experience, or be delivered from a place of anger or dysregulation. For example, if a child breaks an item, they might need help to fix it or to contribute to the cost of replacing it.

It is also important to try and make these consequences as immediate as possible and not to drag out difficult situations. The young person needs to know that things will be OK again, that they are forgiven (this is called relational repair), and that it is the behaviour that is not OK and not them as a person. This fits with the concept of "connection before correction" (Hughes, 2011).

Praise, encouragement, and positive reinforcement

Praise, encouragement, and positive reinforcement are fundamental and can often dilute trickier behaviours. In essence, the more one looks for and magnifies the positive behaviours, the more one will notice them and the more they will grow. This fits with Fletcher Peacock's saying "Feed the flowers, not the weeds" (Peacock, 2001). Therefore, it is important to find ways to celebrate, notice, and build on children's strengths and to support children to power their positive magnets up and fill their treasure boxes with positive memories, experiences, and qualities. This is especially important for children who have experienced relational and developmental trauma, as they will often have low self-esteem, poor self-worth, and a fragile sense of self and be more likely to have learned that negative behaviours get more attention and responses than positive behaviour.

Praise, strengths-based practice, and positive feedback tools are described in detail in Chapter 5 and should be interwoven with the strategies described in this chapter.

Mastery and a sense of agency

Providing children with a safe sense of control can be beneficial, particularly when they have had earlier experiences of feeling powerless and helpless. This sense of feeling out of control and powerless can often show itself understandably in children trying to find ways of regaining or establishing control such as through outbursts. Supporting children to have a sense of agency and mastery opens up more opportunities for them to be facilitators of change and to be the authors of their own story.

Picking one's battles and problem-solving

During some forms of distressed dysregulation and rage, it is important to hold in mind that at the heightened point and pinnacle the child is generally functioning in their primal survival brain. Therefore, talking and problem-solving at that time can be likened to trying to rationalise with a baby or a young infant. At these times, safety and practical considerations need to be prioritised, and it can also be helpful to try to wait and pick the moment wisely to rationalise and debrief. Once the child/caregiver has down-regulated, is in their thinking brain, and in a good learning moment, it can then if appropriate, be useful to discuss what possible alternatives there might have been and think with them about problem-solving and other options for managing difficult feelings (see Box 6.6). In essence, the more regulated, organised, and grounded children are; the more able they will be to learn, process the information, reflect and engage.

Creative and playful ways of exploring and externalising "the anger/aggression/outbursts"

Exploring, describing, and reflecting on the feeling of anger

It is important to support children to increase their awareness of feeling states and to develop richer ways of describing feelings (see Chapter 4). Children can be supported to begin this process by reflecting on what anger is, what anger looks like, what anger feels like, what anger means, what other emotions anger is a bodyguard for, what function anger serves, etc. Worksheets 8.1–8.6 can help thicken this process and offer some useful avenues of questions to explore feelings and metaphors associated with anger.

In addition, children can also be supported to make collages, sculpt, draw, write, dance, or depict in sand what anger means to them, looks like, feels like, etc. Children can also be supported to use games, crosswords, and quizzes, such as using sentence-completion cards (e.g. "The things that get under my skin are...", "The things that make the anger visit are...", "The thing I need most is...", "The thing I am fighting for is...", etc.) to explore the feeling of anger. (See Photos 8.6–8.8.)

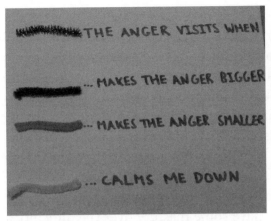

Photo 8.6 Anger-themed pipe cleaner game

Photo 8.7 Anger-focused collage

Photo 8.8 Anger-inspired sand image

Making links between the mind and the body through body-mapping

It is helpful to support children to connect to what happens in their body when they are about to be in and/or are in a heightened state. One way of supporting them in doing this (if appropriate and ready, as safety is first) is through making a body-map about how anger is felt and shown in their and/or others' bodies and how different this might be to how their/others' bodies feel when calm (see Photo 8.9). Chapters 3 and 4 contain various questions, ideas, and photographed examples around body-mapping exercises. Other ways might include a range of trauma-informed body-based techniques such as breathing, yoga, grounding, and relaxation exercises (See Chapter 4 for a range of other mind-body exercises).

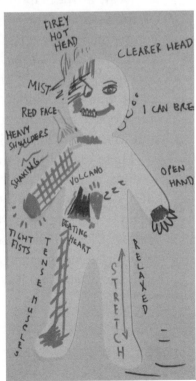

Photo 8.9 Body-mapping: left – how anger feels in the body; right – how calm and relaxed feelings feel in the body

Externalising the difficulties

Externalisation strategies (from Narrative Therapy) can be helpful in responding to difficult behaviours, such as aggression and outbursts. To avoid labelling, reinforcing negative self-beliefs, and creating a self-fulfilling prophecy, it is helpful to take the position that "the problem is the problem, not the person" (White, 1990). For example, it is not the child that you are angry and upset with, but it is the behaviour and the actions. Instead of "You are so naughty", one might label the behaviour by saying something like "I understand why things feel so unfair, but it makes me feel upset when you hit…" or "When you hit your brother I was upset because…". This supports the young person/surrounding adults in seeing the difficulty as separate from themselves and allows them to have some mastery over the difficulty and to gain some distance in evaluating what it is, what its effect is, and how to problem-solve and respond to it.

To facilitate this process, children might like to name, describe, or externalise the feeling/"difficulty". For instance, a child may externalise "the anger" as a character and choose an item, creature, weather, or being to describe and name it. Some common choices have included: a volcano, a wave, a tornado (see Photo 8.10), thunder, red mist, lightning, a bursting balloon, a boxing glove, a shark, a bull, or bubbling water (see Worksheet 8.1 for other commonly used metaphors). Children can then be supported to bring their character to life. They might like to draw, collage, mosaic, depict it in sand, or sculpt it. This can then lead to child-friendly conversations around, for example, how you can cool the volcano down, not let the water bubble over, turn the red mist to being yellow, surf the angry wave (see Photo 8.11), or calm the whirling tornado down.

It can also be helpful to reflect with the young person on the influence and impact of, for example, "the anger" (using their choice of externalised name). This can be complemented by questions such as: *How does "The Lava" affect you and your life now? What does "The Lava" stop you from doing/getting? What's "The Lava's" cleverest trick or superpower? If "The Lava" were to pack his bags and leave, what would you miss about him?* (See Worksheet 8.5 for more sample Narrative Therapy externalising questions that can aid these discussions and Worksheet 8.6 for exploring the hazards and strengths of expressing anger.)

These metaphors can also be built on further by supporting the young person to draw, sculpt, act out, collage, or depict in sand how they felt before, during, and after a specific incident (see Worksheet 8.7) when the "tornado" visited. They can then be supported to reflect on what thoughts, physical sensations, reactions, and feelings they had at those different times. These thoughts and feelings can also be helpfully demonstrated using a head with blank spaces around it or a 3D head or hat with sticky labels on it as shown in Photo 8.12.

Photo 8.10 Anger externalised as a tornado

Photo 8.11 A replica drawing of a child surfing the stormy waves

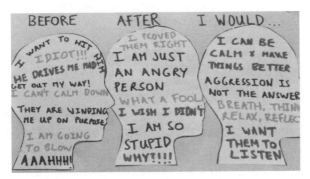

Photo 8.12 Head of thoughts before/during, after, and in hindsight

Another way of externalising can be to talk about the different parts/pieces/sections of the child. This can be illustrated in different ways, including through drawing or making their different parts or pieces on a puzzle, patchwork of parts, body cut-out (see Photo 8.13), or set of Russian dolls (see Worksheets 2.2–2.4 for various examples of these exercises). This acknowledges, respects, and celebrates the whole child, and positions, for example, "the aggression" as one part of them rather than as their master identity and their dominant, defining feature. So, one might say "Oh, you are letting me know you are feeling your sad part today", "Wow, how nice to meet your adventurous part" or "We need to practise taking your kind hands part to the gym".

Alternatively, some young children might relate well to the concept of body muscles (see Photo 8.14). One might explain to a young person that if they have one big muscle that's strong, for example the aggressive muscle, and the other one is smaller and limp, this means they will be off balance, lopsided, and wonky, so, to make them balanced, big, and strong, they need to practise and take, for example, the calm muscles to the gym (see Photo 8.15). These concepts can also be complemented by the inside/outside masks and dual portrait exercises discussed in Chapter 4.

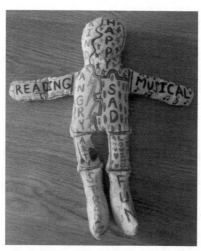

Photo 8.13 Different parts expressed on a doll

Photo 8.14 Muscles that are strengthened compared with those that are not

Creatively exploring the functions and consequences of "the anger"

It can be helpful to explore with the young person what "the aggression/anger/ outbursts/rage" is preventing them from doing or being. This said, it is important to remember to convey the underlying messages that the anger is OK and valid, but it is the way of expressing it, for example through physical aggression, that is not. It is also useful to acknowledge that the anger serves a function and has developed for a reason and therefore needs to be respected and explored. To support the young person in exploring the influence of "the aggression", it can be useful to write a physical list of the advantages and disadvantages of "the aggression" (these can also be drawn, acted out, sculpted, etc.) and link this back to the young person's thoughts, feelings, behaviours, and sensations. An example is given below.

Andy shared that being physically aggressive at school had resulted in him being sent out of lessons, which had led to him feeling disappointed in himself, as well as his parents being upset with him. This also meant that he wasn't learning, which was keeping him further from his goal of working in sports science. He had also noticed that his peers were increasingly distancing themselves from him or expecting him to respond aggressively. He was also aware that he was regularly feeling stiff and achy from the stress and physicality of his responses.

Metaphors can be a powerful way of illustrating the different ways that "the aggression" might be hurting a young person, preventing them from achieving something, or holding them back. Some metaphors that I commonly use and young people often choose include a ball and chain, a burning fire, a fence, a net, handcuffs, and a wall. These can be drawn, sculpted, and moulded to visually depict the influence and consequences of "the aggression" (see Photos 8.15 and 8.16).

For other young people, I sometimes bring this concept alive by supporting them to wear a backpack that is filled with beanbags/weights (this should only be done in the context of a safe and informed therapeutic relationship and after a thorough assessment).

Some questions using the example of a ball and chain (this can be adapted for any appropriate metaphor) to enhance these discussions are given below.

What is inside the ball and chain? What is the ball and chain made of? How long has the ball and chain been there? How did it develop/get put there? What is the ball and chain blocking you from doing/being/achieving? How is the ball and chain weighing you down/restricting you/slowing you down? What does it feel like physically and emotionally to be weighed down by the ball and chain? Who else do you know who is weighed down by a ball and chain? What do people not see within you because they are distracted by seeing the ball and chain? What would it feel like to be free from the ball and chain? What could you do/achieve if you were free from the ball and chain?

Photo 8.15 Being held down by a ball and chain

Photo 8.16 The anger walled in

It is important to think with the young person about what purpose/functions "the aggression" (other terms and externalised names can be used instead of "the aggression") serves and to support them in problem-solving different ways of responding to these feelings. We can't expect young people to stop doing something without first understanding it or without them having something else to do as a healthier replacement. Some questions that I find useful for exploring the function/purpose of the behaviour with older children are given below (these will need to be adapted for the individual practitioner and child and used alongside the other strategies).

What would you miss if "the aggression" packed its bag and went away? When is "the aggression" your friend/helper? When is "the aggression" your enemy? What could you do more of if you were more in charge of your emotions than "the aggression"? What do the different paths of your life look like if you carry on as you are, or if you...? (It can be helpful to draw the two different paths and/or the different future scenarios as road maps, paths, or side-by-side images.)

What emotional needs do you think you were expressing through your behaviour? What were you trying to say/ask for? If "the aggression" could talk, what might it say/tell you/explain/describe? What other ways might there be of communicating and getting your needs met? What were the negative consequences/ripple effects/cycles of that situation?

If you had a time machine, what would you have done differently? If you had a magic wand, how would you wish for it to be different?

What has your experience been of "conflict"? (Other terms and externalised names can be used instead of "conflict", such as aggression, pain, violence, etc.) What are some of the hazards and disadvantages of conflict? What are some of the strengths and advantages of conflict? How would you like someone to respond to you in a conflict? How do you know you're being truly listened to and heard? Can you recall an example of when you felt truly listened to and connected – what did it feel like emotionally, cognitively, and physically? What might have to change for you to be able to be listened to and to be heard, and vice versa?

These avenues of exploration should be enhanced and embedded further through exploring the responses through creative means such as drawing, writing a song, making a collage, making a sculpt, etc. An example is given below.

Seventeen-year-old Eric had been so hurt and let down throughout his childhood that he had developed ways to keep himself safe and protected. Over time, it seemed he had metaphorically layered on his trauma jacket. Each time he did this, the padding got thicker and the zip was zipped up tighter and tighter. In therapy, we explored how the jacket had come to be there, what the jacket symbolised, what function the jacket served, what need the jacket met, and how the jacket felt when it was on. We also thought about the different layers of the jacket and what they represented. I then supported Eric to draw and sculpt the different people who had hurt him and let him down over the years. We then did various techniques including squashing/erasing the people, writing letters to them (not to be sent), and detailing the evidence that disproved the things that they had repeatedly said to him over the years, such as "You are a waste of space". We then reflected on how things were different and felt different, and then Eric was supported to draw and act out what having some of the layers of the jacket come off looked and felt like.

Role-play and practising

When the young person is regulated and in a learning mode, it can be helpful to role-play and practise different scenarios and responses in a playful and problem-solving way. This can be a helpful way to link the outburst to a trigger, to explore alternative responses, and then to be able to rehearse it repeatedly with a more positive outcome. This can be done through acting, making a video, drawing a comic strip, or playing it out through using masks/dolls. It can be useful to use third-person narrative stories, TV programmes, and puppet shows to explore scenarios and different outcomes (see Photo 8.17). Another useful way can be to ask the child to pick a different way that they could have potentially responded. You can also ask them to imagine that they were faced with a similar situation again or that they could turn back time or travel back in a time machine and to draw themselves responding in another way. They can then reflect on/draw how they think the outcome would be different if they had responded differently (see Worksheet 8.7).

Photo 8.17 Role-playing with puppets – trying to stay grounded like a tree

Stop, think, and go

When they feel their emotions taking over, some young people find it helpful to visualise a stop sign in their mind or to think of the traffic light metaphor (stop – red; think – amber; go – green). This can be represented visually, for example by having a traffic light poster with orange or saying something like "Take three long, deep breaths", "Do some star jumps", "Squeeze your stress ball", etc. Another useful way l have found to support some children to stop and reflect on some of their ways of expressing themselves (where appropriate) is to use a shampoo bottle. I ask them to squeeze the contents of the shampoo bottle out into a sink, into a container, or onto a piece of cardboard (see Photo 8.18). I then ask the child to try and put the shampoo contents back into the bottle (see Photo 8.19). This is a playful way of demonstrating that it is easier to get words or actions out than to put them back in. This said, it is important that this explanation is given in a way that conveys that the contents can still be put back in but it is trickier: we do not want to push a child into a place of shame or for them to feel that once something is done it cannot be repaired.

Photos 8.18 and 8.19 Illustrating that words are easier to take out than to put back in

Sensory, body-based, and regulating activities

During a rage, period of dysregulation, or outburst, the young person needs some non-verbal, soothing, sensory, rhythmic, and regulating strategies to support them to move back to their rational brain and to ground and re-centre themselves (e.g. using a sensory box, going to their safe place, smelling lavender, blowing bubbles, saying positive affirmations, using a weighted blanket, giving themselves a butterfly hug, ripping paper up, crawling, listening to music, doing relaxation exercises, etc.).

These regulating strategies are so important in providing the child with a wealth of alternative and tangible coping strategies that they can have to hand. Worksheets 3.9 and 7.9 contain some ideas of grounding, regulating, and soothing techniques and ideas presented as cards that can be cut out, laminated, or added to the child's sensory box, coping card, octopus of options, etc. These have been deliberately left blank so that the child can draw, decorate, and tailor them. In addition, the sensory box and safe place exercises that are detailed in depth in Chapter 3 can also be particularly helpful when addressing outbursts. Which cards from Worksheets 3.9 and 7.9 do you think might be helpful?

Coping and option cards – keeping a record of what works

Once the young person has found some tools that work for them from the strategies discussed and the regulating cards, it is useful to record these in a child-friendly way. This helps to keep them in the young person's mind and means they are more accessible in moments of dysregulation. The records could be kept in a range of ways such as: my coping card (see Photo 8.20), my treasure box of tools (see Photo 8.21), my coping cookbook, my cue/stress cards, my protective palm (where they write a coping strategy on each finger) poster, my calm-down superpowers (see Photo 8.22), my octopus of options (with each coping strategy written on its tentacles) (see Photo 8.23), my chill skills, my ice cubes of cooling down ideas (see Photo 8.24), my bag of ideas, etc. Additional photos of these strategies can also be found in Chapter 3.

Photo 8.20 A sample coping card

Photo 8.21 A treasure box of tools

Photo 8.22 My calm-down superpowers

Photo 8.23 Octopus of options

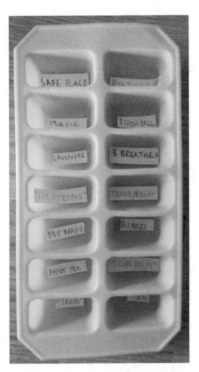

Photo 8.24 Ice cubes of cooling down ideas

Anger is (using metaphors)...

Anger

The feeling of "anger" is like...

If I gave the "anger" a name I would call it...

I would describe the "anger" as being like...

Avalanche	Volcano	Fire	Shark	Lion hunting
Boiling blood	Banging drum	Tidal wave	Monster	Dragon
Thunder & lightning	Adrenaline rush	Spiked ball	Red mist	What else?

Copyright © Karen Treisman – *A Therapeutic Treasure Box for Working with Children and Adolescents with Developmental Trauma* – 2018

About the "anger" (replace "anger" with your own choice of name)

» If the "anger" was a colour, it would be…

» If the "anger" was a shape, it would be…

» If the "anger" was an animal, it would be…

» If the "anger" was an object/item/metaphor, it would be…

» If the "anger" was a flower, a tree, or something from nature, it would be…

» If the "anger" could talk, it would say… (What would its voice sound like?)

» The "anger" stops me from…

» The "anger" helps me…

» Without the "anger", I would…

» If the "anger" disappeared, I would miss…

» …makes the "anger" much bigger.

» …makes the "anger" smaller.

» I am stronger and bigger than the "anger" when…

Expanding creatively on the metaphor

Once a metaphor/name/item/object has been chosen and discussed in detail, it can be helpfully embedded and expanded on by carrying out related expressive and creative activities.

For example, if a child says that their feeling of "anger" is like a shark, they might sculpt, mould, draw, paint, or make "the shark". Similarly, the child might be encouraged to act as if they are "the shark" or fleeing from "the shark"; they may be supported in using physical movement, puppets, masks, or a sand-tray exercise to explore this metaphor further.

The above questions can be used to bring the metaphor to life; for example: What is "the shark's" name? What does "the shark" sound like? If "the shark" could talk, what would it say? What makes "the shark" stronger? What scares "the shark"?

Additionally, the metaphor can be played with according to the need. For example, the ocean, other sharks, boats, dolphins, divers, fish, seaweed, and waves can be discussed as being symbolic.

Photo 8.25 Anger externalised as a "Spike the Snappy Shark"

Copyright © Karen Treisman – *A Therapeutic Treasure Box for Working with Children and Adolescents with Developmental Trauma* – 2018

Worksheet 8.2
What does...look like?

Use Play-Doh, clay, pens, pencils, or collage to depict the emotion.

Copyright © Karen Treisman – *A Therapeutic Treasure Box for Working with Children and Adolescents with Developmental Trauma – 2018*

Worksheet 8.3
I recognise when I am feeling...because I show it through my...

Draw, sculpt, write, collage, or depict in sand your responses.

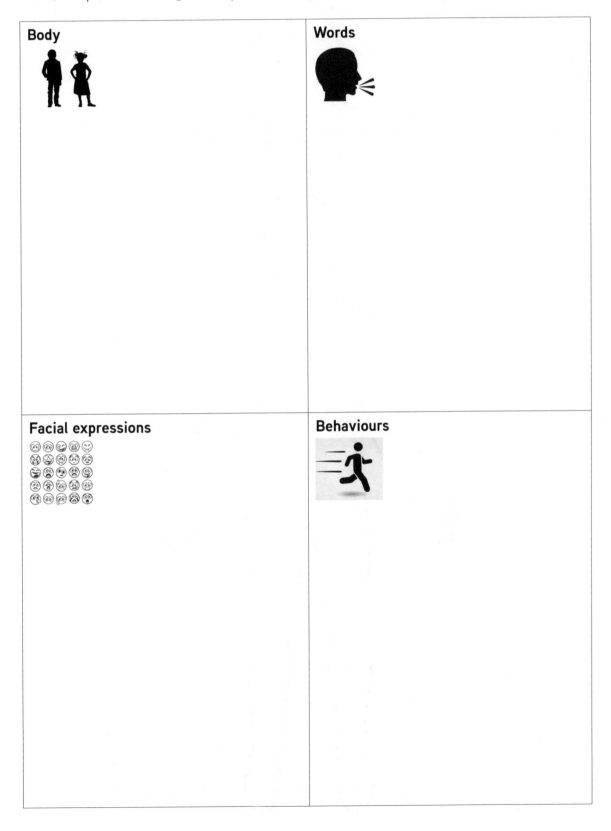

Copyright © Karen Treisman – *A Therapeutic Treasure Box for Working with Children and Adolescents with Developmental Trauma* – 2018

Colour, draw, or design where and how you feel the different core emotions in your body

Colour, draw, or design where and how you feel the different core emotions in your body.

If these emotions were a colour, a shape, or a thing, what would they be? If they had a voice, what would they say? Can you think about a specific time or story when you felt these emotions?

Sadness	Fear	Anger	Shame	Joy/ excitement	Curiosity	?	?

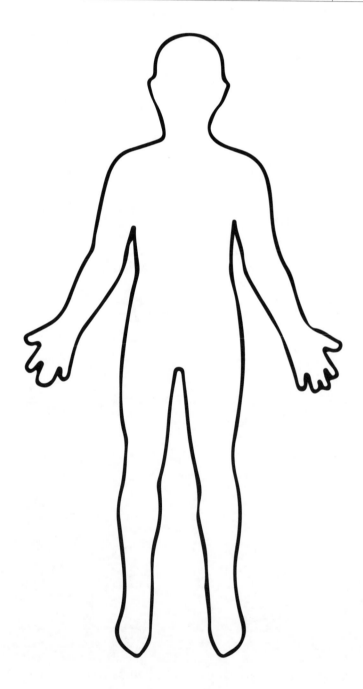

Copyright © Karen Treisman – A Therapeutic Treasure Box for Working with Children and Adolescents with Developmental Trauma – 2018

Externalisation and Narrative Therapy example questions

What is…called? What does it look like? What does it sound like? What does it say? What does it do?

It can be very helpful for children to draw, paint, sculpt, or mould the character they create. Various therapeutic avenues could then be followed, like the examples given below (examples of names children have chosen for aggressive behaviour are used):

How did you manage to outsmart "Raging Roy"? How much bigger or stronger are you than "Vaughn the Volcano"? What skills and strengths did you use to conquer "Spike the Smasher"? Who would you rather have in charge of your life – "Thor the Thunder" or you? What is it like to share your life with "Strangling Stan"? What plans does the "Kicking Ninja" have for your life? What is "Raging Bull" stopping you from doing?

How is "The Fire" affecting your life? When the voice of "The Crusher" is less strong, what will you be doing that you're not doing now? How are "The Shards of Glass" attempting to prevent you from enjoying the calm you were able to acknowledge before the trauma? What plans does the "Farryl the Fist" have for your life? When "The Volcano" is about to erupt, what can you do to lessen the effect of the lava?

When did "The Lava" first appear in your life? Was "The Lava" around in your family?

What purpose did "The Lava" serve for you back then? In what ways did "The Lava" help you? How does "The Lava" affect you and your life now? What does "The Lava" stop you from doing/getting? What's "The Lava's" cleverest trick or superpower? If "The Lava" were to pack his bags and leave, what would you miss about him? What have you learned from him that can be useful in your life? Have you ever managed to deal with a conflict in a different way, without "The Lava"; if so, how?

Copyright © Karen Treisman – *A Therapeutic Treasure Box for Working with Children and Adolescents with Developmental Trauma* – 2018

Worksheet 8.6

Strengths (advantages) and hazards (disadvantages) of expressing the anger

Strengths and advantages of expressing anger	Hazards and disadvantages of expressing anger

Copyright © Karen Treisman – *A Therapeutic Treasure Box for Working with Children and Adolescents with Developmental Trauma – 2018*

Worksheet 8.7

Thoughts, feelings, and actions diary and reflection log

What was going on around me at the time?	How was I feeling emotionally and in my body?	What was I thinking?	What did I do?	What happened?	If I could go back in time, what would I do differently?

Copyright © Karen Treisman – A Therapeutic Treasure Box for Working with Children and Adolescents with Developmental Trauma – 2018

Worksheet 8.8
Different responses and reflection

Choose one way of responding differently to a particular situation.

What is this way?

What are some of the advantages of responding in this way?

Draw yourself (or sculpt, act, or depict it in sand if you prefer) responding in this way.

Copyright © Karen Treisman – *A Therapeutic Treasure Box for Working with Children and Adolescents with Developmental Trauma – 2018*

The Pot of Bubbling Feelings

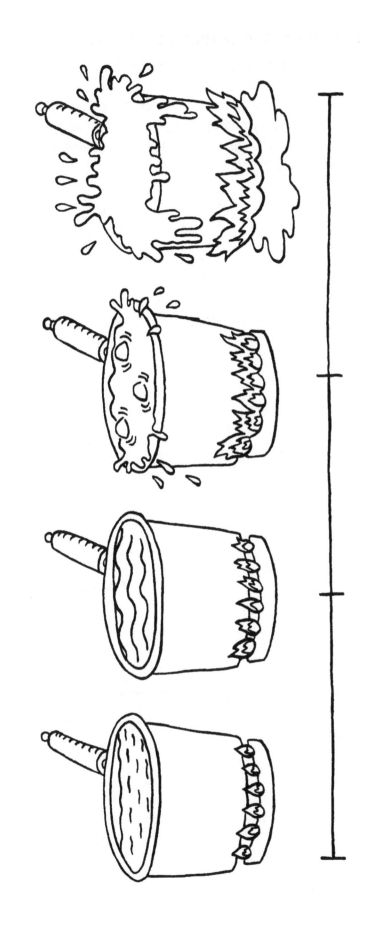

Copyright © Karen Treisman – *A Therapeutic Treasure Box for Working with Children and Adolescents with Developmental Trauma – 2018*

Worksheet 8.10
Thermometer of feelings

Choose a different word or statement to represent the feelings for each colour, for example green being calm and cool as a cucumber and black for being raging like an exploding volcano. Then you can colour in the blocks below and choose which colour you would place yourself on at different times.

Black
Red
Orange
Yellow
Blue
Green

Copyright © Karen Treisman – *A Therapeutic Treasure Box for Working with Children and Adolescents with Developmental Trauma* – 2018

Crib sheet: strengthening and supporting the development of executive function and cognitive skills

Introduction

Executive function difficulties are more common in children who have experienced relational and developmental trauma. These pockets of difficulties can have multi-layered implications for children's learning and life skills (Loman *et al.*, 2013; Spann *et al.*, 2012). Executive function difficulties can include struggling with: planning, organising, completing tasks, goal-setting, anticipating consequences, orientation, spatial awareness, initiating, attending, memorising, processing information, concentrating, exerting self-control, switching focus, managing impulse-control, utilising cognitive flexibility, problem-solving, abstract thinking, reasoning, making inferences, and understanding object permanency (Pollak *et al.*, 2010; Samuelson *et al.*, 2010).

This worksheet will offer some activities and strategies to support the development and strengthening of these skills. This list is not exhaustive or prescriptive, needs to be informed by a thorough assessment and formulation, and needs to be tailored to the specific individual/situation. Keep in mind that every child is unique and is living within a unique context.

These activities may give some ideas that can be helpful for caregivers, teachers, etc. in supporting children to optimise their learning. They could be tailored and adapted to be interwoven with recommendations on neuropsychological assessments. These strategies are just one piece of the overall puzzle of supporting children with executive function difficulties. They need to be complemented by other pieces of the puzzle, such as strategies around sensory processing and sensory integration, regulating emotions, and increasing feelings of safety.

Practical and creative strategies for strengthening and supporting the development of executive function skills

» Information should be communicated in the most accessible way possible. This includes using short and concise sentences that use child-friendly and "age"-appropriate language and where necessary are broken up into smaller, more manageable parts (think about SMART goals; see Worksheet 5.6). For the majority of children, starting small and having fewer choices to begin with supports their ability to grasp new concepts.

» Children will generally benefit from having more time than required to absorb and process information. Children are likely to need key information shared and repeated several times in different ways and using different communication styles.

» Where possible, children should understand the rationale, expectations, and steps of a task/instruction. These should be as sequenced and as coherent as possible. It is important that children's understanding of the information is checked. Space should

Copyright © Karen Treisman – *A Therapeutic Treasure Box for Working with Children and Adolescents with Developmental Trauma* – 2018

be made, and children should feel safe and able, to ask questions and for clarity and for repetition.

» Key information should be shared when the child is in a learning and thinking mode, rather than when dysregulated, distracted, and/or full up. This includes finding ways to increase their feelings of safety and decrease their feelings of danger/threat. See Chapter 3 for different ways of supporting multi-levelled safety and of identifying multi-sensory triggers.

» Poignant information should be shared with a child when they have had sufficient sleep, have eaten, have been to the toilet, and have limited external distractions.

» Children will often benefit from having brain breaks in between information and buffered around transition points, as well as having regulating items to hand. This might also include integrating physical activities, art activities, relaxation-based activities, or sensory-based activities into these brain breaks. See Chapter 3 for a range of ideas on supporting this, as well as Worksheet 3.9, which provides a range of regulating activities on a set of cards.

» Information should be communicated and contextualised using multi-modal and multi-approach tools. For example, in addition to explaining a concept, it is helpful to employ other modes such as using visual aids, props, diagrams, flow charts, pie graphs, video recordings, photos, etc. For example, if someone is explaining the brain, the information is likely to be embedded further and engaged more if using brain models, brain puzzles, brain drawings, metaphors about the brain, podcasts about the brain, etc. Similarly, if someone is discussing and describing a tree, it is likely to be more interactive and absorbed if a child is shown a tree, encouraged to touch a tree, looks at pictures of a tree, makes art out of the bark and the leaves of the tree, etc. This style incorporates the left and the right brain, as well as utilising and activating multiple senses.

» Role-playing and practising particular skills when the child is in their thinking and learning brain can be very helpful. One can use dolls, teddies, masks, or puppets to enhance these discussions and to make them feel less exposing and more playful.

» Making real-world associations with concepts and items can enhance some children's memory and engagement with them. This includes bringing concepts alive through strategies such as using rhymes, acronyms, poems, catchy sayings, metaphors, etc.

» Children can also be supported to think about the links and connections between different concepts and actions. This can be enhanced through things like making paper chains, links on a chain, or paper dolls, using string on a path, or games like dominoes. Breaking down situations or concepts into smaller steps and looking at them as, for example, pieces of a puzzle, bricks in a house, or parts of a cog can also be useful. Worksheets exploring SMART goals can also be useful in supporting these skills (see Worksheets 4.20, 4.21, and 5.6).

» Problem-solving skills should be modelled by surrounding adults and actively encouraged. This might include things such as writing an advantages and disadvantages list, drawing or sculpting the different potential paths/outcomes/ decisions, making a paper chain of events, drawing a spidergram, or making a visual

Copyright © Karen Treisman – *A Therapeutic Treasure Box for Working with Children and Adolescents with Developmental Trauma* – 2018

representation of possible options (e.g. an octopus of options, the treasure box of tools, the protective palm, and so forth; see Chapters 3 and 8).

» Some children find focusing and filtering information trickier than others. Finding ways to highlight and prioritise information can be helpful for these children. This might include things like underlining or highlighting important information, circling information, using reminder post-it notes, writing lists/checklists, and/or using sorting systems such as colour coding.

» Children may also benefit from having reminder, crib, flash, or cue cards of key information. I often talk with children about the skill of focusing in by likening it to putting a camera on zoom or using a magic magnifying glass. I then support children to practise using their zoom lens or their magic magnifying glass.

» Some children might benefit from having prompts, anchors, or scaffolding techniques. For example, a child writing a story may be supported by having some story starter ideas, looking at a picture book, reading and seeing some actual examples, looking at a physical item for inspiration, or being given a heading/cue word.

» It can also be helpful to support children to have a visual record of the steps that are involved in a particular task, for example through using pictorial/visual checklists, visual diaries, visual calendars, or visual timetables. These can be enhanced by making the steps into comic strips, mental/actual movies, plays, or social stories. These can also be brought to life by supporting the child to draw the pictures of the different steps or taking actual photographs. These can be made more interactive by using Velcro, buttons, plastic sleeves, etc.

» Labelling and sorting items can also be useful, for example having labelled notepads, pencil cases, cupboards, folders, etc. This might be enhanced by having sorting systems such as colour coding or putting things in alphabetical order.

» Children can be supported to have more of a sense of time and movement through using visual timers, alarms, stopwatches, and child-friendly clocks, and through words like "before", "after", and "next". See Chapter 10 for more specific strategies around supporting transitions.

» Games can be great ways of strengthening children's executive function skills whilst also having fun. Games include: Grandmother's footsteps; freeze; musical statues; follow the leader; Simon says; Twister; snap; cards; Connect 4; Jenga; using labyrinths, mazes, or Rubik's cubes; head, shoulders, knees, and toes; Pictionary or charades; and copying games, for example making a Play-Doh sculpture or drawing a picture and asking the child to copy it and vice versa.

» Cognitive games can also be very helpful in practising these skills. These include: crosswords; quizzes; games like I spy, "I went shopping and bought", and "Can you tell me all the countries beginning with the letter A?"; brain gym activities (e.g. cross crawl, number 8, and brain buttons); games such as "How many different ways can you use a hat, table, stick, and so forth?"; giving a child a magazine, piece of paper, or book and asking them to, for example, circle all the words beginning with "F" or look out for all of the animals; finding Wally in Where's Wally picture books; looking at multiple perspectives or finding "hidden" images in optical illusion images or

Copyright © Karen Treisman – *A Therapeutic Treasure Box for Working with Children and Adolescents with Developmental Trauma* – 2018

items in find-it games; playing spot the difference and similarities-themed games; playing sorting games like sorting all the red shapes into one basket or all the green buttons into a jar; and asking children to think about what they would need or what they would pack for when it is, for example, snowing or when they are baking a cake.

» The games described above can also be enhanced by daily activities that can help to integrate and practise lots of different executive function skills. These might include activities such as cooking (following a recipe), baking, gardening, shopping, choreographing a dance, following a map, going on a treasure hunt, putting together a puzzle, building something like a bridge or a tower, playing supermarket sweep, etc.

» Games such as hide and seek, using find-it tubes, playing treasure hunts, and using hideaway puppets can be useful for supporting the concept of object permanence.

» These ideas can be enhanced by apps and computer programs that are designed to support children to strengthen their executive function skills.

» Children should be encouraged to use and be acknowledged and praised for using/ trying to use these skills such as their concentration part or their memory muscle. Chapter 5 contains some strategies for supporting and expanding on children's strengths.

Copyright © Karen Treisman – *A Therapeutic Treasure Box for Working with Children and Adolescents with Developmental Trauma* – 2018

CHAPTER 9

Supporting Children who are Experiencing Nightmares and Sleep Difficulties[1]

Introduction and reflecting on nightmares in the context of trauma

Nightmares are a common and normal occurrence, particularly during childhood; we have all had them at one point or another. In most cases, they are scary but harmless, will fade naturally, and do not require a specific therapeutic intervention. This chapter focuses on suggestions and tools for when the nightmares, night terrors, or sleep difficulties become frequent, distressing, are having an impact on the child's day-to-day life, and are being experienced in the context of relational and developmental trauma. Many of the strategies and tools presented in this chapter can also be applied and adapted to working with children with other worries, fears, and anxiety-related difficulties.

There are many different theories about and explanations for why nightmares occur and why they are maintained. Many suggest that, in the context of trauma, nightmares represent different fragments and pieces of children's sensory, imagery, perceptual, and body-based traumatic memories. These memories and experiences are often raw, unresolved, unintegrated, and unprocessed, so the nightmares and flashbacks can act as a reminder of them, a representation of their stuckness, and/or the child's mind's way of trying to process and make sense of them. Within this, nightmares can be emotionally intense, feel very real, be intrusive, and have associated physical (e.g. sweating, heart beating faster, muscles tensing) and emotional associations. Like traumatic events, they can have a multi-sensory and whole-body impact, which requires multi-sensory and body-based responses (see the case examples in Chapter 3).

The content and nature of the nightmares can vary significantly. Nightmares can be a reoccurring, a re-enactment, and a recall of the actual traumatic event (in the literature this is often referred to as post-traumatic nightmares) or they may appear to be singular and unconnected but still elicit an extreme fear response (this is often a feeling that has been experienced in previous times). They may represent an associated theme of the trauma/s (often referred to as idiopathic nightmares). For example, a child may have several nightmares of being chased, but the person chasing them may vary and they may be in different contexts or a child may have

---

[1]   These strategies are equally relevant for supporting children with a variety of worries, fears, and anxieties.

nightmares about getting lost and of being abandoned, but the place they get lost in or the person who abandons them may change.

For many children who have experienced relational and developmental trauma and toxic stress, nightmares can resurface and retrigger past negative experiences and can be linked to an array of feelings, themes, and lived experiences. These might include fear, abuse, neglect, separation, feeling trapped, being chased, anxiety, loss, feeling/being abandoned, having to be hyper-vigilant and on edge, feeling unsafe and in danger, feeling alone, insecure, or powerless, and being out of control. It is helpful to view nightmares as a form of communication, and in turn they can provide us with valuable windows into and maps of children's inner worlds and emotional landscapes.

The associated feelings, themes, and triggers can be further complicated due to the very nature of the task of being able to sleep well. Sleep, in itself, requires children and their bodies to be down-regulated, relaxed, grounded, and calm. This can be extremely difficult for children who may be functioning predominantly in their fight, flight, or freeze survival mode and who already have increased levels of adrenaline and cortisol flowing through their bodies. This is heightened for children who have sensory processing, sensory integration, and regulating difficulties. Children can struggle with regulating their bodies and their overall arousal levels to be able to be in a place where good-quality sleep is possible. For some children, being able to be and stay calm, down-regulated, and still for a prolonged period can be likened to telling them to try to do aqua aerobics or synchronised swimming whilst in shark-infested waters. Case examples of how relational and developmental trauma may be demonstrated or triggered at night time are given below.

Reports described how Cairo would be locked in his bedroom and physically restricted by having large items placed against the door that wedged him in so that he could not leave his room or interrupt his parents.

Tilly told her adoptive father that she remembered being told by her birth mother that if she was naughty, the devil would come and get her in the middle of the night. She went on to describe how, if she had a nightmare, she was told by her birth mother how "babyish, stupid, and gullible" she was. She said that there was a time when her cousin was encouraged to wear a devil's mask and jump on top of her during the night whilst she was sleeping, and she could hear her mother and a few of her mother's friends outside her door laughing hysterically at her shock and fear of this mask.

Nyle shared how he would be petrified each time he knew his grandfather was visiting and babysitting, as he would come into his bedroom and touch him in places that he didn't like and didn't want to be touched.

Lili would often be scared to go to bed at night because of the fear that her mother would not be there when she woke up or would be hurt. She felt she needed to be there to protect her or call the police.

Oliver's foster carer reported that each morning she would find Oliver sleeping on wet linen or would find the wet linen hidden under his bed. Social service reports had described Oliver being given extreme physical chastisement and verbal humiliation if he wet the bed when he was younger.

Carrie associated bedtime with screaming, shouting, and fear. She remembered that when she was younger, more often than not she would lie in bed hearing her parents arguing aggressively, breaking items, and slamming doors.

Abdul, an unaccompanied asylum-seeking young person, shared how when he was tortured he was made to sit in a room with a bag over his face with blaring, loud music being played for hours on end. Each time he nodded off to sleep, he was hit and forced to stay awake. These negative experiences around sleep and of darkness were exacerbated, as when Abdul was fleeing from his country, he was made to hide for days in a pitch-black cargo container behind some large boxes, constantly on high alert in case someone found him.

Cycles and patterns of nightmares

The presence of nightmares can be perpetuating and in turn lead to an unhelpful and reinforcing cycle and pattern. An example is given below.

Brayden repeatedly had nightmares of a traumatic incident. After having several of these nightmares, he learned to associate sleep and bedtime with having nightmares of the traumatic event. He developed anticipatory worry about going to sleep or lying in bed because he was scared the nightmares would visit again. This made night time more difficult and dreaded, and he tried lots of different ways to avoid going to sleep. This also increased the intensity of the anticipation and of the occurrence of nightmares.

This anticipatory worry, and being on high alert, is also likely to raise children's arousal levels (these children often have raised baseline levels already due to toxic stress), which makes going to and staying asleep more difficult.

This avoidance cycle can also be fuelled and reinforced by children trying to push the thoughts out of their head (this is called cognitive avoidance) and trying not to think of the nightmares or their content. Unfortunately, this can have the opposite effect, as this cognitive avoidance strategy comes with hazards. First, it does not allow the child to have the opportunity to process, make links with, and integrate the nightmare and its content into their autobiographical memory. Second, it doesn't allow for normalisation and familiarisation of the nightmare, which instead can increase the nightmare's power, hold, and intensity. It also prevents the child from being able to think about other alternatives and different aspects of the nightmare/ theme, which could widen the frame and bring new understandings into the picture, for example the fact that the person's face was empty, that there was a door they could escape from, or that the story did not actually flow or make sense.

Assessment of nightmares

The variation and multiple layers of nightmares and sleep difficulties lends itself to highlighting why information-gathering, formulating, and carrying out thorough trauma-informed assessments is so important in ascertaining whether the following strategies are appropriate and, if so, when it is suitable to use them.

Some suggested nightmare-specific questions have been presented in Box 9.1. However, it is important when assessing nightmares to think about the whole child and to view nightmares as one symptom within their wider frame and context (see

Chapter 2 for more information about this and Chapter 5 in *Working with Relational and Developmental Trauma in Children and Adolescents*, Treisman, 2016, for a more detailed discussion on trauma and attachment-informed assessments).

Nightmares can be interpreted differently, and the meaning and sense-making around them can vary significantly. For example, in some cultures, nightmares are seen as: a vehicle for ancestors or G-d sending powerful messages; guidance in times of crisis; and clues to helping people with making key life decisions. It is vital to explore the meaning and attributions made about them and view them within a wider context.

Box 9.1 **Assessments around nightmares some suggested questions**

These should be used within the context of a wider, whole-child, and trauma-informed assessment.

- What is the child's bedtime routine? What does this look like and involve? Has this always been the case? (For example, children in care are likely to have had different experiences of bedtime and of night time.)

- When did the nightmares start? Why might the nightmares have started at that time? Were there any triggers, changes, transitions, or incidents that co-occurred?

- How frequently do the nightmares occur? Where and when do the nightmares occur? (It can be helpful to visually track, map, chart, and/or diarise the patterns of the nightmares.)

- What other variables impact the occurrence of the nightmares? Are there any particular patterns of when they occur more or less or are stronger or weaker?

- What triggers, hotspots, variables (e.g. environmental, sensory, autobiographical, physical, cognitive, relational, emotional, or situational) make the nightmares bigger, smaller, absent, present, etc.?

- What happens in the times when the nightmares are absent or less frequent/intense/distressing? What is different and why? How can these times when they are absent or less intense be magnified, increased, and celebrated?

- Is the child able to recall the content of the nightmare? Is the content the same each time or is there a common theme or feeling?

- What is the impact of the nightmares on the child and those around them? What does the child do differently as a result (e.g. try to stay awake, play with their phone, wake the other children up, sleep in their carer's room, etc.)?

- What do we think the nightmares or themes within them may be communicating? What function are they serving? What might be the story behind them and underneath their surface?

- What are the child's sense-making, meaning-making, attributions, and explanations about the nightmares? How are these similar or different to other surrounding people's conceptualisations of the nightmares?

- What strategies/interventions have been tried already? What bits of these were helpful or less helpful and why?

Psychoeducation techniques

Depending on the assessment, the child's presentation, and their unique needs, it feels important that the child and their supporting adults have the opportunity to learn through psychoeducation about why anxiety, trauma, flashbacks, memory systems, and nightmares might be occurring. There are various ways of doing this (depending on one's model and selection of language); however, I often use sculptures and models of the brain and the commonly used metaphors in the field (e.g. the "linen cupboard", "filing cabinet", or "film projector"). I also find it helpful to use props, diagrams, drawings, and video clips to bring these concepts alive and to think about them on a multi-sensory, whole-brain level.

Normalising, empathising, and modelling

It also feels important to normalise the experience of nightmares with the child and to let them know that we all have nightmares and bad dreams at different times and they are not alone. This fits with really listening (active and whole-body listening – see Worksheet 6.3) and empathising with how the child is feeling and what might be being triggered for them or communicated via this nightmare or sleep difficulty. It is also helpful to convey the message that nightmares can go away or occur less frequently and that you feel you can support them to sleep better and to feel safer.

Meaning-making, sense-making, and reflecting on the associated thoughts and feelings

For some children, the experience of the nightmares will re-trigger difficult feelings, body memories, and/or other triggers. Therefore, making sense of and finding meaning in the nightmare (such as their underlying feelings and communication), the associated themes, and their relationship to them feels as if it is a crucial step to take before progressing to the more practical and tangible techniques. See Chapters 3 and 4 for different ways of doing this.

From a Cognitive Behavioural perspective, the occurrence of the nightmares may lead to certain thoughts such as "Something bad is going to happen to me", "It is all my fault", "I am going mad", and "Something is very wrong with me". These distressing thoughts need to be examined, reflected on, and processed.

Some practical and creative tools to help make night time feel and be more comforting

The following ideas and strategies contain some suggestions on different ways of making night time more comforting, relaxing, down-regulating, safe, and containing for children. Some specific strategies for addressing nightmares are also presented. These ideas are intended to be used in conjunction with the strategies in Chapters 3 and 4.

These strategies should be delivered in the context of a safe, positive, and containing relationship. Some are intended to be used within a therapy setting and others would ideally be implemented by a child's caregiver under the guidance and advice of a trauma-informed therapist. Please see Chapter 1 for other considerations and factors to hold in mind whilst implementing these strategies.

Things to avoid

It is helpful to try to ensure that the child is not being exposed to frightening, adrenaline-pumping, or up-regulating situations, TV, and/or computer games before bed. It is also important to ensure that the child is not being threatened, even in a joking manner, with scary creatures or the consequences of not sleeping (e.g. the boogie monster or being locked in the naughty attic). It is also advisable to limit the child's sugar and caffeine intake before bed.

Calming and comforting experiences before bed

It is important to try to support caregivers to try to make a child's night-time experience and bedroom space feel as comforting, safe, relaxing, and calming as possible. Children need to feel safe and down-regulated in order to be able to sleep, feel relaxed, and rest their minds and bodies, as night time may have been associated with negative memories, themes, and experiences.

Some practical ways to enhance this are suggested below.

- Listening to gentle, soothing, positive-association music.

- Having a white-noise machine.

- Snuggling under a weighted or heated blanket.

- Putting on a light show and/or using items such as a lava/glow/bubble lamp or glow-in-the-dark stars that go on the ceiling. If the child fears the dark, it can be helpful to play games in the dark, like making patterns with torches or having a treasure hunt (if this is appropriate and safe).

- Reading a calming, positive story or singing a lullaby to them.

- Drinking a hot, down-regulating drink before bed.

- Having a warm bath.

- Having their pillow sprayed with relaxing and down-regulating oils and scents, such as lavender, camomile, or jasmine. These can be given child-friendly names, for example "magic dreaming dust" or "relaxing rainbow dust".

- Doing some relaxation, breathing, mindfulness, and/or yoga exercises before bed as part of their winding-down routine (it is important to address both the mind and the body). There are endless books, internet resources, and apps that offer a huge range of child-friendly relaxation exercises and activities. Some of my favourite relaxation exercises include: going from being a tall giraffe to a tiny mouse, going from being a stiff robot to being a floppy toy (see Photo 9.1), tensing and relaxing all of their muscles from their head to their toes, and/or imagining they are floating on a fluffy cloud.

- Having a gentle hand or back massage (this should be done with caution and be guided by the child's comfort level and their relationship to touch, their body, and the adult delivering the massage) and/or to have soothing oils applied to their skin.

- Having a special object to keep by their bed, such as a magic pebble, a precious stone, a photo of their family, a comforter, a scarf with their caregiver's perfume sprayed on it, their sensory box (see Chapter 3), or a favourite toy. This can support them to feel safe, connected, and held in mind.

- Some children might find the thought/feeling of being alone or separated from their caregiver distressing, so it can be comforting to feel another presence in the room. This can be supported by playing music or having a fish bowl (this could be electronic), a heartbeat teddy bear, or a toy that has a voice recorder inside it. I also like the teddies that can have a photo on their T-shirt or using Huggee Miss You dolls (see Photo 9.2), which can hold a photo or picture in the doll's face and have a voice recorded in them (see www.huggeemissyou.com).

Photo 9.1 Relaxation exercises using a robot and a floppy toy

Photo 9.2 A Huggee Miss You doll

Routine and rituals

To help to make night time feel safe and familiar, children should have bedtime routines and rituals that are kept as consistent and predictable as possible. They should be aware of the different steps and stages involved in their bedtime routine and have some ownership within them, for example choosing which book to read, song to listen to, or pyjamas to wear. To embed these routines further, it can be helpful to make visual checklists, visual diaries, or visual step guides of the different steps (see Photos 9.3 and 9.4). Where possible, it is also helpful to allow for more wind-down time to avoid the child feeling rushed and so they have more processing time to down-regulate.

Some children enjoy having a special goodbye ritual that is done every night and is unique to that relationship, such as a special handshake, a tucking-in method, reading a story, a saying (e.g. "I love you to the moon and back"), or a specific number of kisses.

It can also be helpful to support the child to go to bed with a positive thought or a positive memory in their mind, for example saying out loud, drawing, writing down, painting, or acting out the three best things of that day, the things that day that made them smile, or the things that they are looking forward to the next day (see Chapter 5 for ways to embed these strengths-based ideas further).

It can be useful to support caregivers to verbalise what the plans are for the next day and to remind the young person where they are, that they are in their bed/bedroom, that they are safe, and that the caregiver is in the house making sure that they are safe and doing their job of keeping the child safe. This can be embedded further by doing several safety tours of the bedroom and the house (see the "Safety tour" section in Chapter 3).

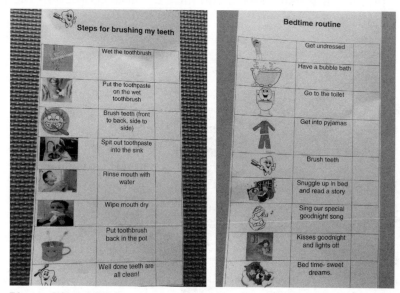

Photos 9.3 and 9.4 Brushing teeth and bedtime step-by-step routine checklists

Holding children in mind and showing children that they are held in mind

It can be important for children to know that they are still in their caregiver's mind, even when they are not physically with them. This is even more important for those who have previously had experiences of feeling/being forgotten, neglected, ignored, dismissed, abandoned, and not being held in mind. This can be further exacerbated by night time feeling like a long and fear-eliciting period of time, especially from the eyes of a child who has a less developed concept of time and orientation. Children who have experienced relational and developmental trauma often have not fully developed their concept of object permanence (this is the understanding that objects continue to exist even when they cannot be observed, seen, heard, touched, smelled, or sensed in any way).

This can be supported in various ways, including showing the child that they are important and that they have actively been kept in mind (e.g. having daily check ins, remembering things that they said to you, being their memory bank, noticing when they are absent, making an intentional effort to see things from their perspective or through their eyes, being attuned and sensitive to their signals and cues, naming, labelling, and responding to their feelings, etc.). This can also be a nice opportunity for the caregiver to talk with the child about how they are in their heart and head, even when they are not physically there.

Some caregivers find it helpful to swap a special item before bed or to have matching items such as jewellery, pyjama bottoms, or key rings (see Photo 9.5). Others might find it helpful to talk about the concept of an invisible string, a golden thread, or magic glue that always connects and ties them together. This can be a fun concept to act out or demonstrate creatively, for example being tied and connected together or stuck like glue. Another fun way of talking about this concept is to have mini models of brains and explain to the child how they symbolise always being in each other's minds and thoughts. Additionally, a nice gesture is to write loving post-it notes and put them by the child's bed, in their school box, or on their mirror. This can be enhanced by, for example, recording a voice message of support, giving them a cuddly toy with family photo in it, or writing supportive messages on a cushion/doodle bear.

Other activities can be done throughout the day to build on the concept of object permanence, such as playing games like peek-a-boo, hide and seek, knock knock who's there?, playing with find-it tubes, or engaging in treasure hunts and/or using hideaway puppets (see Photo 9.6).

Photo 9.5 People key rings

Photo 9.6 Hideaway puppets and find-it game

Making a worry/nightmare box or keeping a worry/nightmare diary

Worry boxes can be a great way of supporting children to externalise their worries and nightmares and to put their worries and nightmares away physically. Worry boxes can be purchased through various retailers or children can be supported in making and decorating their own worry box/jar/bag/container (this is nice, as it creates more of a relational memory, supports mastery over the exercise, and allows for the box to be individualised). Children can choose a name for their worry box and be supported to write down, draw, mould, or sculpt their different worries, which can then be placed in the box. These worries can also be represented by tangible items, such as putting something in a container, worry butterflies, worry worms, worry warriors, worry weights, or worry stones. Other commonly used metaphors for expressing more generalised fears and worries can be found in Worksheet 9.1.

Children tend to vary in how and when they would like to use their worry box, so it is helpful to offer them some choices and then to be led by them (this should be reviewed, tweaked, and adapted accordingly). For example, some children might like to hide their box away, lock it up, have their caregivers keep it, or have a certain time when they share a worry with someone else. It can also be useful to have a worry box that can be filled with children's worries and nightmares (see Photo 9.7) and a happy box (described below) where they can record and celebrate their happy, special, and positive memories and dreams.

A similar concept can be used with making or keeping a worry/nightmare diary (see Photo 9.8), where children are encouraged to write down/draw their worries and the nightmares and then to put the diary away or lock it up.

Photo 9.7 A nightmare/worry box

Photo 9.8 A nightmare/worry diary

Worry monsters and worry eaters (see Photo 9.9)

Some children might like to put their worries and nightmares into a worry/nightmare monster's mouth or tummy. You can buy a worry monster or worry eater from a range of suppliers (see the "Resources" tab at www.safehandsthinkingminds.co.uk for some suggestions and links to related products) or make your own worry eater, worry creature, worry superhero, or worry monster using everyday materials, such as pipe cleaners, cereal boxes, foam, Fimo, and toilet rolls. A more expensive, but also potentially more magical, version is for the child to name, describe, and draw their worry monster, animal, item, creature, superhero, or protector and for you to have this transformed into a real-life version of the toy (there are companies that specialise in making children's drawings into toys).

Some characters that other children have created when externalising a worry monster, a worry eater, or a protective figure are "Rainbow of Joy", "Mr Brave", "Hugging Harry", "Derek the Dream Catcher", "Barry the Battler of Bad Dreams", and "Gary the Gobbler".

Questions that can explore the worry monster concept more include: *What is your worry monster's name? What does...look/sound/smell like/say/do? What is...'s job? What special powers does...have? How does...protect you? How does...gobble up/scare away/crush/squeeze/eat/jump on/catch the worries? How does...keep the dreams safe? How much safer does knowing...is with you at night make you feel?*

Children can be supported to sculpt or draw their worry monster eating the nightmares up (or any chosen way for the worry monster to get rid of the nightmares) and then to put the nightmares in the monster's mouth, to act out/role-play the monster getting rid of the nightmares, and/or to write a letter to the worry monster asking for its help and support in taking the nightmares away.

I have also discussed these concepts with children using the character of a "nightmare ninja" and supported them to create and explore the above questions with respect to the "nightmare ninja". See Worksheet 9.2 for some more questions around a "nightmare ninja".

These worry creatures should be personalised to the individual child. Case examples are given below.

Andy was fascinated by insects and flies and he also really liked Spider-Man. Building on this concept, we made a special corner in his room using sticky fly paper, which was guarded by a figurine of Spider-Man. We then talked about how the nightmares would not be able to get to him, because they would get stuck on the sticky paper and caught in Spider-Man's sticky and twisted web. For him this worked wonders!

Gia spoke about how she wished someone would suction away her worries, so we created a homemade "suction machine" and her caregiver vacuumed the room before Gia went to bed.

Elva created a monster called Carlos the Crusher, whose job it was to crush the nightmares and to protect Elva's dreams. We were then able to draw and make a sculpt of Carlos the Crusher and to find ways to connect with him before she went to bed.

Photo 9.9 Different worry monsters and worry eaters

Happy, calming, positive, and safe box

An alternative or addition to the worry/nightmare box concept is to make a safe, positive, and calming box that can be kept next to the young person's bed so that they can look at it before going to sleep or if they wake during the night. As illustrated in Photo 9.10, this can be decorated and filled with lots of happy and soothing images, memories, sparkle moments, inspirational quotes, photos, drawings, and sensory items. This can be a version of the sensory safety box (see the "Creating a calming, soothing, and self-regulating box" section in Chapter 3 for instructions).

Photo 9.10 Calming and soothing box decorated with a wishing fairy, feathers, angel clouds, and fairy dust

Happy, calming, positive, and safe poster (see Photo 9.11)

It can also be useful to design a safe/happy/positive poster, sign, canvas, or collage that includes all of the things (thinking across all of the senses) that make the child feel safe, calm, and positive. This can include using images from magazines, photos, pictures, stickers, written messages, soothing materials, inspirational quotes, etc. This piece of art can be put somewhere where the child will see it if they wake up. This image can also be photographed, or a smaller version made, to make it portable and to put in a photo key ring, on a photo teddy bear, or in a personalised snow globe.

Photo 9.11 Happy and positive poster

Safe place pillow, blanket, or doodle bear

A lovely way of facilitating relaxation and calm feelings is to go to and connect with one's safe place. See Chapter 3 for instructions about creating and travelling to one's safe place. It can also be a helpful integrated part of a child's bedtime routine to be supported to go to their imagined safe place. It can be useful to have those positive and soothing images and thoughts close by to embed the concept of a safe place further. Several safe place creative extensions are described in Chapter 3. Creative extensions specifically for bedtime include having the safe place represented on a blanket, pillow (see Photos 9.12 and 9.13), clock, poster, glow lamp, pyjamas, or doodle bear. The positive images can be applied using transferred photos, stitched designs, and iron-on images, or decorating the items with fabric pens.

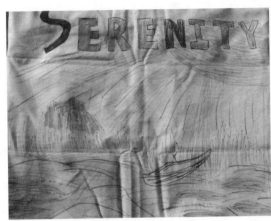

Photos 9.12 and 9.13 Safe place pillows

Dreaming diary, book of beauty, positive pad, or artwork of dreams

Children can also be supported to keep a written or audio record of all of their positive thoughts, moments, and magical dreams in a "dreaming diary", a "positive pad", or a "book of beauty". Children can list these moments, write a story about them, draw them, or sculpt them. This artwork, scrapbook, or diary can be kept by their bed and looked at as a reminder before they go to sleep.

Sleeping well accessories – worry dolls, dream catchers, wishing fairies, magic fairy dust, and guardian angels (see Photo 9.14)

Many children find it comforting to have something tangible that they can feel protected by and transfer some of their worries to. This can be through a range of accessories and can vary a lot depending on the individual child and context; however, I find popular ways include: Guatemalan worry dolls, a dream catcher, wishing fairies, wishing stones, a wishing well, magic fairy dust, or a guardian angel (see the "Resources" tab at www.safehandsthinkingminds.co.uk for specific links to related products). It can be powerful and positive to make items such as worry dolls, dream catchers, and guardian angels together using a range of materials to enhance the relational element.

Photo 9.14 Sleeping well accessories

Safety and protective items and people

Children who are feeling alone, unsafe, or unprotected at night may find it helpful to have/make a safety shield, magic blanket, superhero mask, invisible cape, or safety bubble put around them (see Photo 9.17). These concepts can then be drawn, acted, or made and be a springboard for thickening discussions (see the "Safe person/ people" section in Chapter 3 for ways to bring these concepts to life).

Other children might like to have "magic fairy dust" or "dreaming dust" sprinkled on them, "keep away nightmares" sprayed on them, or "magic lotion" put on them (see Photo 9.18). Other children might like to write their own "magic smell" or make a "nightmare potion" to make the nightmares go away. Some children might like to make a keep-out sign or poster that says, for example, "Stay away nightmares!" or "Nightmare-free zone" (see Photo 9.16).

Children can draw, sculpt, or collage the nightmare and then depict all of their life cheerleaders and team supporters around them who are keeping the nightmares away (see Photo 9.15). They could write a letter from themselves and/or from their team around them (e.g. superheroes, celebrities, historical figures, friends, family, etc.) telling the nightmare to go away and to keep away.

Photo 9.15 A replica of a drawing of a child's team of life cheerleaders fighting against the spiky hand nightmare

Photo 9.16 A "nightmares keep away" poster

Photo 9.17 A replica drawing of a child inside a protective safety bubble

Photo 9.18 Magic nightmare spray

Celebrate and notice when the nightmares are absent

If there are times when the young person does not have nightmares, or has fewer or less intense ones, it is helpful to name, notice, appreciate, and bring attention to these "unique exceptions/outcomes" and to have thickening and embedding discussions around them. It can also be beneficial to think about, list, draw, or sculpt all of the times the young person has overcome other challenges and tricky times and to reflect on what skills and positive qualities they used to achieve this (see the "Reflecting on past challenges, what skills the young person has overcome, and what journey they have travelled" section in Chapter 5).

Externalising and creatively expressing the nightmares

The concept of externalising can be supported by externalising the actual nightmare (if it is a recurring theme/picture). This should happen in a safe, therapeutic context and done or supported by a trained therapist. If a child is having a repeated distressing nightmare, it can be helpful to name and describe the nightmare.

For example, *if the nightmare was an item, type of weather, animal, shape, colour, or creature, what would it be like/look like/smell like/do/sound like/say? Draw, sculpt, collage, mould, or depict in sand what keeps you up at night. What thoughts or feelings are whirling around in your head and in your body?*

Children can be supported to write the story of the nightmare down or to draw, collage, sculpt, mould, or represent it through sand. Within the context of therapy, it can be useful, particularly when addressing the potential cognitive avoidance of trying not to think about the nightmare, to write it down, tell the story of the nightmare, or record it and to repeat this process several times.

Discussions can be had around different ways of responding to "the nightmare" (the chosen name of the nightmare should be used), such as locking it up, squashing it, tearing it up, burying it, scribbling it out, squeezing it, flushing it down the toilet, shouting at it, burning it, etc. It can also be advantageous to reflect with the young person on how much bigger and stronger they are than the nightmare. Examples of externalising, imagery re-scripting, and ways of responding to nightmares are given below.

Jaxon shared how his nightmare centred on a scary pair of hands reaching out and coming to catch him. This image and the associated memories were explored and processed through validating his emotions, making connections with past experiences, and using some cognitive therapy techniques. Jaxon was then supported to name this image. He chose to call them "Razor Hands". He was then supported to draw and make the "Razor Hands" and to reflect on how much bigger and stronger he was than them. He was supported in responding to the "Razor Hands" in lots of different ways, including colouring the hands in black and white, cutting the hands into small pieces, blunting the sharp bits, and turning the hands into floppy hands. He also drew and visualised other guards around and protecting him, like a bubble, a tree of his team of life's hands, and a shield.

Maxine had a recurring nightmare about drowning in the bath. After doing some integrating and processing techniques, she externalised this nightmare by saying it was as if she was caught under a heavy wave and couldn't breathe. She was supported to draw the wave that was overwhelming her and reflected on the associated emotional, sensory, and physical feelings of being weighed down and trapped. She was then supported to draw her riding, jumping through, and surfing the wave (see Photo 9.19). She was also supported to practise and learn about breathing and relaxation techniques. Building on this concept, and led by Maxine, she was supported to imagine pulling the plug out of the water and the water turning into drinking chocolate.

Photo 9.19 Surfing and surviving the wave

Imagery re-scripting

In the context of a safe, therapeutic relationship, children might also find it valuable to use imagery re-scripting techniques when responding to nightmares. This is where a negative mental image is transformed into a more benign image; for example, imagining the nightmare: as being on a TV channel that is changed; with a different ending; on mute or in black and white; and stuck behind a screen, piece of glass, or wall (see Photo 9.20).

Photo 9.20 Imagery re-scripting of a nightmare

Recording what works: coping and option exercises

It can be helpful to reflect with the young person on all of the different tools, skills, and strengths they have to keep the worries and nightmares away. This can be recorded through tools such as: my treasure box of tools, my coping cookbook, my cue/stress cards, my chill skills, my protective palm poster, my octopus of options, my bag of ideas, my calm-down superpowers, etc. (see examples of these and some worksheet templates in Chapters 3 and 8).

Worksheet 9.1
Worry is (using metaphors)...

Worry and Fear

The feeling of "worry/fear" is like...

If I gave the "worry/fear" a name I would call it...

I would describe the "worry/fear" as being like...

Butterflies in stomach	Wobbly jelly	Tornado	Thoughts whirling like a washing machine	Bursting pipe (under pressure)
Being strangled	Ant on somebody's shoe	Racing heart	Runaway train	Lost in a maze
Trapped	Feeling tiny	Heavy load	Mr Stretchy (pulled in different directions)	What else?

Copyright © Karen Treisman – *A Therapeutic Treasure Box for Working with Children and Adolescents with Developmental Trauma – 2018*

About the "worry/fear" (replace "worry/fear" with your own choice of name)

» If the "worry/fear" was a colour, it would be…

» If the "worry/fear" was a shape, it would be…

» If the "worry/fear" was an animal, it would be…

» If the "worry/fear" was a flower, a tree, or something from nature, it would be…

» If the "worry/fear" was an object/item/metaphor, it would be…

» If the "worry/fear" could talk, it would say… (What would its voice sound like?)

» The "worry/fear" stops me from…

» The "worry/fear" helps me…

» Without the "worry/fear" I would…

» If the "worry/fear" disappeared I would miss…

» …makes the "worry/fear" much bigger.

» …makes the "worry/fear" smaller.

» I am stronger and bigger than the "worry/fear" when…

Expanding creatively on the metaphor

Once a metaphor/name/item/object has been chosen and discussed in detail, it can be helpfully embedded and expanded on by carrying out related expressive and creative activities.

For example, if a child says that their feeling of "worry/fear" is like "butterflies in their tummy", they might sculpt, mould, draw, collage, paint, or make "butterflies in their tummy". Similarly, the child might be encouraged to act using physical movement, puppets, masks, or a sand-tray exercise to explore the "butterflies in their tummy" further.

The above questions can be used to bring the metaphor to life; for example: What are the different butterflies' names? What do "the butterflies" sound like? If "the butterflies" could talk, what would they say? What makes "the butterflies" stronger and flitter more? What would make "the butterflies" fly away? When do "the butterflies" sleep and rest?

Additionally, the metaphor can be played with according to the need. For example, caterpillars, flying, wings, butterfly hugs, and butterfly kisses can be symbolically discussed as being symbolic.

Photo 9.21 Butterflies in my tummy artwork

Copyright © Karen Treisman – *A Therapeutic Treasure Box for Working with Children and Adolescents with Developmental Trauma* – 2018

Worksheet 9.2
My nightmare ninja

What does my nightmare ninja look like?
Draw, sculpt, write, or collage your responses.

What does my nightmare ninja sound/smell like? What would my nightmare ninja say if it had a voice? What does my nightmare ninja do?
Draw, sculpt, write, or collage your responses.

Copyright © Karen Treisman – *A Therapeutic Treasure Box for Working with Children and Adolescents with Developmental Trauma – 2018*

CHAPTER 10

Preparing, Planning, Reflecting on, and Expressing Endings, Changes, Goodbyes, and Transitions

Why are endings and transitional work so crucial in the context of relational and developmental trauma?

This chapter is the last in the book to represent and model the ending process. The ending within the therapeutic process, or within an attachment-facilitating environment, needs to be thought about from the beginning. Many children have experienced traumatic endings and goodbyes, which are often characterised by powerlessness, unpredictability a lack of thoughtfulness/preparation, feeling out of control, a lack of emotional containment scaffolding, and co-regulation.

Endings, changes, goodbyes, and new beginnings can evoke a range of feelings, including resurfacing and re-triggering past experiences of rejection, sadness, being disposed of, being let down, being insecure, deprivation, abandonment, pain, grief, and/or loss of a meaningful relationship. Some examples of unresolved and challenging endings in the context of trauma are given below.

Delta had been moved to nine different foster care placements and nine different schools. Each one further reinforced her belief system that she was "disposable and damaged goods". Delta described one placement where her foster carer had adopted the other child in the home, to whom she had become close, and had given notice on Delta's placement. Delta spoke of another time when she had come home from school to find her social worker waiting for her to take her to a different placement, with her possessions packed in black bags.

Bobby's last memory of his mother, Nancy, was when the police raided his house. Nancy resisted arrest, so the intensity of the situation increased, and she was subsequently arrested and driven off in a police car. Bobby was taken to a respite foster carer.

When Hassan's village was attacked, he witnessed his mother being brutally murdered, followed by his older brother being kidnapped and placed into the soldier's van. Shortly after, with little time to grieve or process, he had to flee and start the arduous journey to his new host country.

Shayla's mum kissed her goodnight and then left the house and did not return until five months later. During this time, there was no contact between them.

> Ben had been in several foster placements. He was eventually placed somewhere that he felt safe and settled. However, the foster carer's elderly mother, who lived abroad, became unwell, so she had to emigrate quickly, which resulted in the placement ending.

> Noa's mother and step-father's relationship (they had been together since Noa was three months old) ended abruptly and in a turbulent manner. Noa's mother stated, "He was gone and not coming back", and his presence and absence was never discussed again.

Future-thinking and planning may be further impeded by children functioning more in their fight, flight, or freeze survival mode (being hyper-aroused, hyper-vigilant, or cut off). This can leave less room for children to be in their thinking and learning mode. Endings and goodbyes can often create a storm and/or rupture in relationships and can trigger emotional and behaviour dysregulation and one's defence and survival strategies to be activated (see Worksheet 10.1). Children may also be contending with questions such as: Can I manage on my own? Will they miss me? Will they forget me? What if I need them again? Have I done something wrong? Who am I being replaced by?

It is common for children/parents to respond to endings and goodbyes in a variety of ways, including sadness, anger/rage, hurt, confusion, disappointment, rejecting the person they are saying goodbye to, sharing ambivalent feelings, denigrating the person they are saying goodbye to, disengaging, and shutting off, or, on the other side, magnifying difficulties, reporting new crises, presenting difficulties, or presenting with an increased sense of helplessness and vulnerability.

The ending is therefore a significant process and a vital time to provide children/parents with a reparative ending and a further opportunity to process, revise, and refine their previous distressing endings and relational ruptures. The ending is also a powerful opportunity to convey the message to the young person/parent that they are ready to celebrate the journey which they have travelled and connect with their future hopes and plans and to emphasise that they have been the agent and vehicle of their own change and journey.

This reparative ending can be difficult to achieve and can be a source of frustration and disappointment if it is not made possible, particularly if the ending occurs prematurely or unexpectedly or is enforced (e.g. placement breakdown, geographical change, restricted session amounts permitted by the service, the client disengages, etc.). In these cases, it is still important to mark and process the ending in the best way possible.

Therapists' own experiences of endings

Endings and transitions can trigger similar feelings in the therapist, social worker, caregiver, teacher, etc. and in turn can colour, shape, and permeate the ending process. Some of the following questions might be supportive in reflecting on this process.

> What have been some of your own personal and professional experiences of and relationships to endings, goodbyes, losses, changes, and transitions? Do you have a pattern or learned way of responding to endings, goodbyes, losses, changes, and transitions? What are some of your hopes, fears, worries, and expectations about ending the therapeutic relationship? What role does the particular child/caregiver/piece of work

play and fill in your week/month/life/therapy journey? What implications or feelings might there be of that role or space no longer occurring?

Structure of the chapter: transitions and endings

To capture some of the complexity of endings and transitions, this chapter will focus on the following. First, some ideas and strategies will be offered for supporting transitions, such as moving from one activity to another, breaking up for the school holidays, or moving to another class. Second, some ideas and strategies will be offered to reflect on the ending of a therapeutic relationship.

Strategies from both may be interwoven, adapted, and drawn on. It should be noted that these are intended to complement existing therapeutic models and styles and are not standalone techniques.

Preparing for and supporting transitions

The skill of managing transitions is commonly reported as being difficult for children who have experienced relational and developmental trauma. Reasons for this include children:

- having had difficult, and at times traumatic, previous experiences of losses, changes, endings, and goodbyes, including feelings of unpredictability, abandonment, powerlessness, and so forth, which are triggered by day-to-day transitions, changes, and moves. Including these transitions not being supported, contained, or in a context of co-regulation.

- struggling with regulating their emotions and alternating between arousal and regulation states and levels

- having difficulties with their executive function and cognitive skills, such as around cause and effect, consequential thinking, and planning skills

- having difficulties with their impulse control skills

- having increased difficulty with their sensory processing and sensory integration skills

- having high levels of anxieties and worries

- having to live in the present survival mode.

It is advantageous to keep in mind that transitioning can include transitioning one's physical body and/or transitioning one's mind. These day-to-day transitions can include transitioning from one task to another, changing from one environment to another, and moving from primary to secondary school. Where possible, transitions should be minimised, planned for, and linked to the associated trigger. As with all the strategies, they are generally much more effective and meaningful when they are done in the context of a positive, trusting, and safe relationship and when the relationship can be used as an anchor and a co-regulator. Some strategies to support transitions are listed below, although these will vary according to the individual and context.

- Noticing, acknowledging, and naming what constitutes a transition for that child and providing them with opportunities to express the associated feelings, hopes, fears, and expectations (the feelings and safety-focused strategies detailed in Chapters 3 and 4 can be used to support these conversations with a focus on transitions and endings). Using picture books around transitions or sentence-completion cards can support these discussions.

- Planning, preparing, and anticipating any transitions. Where possible, trying to keep as many things the same and unchanged, allowing for adjustment and processing time, staggering endings and changes, taking a bite-size SMART approach, and facilitating opportunities for the child to have some choice and mastery over the change.

- Supporting the child to have a clear idea of what the transition is, what is expected, and what is required, for example "My body needs to move from... to...", "My brain needs to move from...to...", and "When the chime rings, we all will...then we will...".

- The planning and preparing part can also be worked towards by decreasing the child's uncertainty and explicitly talking about and showing them on visual timetables and checklists what will happen before, during, and after the transition. An example is given in Box 10.1.

- Reflecting on previous transitions that the child has mastered and achieved and magnifying the lessons learned from these and the factors and skills that made this possible. This includes thinking about "smaller" tasks, such as reviewing lots of transitions in the day that they do successfully, for example "Every day I move from...to...".

- Finding ways to show the child that they are kept in mind. It can be very important for children to know that they are still in their caregiver's mind, even when they are not physically with them. This is heightened for children who have had experiences of feeling/being forgotten, neglected, silenced, ignored, dismissed, abandoned, or not being held in mind, and/or having their feelings minimised, denied, or misinterpreted. This is exacerbated for children who have experienced relational and developmental trauma, because they often have not fully developed their concept of object permanence (the understanding that objects continue to exist even when they cannot be observed, seen, heard, touched, smelled, or sensed in any way). This can be supported by their caregiver/supporting adult naming, validating, and responding to their feelings (see Chapter 4) and verbalising how much they were missed and were kept in mind. See Chapter 6 for ideas around supporting this.

- Anticipating difficulties and formalising and teaching transition skills by having clear systems in place to facilitate this process. These might include a traffic-light system, movement cards, a drum sequence, music playing, switching the lights on and off, or using visual timers (e.g. stopwatches, child-friendly clocks, or sand timers).

- Using transition-focused, step-by-step, clear, visual, colourful, and pictorial photo books, moving calendars, handover books, social stories, comic strip conversations, and communication books.

- Practising and role-playing transitions and scenarios. This can be done with masks, puppets, dolls, or teddies. The transition can be made into a game or an adventure.

- Supporting children during transitions with the commonly recommended parenting strategies, such as using humour, playfulness, rewards, incentives, encouragement, praise, and distraction techniques.

- Ensuring that the child has their toolbox of self-regulation techniques to hand during the transition (e.g. their safe person, down-regulating, comforting smell/scent item, sensory box, or transitional object). See Chapters 3 and 7 for a variety of grounding and regulating activity suggestions.

- Facilitating graded visits, tours, and handovers, ideally with the child seeing their caregiver and, for example, school having a dialogue and being partners.

- Finding fun and child-friendly ways for the child to get involved in and to take some ownership of the transition, such as taking photos of their new school/journey, decorating their new notebook, and/or making an "All About Me" book (see Chapter 2).

Box 10.1 **A case example of supporting a child around transitions**

A child who struggles to transition to break time at school (following an assessment and reflecting on his unique needs) may be supported to have:

- his feelings named, validated, and acknowledged by thinking adults and to have some exploration and reflection on what he is finding difficult and why it might be tricky

- a visual calendar and child-friendly clock so that he knows what he is doing when and where

- anchoring words used, such as "when and then", or "before, after, and next"

- a staged warning system that signals impending transitions, like countdowns, cue cards, or a light changing system

- regulating and grounding activities integrated before and after break time and a winding-down, processing time incorporated into the different transition points

- a reminder of what would happen during the break and what he would be doing after

- opportunities to gain some mastery, such as choosing where he will go at break time or what toy he will play with

- support during the break if necessary, such as from a peer helper or key adult and/or by having a transitional object available

- the transition task reduced, for example starting with just a five-minute break time (or whatever is manageable) and gradually increasing the time

- encouragement and praise for his effort and towards the steps he takes and tries to take.

Supporting significant endings and working towards reparative endings

Many of the transition strategies described above can also be useful when moving towards a therapeutic ending; however, some complementary ideas to support more significant long-term endings will now be presented. The extent and use of the following ideas will depend on the quality and nature of the therapy, relationship, and collaborative end goals and hopes for the ending. The ending gives a great opportunity to expand on and play with metaphors that were used during the course of therapy and to find ways to reflect on the overall journey. Some young people may choose to mark the ending with a meal and/or by inviting other key people to one of the lead-up sessions.

Ideally, endings of a long-term piece of therapeutic work will naturally and organically come towards an end and often be led or indicated by the child/caregiver. It is also important to support the young person to see themselves as an active agent of the change and see that they possess the necessary skills and tools to move forward in a positive way and make it through any future setbacks. This extends to giving hopeful and permissive messages for any future work that they may go on to do with other therapists/organisations.

Some strategies to support significant endings and goodbyes

Naming, acknowledging, and validating the range of feelings evoked by endings, including some mixed feelings

Endings can evoke a range of feelings, including resurfacing and re-triggering past challenging experiences and difficult feelings. It is important to allow space and time to explore and discuss the different feelings, including worries and fears, that might be experienced because of the ending. These discussions should be paced and should give the young person plenty of time to process and integrate the ending. They can be guided and enhanced by some of the exercises described in Chapter 4.

For example, activities such as exploring the various different feelings associated with the ending can be supported through exercises like the feelings wheel, the feelings pie, sentence-completion cards, the head of thoughts and emotions, or the feelings tower.

It can be helpful to explore the mixed feelings which ending can stir up through exercises such as: a feelings wheel (see Photo 10.1), a puzzle of feelings, a bag of feelings, a sand jar of feelings (see Photo 10.2), patchwork of feelings (see Photo 10.3), and a kaleidoscope of feelings.

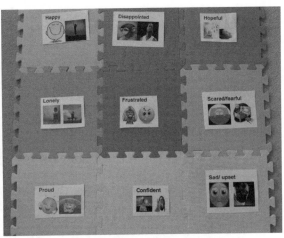

Photo 10.1 Feelings wheel about endings

Photo 10.2 Sand jar of feelings

Photo 10.3 Patchwork of feelings about the ending

Punctuating the stages

It can be helpful to mark the stages leading up to the ending, as children often find the concept of time more challenging to grasp and this can be heightened by the impact of the trauma on orientation and concept of time. It can be useful to have a visual countdown calendar or a diary that marks each week and verbal reminders of the time that is remaining. This can feel too overwhelming for some children who struggle with anxiety around transitions, so the strategies need to be evaluated and planned around the individual child and their needs. The ending and transitions should also be modelled within the session, so, for example how the sessions begin and end each week.

Creatively reflecting on the journey

The ending and nearing the end of the therapy feel like important stages at which to reflect on the journey that has already been travelled. I find it beneficial and powerful to make sure that, in whichever way I am creatively reflecting on the journey, I also leave physical, emotional, and symbolic room and space for more to be added, to convey the message that the ending of the therapy is not the ending of the work or of future possibilities.

Some ways that I have used to mark the journey (I usually use several of them in combination) include:

- a "then, now, and future" or "dual portrait" picture, sculpt, or collage

- a visual path, road, track, map, and/or a fairground that marks their journey during and beyond therapy

- a visual representation of some of the challenges and obstacles faced and overcome, such as making or drawing this as snakes and ladders (see Photo 10.4), a labyrinth, a maze (see Photo 10.5), an obstacle course (see Photo 10.6), a jungle, or a rollercoaster

- a sand tray, sculpt, or drawing representation of the journey

- a story, poem, rap, or song of the therapy journey

- making art pieces and using selected words for different feelings that children have felt throughout the therapy – the ending can be a powerful way of displaying these art pieces (like a personal art gallery), or photos of them, to track and to visually see the transformation.

These ideas can be optimised by supporting the child to think of a word, sentence, song, poem, or film to represent and describe the journey.

Photo 10.4 Snakes and ladders of the relationship

Photo 10.5 Labyrinth/maze of the relational journey

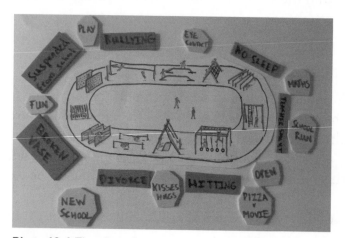

Photo 10.6 The obstacle course of the relationship

It is helpful to use a multi-sensory approach with each of the ideas. For example, children might be given an array of materials, such as pipe cleaners, glitter, stones, flowers, butterflies, velvet, etc., to use to represent their feelings when making their journey.

Each response can be thickened through expanding discussions and creative representations. Examples are given below.

Gem drew a labyrinth to represent the different obstacles and challenges that she had faced during therapy. These challenges spanned multiple spheres – for example: at school struggling with being bullied by a group of girls; finding it difficult to make friends; falling behind with her work; at home feeling hurt and humiliated by her mother's comments to her and her step-father's behaviour towards her mother; struggling to trust the therapy relationship and process; and finding it difficult to show any form of raw emotion or vulnerability. Once these challenges were labelled and positioned on the labyrinth, Gem was supported to reflect on what it had felt like to be in the labyrinth and what skills and strengths she had used to find her way out. Each of these was expanded on and used to plan for how she would manage if she found herself in another labyrinth. We also reflected on what she could teach others about navigating through a labyrinth and what she had learned about herself, her life, and from being in one for so long.

Mohammad had experienced frequent and distressing headaches. He had externalised these headaches as "The Hammer". Throughout therapy, alongside other strategies, Mohammad was supported to draw, sculpt, collage, and write about "The Hammer" and to depict himself in a series of art-based tools and through various body-mapping techniques. Mohammad was then supported to respond to "The Hammer" through a range of imagery re-scripting and reshaping exercises. As the therapy was coming to an end, Mohammad was supported to display the artworks of "The Hammer" throughout the room and to reflect on the shifts and changes seen. This included images about being free from "The Hammer" and being stronger and bigger than "The Hammer".

Reflecting further on changes and progresses made

Magnifying the strengths, skills, and resiliencies that were used to overcome obstacles and challenges is important (see the exercises in Chapter 5). This can be summarised and expanded on by making a list, collage, picture, sculpt, or poem of things such as "The changes I have made", "The leaps I have taken", "I am proud of…", "I have learned…", "Now I can…", "Now I am…", "All of my achievements", and "The good choices I have already made". (See Photos 10.7 and 10.8.)

Photo 10.7 Challenges I have overcome   **Photo 10.8** Record of changes made

Expanding on the journey, the changes, and the strengths of the therapeutic process and how to take some of those lessons with them

It can be helpful to reflect on the therapeutic journey and in turn on what parts and components of the process and time can be carried forward. These exercises can marry up nicely with the other strategies described throughout this chapter. Some examples of the ways to reflect on the journey are listed below.

- Creating, decorating, and starting to fill up a treasure box with special moments, memories, hopes, dreams, wishes, and lessons learned.

- Making a skyscraper of strengths, or therapy tower (see Photo 10.11), that is made up of the bricks of the therapy and the time that has passed, including the special moments, memories, hopes, dreams, wishes, and lessons that have been learned and appreciated. It is also helpful to discuss how all of the pieces are still there even if the tower falls down, and these can be put together again, sometimes in a different, even stronger, formation.

- Placing or drawing special moments, wishes, hopes, lessons learned, and so forth in a time capsule (see Worksheet 10.4), into pieces of a therapy puzzle (see Worksheet 2.3 in Chapter 2), or into bottled-up feelings (see Worksheet 10.5).

- Supporting children to think about what parts of their experience have stuck to their positive magnet (see Photo 10.9 and Worksheet 10.6) and which parts, if any, they want to drink and breathe in.

- Thinking with children can also think about what lessons, memories, or moments they are putting in their invisible travelling suitcase, safety kit, such as their protective vest, as well as their and their lifeboat (see Photo 10.10 and Worksheet 10.10).

- To promote the idea of continuing to work on the process, and to prioritise self-care, children can be supported to think of a flower and what they need to do to water and feed the flower in the future to keep it nourished and sustained. They can also think of the tower of strength and what they need to do to maintain and strengthen it (see Worksheet 10.10).

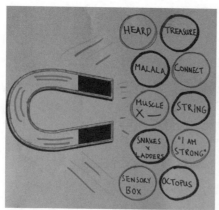

Photo 10.9 Magnetic thoughts, memories, and moments that I want to stick

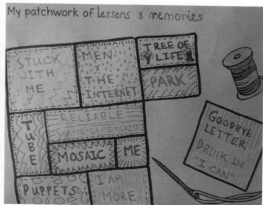

Photo 10.10 Patchwork of lessons and memories

Photo 10.11 Therapy tower of lessons and memories

Hopes, fears, and expectations for the future

It is important to create a future-oriented, hope-filled approach throughout the therapy, particularly towards the ending and moving-on stage. This might include reflecting with children about how they see their future self, how they would like to be, feel, think, act, believe, and achieve, and what their various hopes, goals, dreams, and wishes are. This can be supported by exercises such as:

- writing a letter from their future to their current self

- making a time capsule (see Worksheet 10.4 and Photos 6.9 and 10.12)

- creating a bridge, magic door, or key for getting to their future place

- drawing a "then, now, and future" picture/portrait.

Discussions about wishes, hopes, dreams, and aspirations can be complemented by props or making or drawing things like magic wands, genies (see Worksheets 10.8 and 10.9), fortune-teller balls, dream catchers, a wishing well, and/or wishing dandelions. It is a good idea to thicken the discussions of each wish or goal so that they become and feel richer and more energised. Examples of thickening wishes are described in Chapter 5.

Photo 10.12 Time capsule and letter to one's future self

Tree of Life (Ncube, 2007)

The Tree of Life is a wonderful Narrative Therapy tool that traditionally uses the tree as a metaphor for children's lives, experiences, roots, identity, connections, resiliencies, and skills. It also provides the opportunity to talk about the storms and hazards that they have faced. I have found it to be a powerful tool to use towards the ending of therapy and to span over several sessions. It can be creatively represented through painting, sculpting, mural, mosaic, etc. and can be a very tangible strengths-based piece to take home or to have framed. Worksheet 5.13 offers more guidance on the different steps of the Tree of Life.

A take-back practice letter

This can be a powerful letter, card, or recording to give to the young person to mark their various strengths, skills, and resiliencies, to validate the reciprocal nature of the therapeutic relationship, and to share with them the influence they have had on you. See Worksheet 10.11 for guidance on what types of questions and themes can be included in a take-back practice letter.

Ending gifts and transitional objects

There are mixed feelings in the therapy world about giving clients gifts, so this will depend on one's personal views and training, alongside the context in which you work. Personally, providing I have reflected on why I am giving the gift, how I will present it, what purpose/function it is serving, and how it is contributing to the overall aims of the therapeutic process, I tend to like to give a symbolic gift that is a reminder of the journey. Some examples are given below.

I worked with one young person who was religious and spiritual and for whom angels had featured regularly throughout our therapy, so, as a parting gift, I gave her a guardian angel.

With another young person, our work had often used the metaphor of a tree, so, alongside framing her Tree of Life piece of art, I gave her a small tree sculpture.

I gave a young boy a treasure box to symbolise the importance of acknowledging and celebrating strengths and a sparkle moments diary to fill up with memories.

It can be useful to make children a certificate or an award to mark the end of therapy. In addition, depending on the appropriateness and the situation, it might be helpful to do something like plant a tree, name a star, make a plaque, or sign a wall.

Future problem-solving and creating coping cards

It is likely that the young person will have identified and tried a range of tools that they have found helpful throughout the therapeutic process. As part of the ending experience, it is important to revisit and rehearse these tools and to normalise, plan for, anticipate, and problem-solve possible obstacles, setbacks, and barriers that may occur.

It is also helpful to find a child-friendly way to record these coping strategies. This could be done in a range of ways, including: my treasure box of tools, my coping cookbook, my cue/stress cards, my chill skills, my protective palm, my octopus of options, my bag of ideas, my calm-down superpowers, etc. This could also be translated onto a self-care pledge (see the example on Worksheet 7.11). Photos and worksheets for these strategies are presented in Chapters 3 and 8.

Feeling Unsafe/Putting Up Defences

When I am feeling "unsafe" and need to protect myself I ...

Surround myself with barbed wire	Go into attack mode like a hungry shark	Go into my own protective bubble	Put on my bulletproof vest	Retreat into my tortoise shell
Make myself small/invisible	Hide away in the fog	Freeze on the spot	Whizz around like a dart	Paint on a smile like a clown
Put up my spikes like a hedgehog	Zoom away like a speeding car	Push people away like an opposing magnet	Think in black and white	What else?

Copyright © Karen Treisman – *A Therapeutic Treasure Box for Working with Children and Adolescents with Developmental Trauma – 2018*

Then, now, and in the future

Write, draw, collage, depict in sand, or sculpt your journey and the changes you have made, and hope to make, in relation to a range of situations such as relationships and difficulties.

Then	Now	My future

Copyright © Karen Treisman – *A Therapeutic Treasure Box for Working with Children and Adolescents with Developmental Trauma* – 2018

Worksheet 10.3
Sentence-completion ideas and discussion points for the ending experience

These responses can be collaged, drawn, acted out, sculpted, depicted in a sand tray, etc. They are intended as ideas and need to be adapted and selected dependent on the individual and the specific situation.

When I think about endings and goodbyes I think…

When I think about endings and goodbyes I feel…

When I think about endings and goodbyes I remember…

My wishes and hopes for this ending are…

My fears and worries for this ending are…

The highlight of this journey has been…

The things that will stay with me from this journey are…

If I could bottle up a moment or lesson it would be…

The hardest part was…

If I could go back and do things differently, I would…

A word to describe my therapy journey would be…

A sentence/song/movie/poem to describe my therapy journey would be…

Copyright © Karen Treisman – A Therapeutic Treasure Box for Working with Children and Adolescents with Developmental Trauma – 2018

I have learned…

The things that are different now are…

The changes I have made…

I know I can…

I am proud of…

I am thankful for…

I overcame…

My coping skills are…

In my treasure box of tools there is…

My safety plan is…

My go-to options are…

I will remind myself of…

I can teach others about…and how to…

My dreams and hopes for myself, others, and the world are…

My future will be…

Copyright © Karen Treisman – *A Therapeutic Treasure Box for Working with Children and Adolescents with Developmental Trauma* – 2018

Inside the time capsule I/we would put ...

DO NOT OPEN UNTIL

2050

Copyright © Karen Treisman – *A Therapeutic Treasure Box for Working with Children and Adolescents with Developmental Trauma* – 2018

Bottle up moments

This is like taking a mental snapshot or soaking in a special moment. Which moments would you bottle up and why? Write or draw on the bottles below and try to give each one a label. If you prefer, you can label and fill actual bottles.
Try and remember and hold on to all the details, the smells, the sounds, the tastes, the feelings, the movements, and more of each memory and moment...

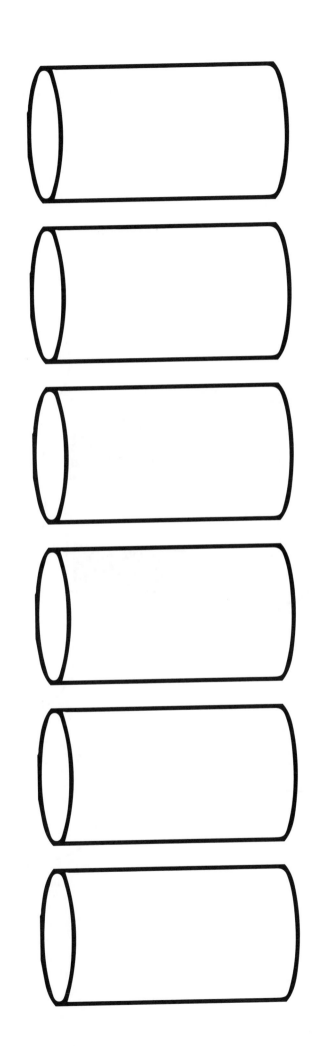

Copyright © Karen Treisman – A Therapeutic Treasure Box for Working with Children and Adolescents with Developmental Trauma – 2018

Worksheet 10.6
Magnetic thoughts, feelings, and sensations

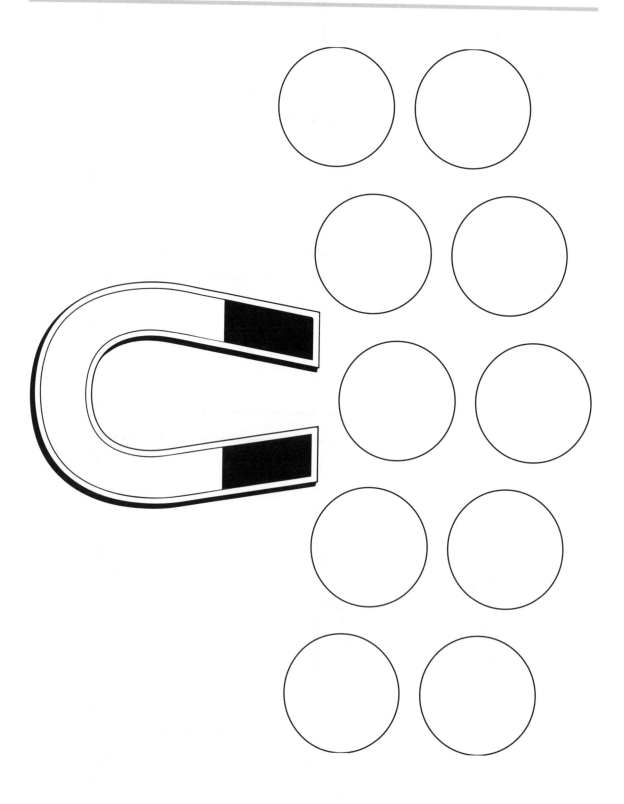

Copyright © Karen Treisman – *A Therapeutic Treasure Box for Working with Children and Adolescents with Developmental Trauma – 2018*

Copyright © Karen Treisman – *A Therapeutic Treasure Box for Working with Children and Adolescents with Developmental Trauma* – 2018

Worksheet 10.8
Wishes for myself, others, and the world

My wishes for myself are... (Draw, sculpt, or collage your responses.)

My wishes for others are... (Draw, sculpt, or collage your responses.)

My wishes for the world are... (Draw, sculpt, or collage your responses.)

Copyright © Karen Treisman – *A Therapeutic Treasure Box for Working with Children and Adolescents with Developmental Trauma* – 2018

My wishes for...
are...

Copyright © Karen Treisman – *A Therapeutic Treasure Box for Working with Children and Adolescents with Developmental Trauma – 2018*

Worksheet 10.10
Feeding and strengthening myself and carrying on with my journey

This worksheet gives multiple options for a similar concept, as different metaphors will resonate with different people.

What can I do to nurture and nourish myself? How can others support me with this? What feeds, waters, strengthens, and protects me like a flower? (Draw, sculpt, collage, or write your responses.)

What can I do to make my tower of life and self stronger and sturdier? What bricks need to be celebrated and noticed? Which bricks need to be added? How can the tower be looked after and maintained? What can be done if some of the bricks chip or break off? (Draw, sculpt, collage, or write your responses, or build your life/self-tower.)

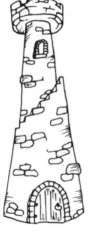

Copyright © Karen Treisman – A Therapeutic Treasure Box for Working with Children and Adolescents with Developmental Trauma – 2018

What lessons, memories, and skills am I taking with me on my journey in my invisible jacket and invisible suitcase? (Draw, sculpt, collage, or write your responses.)

What is in or makes up my safety kit for any future storms? What is my lifeboat, lifejacket vest, and safety ring? (Draw, sculpt, collage, or write your responses.)

Copyright © Karen Treisman – *A Therapeutic Treasure Box for Working with Children and Adolescents with Developmental Trauma* – 2018

Strengths-based approach: writing a take-back practice letter

Guidance on how to use these questions

The following questions offer some possibilities and options for reflecting on and identifying young people's/carers'/families'/parents'/colleagues' strengths, skills, and positive qualities. These can be powerfully pulled together and documented in an ending letter, email, poem, story, or card. Alternatively, these can be recorded on a video camera or phone. They can also draw on responses and input from the Team Around the Child/Family.

This list is not prescriptive or exhaustive. Each question can be expanded on by asking thickening questions and embedding them through creative means.

Think about a young person/parent/carer/colleague/client:

» What has gone well? What has been achieved so far? What steps have been taken? What can they do already? (Think about their journey and the distance already travelled.)

» What hobbies and activities does the young person engage in, enjoy, and excel in? What makes them sparkle/get excited/feel proud/be happy?

» What skills, strengths, successes, and positive qualities of theirs have you been struck/inspired/impressed by? What are their superpowers and magic gifts?

» If you were writing a review or recommendation about this person, what positive things would you say to others about them?

» If you had to give them an award for something positive, what would it be for?

» If you were stranded on an island with them, what skills of theirs would you appreciate?

» If they became a different person, or life changed as you know it, what would you miss about them?

» If you were no longer with them/seeing them, what parts of their personality would you miss?

» How has knowing them made an impression on you? What have you learned from them?

» What will you take forward from what you have learned from them?

» What are your wishes, hopes, and dreams for them?

» How can these skills, strengths, successes, and positive qualities be recognised, acknowledged, noticed, celebrated, and built on?

Copyright © Karen Treisman – *A Therapeutic Treasure Box for Working with Children and Adolescents with Developmental Trauma – 2018*

References

Abidin, R. R. (1995). *Parenting Stress Index, Third Edition: Professional Manual.* Odessa, FL: Psychological Assessment Resources.

Achenbach, T. M. (2009). *Achenbach System of Empirically Based Assessment (ASEBA): Development, Findings, Theory, and Applications.* Burlington, VT: University of Vermont Research Center for Children, Youth, and Families.

Ainsworth, M. D. S., Blehar, M. C., Waters, E., and Wall, S. (1978). *Patterns of Attachment: A Psychological Study of the Strange Situation.* Hillsdale, NJ: Erlbaum.

Ammaniti, M., van IJzendoorn, M., Speranza, A. M., and Tambelli, R. (2000). 'Internal working models of attachment during late childhood and early adolescence: An exploration of stability and change.' *Attachment and Human Development 2,* 328–346.

Armstrong, J. G., Putnam, F. W., Carlson, E. B., Libero, D. Z., and Smith, S. R. (1997). 'Development and validation of a measure of adolescent dissociation: The Adolescent Dissociative Experiences Scale (A-DES).' *Journal of Nervous and Mental Disease 185,* 491–497.

Bates, B. and Dozier, M. (1998). *This is My Baby,* coding manual. Unpublished manuscript. Newark: University of Delaware.

Bavolek, S. J. and Keene, R. G. (2001). *Adult–Adolescent Parenting Inventory AAPI-2: Administration and Development Handbook.* Park City, UT: Family Development Resources, Inc.

Bayley, N. (2006). *Technical Manual of the Bayley Scales of Infant and Toddler Development.* San Antonio, TX: Harcourt Assessment.

Bifulco, A., Jacobs, C., Bunn, A., Thomas, G., and Irving, K. (2008). 'The attachment style interview: A support-based adult assessment tool for adoption and fostering practice.' *Adoption and Fostering 32,* 33–45.

Biringen, Z. (2008). *The EA Professionals and Parent Curricula.* Available at www.emotionalavailability.com, accessed on 27 May 2017.

Bowlby, J. (1980). *Loss: Sadness and Depression. Attachment and Loss* (Vol. 3). London: Hogarth Press.

Briere, J. (2005). *Trauma Symptom Checklist for Young Children: Professional Manual.* Florida: Psychological Assessment Resources.

Britton, R. (1994). *Re-enactment as an Unwitting Professional Response to Family Dynamics: Crisis at Adolescence.* London: Jason Aronson Inc.

Brockington, I.F, Oates, J., George, S., Turner, D., Vostanis, P., Sullivan, M., Loh, C.C., and Murdoch, C. (2001). 'A screening questionnaire for mother-infant bonding disorders.' *Arch Womens Mental Health, 3,* 133–140.

Broughton, C. (2010). 'Measuring Trauma in the Primary Relationship: The Parent–Infant Relational Assessment Tool.' In T. Baradon (ed.) *Relational Trauma in Infancy: Psychoanalytic, Attachment and Neuropsychological Contributions to Parent–Infant Psychotherapy.* Hove: Routledge.

Caldwell, B. and Bradley, R. (1984). *Home Observation for Measurement of the Environment.* Little Rock, AR: University of Arkansas.

Carter, A. S. and Briggs-Gowan, M. (2005). *The Infant–Toddler and Brief Infant Toddler Social Emotional Assessment.* San Antonio, TX: PsychCorp.

Condon, J. T. (1993). 'The assessment of antenatal emotional attachment: Development of a questionnaire instrument.' *British Journal of Medical Psychology, 66,* 167–183.

Cook, A., Spinazzola, J., Ford, J., Lanktree, C., *et al.* (2005). 'Complex trauma in children and adolescents.' *Psychiatric Annals 35,* 390–398.

Cozolino, L. (2002). *The Neuroscience of Psychotherapy: Building and Rebuilding the Human Brain.* New York: W.W. Norton.

Cozolino, L. (2006). *The Neuroscience of Human Relationships: Attachment and the Developing Social Brain.* New York: W.W. Norton.

Cranley, M.S. (1981). 'Development of a tool for the measurement of maternal attachment during pregnancy.' *Nursing Research, 30,* 281–284.

Crinic, K. A. and Greenberg, M. T. (1990). 'Minor parenting stresses with young children.' *Child Development 61,* 1628–1637.

Crittenden, P. M. (2004). *CARE-Index: Coding Manual.* Unpublished manuscript. Miami, FL: Family Relations Institute.

Crittenden, P. M., Kozlowska, K., and Landini, A. (2010). 'Assessing attachment in school-age children.' *Child Clinical Psychology and Psychiatry 14,* 185–208.

Denborough, D. (2005). *Collective Narrative Practice: Responding to Individuals, Groups, and Communities who have Experienced Trauma.* Adelaide: Dulwich Centre Publications.

Denborough, D. (2010). *Kite of Life: From Intergenerational Conflict to Intergenerational Alliance.* Adelaide, Australia: Dulwich Centre Publications.

De Shazer, S. (2012). *More than Miracles: The State of the Art of Solution-Focused Therapy.* Binghamton, NY: Haworth Press.

Evers-Szostak, M. and Sanders, S. (1992). 'The Children's Perceptual Alteration Scale (CPAS): A measure of children's dissociation.' *Dissociation 5,* 91–97.

Figley, C. (1995). *Compassion Fatigue: Coping with Secondary Traumatic Stress Disorder in Those who Treat the Traumatized.* New York: Brunner/Mazel.

Fisher, J. (2006). 'Working with the neurobiological legacy of early trauma.' Paper presented at the Trauma Center Lecture Series, Brookline, MA.

Foa, E. B., Johnson, K. M., Feeny, N. C., and Treadwell, K. R. H. (2001). 'The Child PTSD Symptom Scale: A preliminary examination of its psychometric properties.' *Journal of Clinical Child Psychology 30,* 376–384.

Fraiberg, S., Adelson, E., and Shapiro, V. (1975). 'Ghosts in the nursery: A psychoanalytic approach to the problems of impaired infant–mother relationships.' *Journal of the American Academy of Child and Adolescent Psychiatry 14,* 387–421.

George, C. and Solomon, J. (2008). 'The Caregiving Behavioral System: A Behavioral System Approach to Parenting.' In J. Cassidy and P. Shaver (eds) *Handbook of Attachment: Theory, Research, and Clinical Application, Second Edition.* New York: Guilford Press.

George, C., Kaplan, N., and Main, M. (1985). *The Adult Attachment Interview.* Unpublished manuscript. Berkeley, CA: Department of Psychology, University of California at Berkeley.

Gerard, A. B. (1994). *Parent–Child Relationship Inventory (PCRI) Manual.* Los Angeles: WPS.

Ginott, H. G. (1972). *Teacher and Child.* New York: Macmillan.

Glaser, D. (2000). 'Child abuse and neglect and the brain: A review.' *Journal of Child Psychology and Psychiatry 41,* 97–116.

Goodman, R., Ford, T., and Richards, H. (2000). 'The Development and Well-Being Assessment: Description and initial validation of an integrated assessment of child and adolescent psychopathology.' *Journal of Child Psychology and Psychiatry 41*, 645–655.

Gratz, K. L. and Roemer, L. (2004). 'Multidimensional assessment of emotion regulation and dysregulation: Development, factor structure, and initial validation of the difficulties in emotion regulation scale.' *Journal of Psychopathology and Behavioral Assessment 26*, 41–54.

Grienenberger, J., Kelly, K., and Slade, A. (2005). 'Maternal reflective functioning, mother–infant affective communication, and infant attachment: Exploring the link between mental states and observed caregiving behavior in the intergenerational transmission of attachment.' *Attachment and Human Development 7*, 299–311.

Grotberg, E. (1995). *A Guide to Promoting Resilience in Children: Strengthening the Human Spirit*. Early Childhood Development: Practice and Reflections, Number 8. The Hague: Bernard van Leer Foundation.

Gunnar, M. R. and Fisher, P. (2006). 'Bringing basic research on early experience and stress neurobiology to bear on preventive interventions for neglected and maltreated children.' *Development and Psychopathology 18*, 651–677.

Hobday, A. (2001). 'Timeholes: A useful metaphor when explaining unusual or bizarre behaviour in children who have moved families.' *Clinical Child Psychology and Psychiatry 6*, 41–47.

Holahan, C. J. and Moos, R. H. (1983). 'The quality of social support: Measures of family and work relationships.' *British Journal of Clinical Psychology 22*, 157–162.

Hughes, D. (2011). *Attachment-Focused Family Therapy Workbook*. New York: W.W. Norton.

Johnston, C. and Mash, E. J. (1989). 'A measure of parenting satisfaction and efficacy.' *Journal of Clinical Child Psychology 18*, 167–175.

Jones, R. T., Fletcher, K., and Ribbe, D. R. (2002). *Child's Reaction to Traumatic Events Scale – Revised (CRTES-R): A Self-Report Traumatic Stress Measure*. Blacksburg, VA: Virginia Tech University.

Kaufman, A. S. and Kaufman, N. L. (2004). *Kaufman Assessment Battery for Children, Second Edition*. Circle Pines, MN: American Guidance Service.

Koomar, J. A. (2009). 'Trauma- and attachment-informed sensory integration assessment and intervention.' *Sensory Integration Special Interest Section Quarterly 32*, 266–306.

Koren-Karie, N. and Oppenheim, D. (2004). *The Insightfulness Assessment Coding Manual*. Haifa: University of Haifa.

Korkman, M., Kirk, U., and Kemp, S. (1998). *NEPSY: A Developmental Neuropsychological Assessment*. San Antonio, TX: The Psychological Corporation.

Kumar, R. C. (1997). '"Anybody's child": Severe disorders of mother-to-infant bonding.' *British Journal of Psychiatry, 171*, 175–181.

Lieberman, A. F., Padron, E., Van Horn, P., and Harris, W. W. (2005). 'Angels in the nursery: The intergenerational transmission of benevolent influences.' *Infant Mental Health Journal 26*, 504–520.

Lilas, C. and Turnball, J. (2009). *Infant Mental Health, Early Intervention, and Relationship-Based Therapies: A Framework for Interdisciplinary Practice*. New York: W.W. Norton.

Loman, M. M., Johnson, A. E., Westerlund, A., Pollak, S. D., Nelson, C. A., and Gunnar, M. R. (2013). 'The effect of early deprivation on executive attention in middle childhood.' *Journal of Child Psychology and Psychiatry 54*, 37–45.

Lupien, S. J., McEwen, B. S., Gunnar, M. R., and Heim, C. (2009). 'Effects of stress throughout the lifespan on the brain, behaviour and cognition.' *Nature Reviews Neuroscience 10*, 434–445.

Luyten, P., Mayes, L., Sadler, L., Fonagy, P., Nicholls, S., Crowley, M., and Slade, A. (2009). *The Parental Reflective Functioning Questionnaire-1 (PRFQ-1).* Leuven: University of Leuven, Belgium.

Mann, M., Hosman, C. M., Schaalma, H. P., and de Vries, N. K. (2004). 'Self-esteem in a broad-spectrum approach for mental health promotion.' *Health Education Research 19,* 357–372.

Marschak, M. (1960). 'A method for evaluating child–parent interaction under controlled conditions.' *The Journal of Genetic Psychology 97,* 3–22.

Maslach, C. (2003). *Burnout: The Cost of Caring.* Los Altos, CA: Malor Books.

Masten, A. S., Cutuli, J. J., Herbers, E. J., and Reed, M. G. J. (2011). 'Resilience in Development.' In C. R. Snyder and S. J. Lopez (eds) *Oxford Handbook of Positive Psychology.* New York: Oxford University Press.

Mayer, J. D., Salovey, P., Caruso, D. R., and Sitarenios, G. (2003). 'Measuring emotional intelligence with the MSCEIT V2.0.' *Emotion 3,* 97–105.

McCann, I. L. and Pearlman, L. A. (1990). 'Vicarious traumatization: A framework for understanding the psychological effects of working with victims.' *Journal of Traumatic Stress 3,* 131–149.

Mischenko, J., Cheater, F., and Street, J. (2004). 'NCAST: Tools to assess caregiver–child interaction.' *Community Practitioner 77,* 57–60.

Moos, R. and Moos, B. (1983). 'Clinical Applications of the Family Environment Scale.' In E. Filsinger (ed.) *A Sourcebook of Marriage and Family Assessment.* Beverly Hills, CA: Sage.

Muller, M.E. (1992). 'A questionnaire to measure mother to-infant attachment.' *Journal of Nursing Measurement, 2,* 129–41.

Nader, K., Kriegler, J. A., Blake, D. D., Pynoos, R. S., Newman, E., and Weathers, F. W. (1996). *Clinician-Administered PTSD Scale, Child and Adolescent Version.* White River Junction, VT: National Center for PTSD.

Ncazelo, N. (2007). *The Tree of Life: An Approach to Working with Vulnerable Children.* DVD. Adelaide: Dulwich Centre Publications.

Ncube, N. (2007). *The Tree of Life: An Approach to Working with Vulnerable Children.* DVD. Adelaide, Australia: Dulwich Centre Publications.

Olson, D. H., Gorall, D. M., and Tiesel, J. W. (2006). *FACES IV: Development and Validation.* Unpublished manuscript.

Oppenheim, D. (1997). 'The Attachment Doll-Play Interview for pre-schoolers.' *International Journal of Behavioral Development 20,* 681–697.

Panksepp, J. (ed.) (2004) *A Textbook of Biological Psychiatry.* Hoboken, NJ: Wiley.

Peacock, F. (2001). *Water the Flowers, Not the Weeds: A Strategy that Revolutionizes Professional, Personal, Family Communication and Relationships.* Montreal, Quebec: Open Heart Publishing.

Pelcovitz, D., van der Kolk, B., Roth, S., Mandel, F., Kaplan, S., and Resick, P. (1997). 'Development of a criteria set and a Structured Interview for Disorders of Extreme Stress (SIDES).' *Journal of Traumatic Stress 10,* 3–16.

Perlman, S. B., Kalish, C. W., and Pollak, S. D. (2008). 'The role of maltreatment experience in children's understanding of the antecedents of emotion.' *Cognition and Emotion 22,* 651–670.

Perry, B. D. (2014). 'The Neurosequential Model of Therapeutics: Application of a Developmentally Sensitive and Neurobiology-Informed Approach to Clinical Problem Solving in Maltreated Children.' In K. Brandt, B. D. Perry, S. Seligman, and E. Tronick (eds) *Infant and Early Childhood Mental Health: Core Concepts and Clinical Practice.* Washington, DC: American Psychiatric Publishing.

Pollak, S. D., Nelson, C. A., Schlaak, M., Roeber, B., *et al.* (2010). 'Neurodevelopmental effects of early deprivation in post-institutionalized children.' *Child Development 81*, 224–236.

Praver, F., DiGiuseppe, R., Pelcovitz, D., Mandel, F. S., and Gaines, R. (2000). 'A preliminary study of a cartoon measure for children's reactions to chronic trauma.' *Child Maltreatment 5*, 273–285.

Putnam, F. W., Helmers, K., and Trickett, P. K. (1993). 'Development, reliability, and validity of a child dissociation scale.' *Child Abuse and Neglect 17*, 731–741.

Remen, N. R. (1996). *Kitchen Table Wisdom: Stories that Heal.* New York: Riverhead Books.

Reynolds, C. R. and Kamphaus, R. W. (2004). *BASC-2: Behavior Assessment System for Children, Second Edition Manual.* Circle Pines, MN: American Guidance Service.

Rogers, C. R. (1961). *On Becoming a Person: A Psychotherapist's View of Psychotherapy.* Boston: Houghton Mifflin.

Rothschild, B. B. B. (2000). *The Body Remembers: The Psychophysiology of Trauma and Trauma Treatment.* New York: W.W. Norton.

Rothschild, B. (2006). *Help for the Helper: The Psychophysiology of Compassion Fatigue and Vicarious Trauma.* New York: W.W. Norton.

Saigh, P., Yaski, A. E., Oberfield, R. A., Green, B. L., *et al.* (2000). 'The Children's PTSD Inventory: Development and reliability.' *Journal of Traumatic Stress 30*, 369–380.

Samuelson, K. W., Krueger, C. E., Burnett, C., and Wilson, C. K. (2010). 'Neuropsychological functioning in children with posttraumatic stress disorder.' *Child Neuropsychology 16*, 119–133.

Saunders, R., Jacobvitz, D., Zaccagnino, M., Beverung, L. M., and Hazen, N. (2011). 'Pathways to earned-security: The role of alternative support figures.' *Attachment and Human Development 13*, 403–420.

Shaffer, D., Gould, M. S., and Brasic, J. (1983). 'A Children's Global Assessment Scale (CGAS).' *Archives of General Psychiatry 40*, 1228–1231.

Sharp, C., Pane, H., Ha, C., Venta, A., *et al.* (2011). 'Theory of mind and emotion regulation difficulties in adolescents with borderline traits.' *Journal of the American Academy of Child and Adolescent Psychiatry 50*, 563–573.

Sheeringa, M. S. and Zeanah, C. H. (1994). *PTSD Semi-Structured Interview and Observation Record for Infants and Young Children.* New Orleans: Department of Psychiatry and Neurology, Tulane University Health Sciences Center.

Siegel, D. J. (1999). *The Developing Mind: How Relationships and the Brain Interact to Shape Who We Are.* New York: Guilford Press.

Siegel, D. J. (2012). *The Developing Mind: How Relationships and the Brain Interact to Shape Who We Are.* New York and London: The Guilford Press.

Siegel, D. J. and Bryson, T. P. (2011). *The Whole Brain Child: Revolutionary Strategies to Nurture Your Child's Developing Mind.* New York: Delacorte Press.

Slade, A., Aber, J. L., Bresgi, I., Berger, B., and Kaplan, M. (2004). *The Parent Development Interview, Revised.* Unpublished protocol. New York: The City University of New York.

Slade, A., Patterson, M., and Miller, M. (2007). *Addendum to reflective functioning scoring manual for use with the pregnancy interview, version 2.0.*

Spann, M. N., Mayes, L. C., Kalmar, J. H., Guiney, J., *et al.* (2012). 'Childhood abuse and neglect and cognitive flexibility in adolescents.' *Child Neuropsychology 18*, 182–189.

Sparrow, S. S., Cicchetti, V. D., and Balla, A. D. (2005). *Vineland Adaptive Behavior Scales, Second Edition.* Circle Pines, MN: American Guidance Service.

Squires, J., Bricker, D., and Twombly, E. (2002). *Ages and Stages Questionnaires: Social-Emotional. A Parent-Completed, Child-Monitoring System for Social-Emotional Behaviors.* Baltimore: Paul H. Brookes Publishing.

Stamm, B. H. (1999). *Secondary Traumatic Stress: Self-Care Issues for Clinicians, Researchers, and Educators*. Lutherville, MD: Sidran Press.

Steinberg, A. M., Brymer, M. J., Kim, S., Ghosh, C., *et al.* (2013). 'Psychometric properties of the UCLA PTSD Reaction Index.' *Journal of Traumatic Stress 26*, 1–9.

Stolbach, B. C. (1997). 'The Children's Dissociative Experiences Scale and Posttraumatic Symptom Inventory: Rationale, development, and validation of a self-report measure.' *Dissertation Abstracts International 58*, 1548B.

Streeck-Fischer, A. and van der Kolk, B. (2000). 'Down will come baby, cradle and all: Diagnostic and therapeutic implications of chronic trauma on child development.' *Australian and New Zealand Journal of Psychiatry 34*, 903–918.

Target, M., Fonagy, F., and Shmueli-Goetz, Y. (2003). 'Attachment representation in school-age children: The development of the Child Attachment Interview (CAI).' *Journal of Child Psychotherapy 29*, 171–186.

Teti, D. M. and Gelfand, D. M. (1991). 'Behavioral competence among mothers of infants in the first year: The mediational role of maternal self-efficacy.' *Child Development 62*, 918–929.

Treisman, K. (2016). *Working with Relational and Developmental Trauma in Children and Adolescents*. New York: Routledge.

Van der Kolk, B. (2014). *The Body Keeps the Score: Brain, Mind, and Body in the Healing of Trauma*. New York: Viking Penguin.

Warner, E. and Koomar, J. (2009). *Arousal Regulation in Traumatised Children: Sensorimotor Interventions*. Boston: International Trauma Conference.

Waters, E. (1995). 'Appendix A: The Attachment Q-Set.' In E. Waters, B. E. Vaughn, G. Posada, and K. Kondo-Ikemura (eds) *Caregiving, Cultural, and Cognitive Perspectives on Secure-Base Behaviour and Working Models: New Growing Points of Attachment Theory and Research. Monographs of the Society for Research in Child Development 60*, 234–246.

Wechsler, D. (1967). *Manual for the Wechsler Preschool and Primary Scale of Intelligence*. San Antonio, TX: The Psychological Corporation.

Wechsler, D. (1991). *Wechsler Intelligence Scale for Children – Third Edition*. San Antonio, TX: Psychological Corporation.

Wetherby, A. M. and Prizant, B. M. (2001). *Communication and Symbolic Behavior Scales Developmental Profile Infant/Toddler Checklist*. Baltimore, MD: Paul H. Brookes Publishing.

White, M. (2007). *Maps of Narrative Practice*. New York: W.W. Norton.

White, M. and Epston, D. (1990). *Narrative means to therapeutic ends*. New York: W. W. Norton.

Winnicott, C. (1968). 'Communicating with Children.' In R. Tod (ed.) *Disturbed Children*. London: Longman.

Wolfe, V. V., Gentile, C., Michienzi, T., Sas, L., and Wolfe, D. A. (1991). 'The Children's Impact of Traumatic Events Scale: A measure of post-sexual abuse PTSD symptoms.' *Behavioral Assessment 13*, 359–383.

Zeanah, C. H. and Benoit, D. (1995). 'Clinical applications of a parent perception interview in infant mental health.' *Child and Adolescent Clinics of North America 4*, 539–554.

Zeanah, C. H., Berlin, L. J., and Boris, N. W. (2011). 'Practitioner review: Clinical applications of attachment theory and research for infants and young children.' *Journal of Child Psychology and Psychiatry 52*, 819–833.

ZERO TO THREE (2005). *Diagnostic Classification of Mental Health and Developmental Disorders in Infancy and Early Childhood, Revised Edition*. Washington, DC: ZERO TO THREE Press.

Further Reading

Chapman, L. (2014). *Neurobiologically Informed Trauma Therapy with Children and Adolescents: Understanding Mechanisms of Change.* New York: W.W. Norton.

Cozolino, L. (2014). *The Neuroscience of Human Relationships: Attachment and the Developing Human Brain, Second Edition.* New York: W.W. Norton.

Crenshaw, D. A. (2008). *Therapeutic Engagement of Children and Adolescents: Play, Symbol, Drawing, and Storytelling Techniques.* Lanham, MD: Jason Aronson.

Fogel, A. (2009). *The Psychophysiology of Self-Awareness: Rediscovering the Lost Art of Body Sense.* New York: W.W. Norton.

Fosha, D., Siegel, D. J., and Solomon, M. F. (eds) (2009). *The Healing Power of Emotion: Affective Neuroscience, Development, and Clinical Practice.* New York: W.W. Norton.

Gil, E. (2006). *Helping Abused and Traumatized Children: Integrating Directive and Nondirective Approaches.* New York: Guilford Press.

Herman, J. L. (1997). *Trauma and Recovery: The Aftermath of Violence: From Domestic Abuse to Political Terror.* New York: Basic Books.

Hughes, D. (2009). *Attachment Focused Parenting: Effective Strategies to Care for Children.* New York: W.W. Norton.

Jennings, S. (2005). *Creative Storytelling with Adults at Risk.* Milton Keynes: Speechmark.

Jennings, S. (2010). *Healthy Attachments and Neuro-Dramatic-Play.* London: Jessica Kingsley Publishers.

Levine, P. (2010). *In an Unspoken Voice: How the Body Releases Trauma and Restores Goodness.* Berkeley, CA: North Atlantic Books.

Levine, P. and Kline, M. (2007). *Trauma Through a Child's Eyes: Awakening the Ordinary Miracle of Healing.* Berkeley, CA: North Atlantic Books.

Lowenstein, L. (2006). *Creative Interventions for Bereaved Children.* Toronto: Champion Press.

Lowenstein, L. (2010). *Creative Family Therapy Techniques: Play, Art, and Expressive Activities to Engage Children in Family Sessions.* Toronto: Champion Press.

Malchiodi, C. (2008). *Creative Interventions with Traumatized Children.* New York: Guilford Press.

Malchiodi, C. (2012). *Handbook of Art Therapy, Second Edition.* New York: Guilford Press.

Malchiodi, C. A. and Crenshaw, D. (2017). *Creative Arts and Play Therapy with Attachment Problems.* New York: Guilford Press.

Malchiodi, C. A. and Crenshaw, D. (2017). *What to Do when Children Clam Up in Psychotherapy: Interventions to Facilitate Communication.* New York: Guilford Press.

Oaklander, V. (2007). *Hidden Treasure: A Map to the Child's Inner Self.* New York: Karnac Books.

Ogden, P. and Fisher, J. (2014). *Sensorimotor Psychotherapy: Interventions for Trauma and Attachment.* New York: W.W. Norton.

Panksepp, J. (2004). *Affective Neuroscience: The Foundations of Human and Animal Emotions.* New York: Oxford University Press.

Porges, S. (2011). *The Polyvagal Theory: Neurophysiological Foundations of Emotions, Attachment, Communication and Self-Regulation.* New York: W.W. Norton.

Siegel, D. J. and Hartzell, M. (2003). *Parenting from the Inside Out: How a Deeper Self-Understanding Can Help You Raise Children Who Thrive.* New York: Penguin Putnam.

Tronick, E. (2007). *The Neurobehavioral and Social-Emotional Development of Infants and Children.* New York: W.W. Norton.

White, M. (2011). *Narrative Practice: Continuing the Conversations.* New York: W.W. Norton.

White, M. and Morgan, A. (2006). *Narrative Therapy with Children and Their Families.* Adelaide: Dulwich Centre Publications.

A Therapeutic Treasure Deck of Sentence Completion and Feelings Cards
Dr. Karen Treisman

£22.99 / $29.95
ISBN: 978 1 78592 398 2

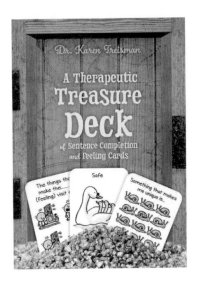

The perfect tool to add to any "therapeutic treasure box", this set of 68 cards provide a way to help open conversations and structure discussions with children and adolescents aged 6+.

The treasure deck offers a fun, non-threatening way to help to build understanding and forge relationships. It also provides a safe, playful way for children to articulate and make sense of their feelings, thoughts, experiences, and beliefs. The deck comes with two different types of card – the "feelings cards" and the "sentence-completion cards" – which can be used separately or together, and the cards are accompanied by a booklet which explains some of the different ways in which they can be therapeutically used.

Designed and tested by specialist clinical psychologist, trainer, and author Dr Karen Treisman, this deck is a little treasure that will have great value for anyone working with children and adolescents aged 6+.

Karen Treisman is a specialist clinical psychologist, trainer, and author, working in London, UK. Karen is also the Director of Safe Hands and Thinking Minds Training and Consultancy services.